HARBINGER WARS 2

MATT KINDT | ERIC HEISSERER | TOMÁS GIORELLO | RAÚL ALLÉN
PATRICIA MARTÍN | ADAM POLLINA | RENATO GUEDES | DIEGO RODRIGUEZ

CONTENTS

Collection Cover: JG Jones
with Andrew Dalhouse

Assistant Editor: David Menchel
(Prelude, #1-4, Aftermath)
Editors: Warren Simons (Prelude) and
Karl Bollers (#1-4, Aftermath)
Executive Editor: Joseph Illidge

VALIANT.

Dan Mintz
Chairman

Fred Pierce
Publisher

Walter Black
VP Operations

Joseph Illidge
Executive Editor

Robert Meyers
Editorial Director

Mel Caylo
Director of Marketing

Matthew Klein
Director of Sales

Travis Escarfullery
Director of Design & Production

Peter Stern
Director of International Publishing & Merchandising

Karl Bollers
Senior Editor

Lysa Hawkins
Editor

Victoria McNally
Senior Marketing & Communications Manager

Jeff Walker
Production & Design Manager

Julia Walchuk
Sales & Live Events Manager

Emily Hecht
Sales & Social Media Manager

David Menchel
Assistant Editor

Connor Hill
Sales Operations Coordinator

Ivan Cohen
Collection Editor

Steve Blackwell
Collection Designer

Russ Brown
President, Consumer Products,
Promotions & Ad Sales

Caritza Berlioz
Licensing Coordinator

Oliver Taylor
International Licensing Coordinator

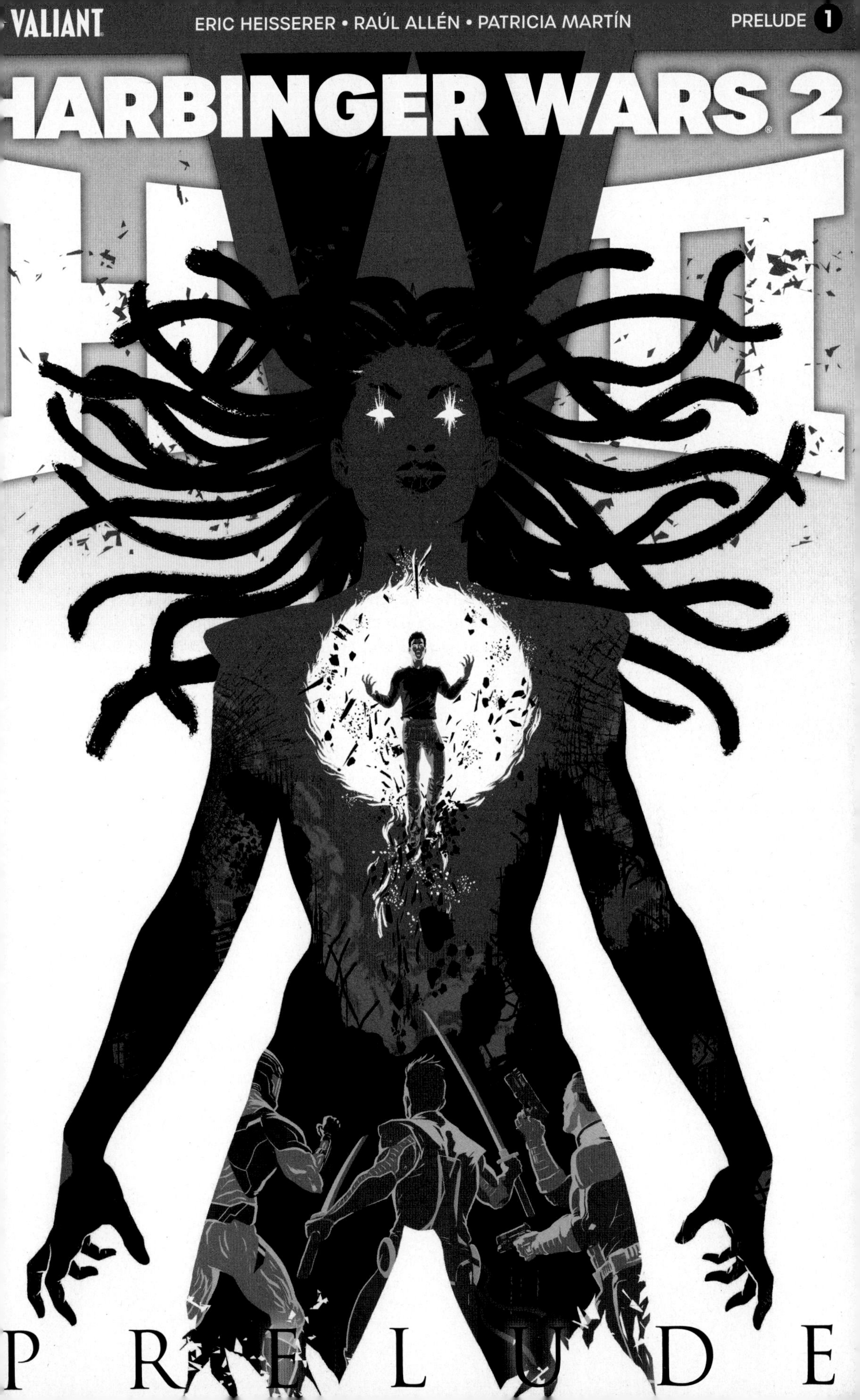
VALIANT
ERIC HEISSERER • RAÚL ALLÉN • PATRICIA MARTÍN
PRELUDE 1
HARBINGER WARS 2
PRELUDE

HARBINGER WARS 2
HWII

Psiots are people born with incredible abilities, and Amanda McKee is one of them. Called Livewire for her power to telepathically interface with technology, Amanda has been a longtime ally to the American government. But, her responsibility is now focused on the well-being of the Secret Weapons, a group of young psiots trying to understand their abilities. As anti-psiot sentiments run high, and with the safety of this new makeshift family to consider, Amanda finds herself at a crossroads as confrontations between psiots and the government flare up across the country...

LIVEWIRE
Utilizing her power to telepathically interface with technology, Livewire had long been considered a friend to the American government–up until they tried to kill her team of untrained psiots. Outraged by their duplicitous actions, Livewire shut down the United States power grid, plunging the country into darkness.

PETER STANCHEK
An omega-level psiot with powerful telepathy and telekinesis, Peter's greatest gift is the ability to activate the dormant powers in latent psiots. With danger just behind him, he has been traveling the continent and activating anyone willing to join his cause. Peter's enemies have embedded a parasite in his mind, betraying his location at all times, allowing them to track his movements.

THE RENEGADES

A team of psiots dedicated to helping others like them. Led by a human named Kris Hathaway, whose ideals and political beliefs guide the team forward. Other members include the flyer, Faith; the strongman, Torque; and the shapeshifter, Animalia.

BLOODSHOT

A soldier with billions of microscopic nanites running through his veins. Bloodshot possesses rapid healing, heightened strength and endurance, and camouflage capabilities. He is the ultimate killing machine.

G.A.T.E.

The Global Agency for Threat Excision, G.A.T.E. is led by Colonel Jamie Capshaw and has long served as the United States' primary response to strange and severe threats.

X-O MANOWAR

Aric of Dacia is X-O Manowar, Earth's most powerful warrior and king of the displaced Visigoth tribe. Armed with the sentient alien armor Shanhara, Aric fights alongside G.A.T.E. for the assured safety of his people.

NINJAK

A master of martial arts, wielding the best high-tech weaponry that money can buy, Colin King is Ninjak–a freelance agent with ties to MI6 and G.A.T.E.

MAJOR CHARLIE PALMER

The leader of H.A.R.D. Corps, OMEN's tactical, anti-psiot unit. Major Palmer has an implant in his head that allows him to access a catalogue of predetermined psionic abilities, with the caveat being he can only use them one at at time.

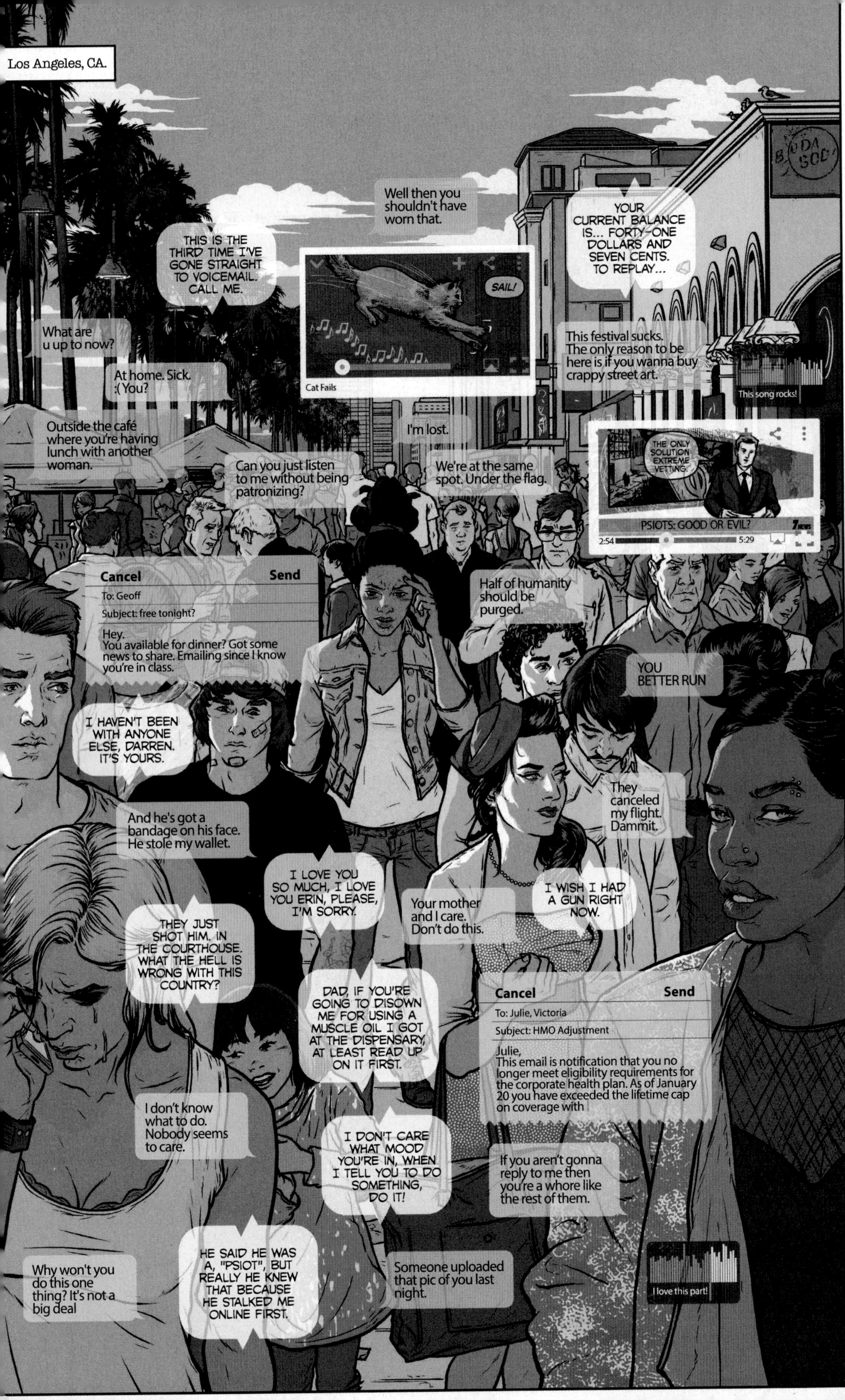
Los Angeles, CA.
Well then you shouldn't have worn that.
THIS IS THE THIRD TIME I'VE GONE STRAIGHT TO VOICEMAIL. CALL ME.
SAIL!
Cat Fails
YOUR CURRENT BALANCE IS... FORTY-ONE DOLLARS AND SEVEN CENTS. TO REPLAY...
BUDA SOD
What are u up to now?
At home. Sick. :(You?
This festival sucks. The only reason to be here is if you wanna buy crappy street art.
This song rocks!
Outside the café where you're having lunch with another woman.
I'm lost.
Can you just listen to me without being patronizing?
We're at the same spot. Under the flag.
THE ONLY SOLUTION: EXTREME VETTING
PSIOTS: GOOD OR EVIL?
7NEWS
2:54
5:29
Cancel
Send
To: Geoff
Subject: free tonight?
Hey.
You available for dinner? Got some news to share. Emailing since I know you're in class.
Half of humanity should be purged.
YOU BETTER RUN
I HAVEN'T BEEN WITH ANYONE ELSE, DARREN. IT'S YOURS.
They canceled my flight. Dammit.
And he's got a bandage on his face. He stole my wallet.
I LOVE YOU SO MUCH, I LOVE YOU ERIN, PLEASE, I'M SORRY.
Your mother and I care. Don't do this.
I WISH I HAD A GUN RIGHT NOW.
THEY JUST SHOT HIM. IN THE COURTHOUSE. WHAT THE HELL IS WRONG WITH THIS COUNTRY?
DAD, IF YOU'RE GOING TO DISOWN ME FOR USING A MUSCLE OIL I GOT AT THE DISPENSARY, AT LEAST READ UP ON IT FIRST.
Cancel
Send
To: Julie, Victoria
Subject: HMO Adjustment
Julie,
This email is notification that you no longer meet eligibility requirements for the corporate health plan. As of January 20 you have exceeded the lifetime cap on coverage with
I don't know what to do. Nobody seems to care.
I DON'T CARE WHAT MOOD YOU'RE IN, WHEN I TELL YOU TO DO SOMETHING, DO IT!
If you aren't gonna reply to me then you're a whore like the rest of them.
Why won't you do this one thing? It's not a big deal
HE SAID HE WAS A, "PSIOT", BUT REALLY HE KNEW THAT BECAUSE HE STALKED ME ONLINE FIRST.
Someone uploaded that pic of you last night.
I love this part!

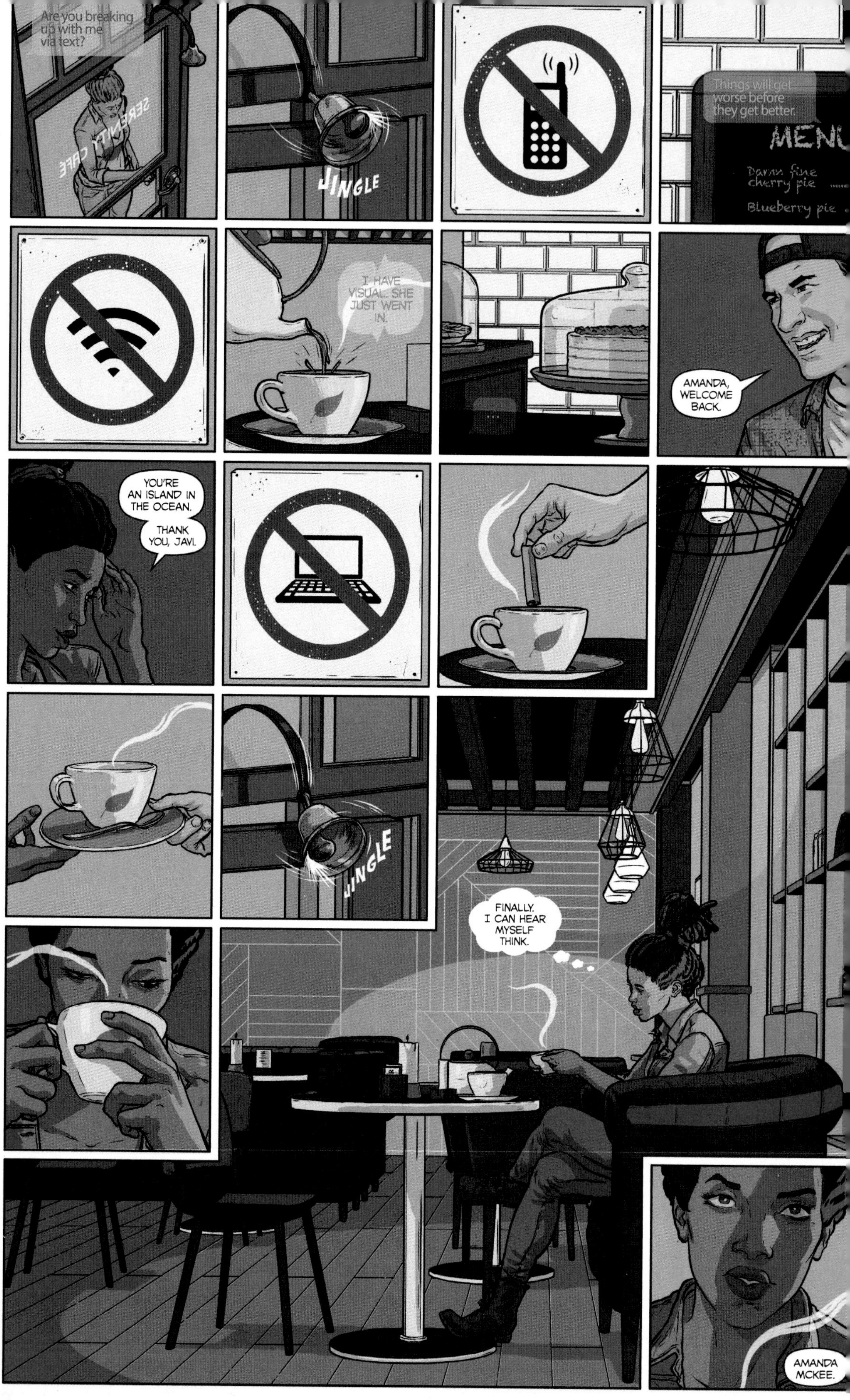

Are you breaking up with me via text?
SERENITY CAFE
JINGLE
Things will get worse before they get better.
MENU
Damn fine cherry pie
Blueberry pie
I HAVE VISUAL. SHE JUST WENT IN.
AMANDA, WELCOME BACK.
YOU'RE AN ISLAND IN THE OCEAN.
THANK YOU, JAVI.
JINGLE
FINALLY. I CAN HEAR MYSELF THINK.
AMANDA MCKEE.

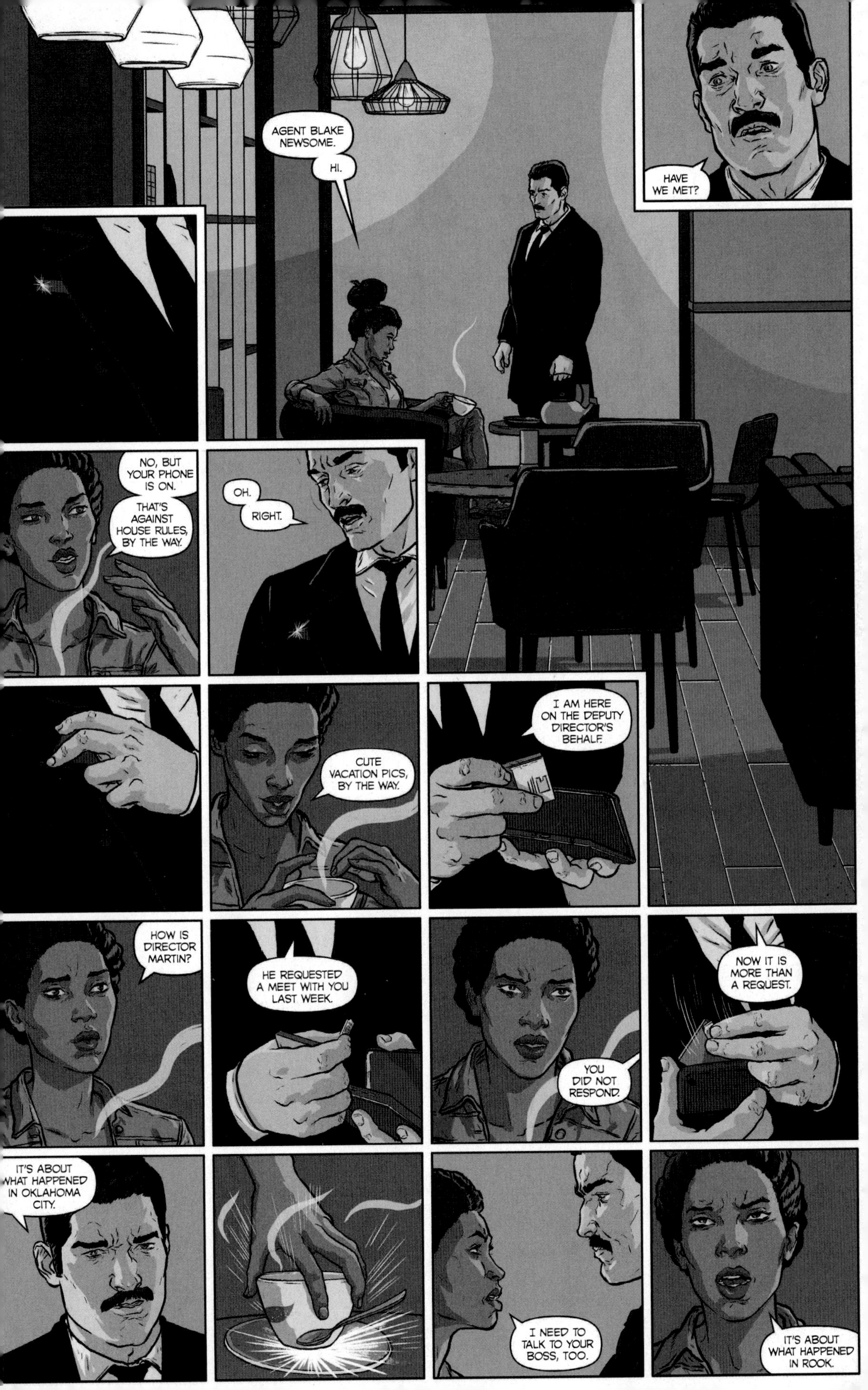
AGENT BLAKE NEWSOME.
HI.
HAVE WE MET?
NO, BUT YOUR PHONE IS ON.
THAT'S AGAINST HOUSE RULES, BY THE WAY.
OH.
RIGHT.
CUTE VACATION PICS, BY THE WAY.
I AM HERE ON THE DEPUTY DIRECTOR'S BEHALF.
HOW IS DIRECTOR MARTIN?
HE REQUESTED A MEET WITH YOU LAST WEEK.
YOU DID NOT RESPOND.
NOW IT IS MORE THAN A REQUEST.
IT'S ABOUT WHAT HAPPENED IN OKLAHOMA CITY.
I NEED TO TALK TO YOUR BOSS, TOO.
IT'S ABOUT WHAT HAPPENED IN ROOK.

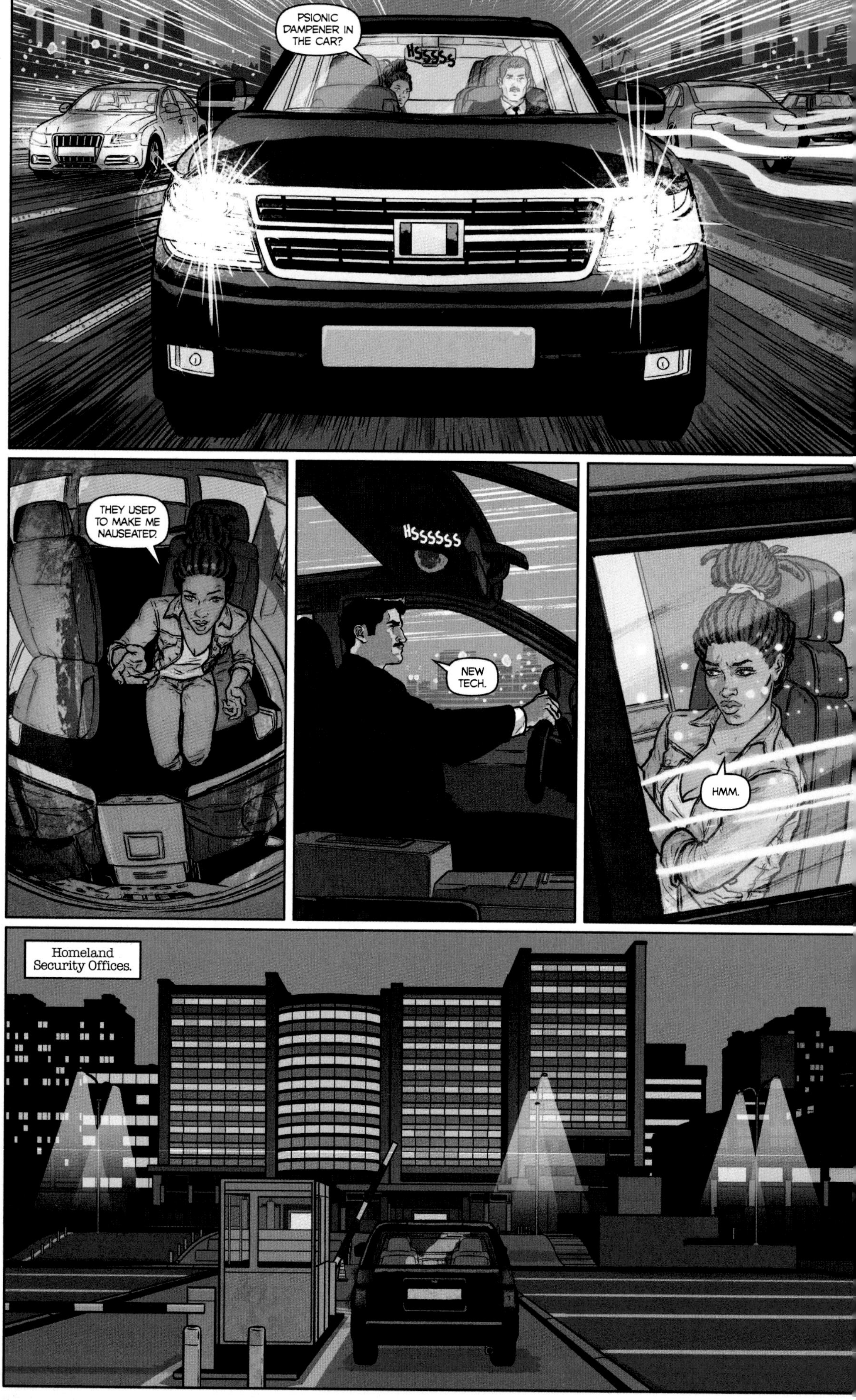
PSIONIC DAMPENER IN THE CAR?
HSSSSS
THEY USED TO MAKE ME NAUSEATED.
HSSSSSS
NEW TECH.
HMM.
Homeland Security Offices.

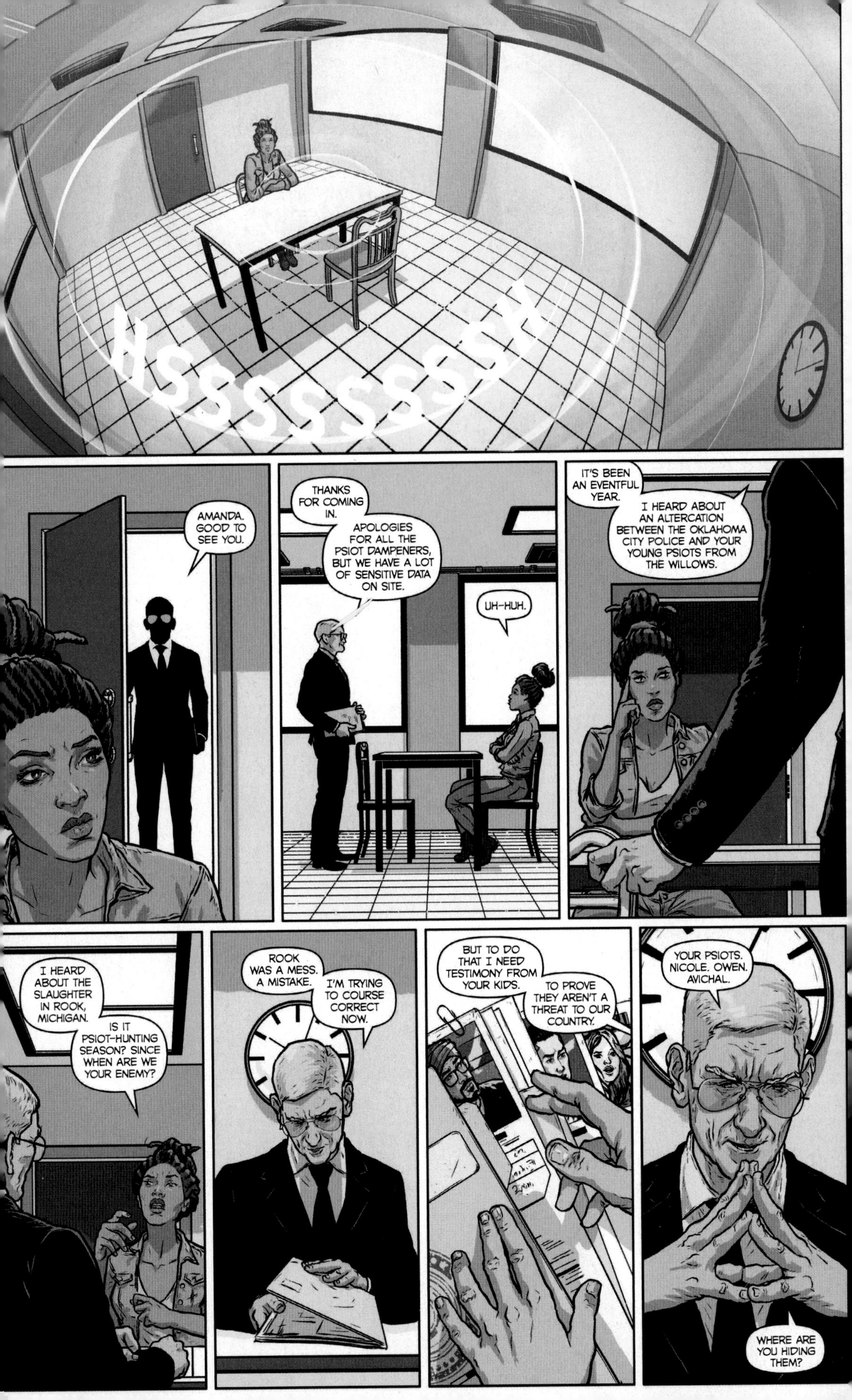
HSSSSSSSSH
AMANDA. GOOD TO SEE YOU.
THANKS FOR COMING IN.
APOLOGIES FOR ALL THE PSIOT DAMPENERS, BUT WE HAVE A LOT OF SENSITIVE DATA ON SITE.
UH-HUH.
IT'S BEEN AN EVENTFUL YEAR.
I HEARD ABOUT AN ALTERCATION BETWEEN THE OKLAHOMA CITY POLICE AND YOUR YOUNG PSIOTS FROM THE WILLOWS.
I HEARD ABOUT THE SLAUGHTER IN ROOK, MICHIGAN.
IS IT PSIOT-HUNTING SEASON? SINCE WHEN ARE WE YOUR ENEMY?
ROOK WAS A MESS. A MISTAKE.
I'M TRYING TO COURSE CORRECT NOW.
BUT TO DO THAT I NEED TESTIMONY FROM YOUR KIDS.
TO PROVE THEY AREN'T A THREAT TO OUR COUNTRY.
YOUR PSIOTS. NICOLE. OWEN. AVICHAL.
WHERE ARE YOU HIDING THEM?

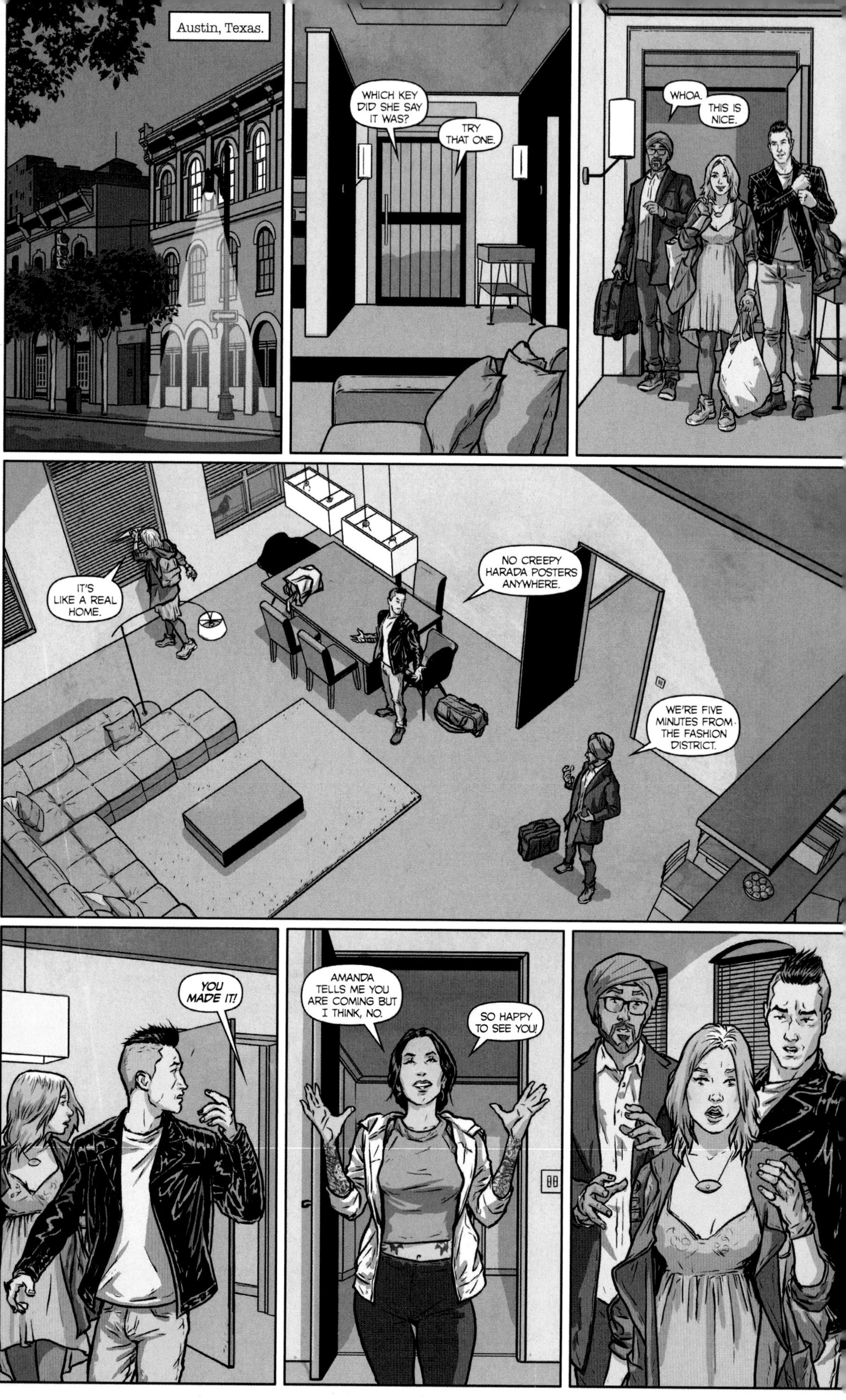
Austin, Texas.
WHICH KEY DID SHE SAY IT WAS?
TRY THAT ONE.
WHOA.
THIS IS NICE.
IT'S LIKE A REAL HOME.
NO CREEPY HARADA POSTERS ANYWHERE.
WE'RE FIVE MINUTES FROM THE FASHION DISTRICT.
YOU MADE IT!
AMANDA TELLS ME YOU ARE COMING BUT I THINK, NO.
SO HAPPY TO SEE YOU!

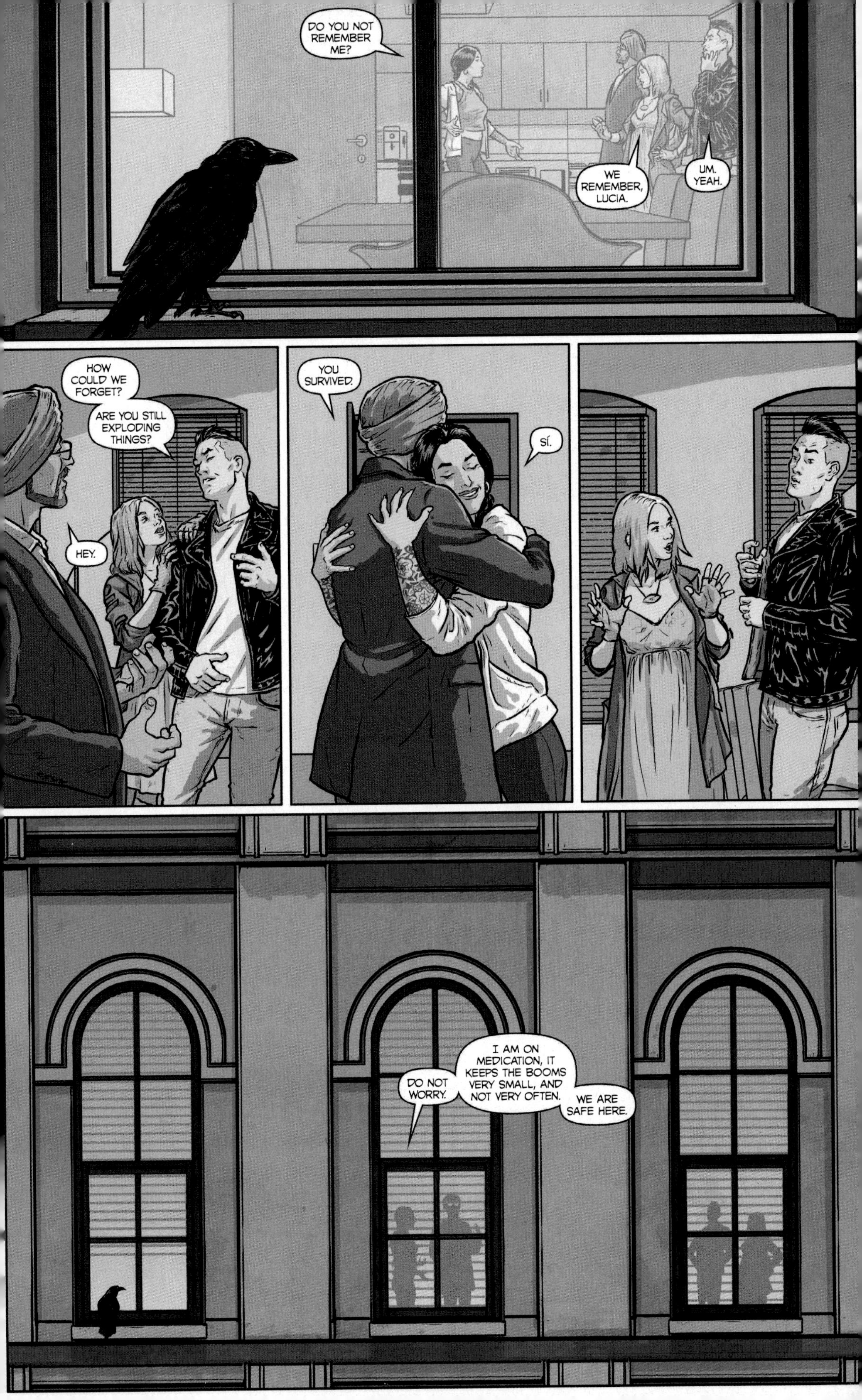
DO YOU NOT REMEMBER ME?
WE REMEMBER, LUCIA.
UM. YEAH.
HOW COULD WE FORGET?
ARE YOU STILL EXPLODING THINGS?
HEY.
YOU SURVIVED.
SÍ.
DO NOT WORRY.
I AM ON MEDICATION, IT KEEPS THE BOOMS VERY SMALL, AND NOT VERY OFTEN.
WE ARE SAFE HERE.

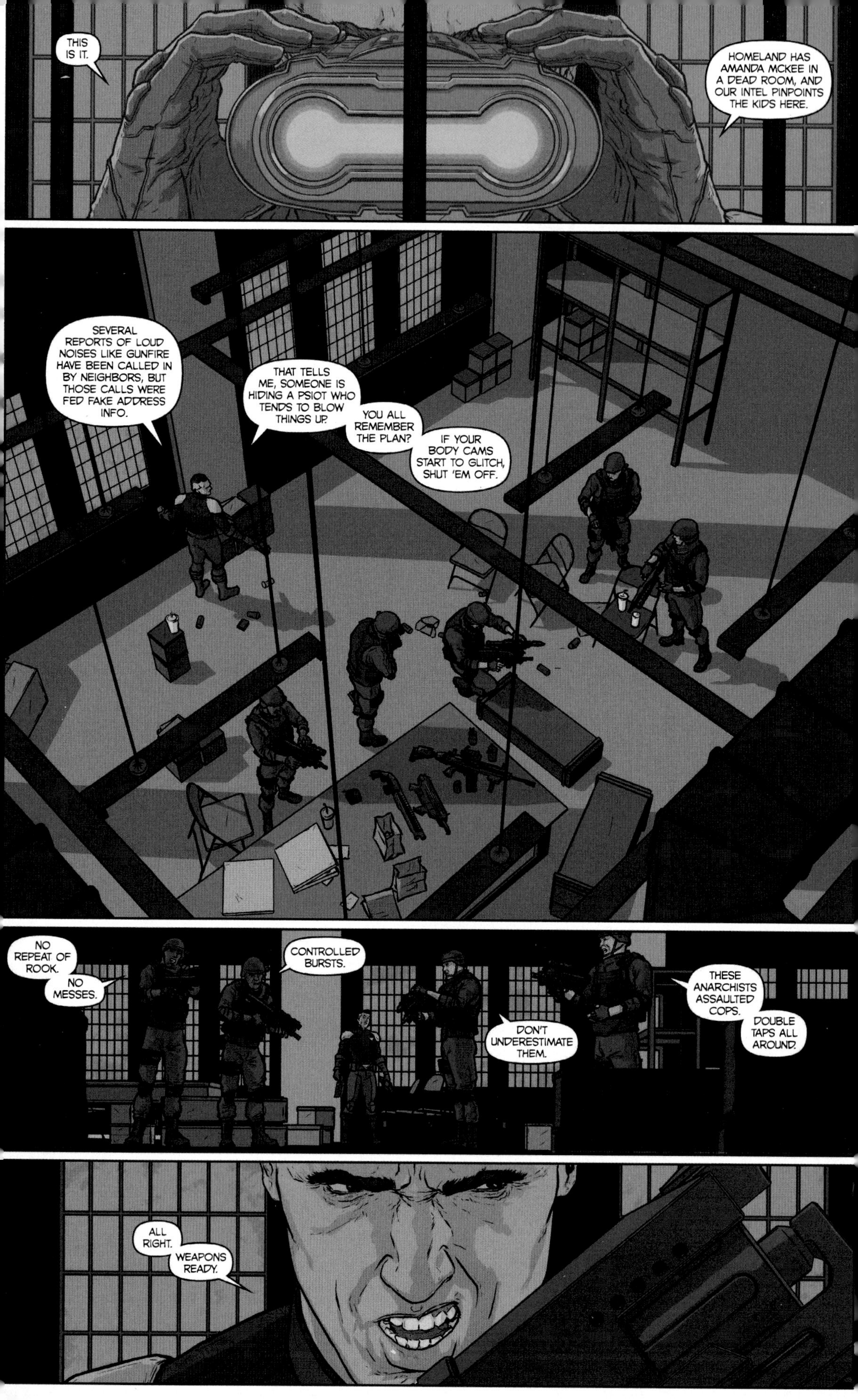
THIS IS IT.
HOMELAND HAS AMANDA MCKEE IN A DEAD ROOM, AND OUR INTEL PINPOINTS THE KIDS HERE.
SEVERAL REPORTS OF LOUD NOISES LIKE GUNFIRE HAVE BEEN CALLED IN BY NEIGHBORS, BUT THOSE CALLS WERE FED FAKE ADDRESS INFO.
THAT TELLS ME, SOMEONE IS HIDING A PSIOT WHO TENDS TO BLOW THINGS UP.
YOU ALL REMEMBER THE PLAN?
IF YOUR BODY CAMS START TO GLITCH, SHUT 'EM OFF.
NO REPEAT OF ROOK.
NO MESSES.
CONTROLLED BURSTS.
DON'T UNDERESTIMATE THEM.
THESE ANARCHISTS ASSAULTED COPS.
DOUBLE TAPS ALL AROUND.
ALL RIGHT.
WEAPONS READY.

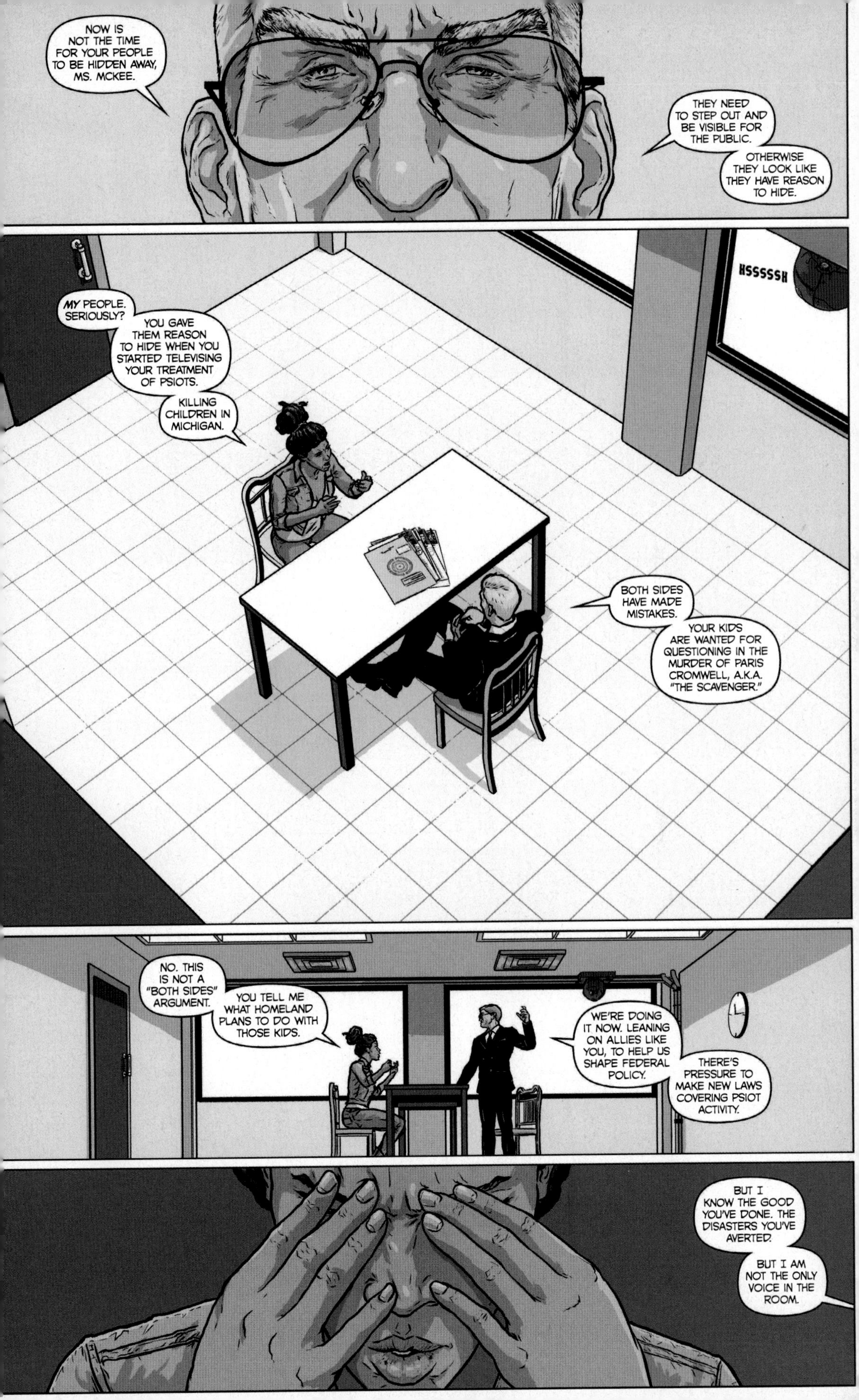

NOW IS NOT THE TIME FOR YOUR PEOPLE TO BE HIDDEN AWAY, MS. MCKEE.
THEY NEED TO STEP OUT AND BE VISIBLE FOR THE PUBLIC.
OTHERWISE THEY LOOK LIKE THEY HAVE REASON TO HIDE.
MY PEOPLE. SERIOUSLY?
YOU GAVE THEM REASON TO HIDE WHEN YOU STARTED TELEVISING YOUR TREATMENT OF PSIOTS.
KILLING CHILDREN IN MICHIGAN.
BOTH SIDES HAVE MADE MISTAKES.
YOUR KIDS ARE WANTED FOR QUESTIONING IN THE MURDER OF PARIS CROMWELL, A.K.A. "THE SCAVENGER."
NO. THIS IS NOT A "BOTH SIDES" ARGUMENT.
YOU TELL ME WHAT HOMELAND PLANS TO DO WITH THOSE KIDS.
WE'RE DOING IT NOW. LEANING ON ALLIES LIKE YOU, TO HELP US SHAPE FEDERAL POLICY.
THERE'S PRESSURE TO MAKE NEW LAWS COVERING PSIOT ACTIVITY.
BUT I KNOW THE GOOD YOU'VE DONE. THE DISASTERS YOU'VE AVERTED.
BUT I AM NOT THE ONLY VOICE IN THE ROOM.

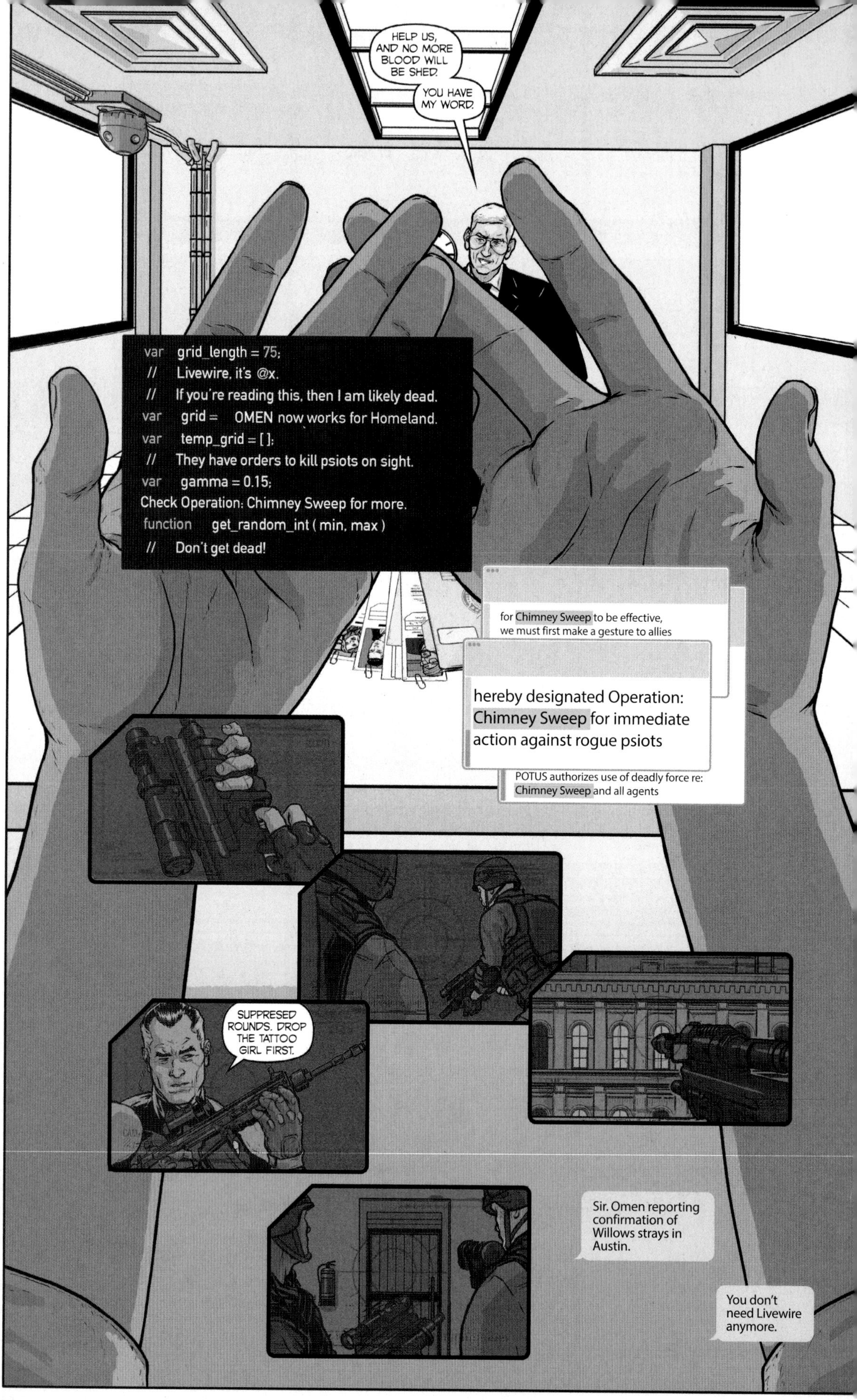
HELP US, AND NO MORE BLOOD WILL BE SHED.
YOU HAVE MY WORD.
var grid_length = 75;
// Livewire, it's @x.
// If you're reading this, then I am likely dead.
var grid = OMEN now works for Homeland.
var temp_grid = [ ];
// They have orders to kill psiots on sight.
var gamma = 0.15;
Check Operation: Chimney Sweep for more.
function get_random_int (min, max)
// Don't get dead!
for Chimney Sweep to be effective, we must first make a gesture to allies
hereby designated Operation: Chimney Sweep for immediate action against rogue psiots
POTUS authorizes use of deadly force re: Chimney Sweep and all agents
SUPPRESED ROUNDS. DROP THE TATTOO GIRL FIRST.
Sir. Omen reporting confirmation of Willows strays in Austin.
You don't need Livewire anymore.

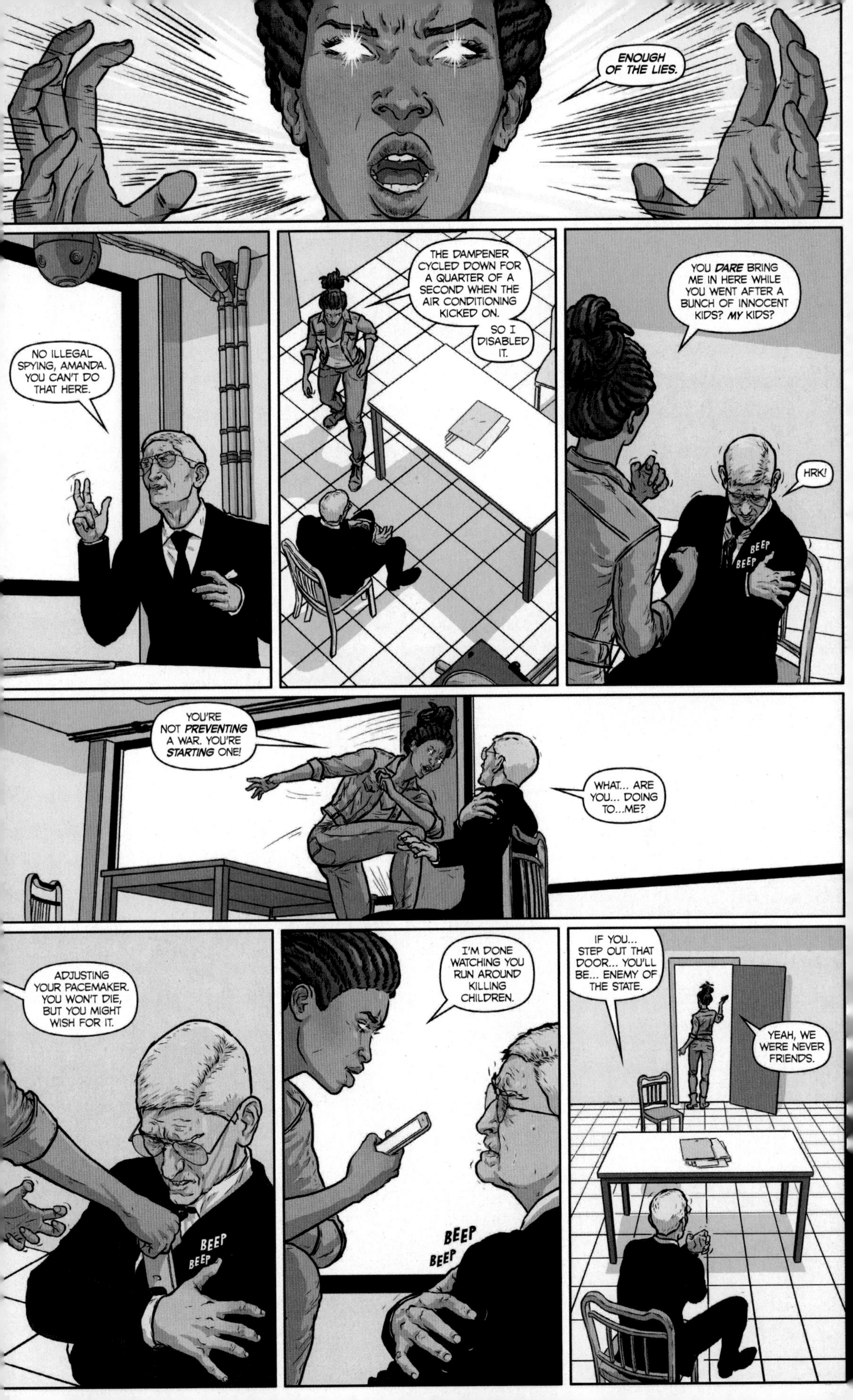
ENOUGH OF THE LIES.
NO ILLEGAL SPYING, AMANDA. YOU CAN'T DO THAT HERE.
THE DAMPENER CYCLED DOWN FOR A QUARTER OF A SECOND WHEN THE AIR CONDITIONING KICKED ON.
SO I DISABLED IT.
YOU DARE BRING ME IN HERE WHILE YOU WENT AFTER A BUNCH OF INNOCENT KIDS? MY KIDS?
HRK!
BEEP
BEEP
YOU'RE NOT PREVENTING A WAR. YOU'RE STARTING ONE!
WHAT... ARE YOU... DOING TO...ME?
ADJUSTING YOUR PACEMAKER. YOU WON'T DIE, BUT YOU MIGHT WISH FOR IT.
BEEP
BEEP
I'M DONE WATCHING YOU RUN AROUND KILLING CHILDREN.
BEEP
BEEP
IF YOU... STEP OUT THAT DOOR... YOU'LL BE... ENEMY OF THE STATE.
YEAH, WE WERE NEVER FRIENDS.

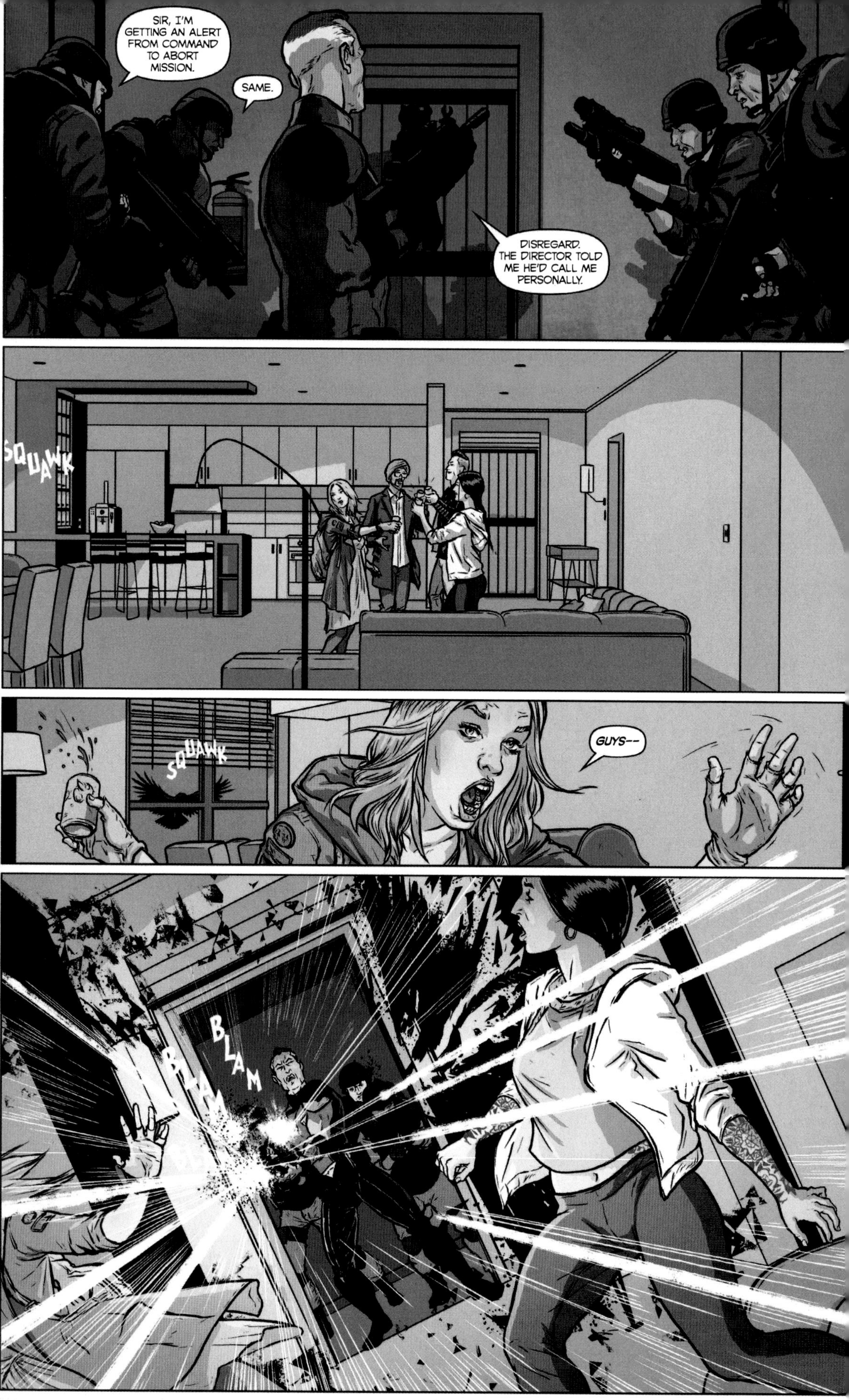
SIR, I'M GETTING AN ALERT FROM COMMAND TO ABORT MISSION.
SAME.
DISREGARD. THE DIRECTOR TOLD ME HE'D CALL ME PERSONALLY.
SQUAWK
SQUAWK
GUYS--
BLAM
BLAM

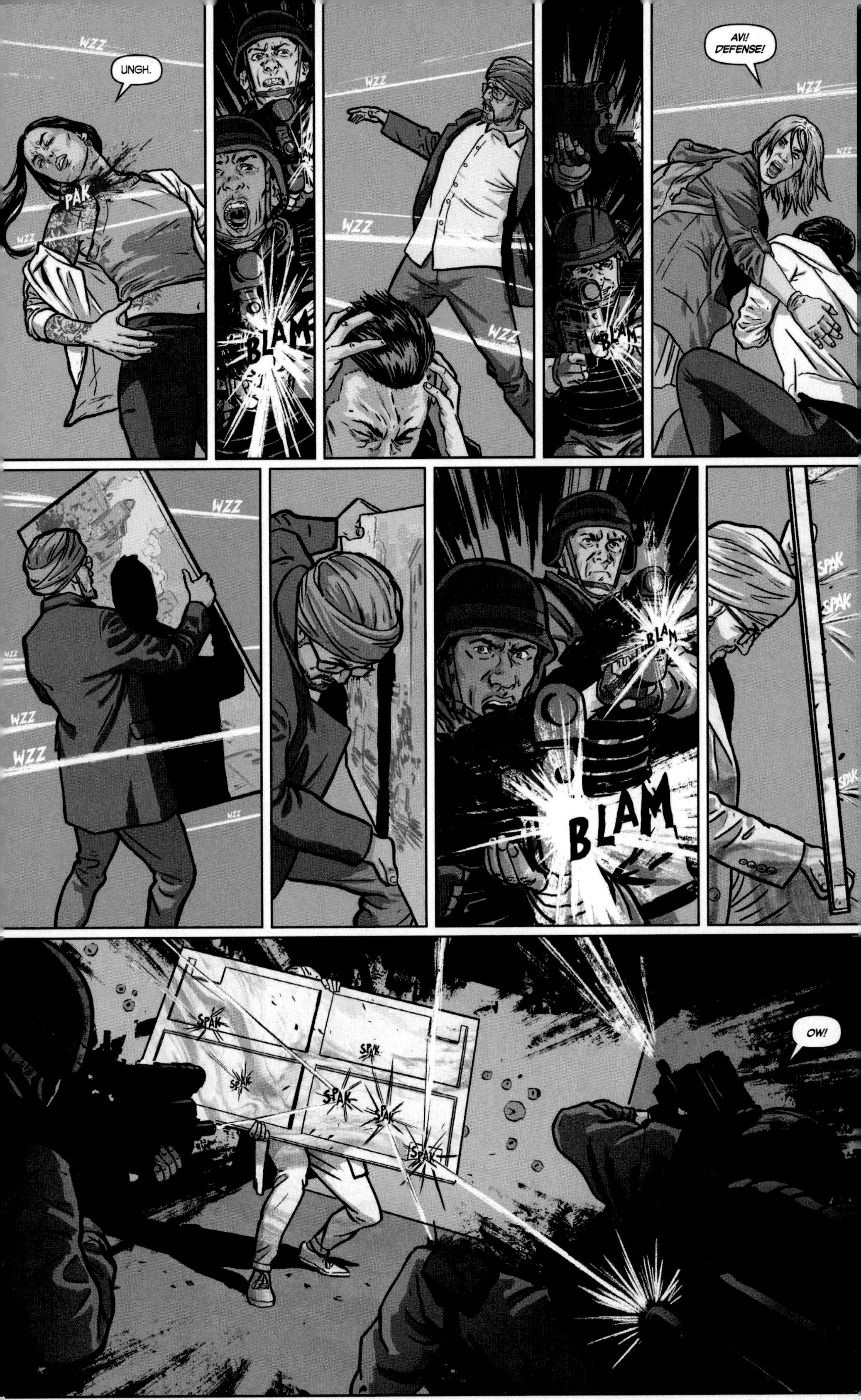
WZZ
UNGH.
PAK
WZZ
BLAM
WZZ
WZZ
WZZ
BLAM
AVI!
DEFENSE!
WZZ
WZZ
WZZ
WZZ
WZZ
WZZ
BLAM
BLAM
SPAK
SPAK
SPAK
SPAK
SPAK
SPAK
SPAK
SPAK
SPAK
OW!

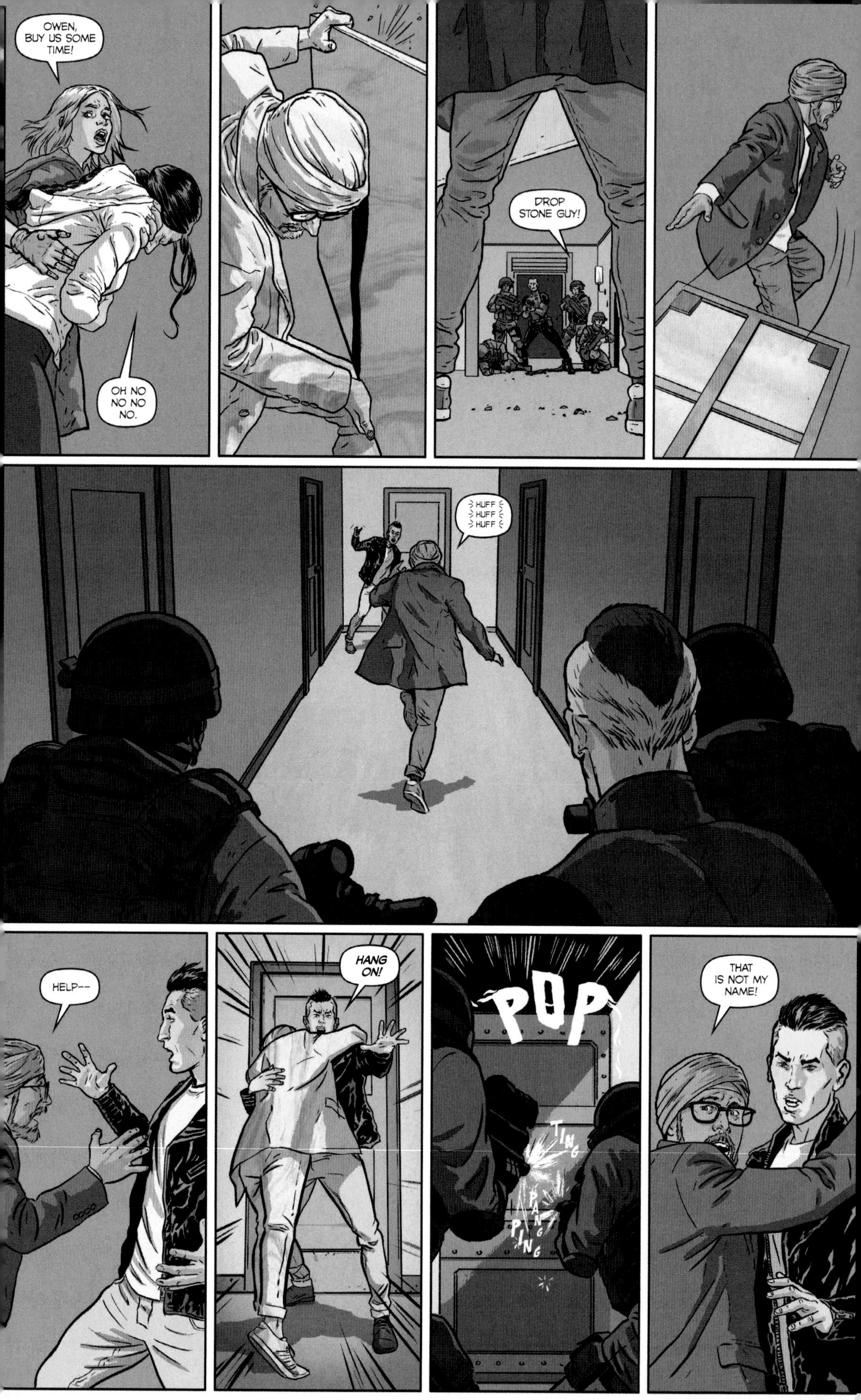
OWEN, BUY US SOME TIME!
OH NO NO NO NO.
DROP STONE GUY!
HUFF HUFF HUFF
HELP--
HANG ON!
POP
TING
PANG
PING
THAT IS NOT MY NAME!

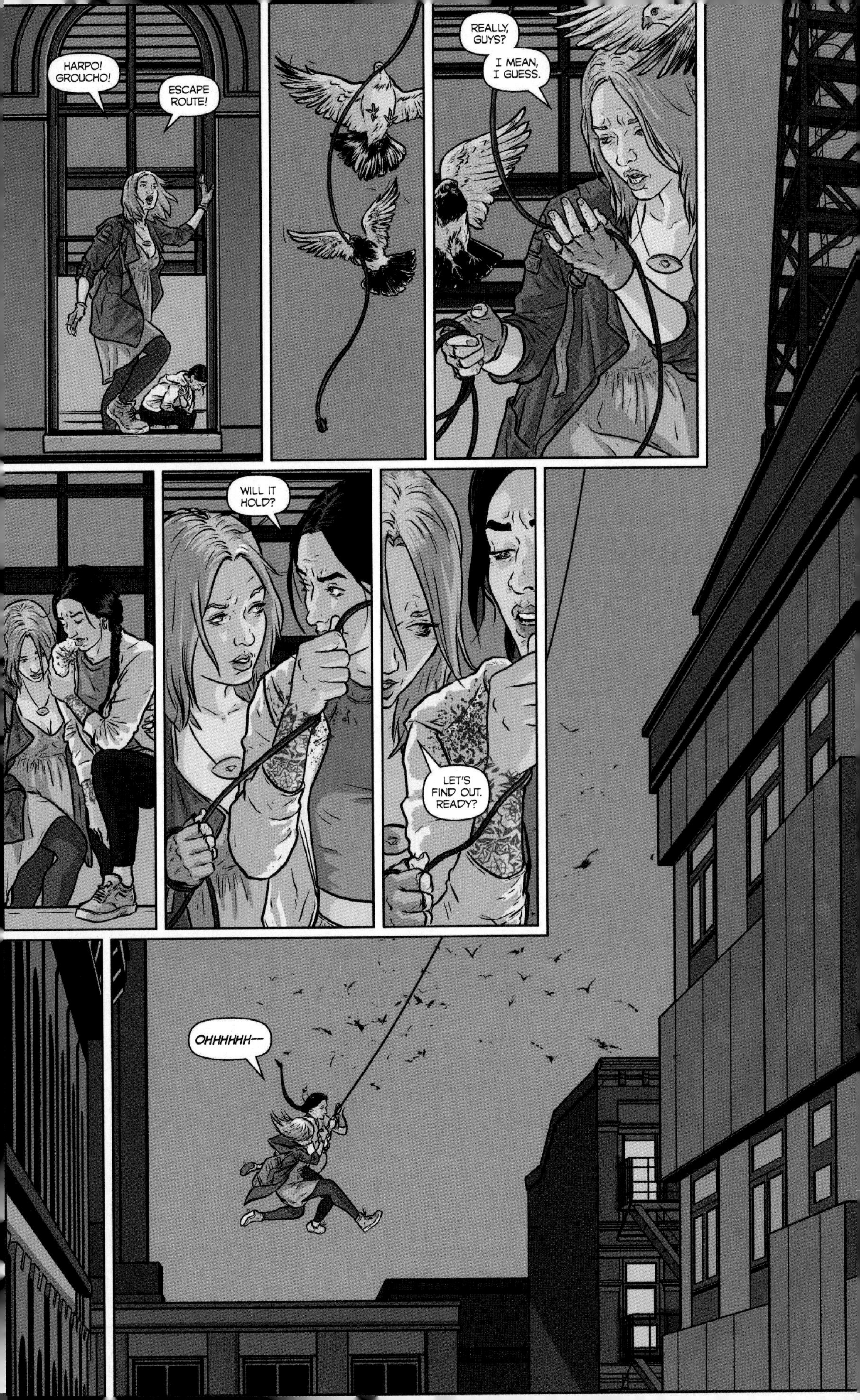
HARPO! GROUCHO!
ESCAPE ROUTE!
REALLY, GUYS?
I MEAN, I GUESS.
WILL IT HOLD?
LET'S FIND OUT. READY?
OHHHHHH--

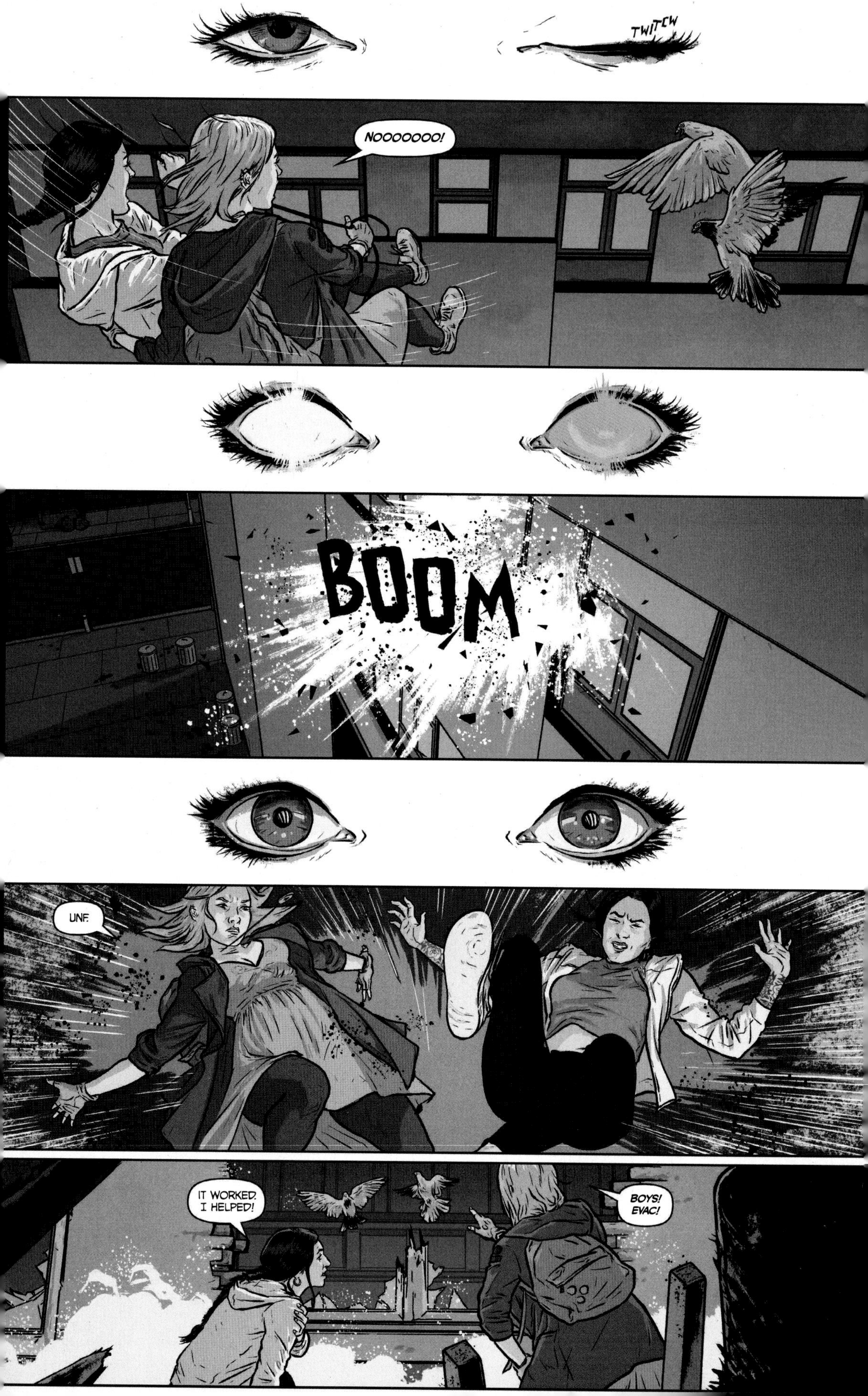
TWITCW
NOOOOOOO!
BOOM
UNF.
IT WORKED. I HELPED!
BOYS! EVAC!

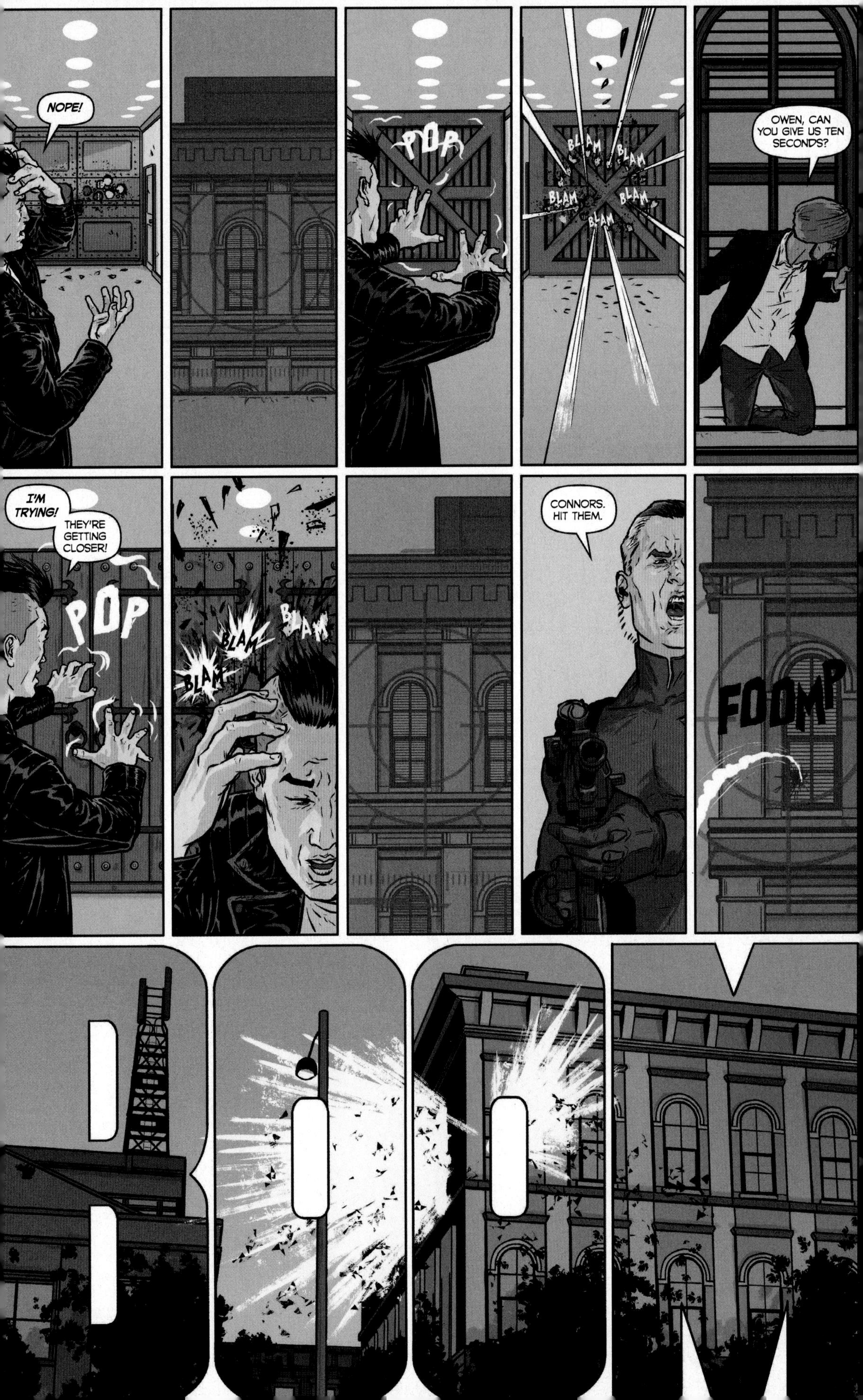
NOPE!
POP
BLAM BLAM
BLAM BLAM
BLAM
OWEN, CAN YOU GIVE US TEN SECONDS?
I'M TRYING!
THEY'RE GETTING CLOSER!
POP
BLAM
BLAM
BLAM
CONNORS. HIT THEM.
FOOMP
BOOM

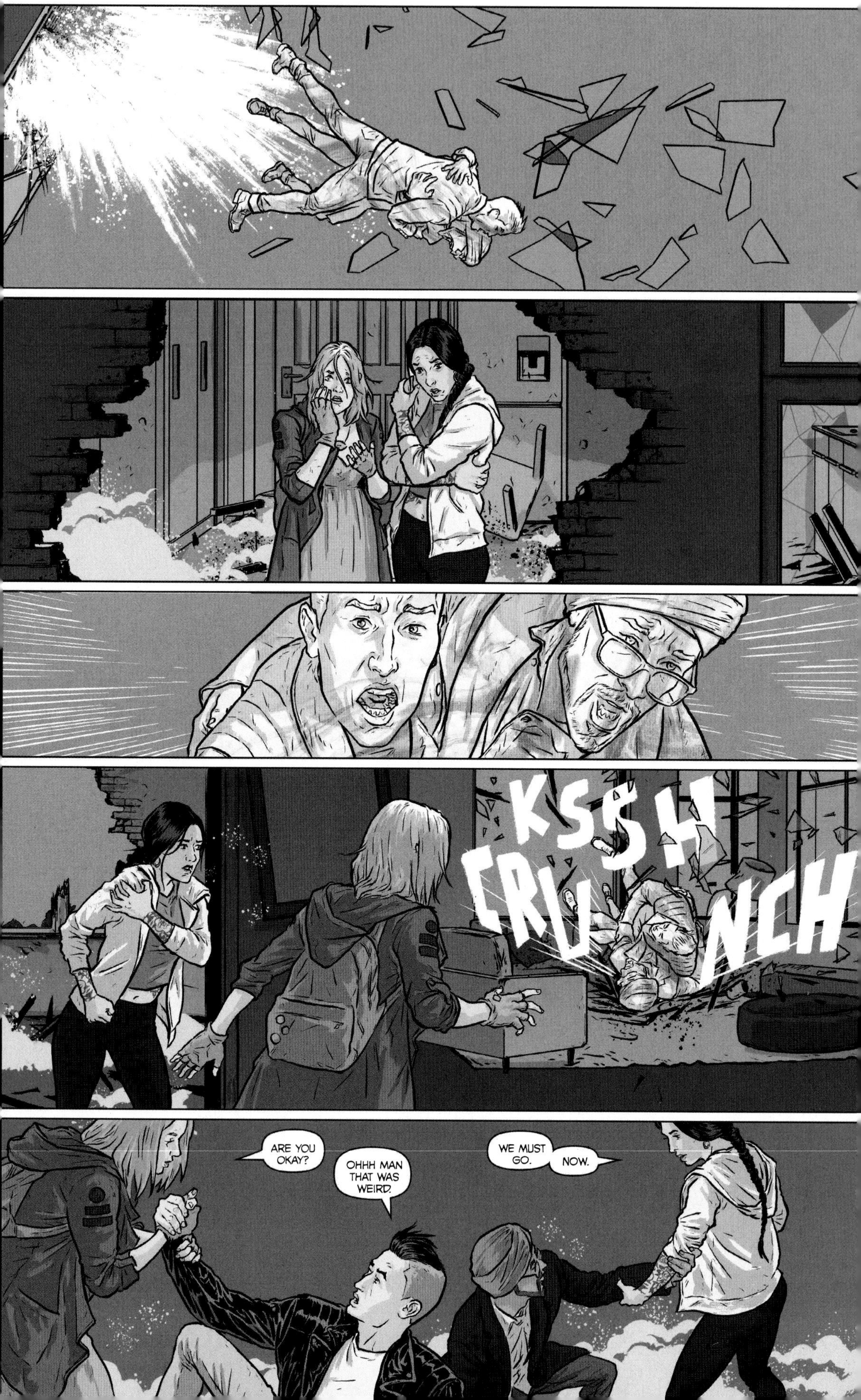
KSSH
CRUNCH
ARE YOU OKAY?
OHHH MAN THAT WAS WEIRD.
WE MUST GO.
NOW.

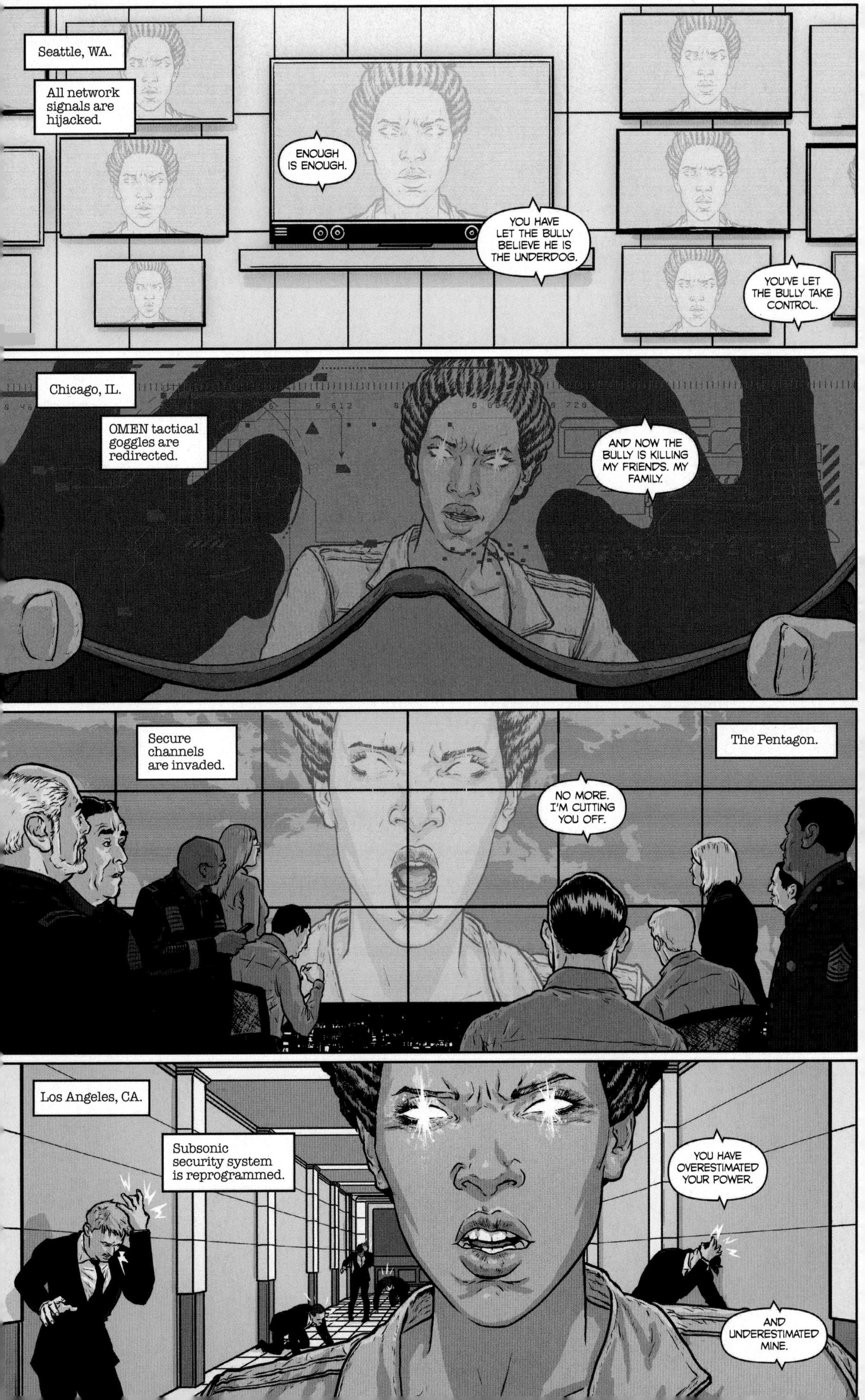
Seattle, WA.
All network signals are hijacked.
ENOUGH IS ENOUGH.
YOU HAVE LET THE BULLY BELIEVE HE IS THE UNDERDOG.
YOU'VE LET THE BULLY TAKE CONTROL.
Chicago, IL.
OMEN tactical goggles are redirected.
AND NOW THE BULLY IS KILLING MY FRIENDS. MY FAMILY.
Secure channels are invaded.
The Pentagon.
NO MORE. I'M CUTTING YOU OFF.
Los Angeles, CA.
Subsonic security system is reprogrammed.
YOU HAVE OVERESTIMATED YOUR POWER.
AND UNDERESTIMATED MINE.

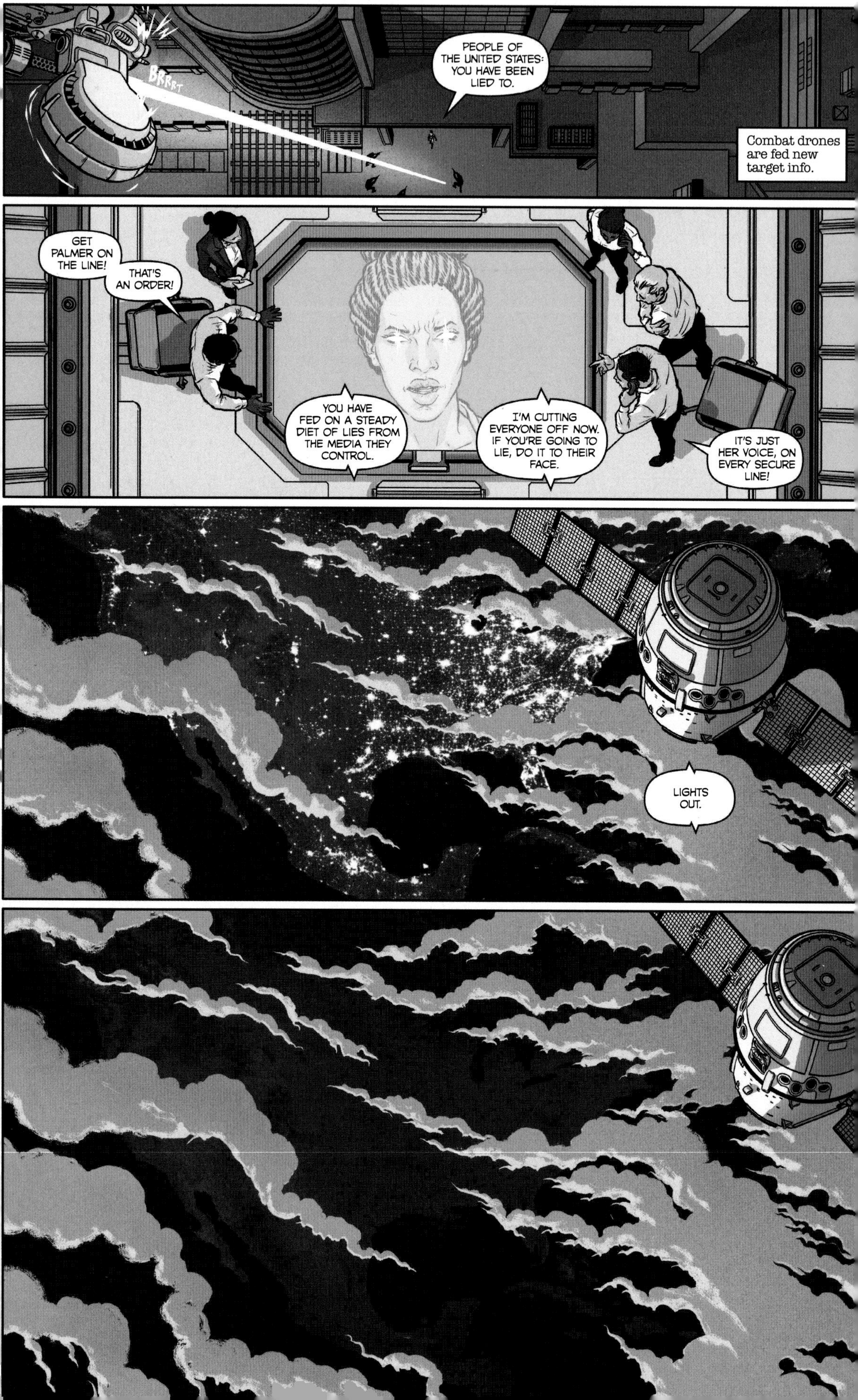
WHIRR
BRRRRT
PEOPLE OF THE UNITED STATES: YOU HAVE BEEN LIED TO.
Combat drones are fed new target info.
GET PALMER ON THE LINE!
THAT'S AN ORDER!
YOU HAVE FED ON A STEADY DIET OF LIES FROM THE MEDIA THEY CONTROL.
I'M CUTTING EVERYONE OFF NOW. IF YOU'RE GOING TO LIE, DO IT TO THEIR FACE.
IT'S JUST HER VOICE, ON EVERY SECURE LINE!
LIGHTS OUT.

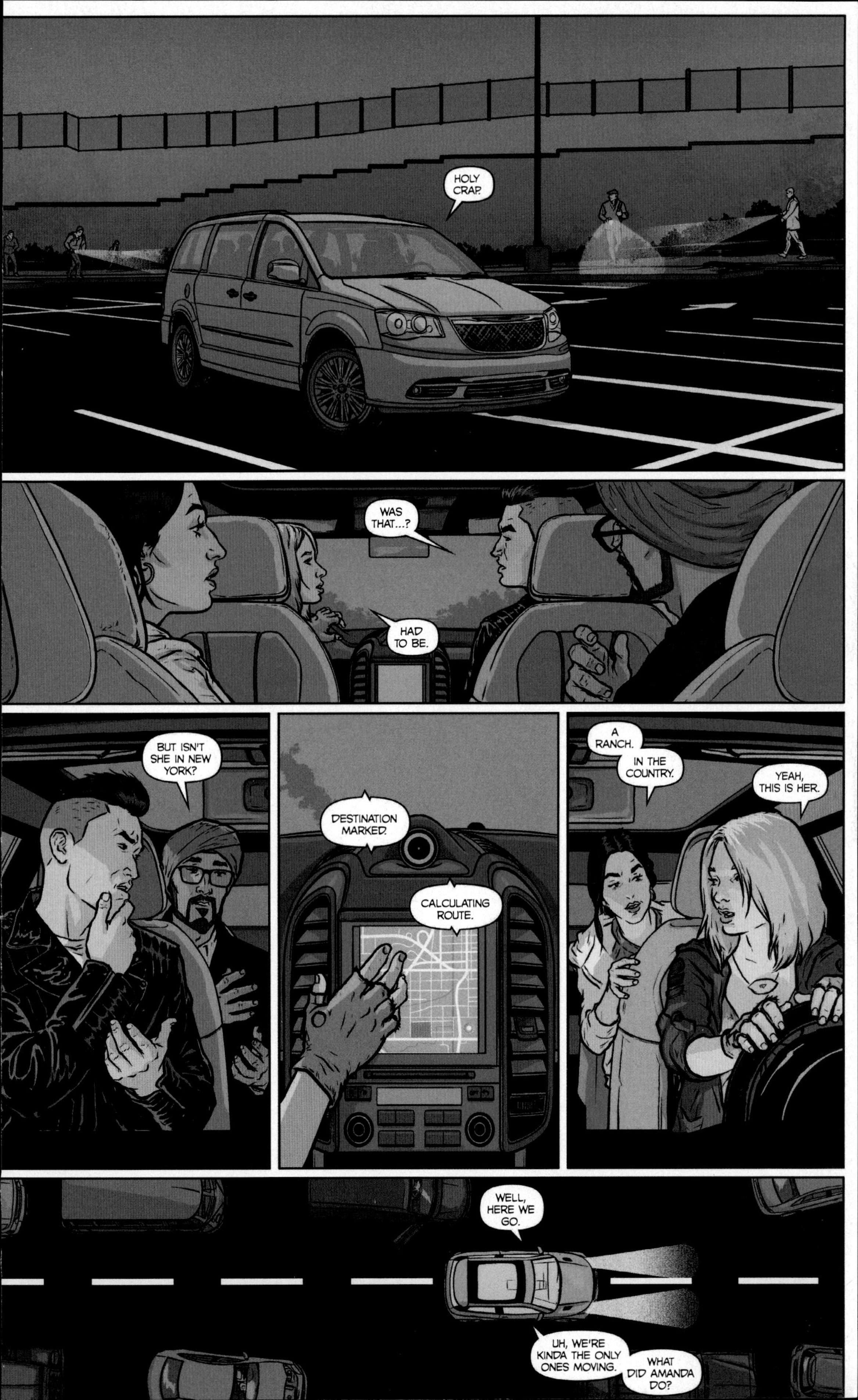
HOLY CRAP.
WAS THAT...?
HAD TO BE.
BUT ISN'T SHE IN NEW YORK?
DESTINATION MARKED.
CALCULATING ROUTE.
A RANCH.
IN THE COUNTRY.
YEAH, THIS IS HER.
WELL, HERE WE GO.
UH, WE'RE KINDA THE ONLY ONES MOVING.
WHAT DID AMANDA DO?

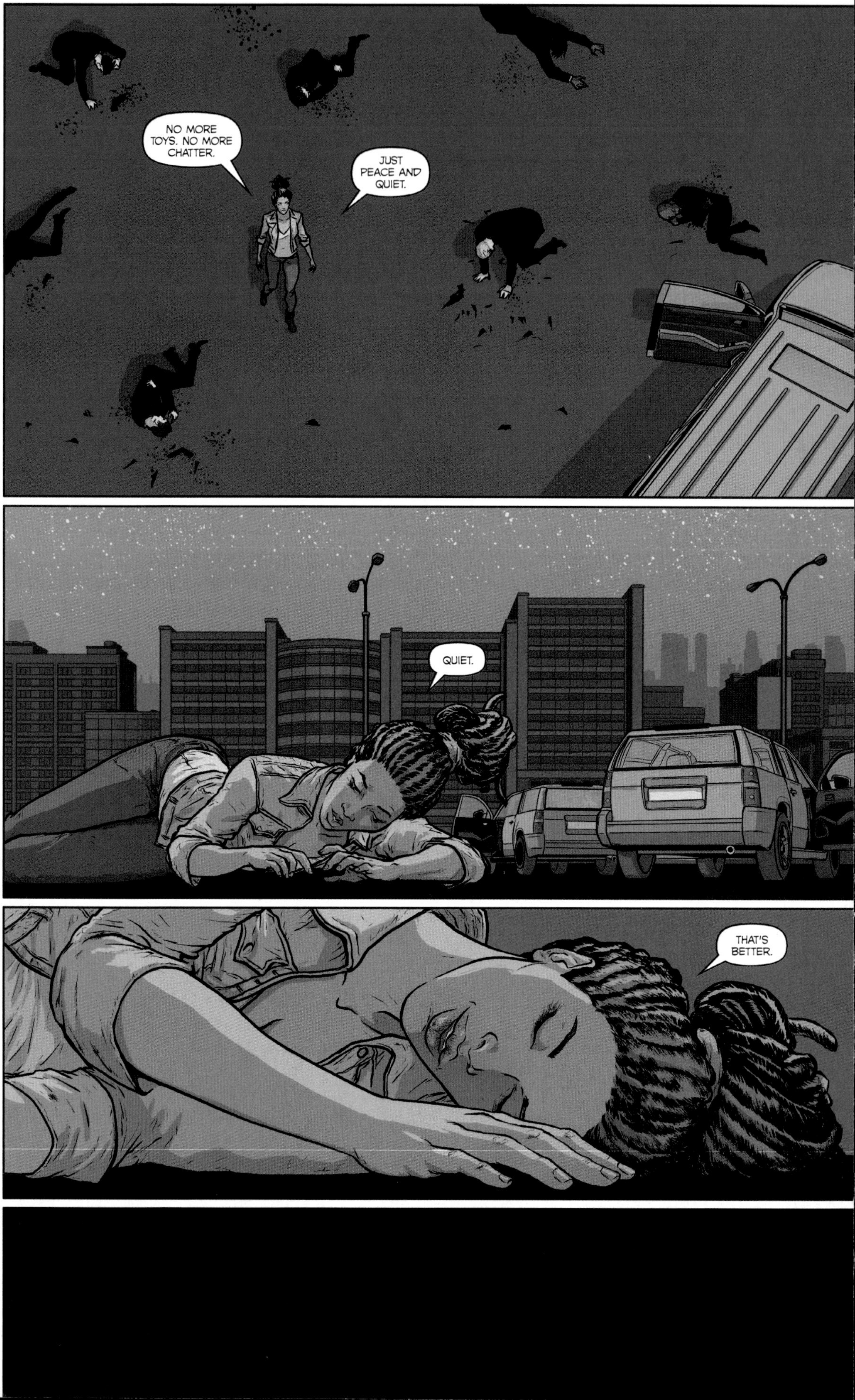
NO MORE TOYS. NO MORE CHATTER.
JUST PEACE AND QUIET.
QUIET.
THAT'S BETTER.

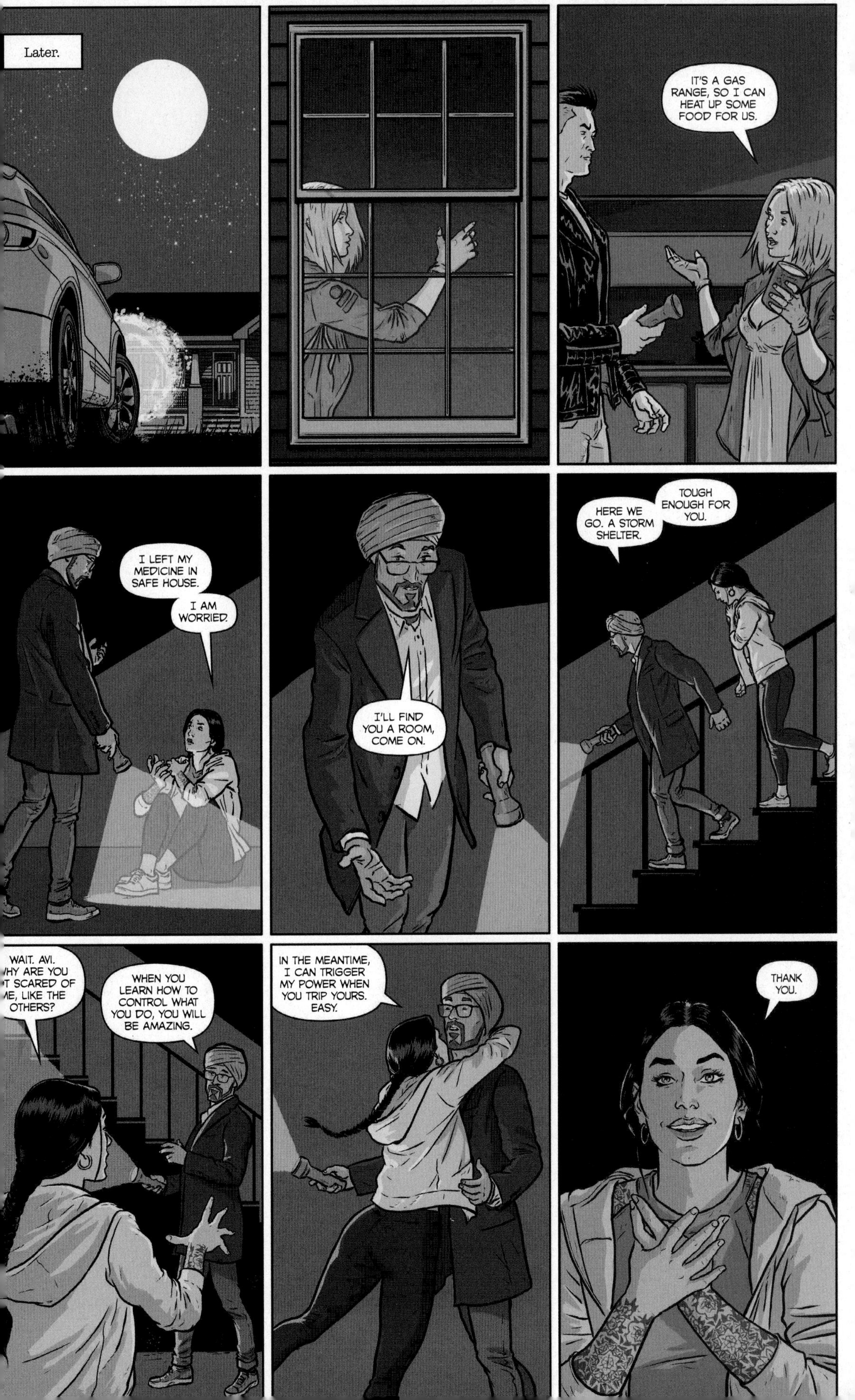
Later.
IT'S A GAS RANGE, SO I CAN HEAT UP SOME FOOD FOR US.
I LEFT MY MEDICINE IN SAFE HOUSE.
I AM WORRIED.
I'LL FIND YOU A ROOM, COME ON.
HERE WE GO. A STORM SHELTER.
TOUGH ENOUGH FOR YOU.
WAIT. AVI. HY ARE YOU T SCARED OF E, LIKE THE OTHERS?
WHEN YOU LEARN HOW TO CONTROL WHAT YOU DO, YOU WILL BE AMAZING.
IN THE MEANTIME, I CAN TRIGGER MY POWER WHEN YOU TRIP YOURS. EASY.
THANK YOU.

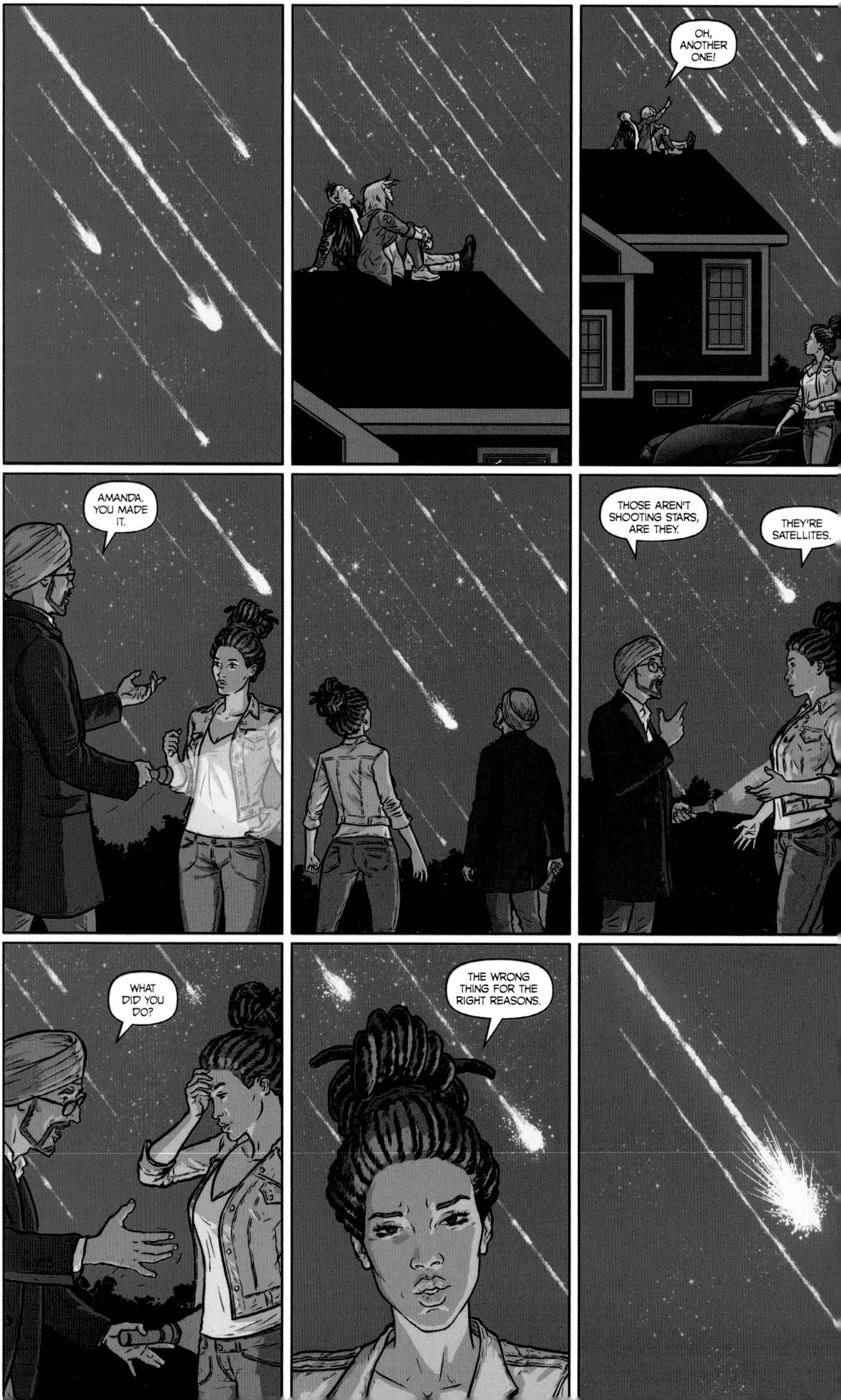
OH, ANOTHER ONE!
AMANDA. YOU MADE IT.
THOSE AREN'T SHOOTING STARS, ARE THEY.
THEY'RE SATELLITES.
WHAT DID YOU DO?
THE WRONG THING FOR THE RIGHT REASONS.

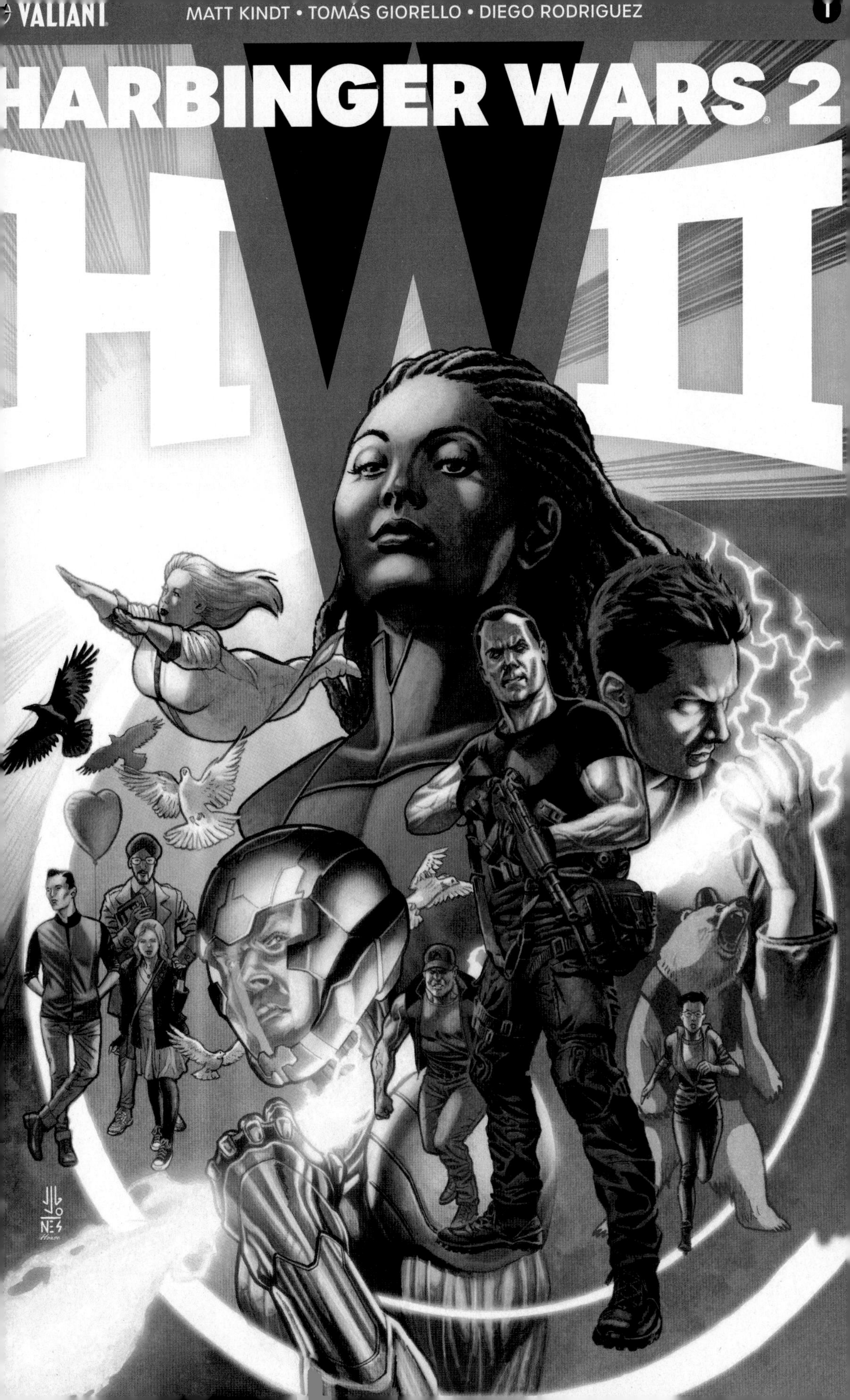
VALIANT
MATT KINDT • TOMÁS GIORELLO • DIEGO RODRIGUEZ
1
HARBINGER WARS 2
HWII

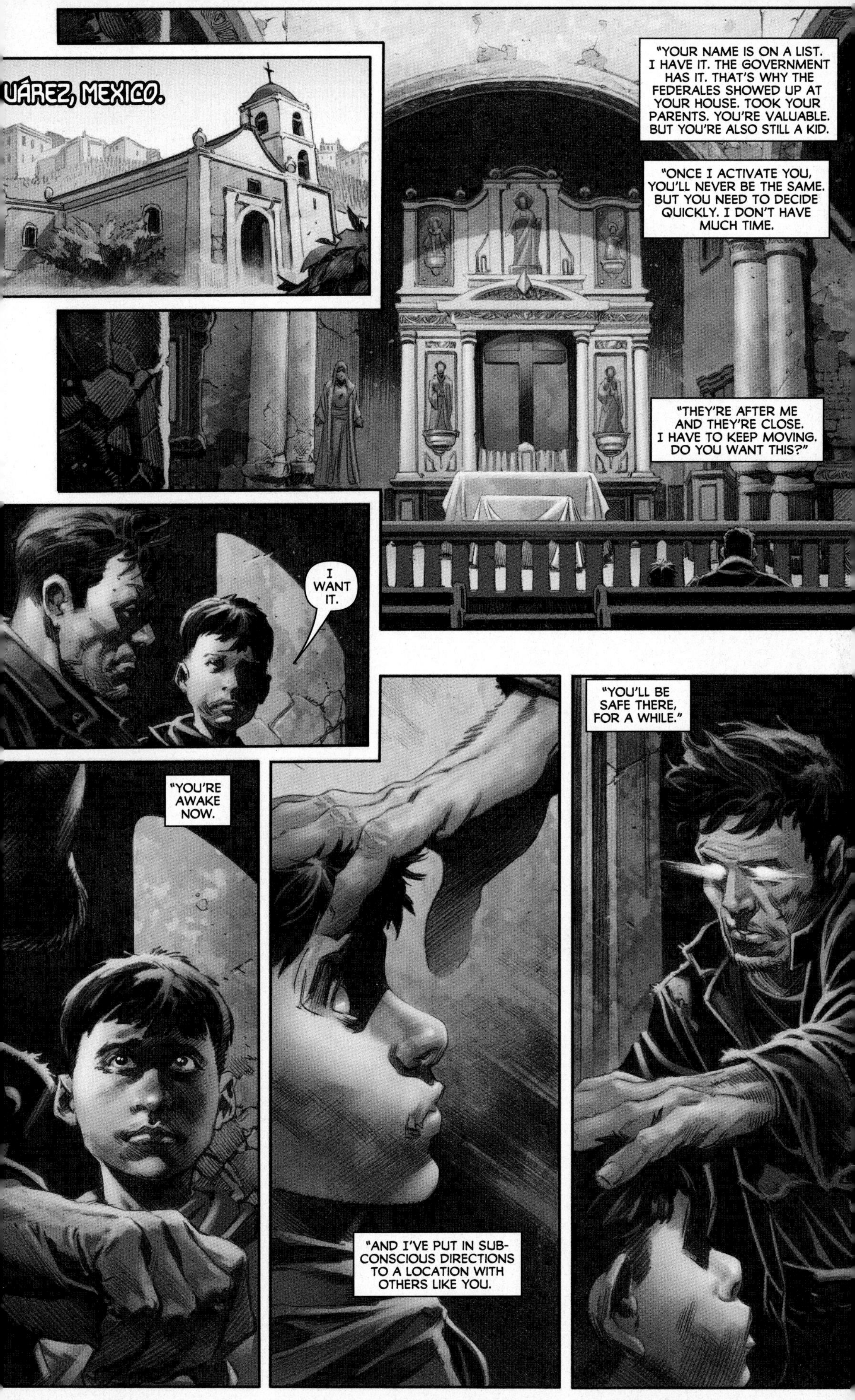
UÁREZ, MEXICO.
"YOUR NAME IS ON A LIST. I HAVE IT. THE GOVERNMENT HAS IT. THAT'S WHY THE FEDERALES SHOWED UP AT YOUR HOUSE. TOOK YOUR PARENTS. YOU'RE VALUABLE. BUT YOU'RE ALSO STILL A KID.
"ONCE I ACTIVATE YOU, YOU'LL NEVER BE THE SAME. BUT YOU NEED TO DECIDE QUICKLY. I DON'T HAVE MUCH TIME.
"THEY'RE AFTER ME AND THEY'RE CLOSE. I HAVE TO KEEP MOVING. DO YOU WANT THIS?"
I WANT IT.
"YOU'RE AWAKE NOW.
"AND I'VE PUT IN SUB-CONSCIOUS DIRECTIONS TO A LOCATION WITH OTHERS LIKE YOU.
"YOU'LL BE SAFE THERE, FOR A WHILE."

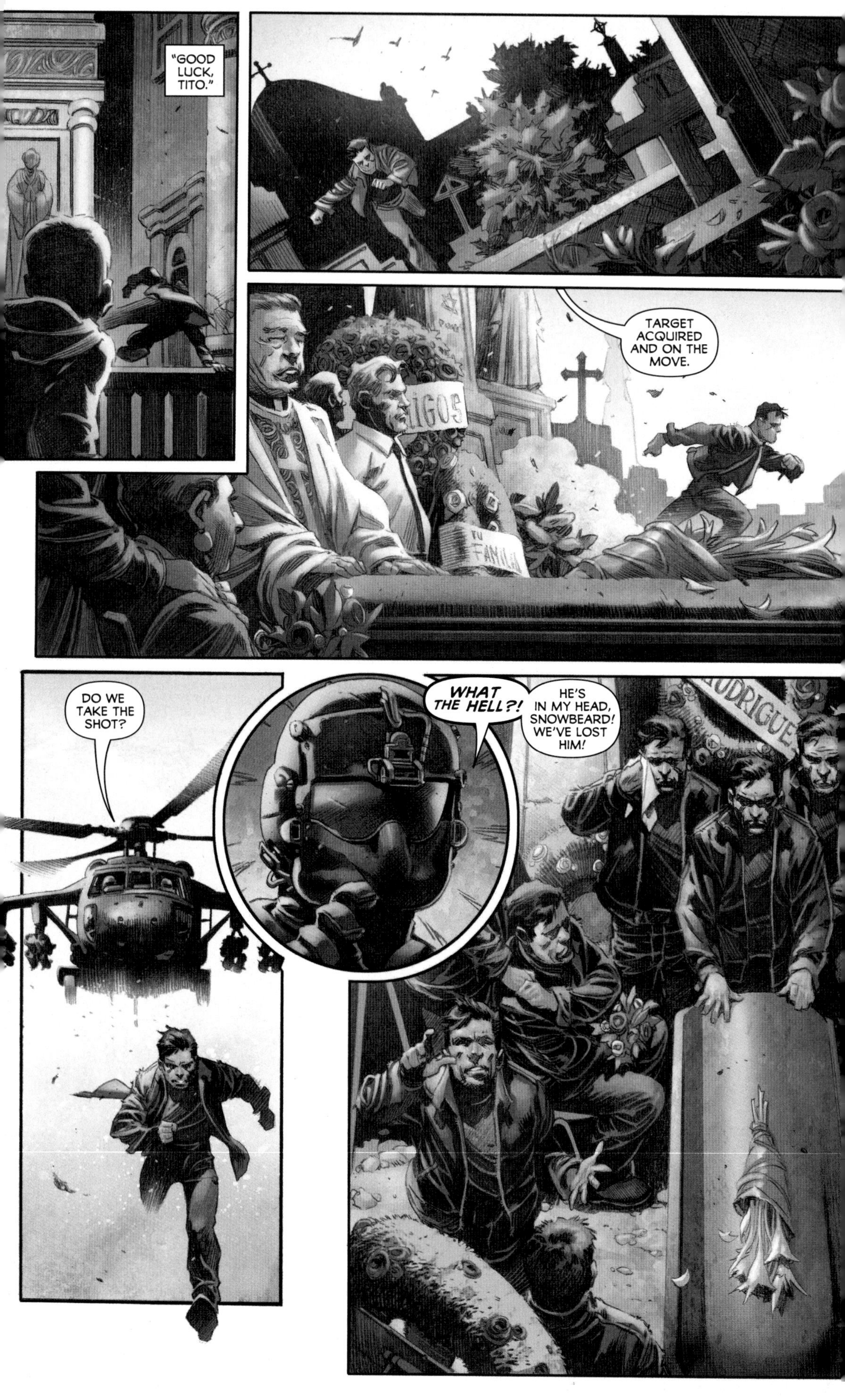
"GOOD LUCK, TITO."
TARGET ACQUIRED AND ON THE MOVE.
DO WE TAKE THE SHOT?
WHAT THE HELL?!
HE'S IN MY HEAD, SNOWBEARD! WE'VE LOST HIM!

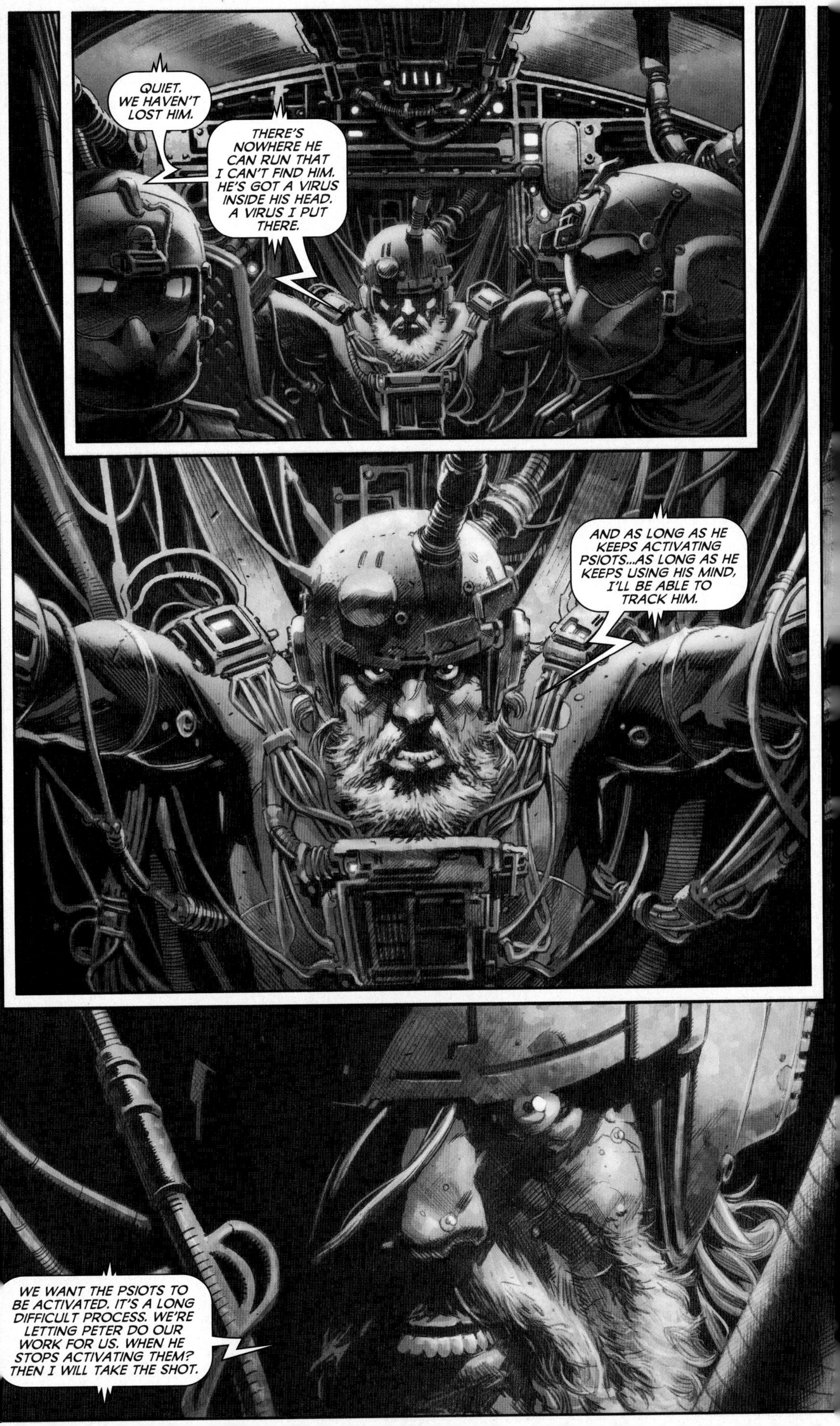
QUIET. WE HAVEN'T LOST HIM.
THERE'S NOWHERE HE CAN RUN THAT I CAN'T FIND HIM. HE'S GOT A VIRUS INSIDE HIS HEAD. A VIRUS I PUT THERE.
AND AS LONG AS HE KEEPS ACTIVATING PSIOTS...AS LONG AS HE KEEPS USING HIS MIND, I'LL BE ABLE TO TRACK HIM.
WE WANT THE PSIOTS TO BE ACTIVATED. IT'S A LONG DIFFICULT PROCESS. WE'RE LETTING PETER DO OUR WORK FOR US. WHEN HE STOPS ACTIVATING THEM? THEN I WILL TAKE THE SHOT.

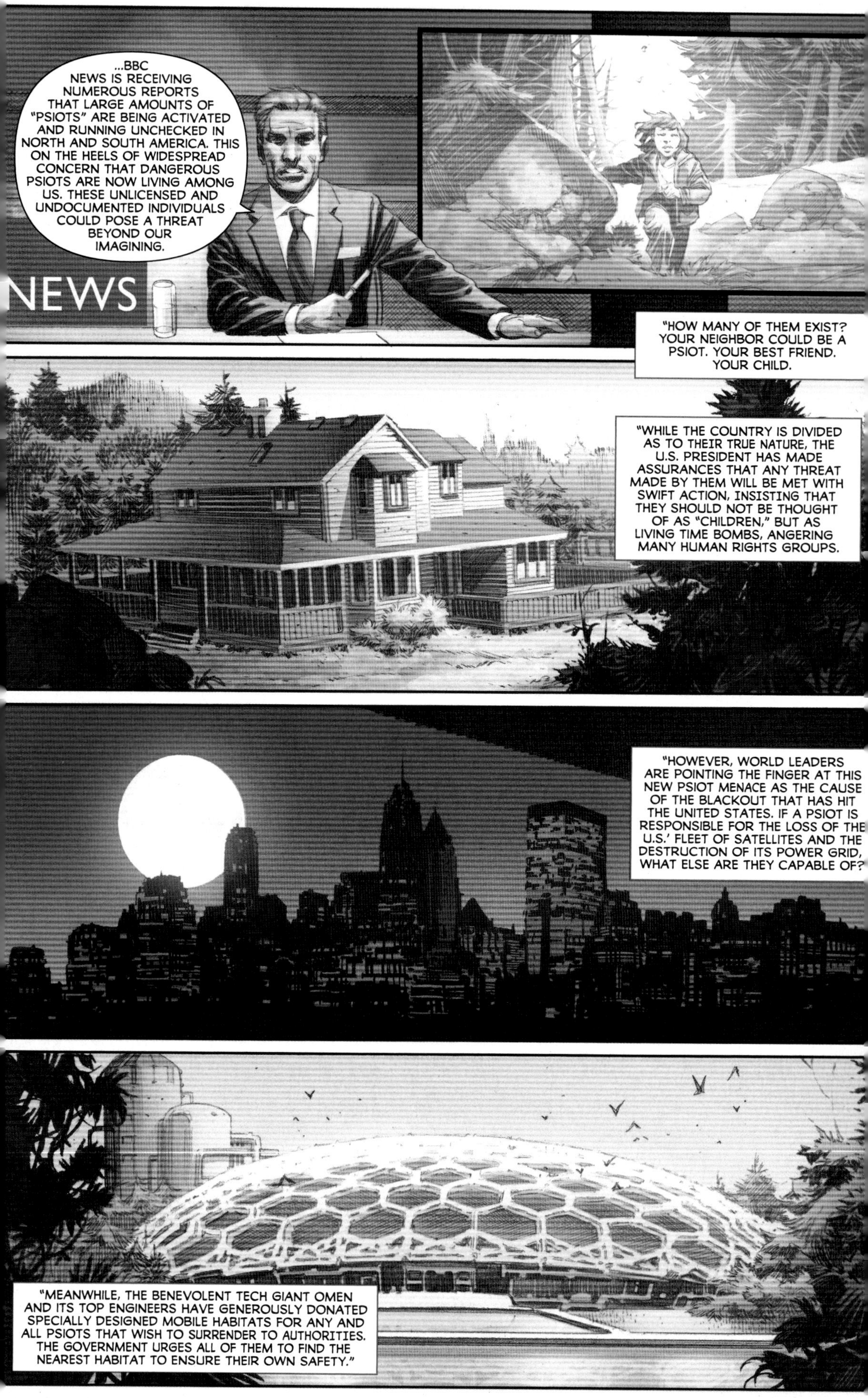
...BBC NEWS IS RECEIVING NUMEROUS REPORTS THAT LARGE AMOUNTS OF "PSIOTS" ARE BEING ACTIVATED AND RUNNING UNCHECKED IN NORTH AND SOUTH AMERICA. THIS ON THE HEELS OF WIDESPREAD CONCERN THAT DANGEROUS PSIOTS ARE NOW LIVING AMONG US. THESE UNLICENSED AND UNDOCUMENTED INDIVIDUALS COULD POSE A THREAT BEYOND OUR IMAGINING.
NEWS
"HOW MANY OF THEM EXIST? YOUR NEIGHBOR COULD BE A PSIOT. YOUR BEST FRIEND. YOUR CHILD.
"WHILE THE COUNTRY IS DIVIDED AS TO THEIR TRUE NATURE, THE U.S. PRESIDENT HAS MADE ASSURANCES THAT ANY THREAT MADE BY THEM WILL BE MET WITH SWIFT ACTION, INSISTING THAT THEY SHOULD NOT BE THOUGHT OF AS "CHILDREN," BUT AS LIVING TIME BOMBS, ANGERING MANY HUMAN RIGHTS GROUPS.
"HOWEVER, WORLD LEADERS ARE POINTING THE FINGER AT THIS NEW PSIOT MENACE AS THE CAUSE OF THE BLACKOUT THAT HAS HIT THE UNITED STATES. IF A PSIOT IS RESPONSIBLE FOR THE LOSS OF THE U.S.' FLEET OF SATELLITES AND THE DESTRUCTION OF ITS POWER GRID, WHAT ELSE ARE THEY CAPABLE OF?
"MEANWHILE, THE BENEVOLENT TECH GIANT OMEN AND ITS TOP ENGINEERS HAVE GENEROUSLY DONATED SPECIALLY DESIGNED MOBILE HABITATS FOR ANY AND ALL PSIOTS THAT WISH TO SURRENDER TO AUTHORITIES. THE GOVERNMENT URGES ALL OF THEM TO FIND THE NEAREST HABITAT TO ENSURE THEIR OWN SAFETY."

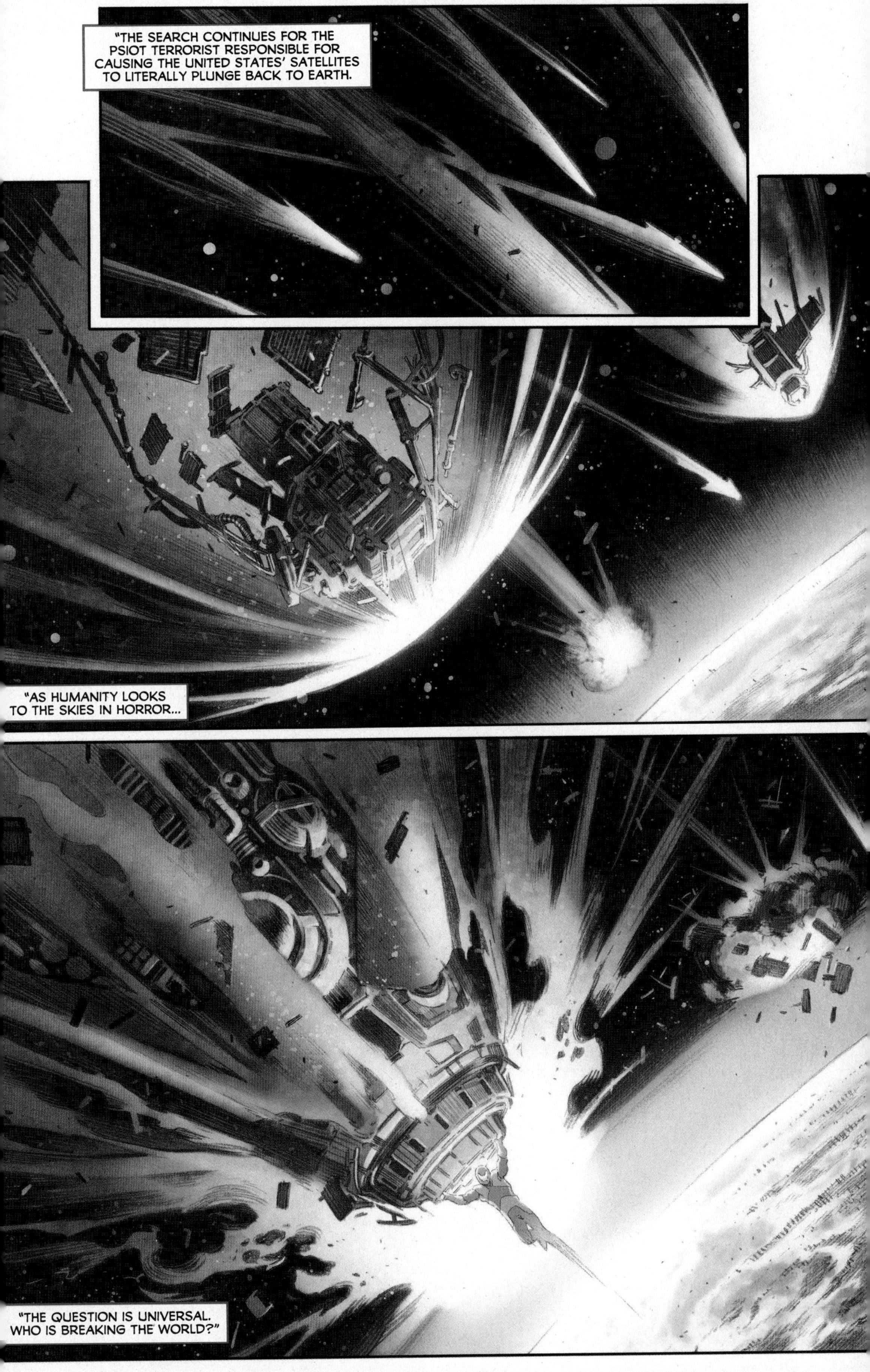
"THE SEARCH CONTINUES FOR THE PSIOT TERRORIST RESPONSIBLE FOR CAUSING THE UNITED STATES' SATELLITES TO LITERALLY PLUNGE BACK TO EARTH.
"AS HUMANITY LOOKS TO THE SKIES IN HORROR...
"THE QUESTION IS UNIVERSAL. WHO IS BREAKING THE WORLD?"

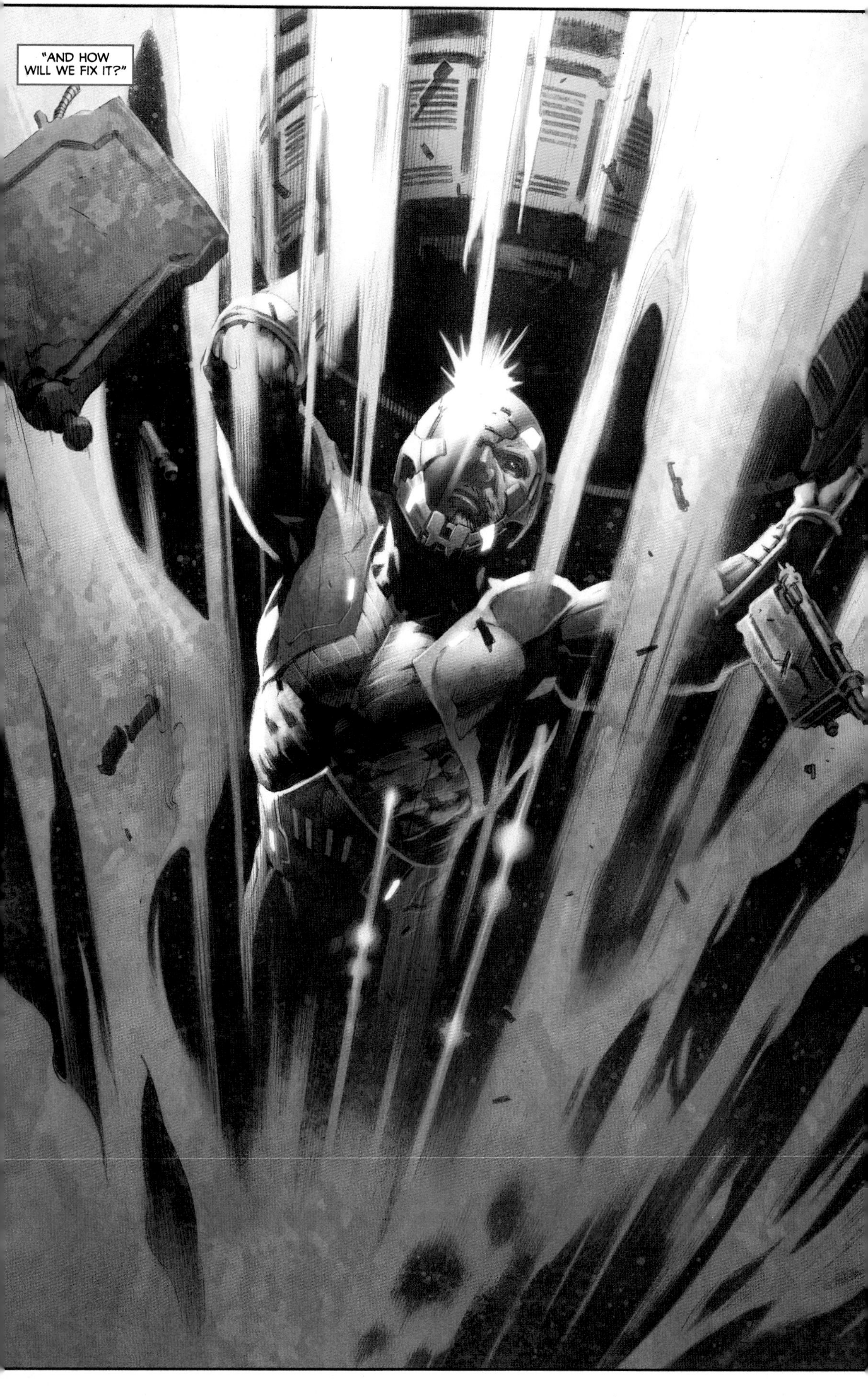
"AND HOW
WILL WE FIX IT?"

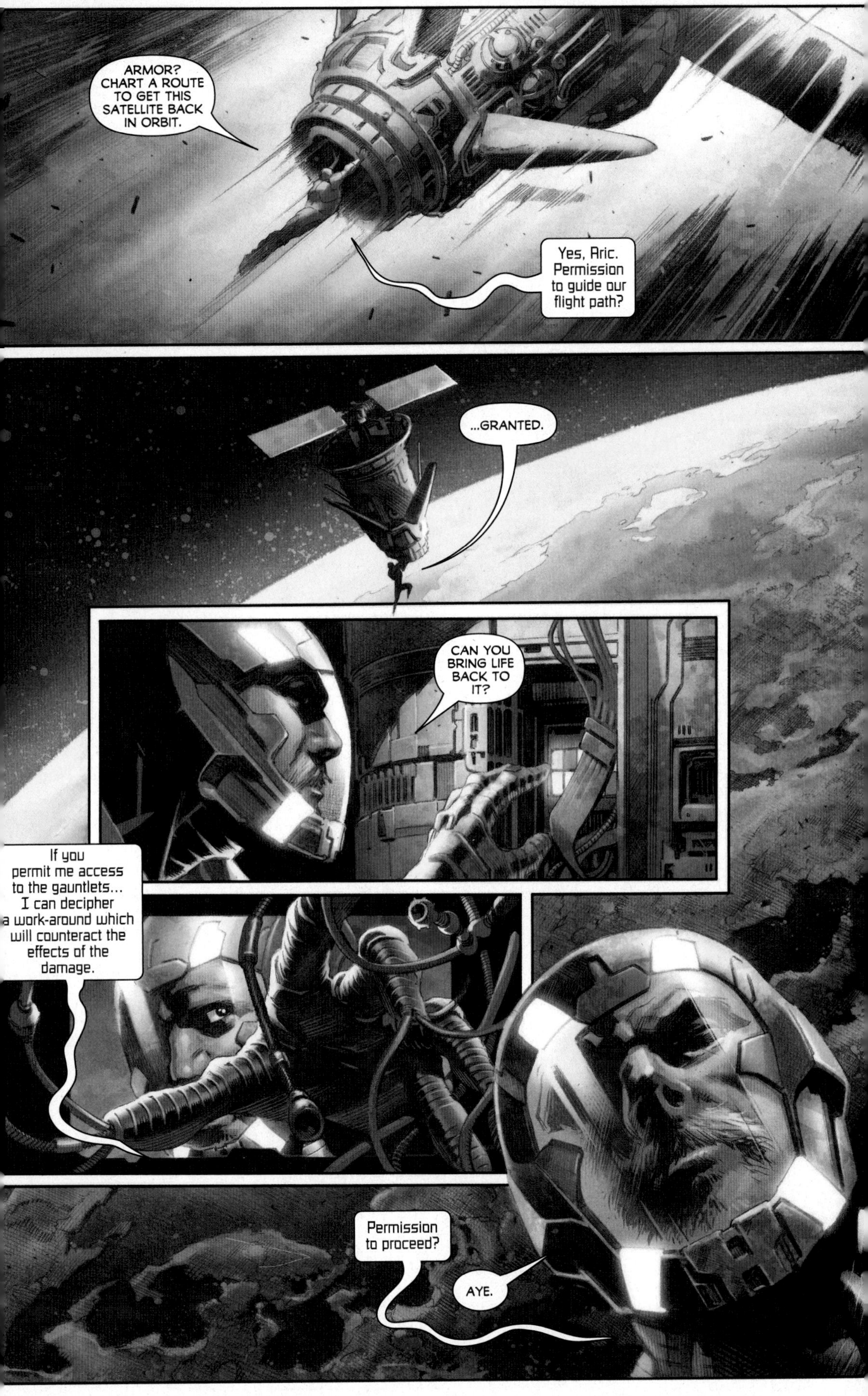

ARMOR? CHART A ROUTE TO GET THIS SATELLITE BACK IN ORBIT.
Yes, Aric. Permission to guide our flight path?
...GRANTED.
CAN YOU BRING LIFE BACK TO IT?
If you permit me access to the gauntlets... I can decipher a work-around which will counteract the effects of the damage.
Permission to proceed?
AYE.

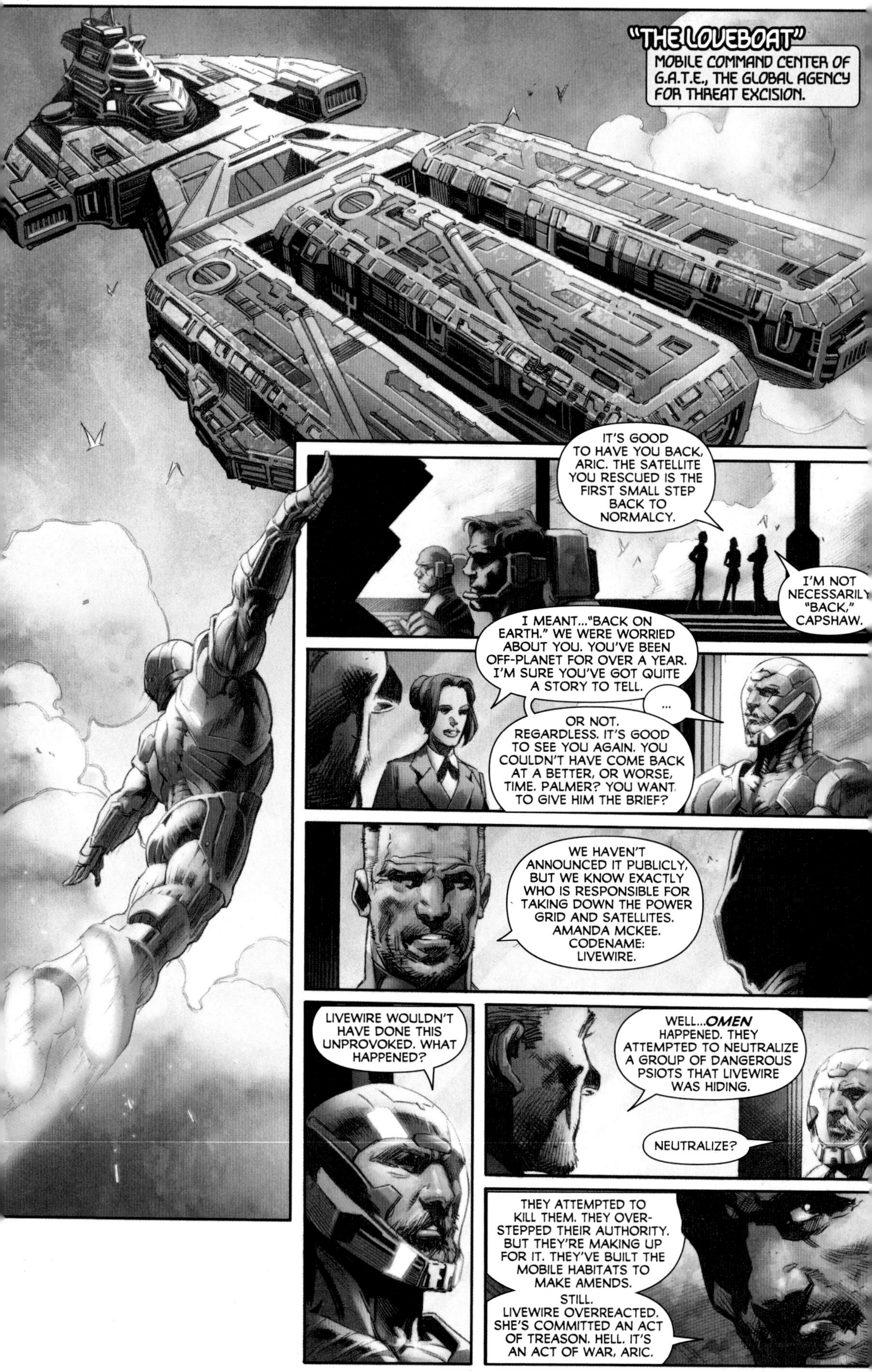
"THE LOVEBOAT"
MOBILE COMMAND CENTER OF G.A.T.E., THE GLOBAL AGENCY FOR THREAT EXCISION.
IT'S GOOD TO HAVE YOU BACK, ARIC. THE SATELLITE YOU RESCUED IS THE FIRST SMALL STEP BACK TO NORMALCY.
I'M NOT NECESSARILY "BACK," CAPSHAW.
I MEANT..."BACK ON EARTH." WE WERE WORRIED ABOUT YOU. YOU'VE BEEN OFF-PLANET FOR OVER A YEAR. I'M SURE YOU'VE GOT QUITE A STORY TO TELL.
...
OR NOT. REGARDLESS. IT'S GOOD TO SEE YOU AGAIN. YOU COULDN'T HAVE COME BACK AT A BETTER, OR WORSE, TIME. PALMER? YOU WANT TO GIVE HIM THE BRIEF?
WE HAVEN'T ANNOUNCED IT PUBLICLY, BUT WE KNOW EXACTLY WHO IS RESPONSIBLE FOR TAKING DOWN THE POWER GRID AND SATELLITES. AMANDA MCKEE. CODENAME: LIVEWIRE.
LIVEWIRE WOULDN'T HAVE DONE THIS UNPROVOKED. WHAT HAPPENED?
WELL...OMEN HAPPENED. THEY ATTEMPTED TO NEUTRALIZE A GROUP OF DANGEROUS PSIOTS THAT LIVEWIRE WAS HIDING.
NEUTRALIZE?
THEY ATTEMPTED TO KILL THEM. THEY OVER-STEPPED THEIR AUTHORITY. BUT THEY'RE MAKING UP FOR IT. THEY'VE BUILT THE MOBILE HABITATS TO MAKE AMENDS.
STILL. LIVEWIRE OVERREACTED. SHE'S COMMITTED AN ACT OF TREASON. HELL. IT'S AN ACT OF WAR, ARIC.

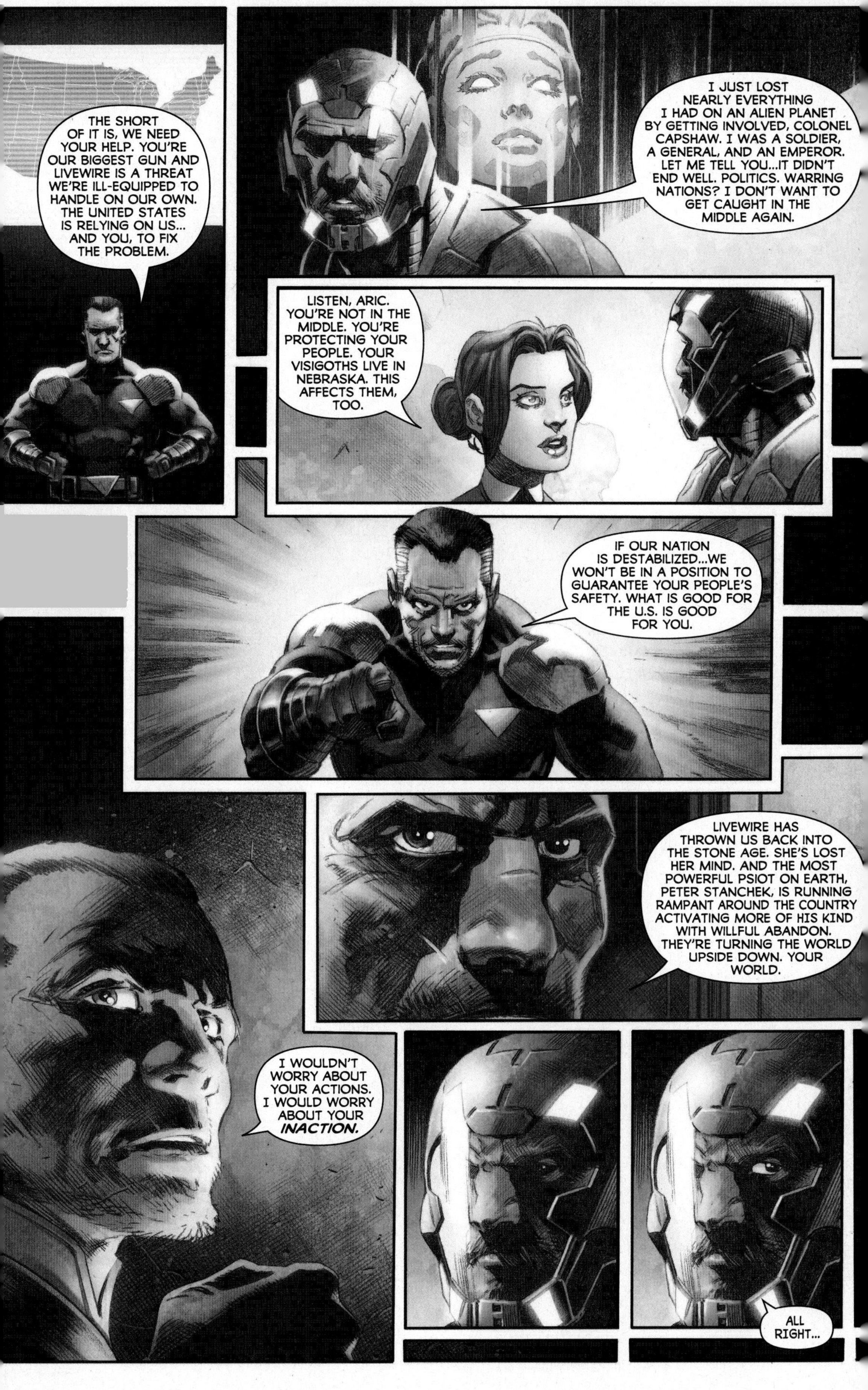
THE SHORT OF IT IS, WE NEED YOUR HELP. YOU'RE OUR BIGGEST GUN AND LIVEWIRE IS A THREAT WE'RE ILL-EQUIPPED TO HANDLE ON OUR OWN. THE UNITED STATES IS RELYING ON US... AND YOU, TO FIX THE PROBLEM.
I JUST LOST NEARLY EVERYTHING I HAD ON AN ALIEN PLANET BY GETTING INVOLVED, COLONEL CAPSHAW. I WAS A SOLDIER, A GENERAL, AND AN EMPEROR. LET ME TELL YOU...IT DIDN'T END WELL. POLITICS. WARRING NATIONS? I DON'T WANT TO GET CAUGHT IN THE MIDDLE AGAIN.
LISTEN, ARIC. YOU'RE NOT IN THE MIDDLE. YOU'RE PROTECTING YOUR PEOPLE. YOUR VISIGOTHS LIVE IN NEBRASKA. THIS AFFECTS THEM, TOO.
IF OUR NATION IS DESTABILIZED...WE WON'T BE IN A POSITION TO GUARANTEE YOUR PEOPLE'S SAFETY. WHAT IS GOOD FOR THE U.S. IS GOOD FOR YOU.
LIVEWIRE HAS THROWN US BACK INTO THE STONE AGE. SHE'S LOST HER MIND. AND THE MOST POWERFUL PSIOT ON EARTH, PETER STANCHEK, IS RUNNING RAMPANT AROUND THE COUNTRY ACTIVATING MORE OF HIS KIND WITH WILLFUL ABANDON. THEY'RE TURNING THE WORLD UPSIDE DOWN. YOUR WORLD.
I WOULDN'T WORRY ABOUT YOUR ACTIONS. I WOULD WORRY ABOUT YOUR *INACTION.*
ALL RIGHT...

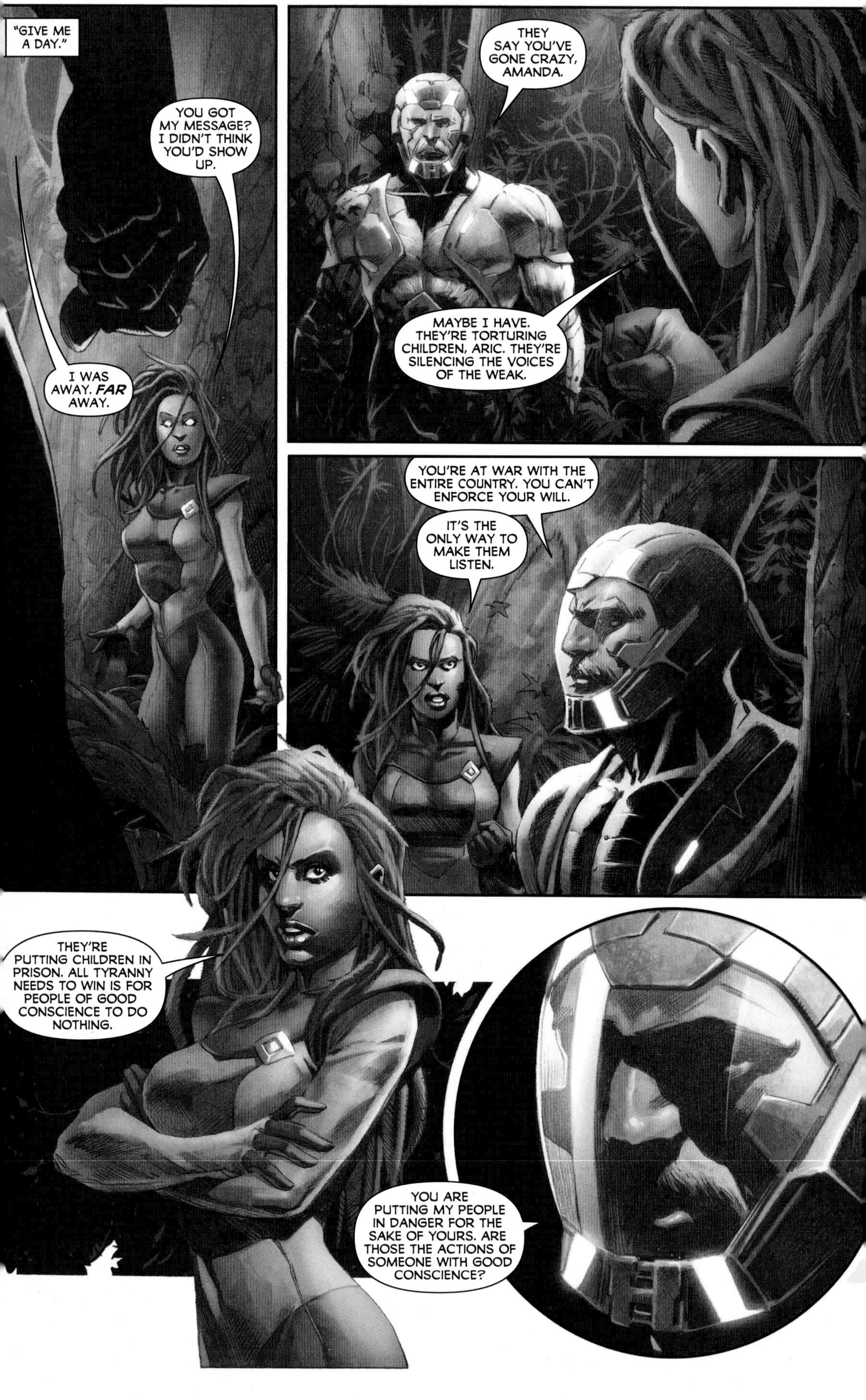
"GIVE ME A DAY."
YOU GOT MY MESSAGE? I DIDN'T THINK YOU'D SHOW UP.
I WAS AWAY. *FAR* AWAY.
THEY SAY YOU'VE GONE CRAZY, AMANDA.
MAYBE I HAVE. THEY'RE TORTURING CHILDREN, ARIC. THEY'RE SILENCING THE VOICES OF THE WEAK.
YOU'RE AT WAR WITH THE ENTIRE COUNTRY. YOU CAN'T ENFORCE YOUR WILL.
IT'S THE ONLY WAY TO MAKE THEM LISTEN.
THEY'RE PUTTING CHILDREN IN PRISON. ALL TYRANNY NEEDS TO WIN IS FOR PEOPLE OF GOOD CONSCIENCE TO DO NOTHING.
YOU ARE PUTTING MY PEOPLE IN DANGER FOR THE SAKE OF YOURS. ARE THOSE THE ACTIONS OF SOMEONE WITH GOOD CONSCIENCE?

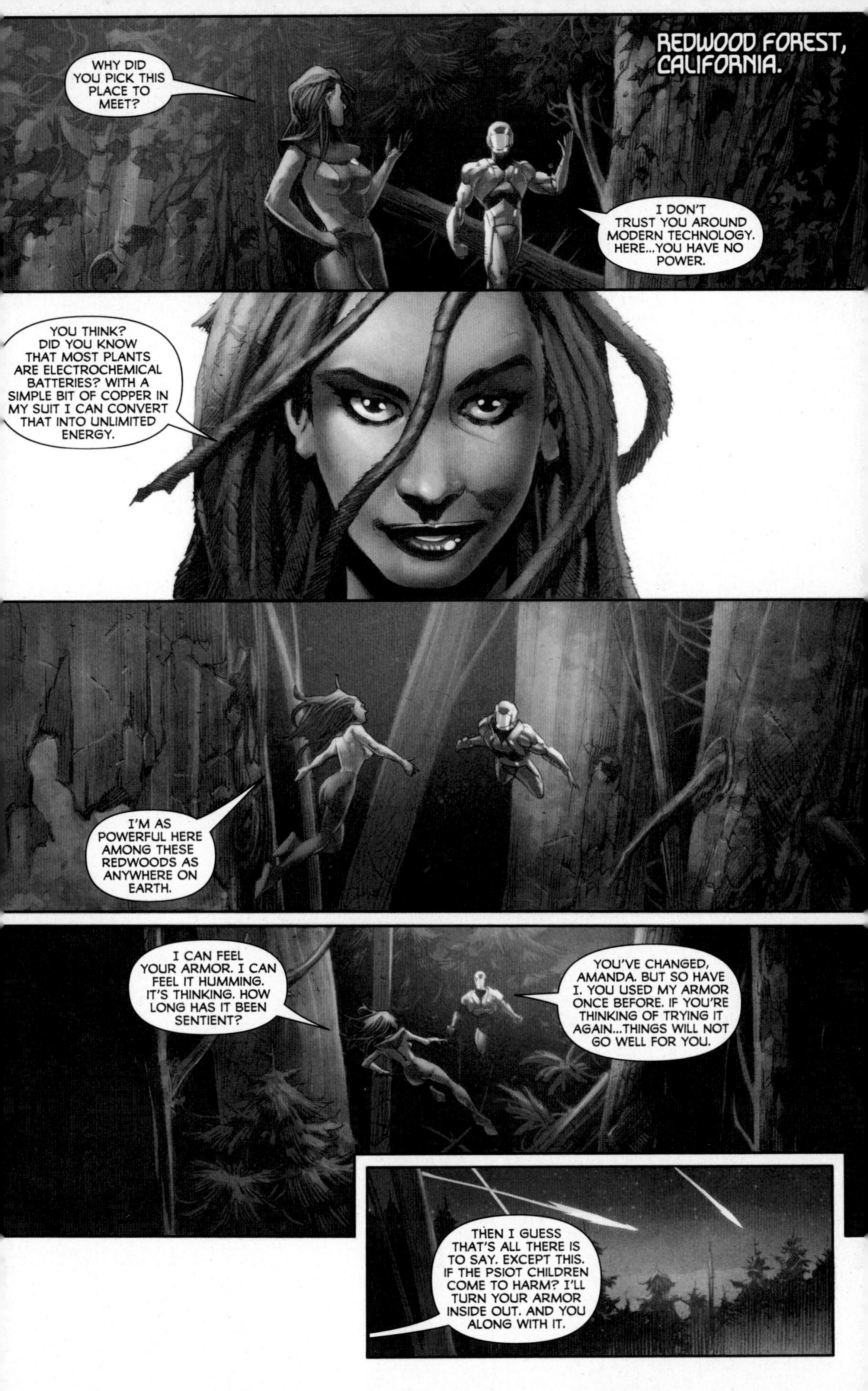
REDWOOD FOREST, CALIFORNIA.
WHY DID YOU PICK THIS PLACE TO MEET?
I DON'T TRUST YOU AROUND MODERN TECHNOLOGY. HERE...YOU HAVE NO POWER.
YOU THINK? DID YOU KNOW THAT MOST PLANTS ARE ELECTROCHEMICAL BATTERIES? WITH A SIMPLE BIT OF COPPER IN MY SUIT I CAN CONVERT THAT INTO UNLIMITED ENERGY.
I'M AS POWERFUL HERE AMONG THESE REDWOODS AS ANYWHERE ON EARTH.
I CAN FEEL YOUR ARMOR. I CAN FEEL IT HUMMING. IT'S THINKING. HOW LONG HAS IT BEEN SENTIENT?
YOU'VE CHANGED, AMANDA. BUT SO HAVE I. YOU USED MY ARMOR ONCE BEFORE. IF YOU'RE THINKING OF TRYING IT AGAIN...THINGS WILL NOT GO WELL FOR YOU.
THEN I GUESS THAT'S ALL THERE IS TO SAY. EXCEPT THIS. IF THE PSIOT CHILDREN COME TO HARM? I'LL TURN YOUR ARMOR INSIDE OUT. AND YOU ALONG WITH IT.

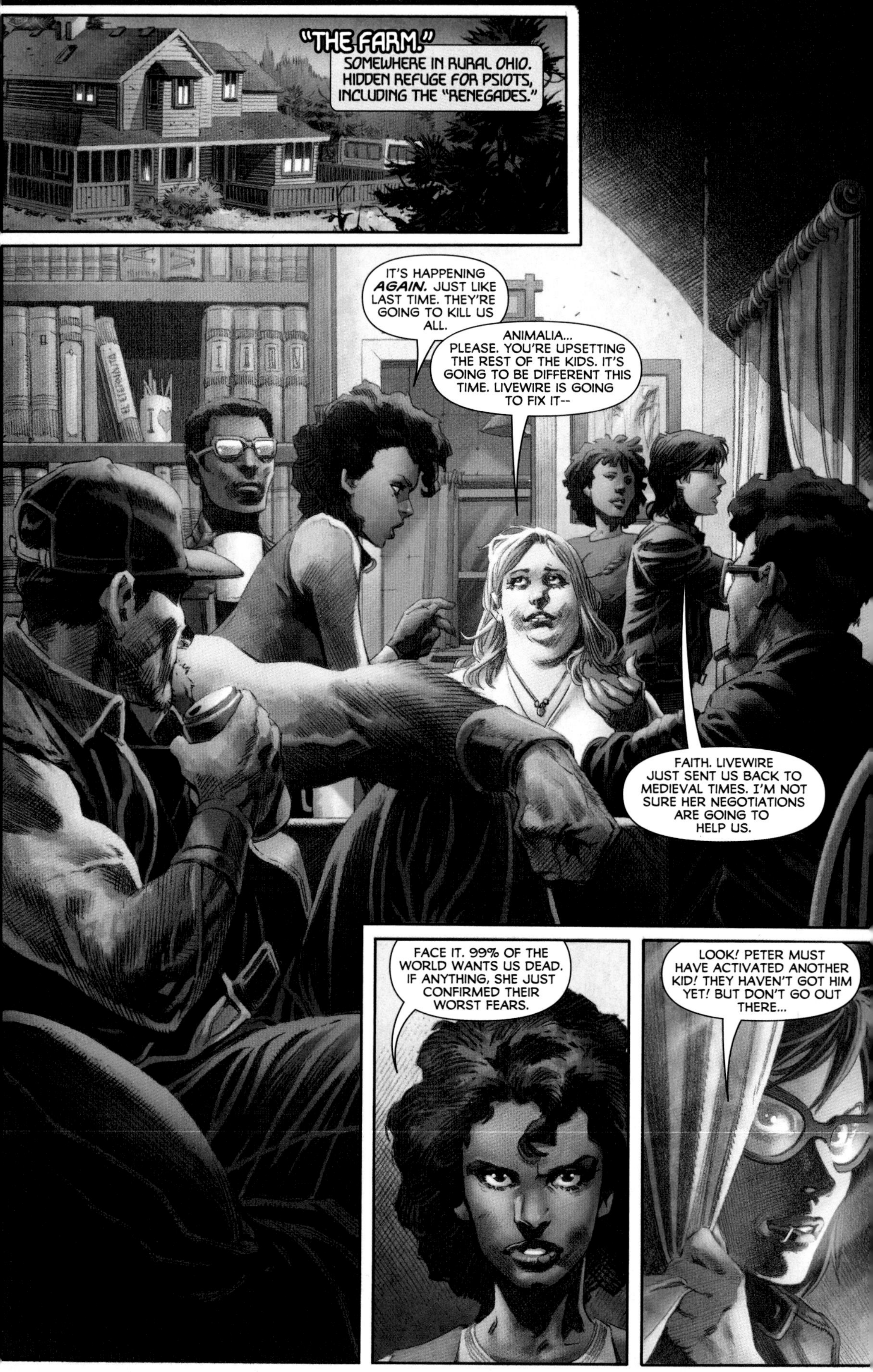
"THE FARM."
SOMEWHERE IN RURAL OHIO. HIDDEN REFUGE FOR PSIOTS, INCLUDING THE "RENEGADES."
IT'S HAPPENING AGAIN. JUST LIKE LAST TIME. THEY'RE GOING TO KILL US ALL.
ANIMALIA... PLEASE. YOU'RE UPSETTING THE REST OF THE KIDS. IT'S GOING TO BE DIFFERENT THIS TIME. LIVEWIRE IS GOING TO FIX IT--
FAITH. LIVEWIRE JUST SENT US BACK TO MEDIEVAL TIMES. I'M NOT SURE HER NEGOTIATIONS ARE GOING TO HELP US.
FACE IT. 99% OF THE WORLD WANTS US DEAD. IF ANYTHING, SHE JUST CONFIRMED THEIR WORST FEARS.
LOOK! PETER MUST HAVE ACTIVATED ANOTHER KID! THEY HAVEN'T GOT HIM YET! BUT DON'T GO OUT THERE...

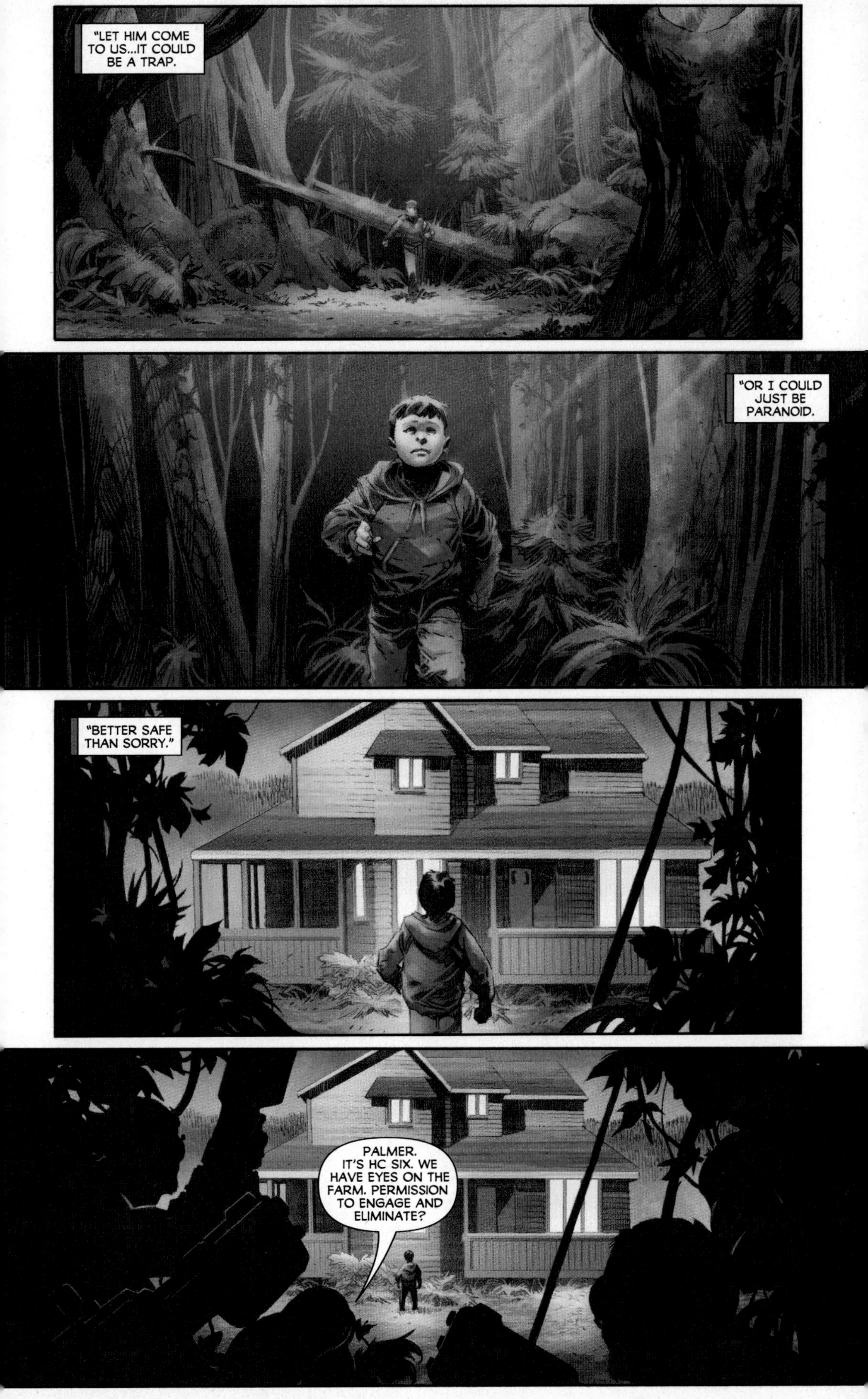
"LET HIM COME TO US...IT COULD BE A TRAP.
"OR I COULD JUST BE PARANOID.
"BETTER SAFE THAN SORRY."
PALMER. IT'S HC SIX. WE HAVE EYES ON THE FARM. PERMISSION TO ENGAGE AND ELIMINATE?

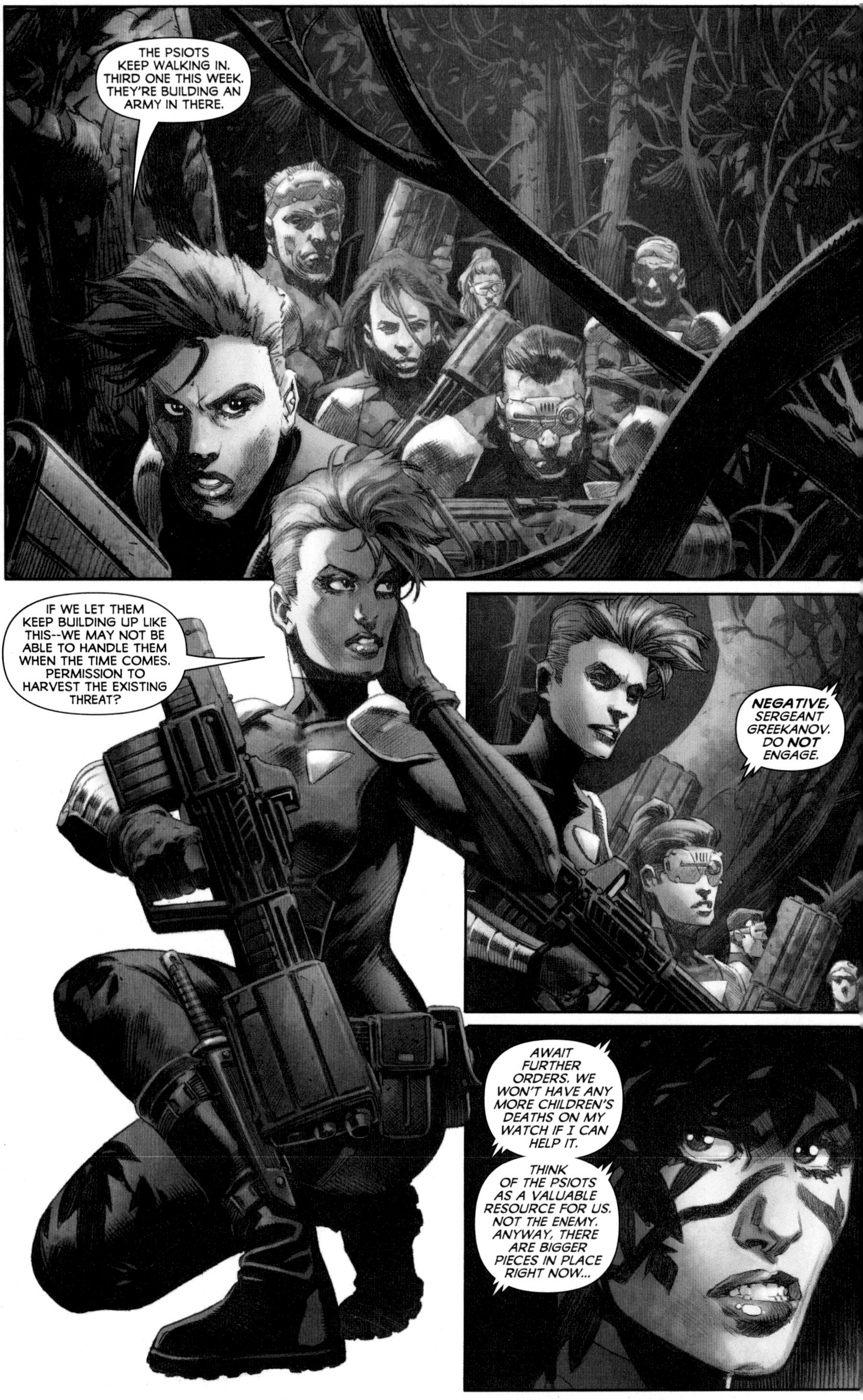
THE PSIOTS KEEP WALKING IN. THIRD ONE THIS WEEK. THEY'RE BUILDING AN ARMY IN THERE.
IF WE LET THEM KEEP BUILDING UP LIKE THIS--WE MAY NOT BE ABLE TO HANDLE THEM WHEN THE TIME COMES. PERMISSION TO HARVEST THE EXISTING THREAT?
NEGATIVE, SERGEANT GREEKANOV. DO NOT ENGAGE.
AWAIT FURTHER ORDERS. WE WON'T HAVE ANY MORE CHILDREN'S DEATHS ON MY WATCH IF I CAN HELP IT.
THINK OF THE PSIOTS AS A VALUABLE RESOURCE FOR US. NOT THE ENEMY. ANYWAY, THERE ARE BIGGER PIECES IN PLACE RIGHT NOW...

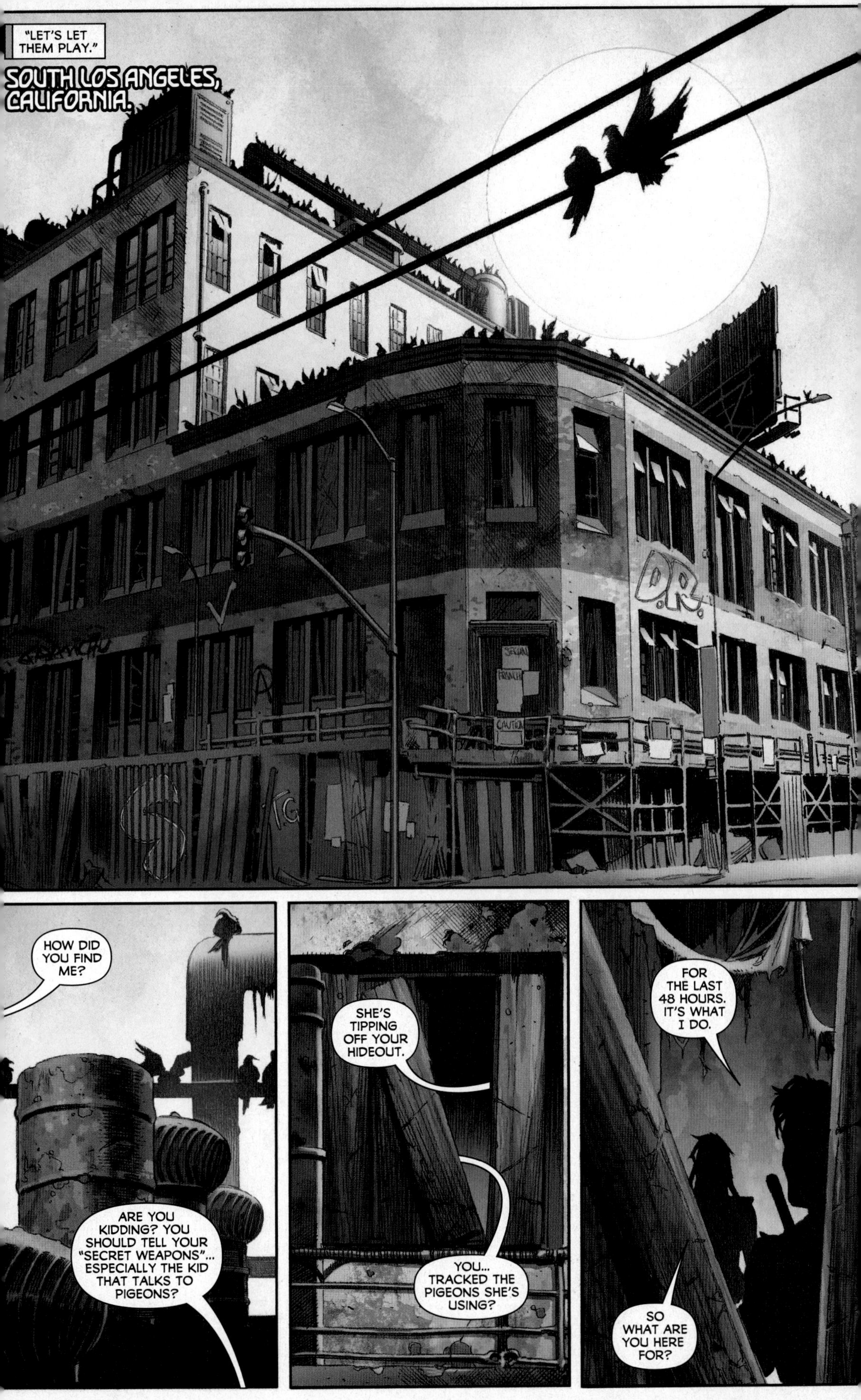
"LET'S LET THEM PLAY."
SOUTH LOS ANGELES, CALIFORNIA.
HOW DID YOU FIND ME?
ARE YOU KIDDING? YOU SHOULD TELL YOUR "SECRET WEAPONS"... ESPECIALLY THE KID THAT TALKS TO PIGEONS?
SHE'S TIPPING OFF YOUR HIDEOUT.
YOU... TRACKED THE PIGEONS SHE'S USING?
FOR THE LAST 48 HOURS. IT'S WHAT I DO.
SO WHAT ARE YOU HERE FOR?

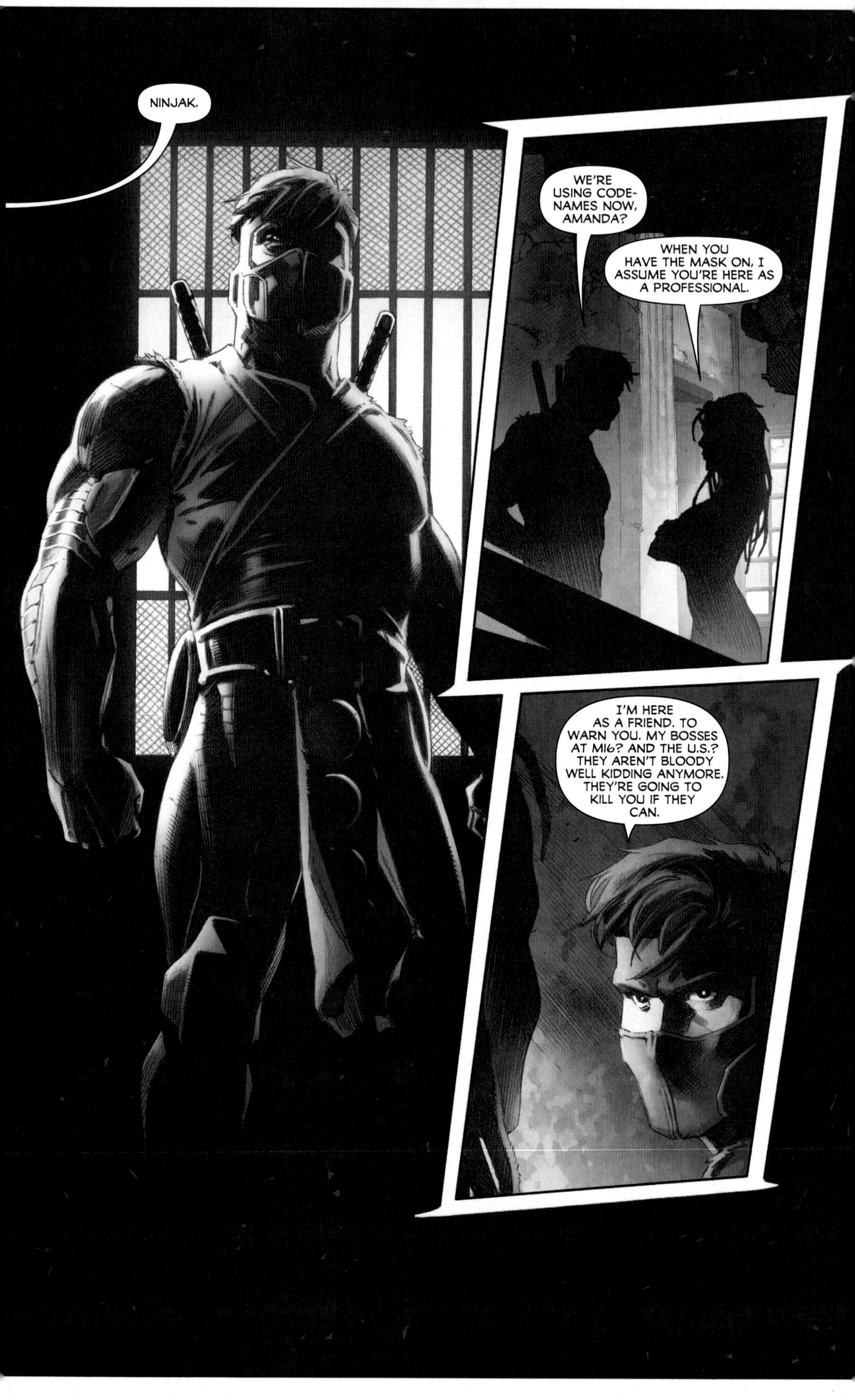
NINJAK.
WE'RE USING CODE-NAMES NOW, AMANDA?
WHEN YOU HAVE THE MASK ON, I ASSUME YOU'RE HERE AS A PROFESSIONAL.
I'M HERE AS A FRIEND. TO WARN YOU. MY BOSSES AT MI6? AND THE U.S.? THEY AREN'T BLOODY WELL KIDDING ANYMORE. THEY'RE GOING TO KILL YOU IF THEY CAN.

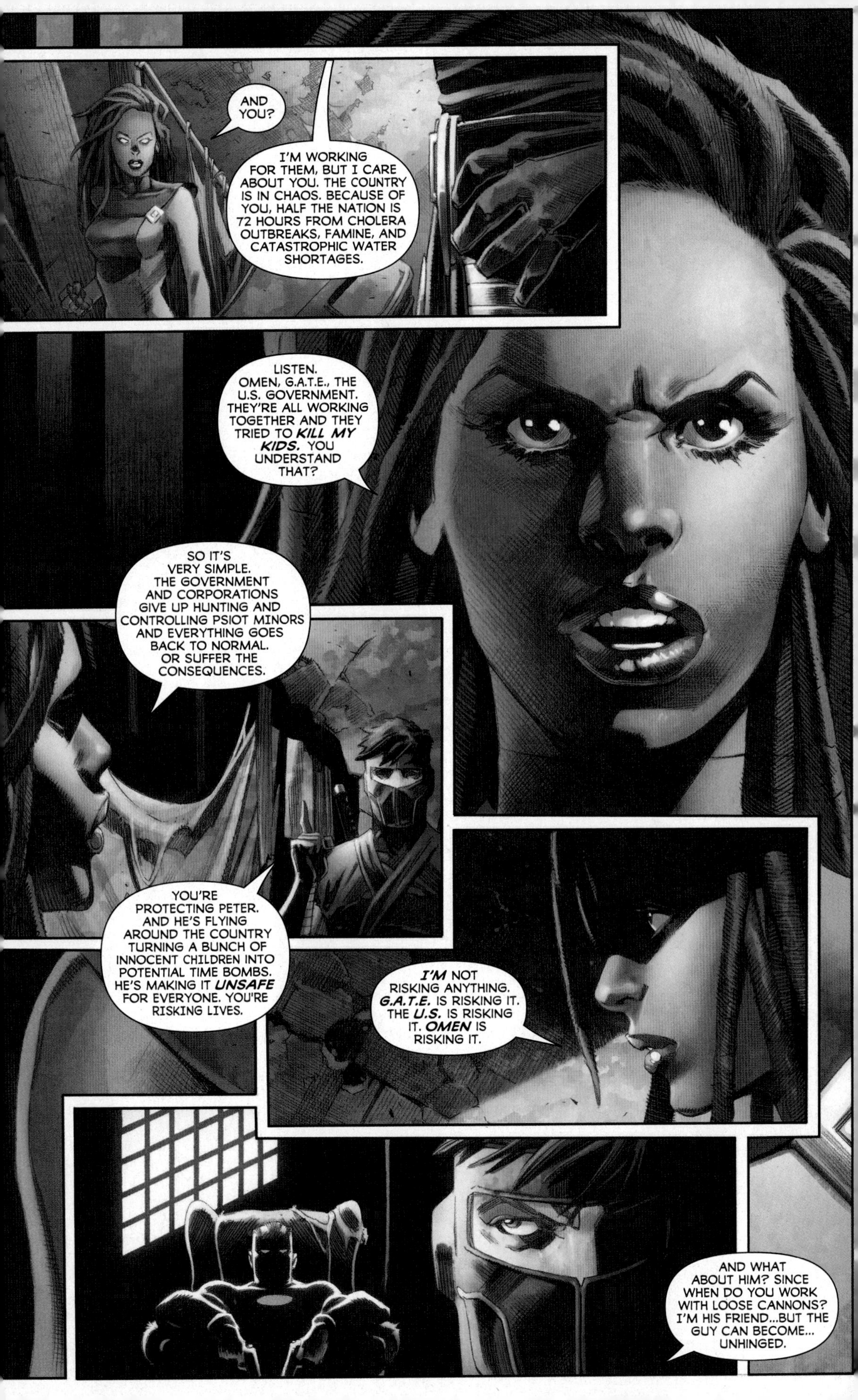
AND YOU?
I'M WORKING FOR THEM, BUT I CARE ABOUT YOU. THE COUNTRY IS IN CHAOS. BECAUSE OF YOU, HALF THE NATION IS 72 HOURS FROM CHOLERA OUTBREAKS, FAMINE, AND CATASTROPHIC WATER SHORTAGES.
LISTEN. OMEN, G.A.T.E., THE U.S. GOVERNMENT. THEY'RE ALL WORKING TOGETHER AND THEY TRIED TO **KILL MY KIDS.** YOU UNDERSTAND THAT?
SO IT'S VERY SIMPLE. THE GOVERNMENT AND CORPORATIONS GIVE UP HUNTING AND CONTROLLING PSIOT MINORS AND EVERYTHING GOES BACK TO NORMAL. OR SUFFER THE CONSEQUENCES.
YOU'RE PROTECTING PETER. AND HE'S FLYING AROUND THE COUNTRY TURNING A BUNCH OF INNOCENT CHILDREN INTO POTENTIAL TIME BOMBS. HE'S MAKING IT **UNSAFE** FOR EVERYONE. YOU'RE RISKING LIVES.
I'M NOT RISKING ANYTHING. **G.A.T.E.** IS RISKING IT. THE **U.S.** IS RISKING IT. **OMEN** IS RISKING IT.
AND WHAT ABOUT HIM? SINCE WHEN DO YOU WORK WITH LOOSE CANNONS? I'M HIS FRIEND...BUT THE GUY CAN BECOME... UNHINGED.

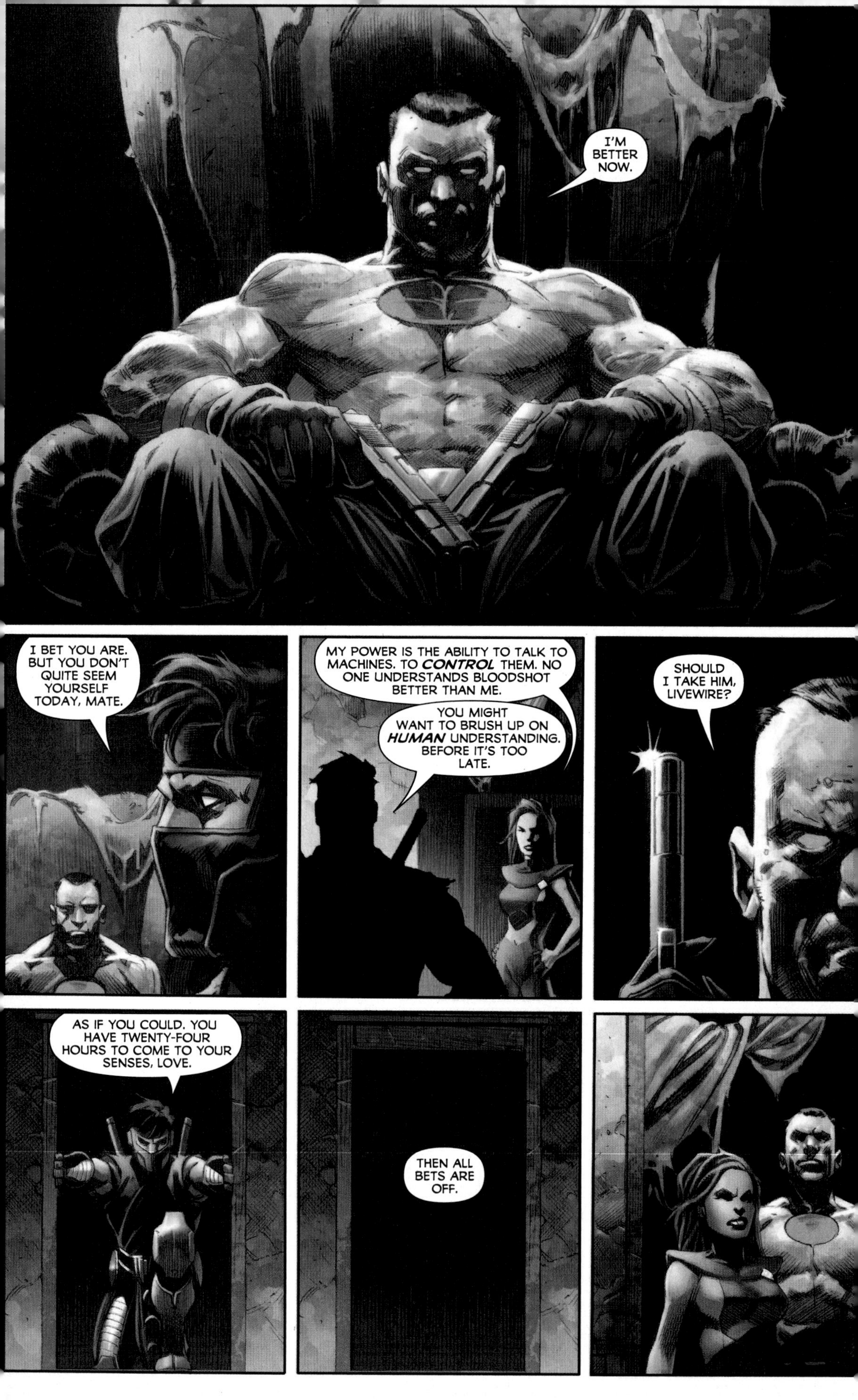
I'M BETTER NOW.
I BET YOU ARE. BUT YOU DON'T QUITE SEEM YOURSELF TODAY, MATE.
MY POWER IS THE ABILITY TO TALK TO MACHINES. TO CONTROL THEM. NO ONE UNDERSTANDS BLOODSHOT BETTER THAN ME.
YOU MIGHT WANT TO BRUSH UP ON HUMAN UNDERSTANDING. BEFORE IT'S TOO LATE.
SHOULD I TAKE HIM, LIVEWIRE?
AS IF YOU COULD. YOU HAVE TWENTY-FOUR HOURS TO COME TO YOUR SENSES, LOVE.
THEN ALL BETS ARE OFF.

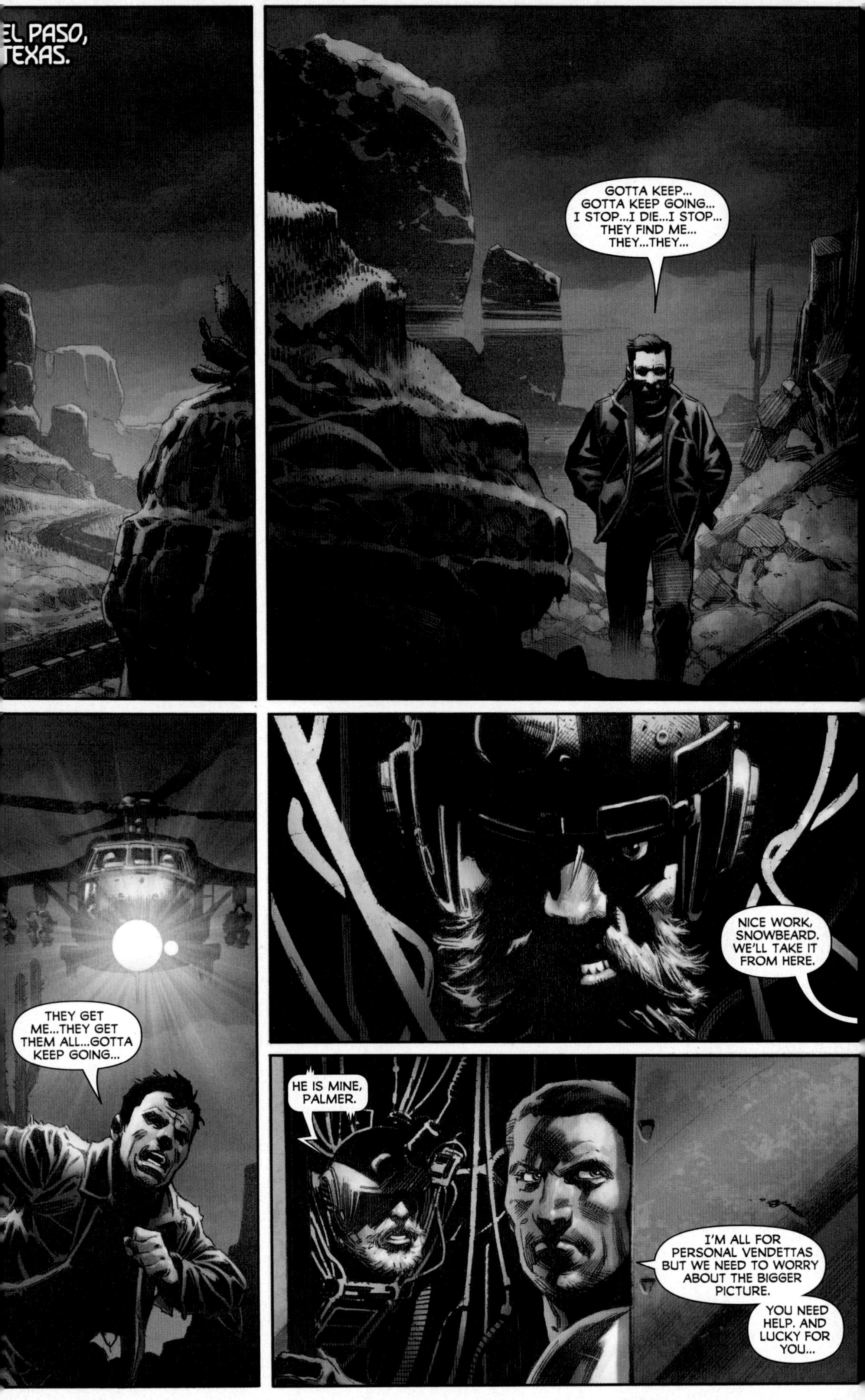
EL PASO, TEXAS.
GOTTA KEEP... GOTTA KEEP GOING... I STOP...I DIE...I STOP... THEY FIND ME... THEY...THEY...
THEY GET ME...THEY GET THEM ALL...GOTTA KEEP GOING...
NICE WORK, SNOWBEARD. WE'LL TAKE IT FROM HERE.
HE IS MINE, PALMER.
I'M ALL FOR PERSONAL VENDETTAS BUT WE NEED TO WORRY ABOUT THE BIGGER PICTURE.
YOU NEED HELP. AND LUCKY FOR YOU...

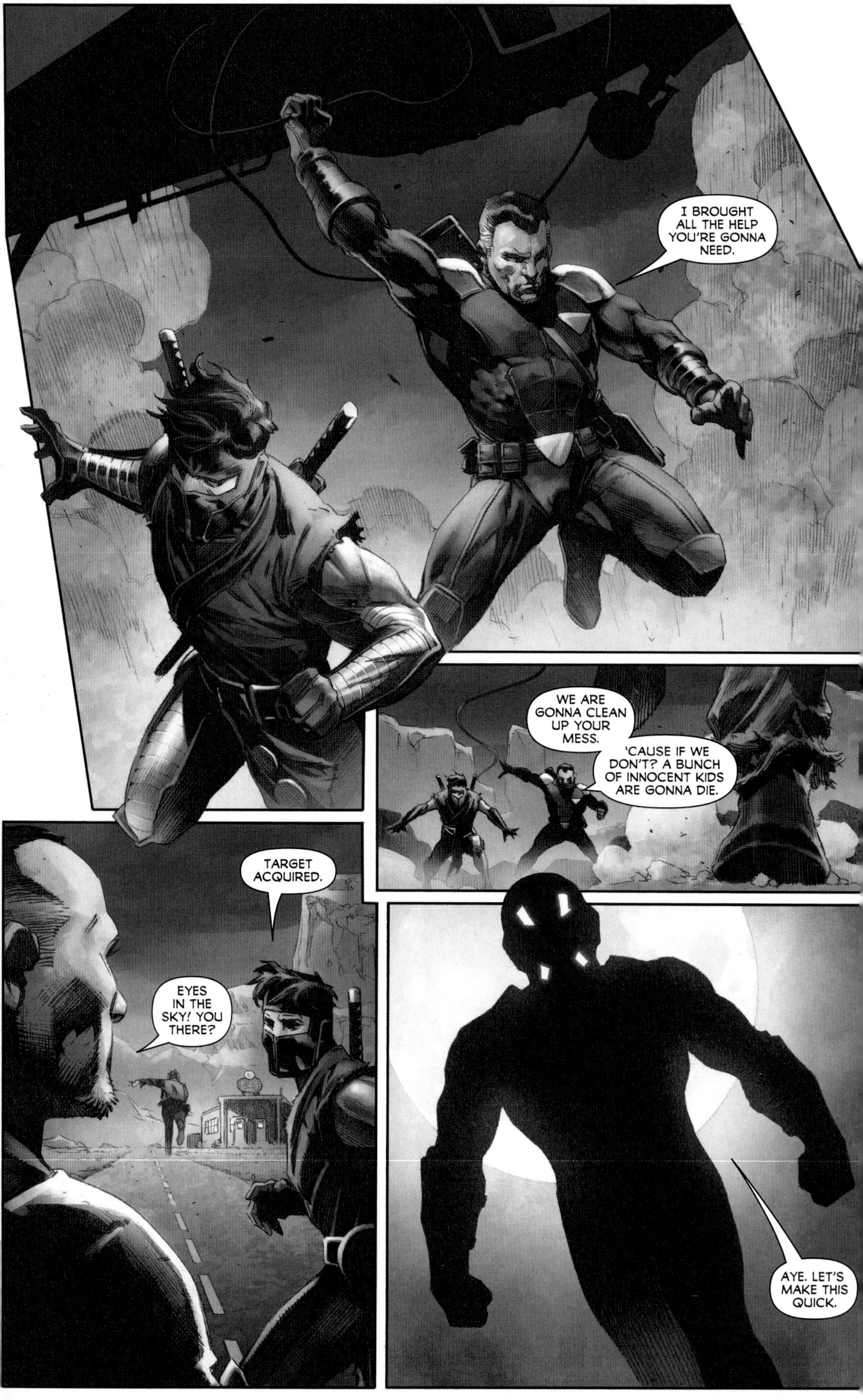
I BROUGHT ALL THE HELP YOU'RE GONNA NEED.
WE ARE GONNA CLEAN UP YOUR MESS.
'CAUSE IF WE DON'T? A BUNCH OF INNOCENT KIDS ARE GONNA DIE.
TARGET ACQUIRED.
EYES IN THE SKY! YOU THERE?
GAS
AYE. LET'S MAKE THIS QUICK.

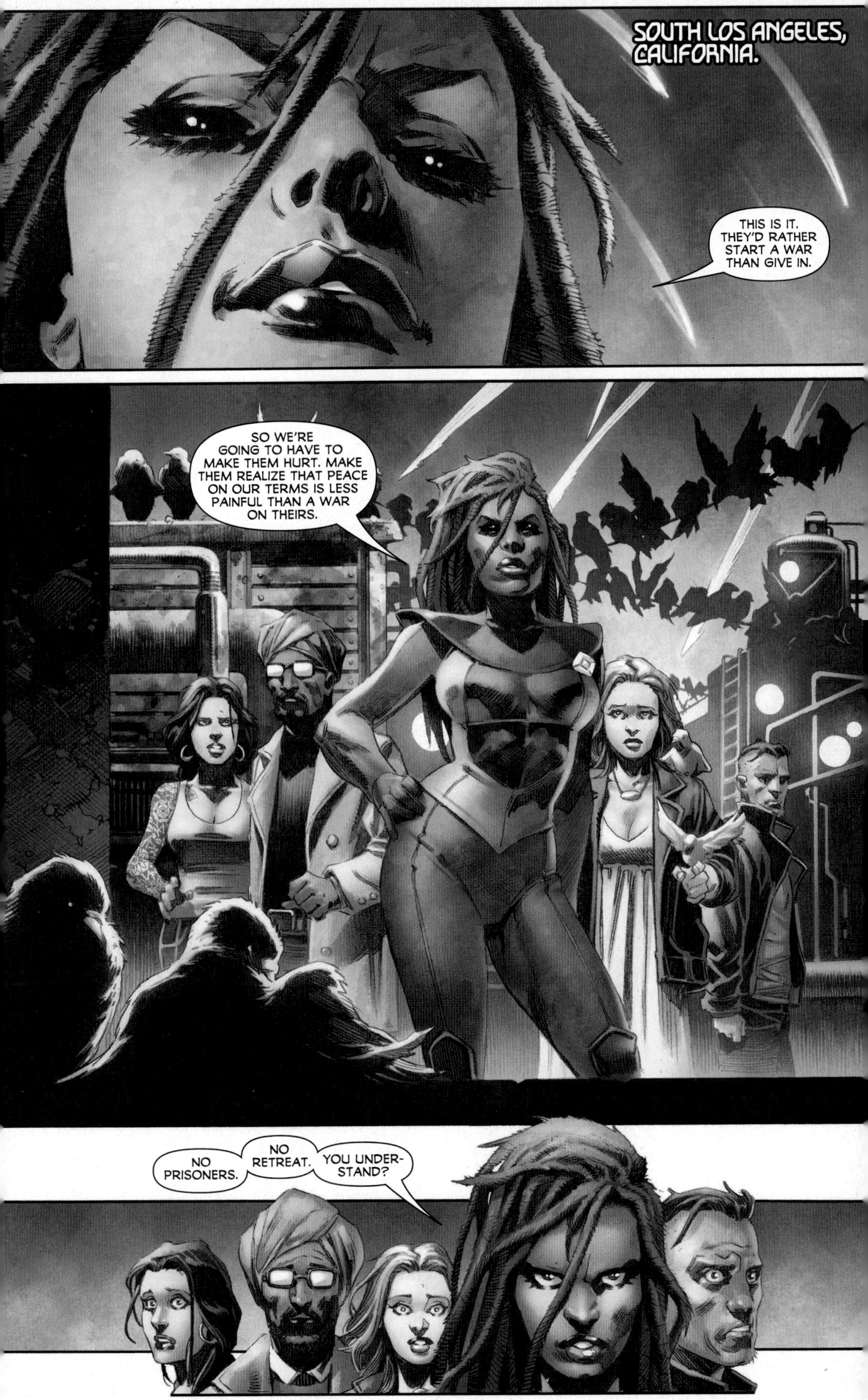

SOUTH LOS ANGELES, CALIFORNIA.
THIS IS IT. THEY'D RATHER START A WAR THAN GIVE IN.
SO WE'RE GOING TO HAVE TO MAKE THEM HURT. MAKE THEM REALIZE THAT PEACE ON OUR TERMS IS LESS PAINFUL THAN A WAR ON THEIRS.
NO PRISONERS.
NO RETREAT.
YOU UNDER-STAND?

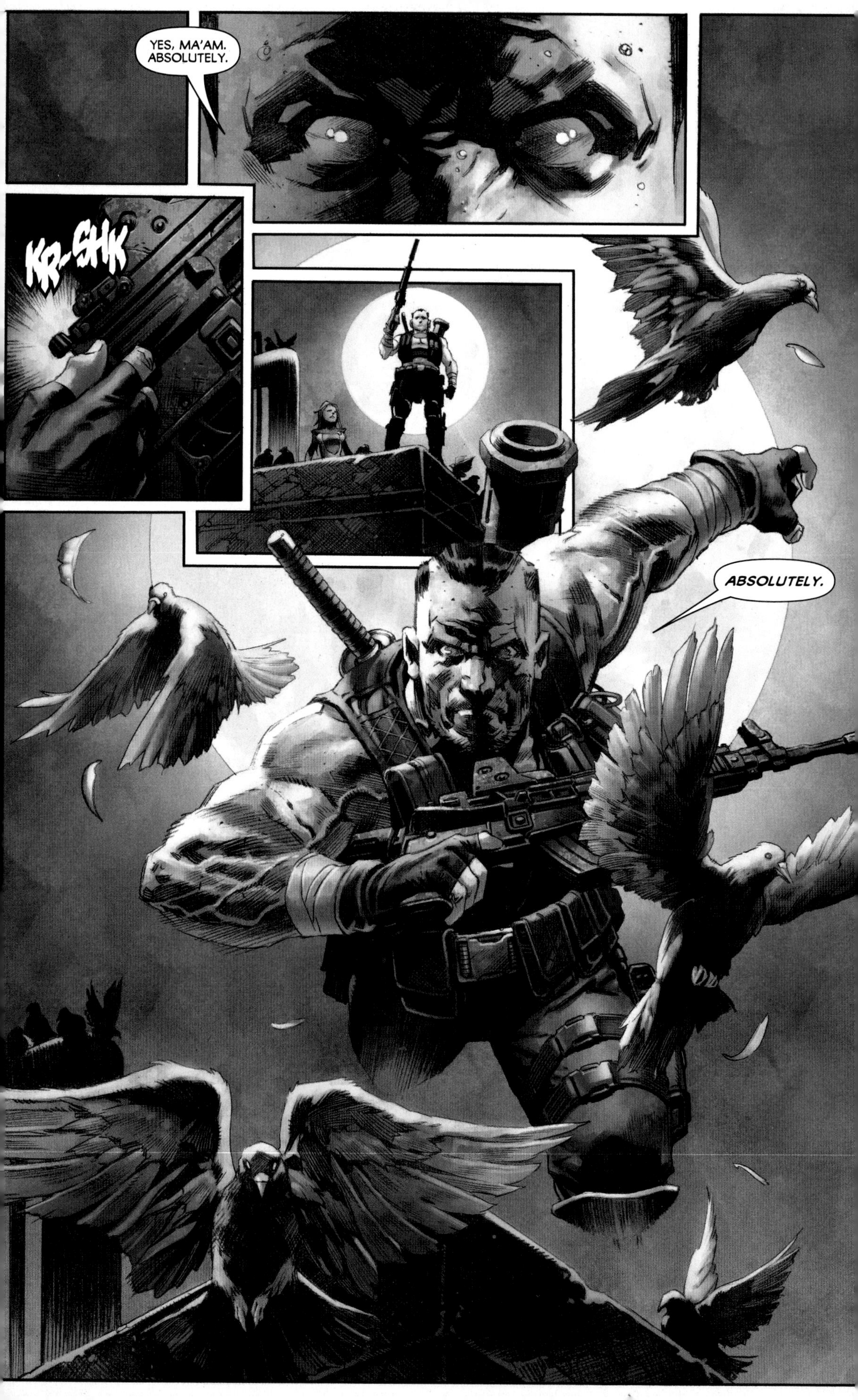
YES, MA'AM. ABSOLUTELY.
KR-SHK
ABSOLUTELY.

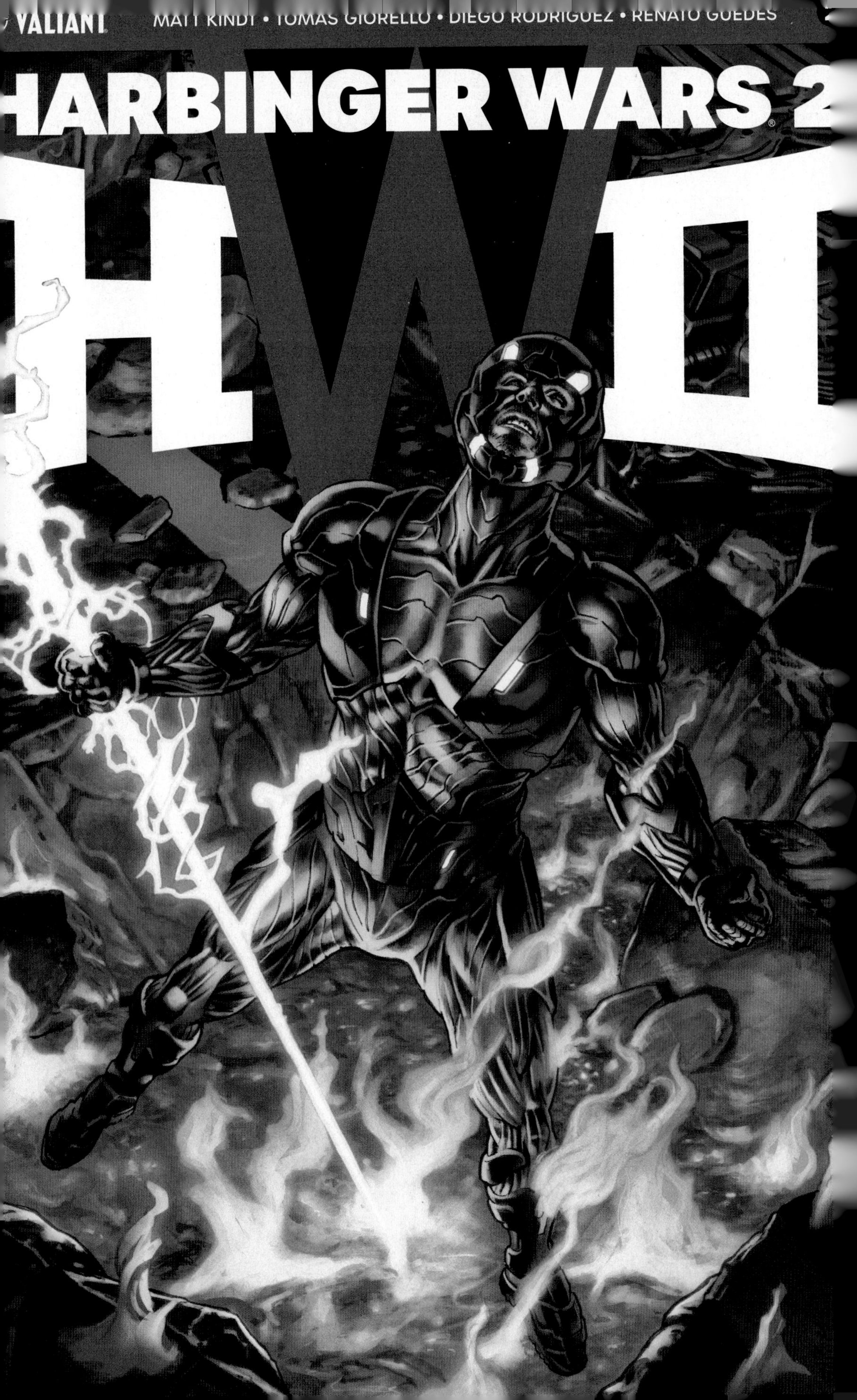
VALIANT
MATT KINDT • TOMAS GIORELLO • DIEGO RODRIGUEZ • RENATO GUEDES
HARBINGER WARS 2
HWII

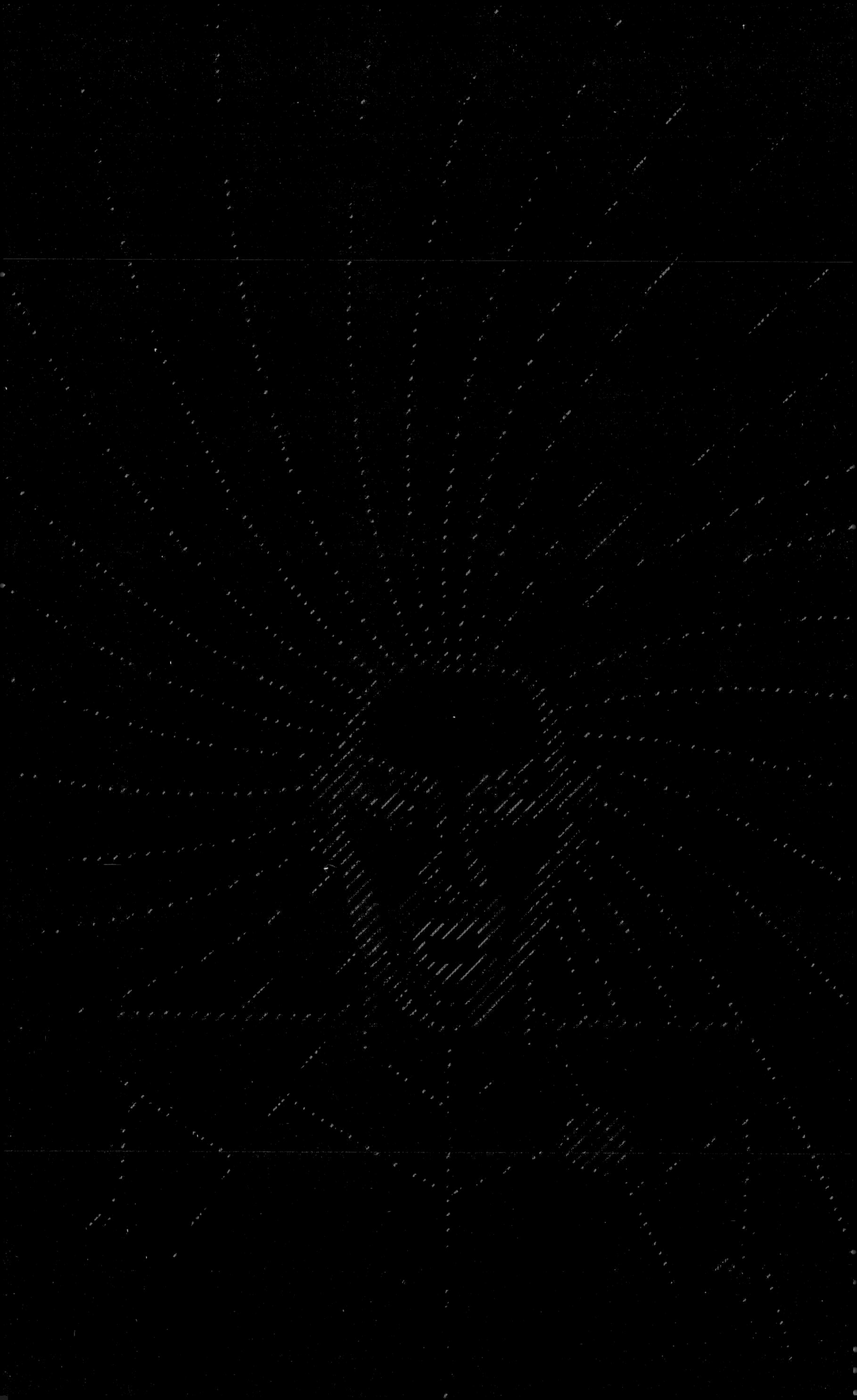

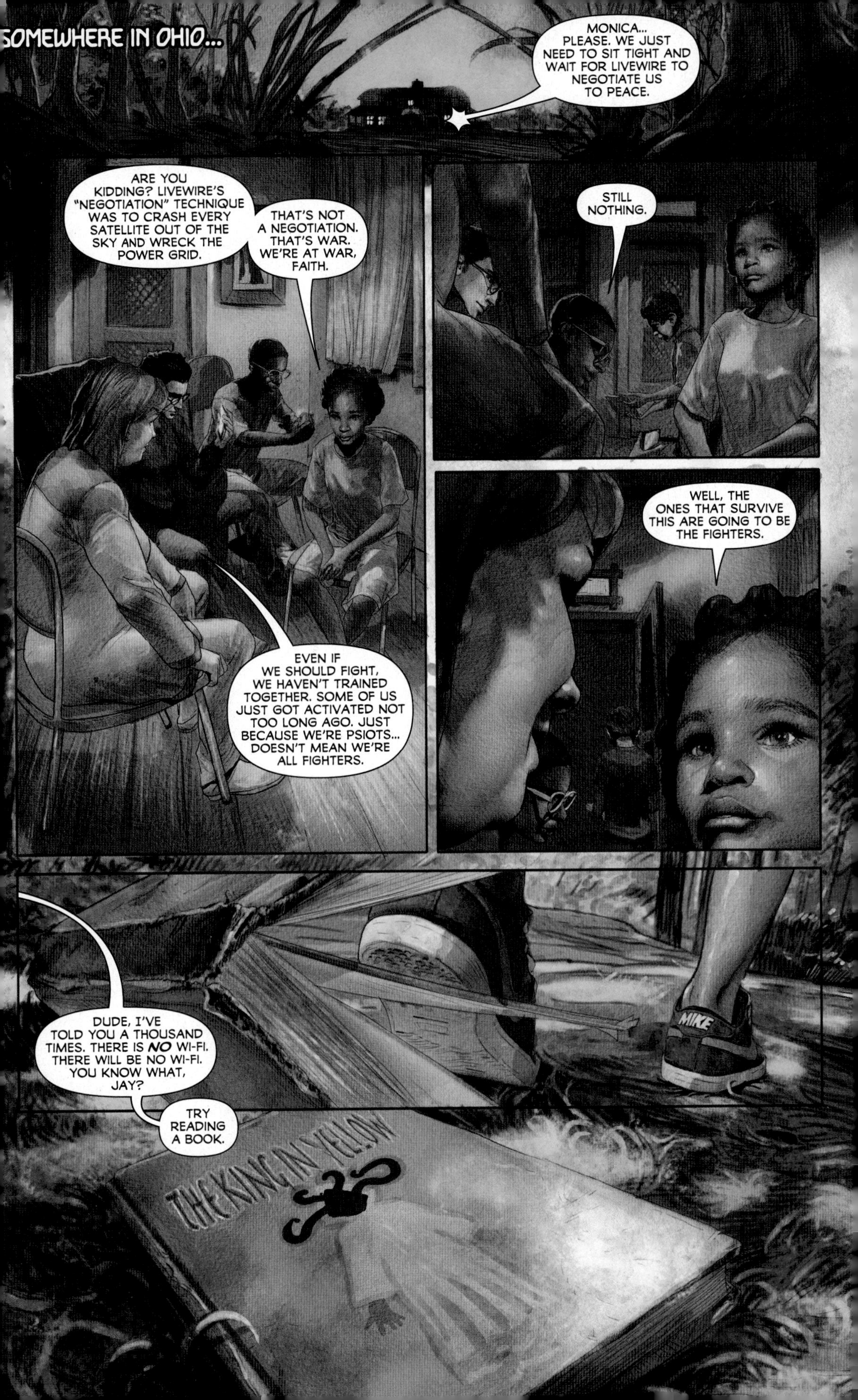
SOMEWHERE IN OHIO...
MONICA... PLEASE. WE JUST NEED TO SIT TIGHT AND WAIT FOR LIVEWIRE TO NEGOTIATE US TO PEACE.
ARE YOU KIDDING? LIVEWIRE'S "NEGOTIATION" TECHNIQUE WAS TO CRASH EVERY SATELLITE OUT OF THE SKY AND WRECK THE POWER GRID.
THAT'S NOT A NEGOTIATION. THAT'S WAR. WE'RE AT WAR, FAITH.
EVEN IF WE SHOULD FIGHT, WE HAVEN'T TRAINED TOGETHER. SOME OF US JUST GOT ACTIVATED NOT TOO LONG AGO. JUST BECAUSE WE'RE PSIOTS... DOESN'T MEAN WE'RE ALL FIGHTERS.
STILL NOTHING.
WELL, THE ONES THAT SURVIVE THIS ARE GOING TO BE THE FIGHTERS.
DUDE, I'VE TOLD YOU A THOUSAND TIMES. THERE IS ***NO*** WI-FI. THERE WILL BE NO WI-FI. YOU KNOW WHAT, JAY?
TRY READING A BOOK.
MIKE
THE KING IN YELLOW

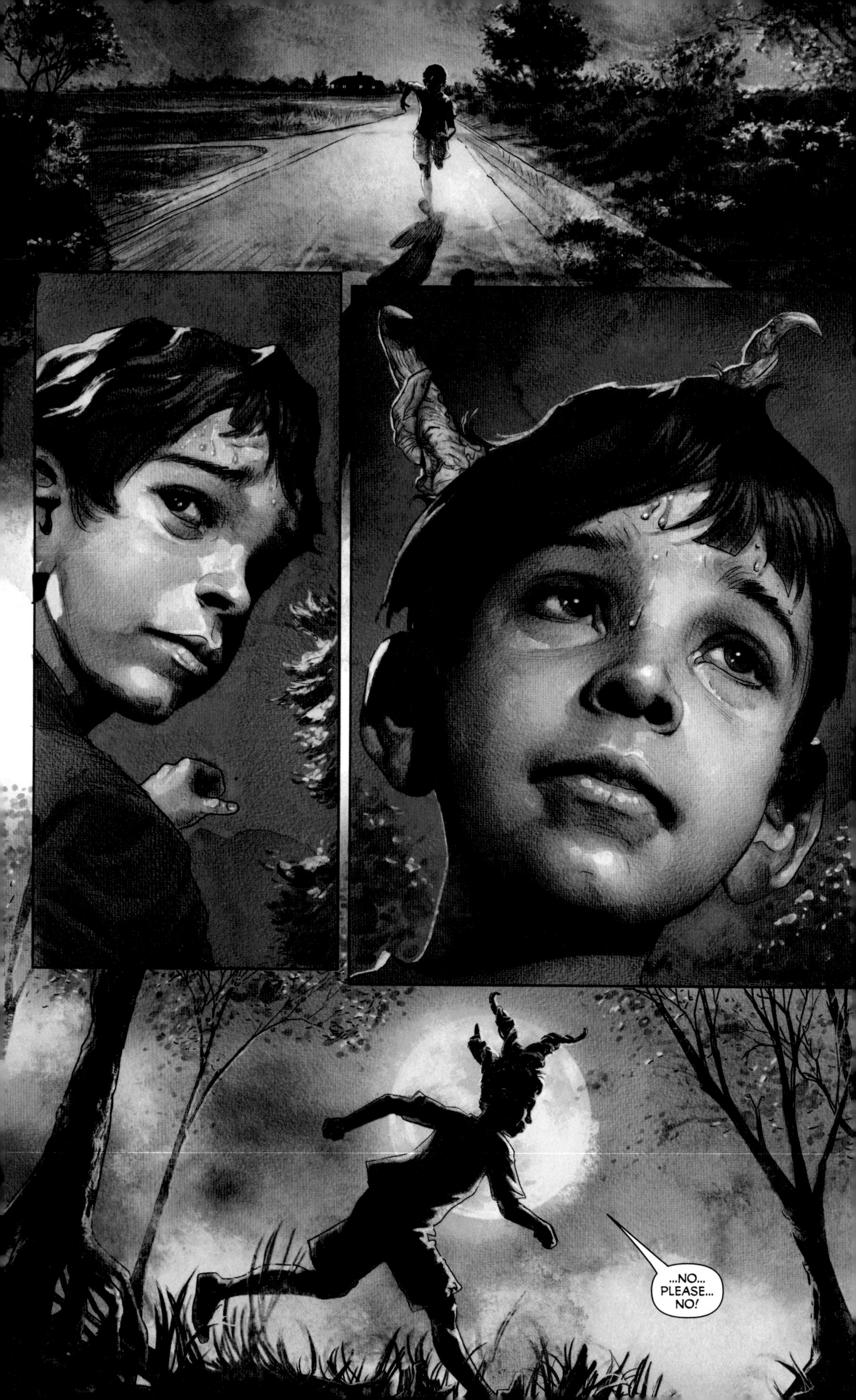
...NO... PLEASE... NO!

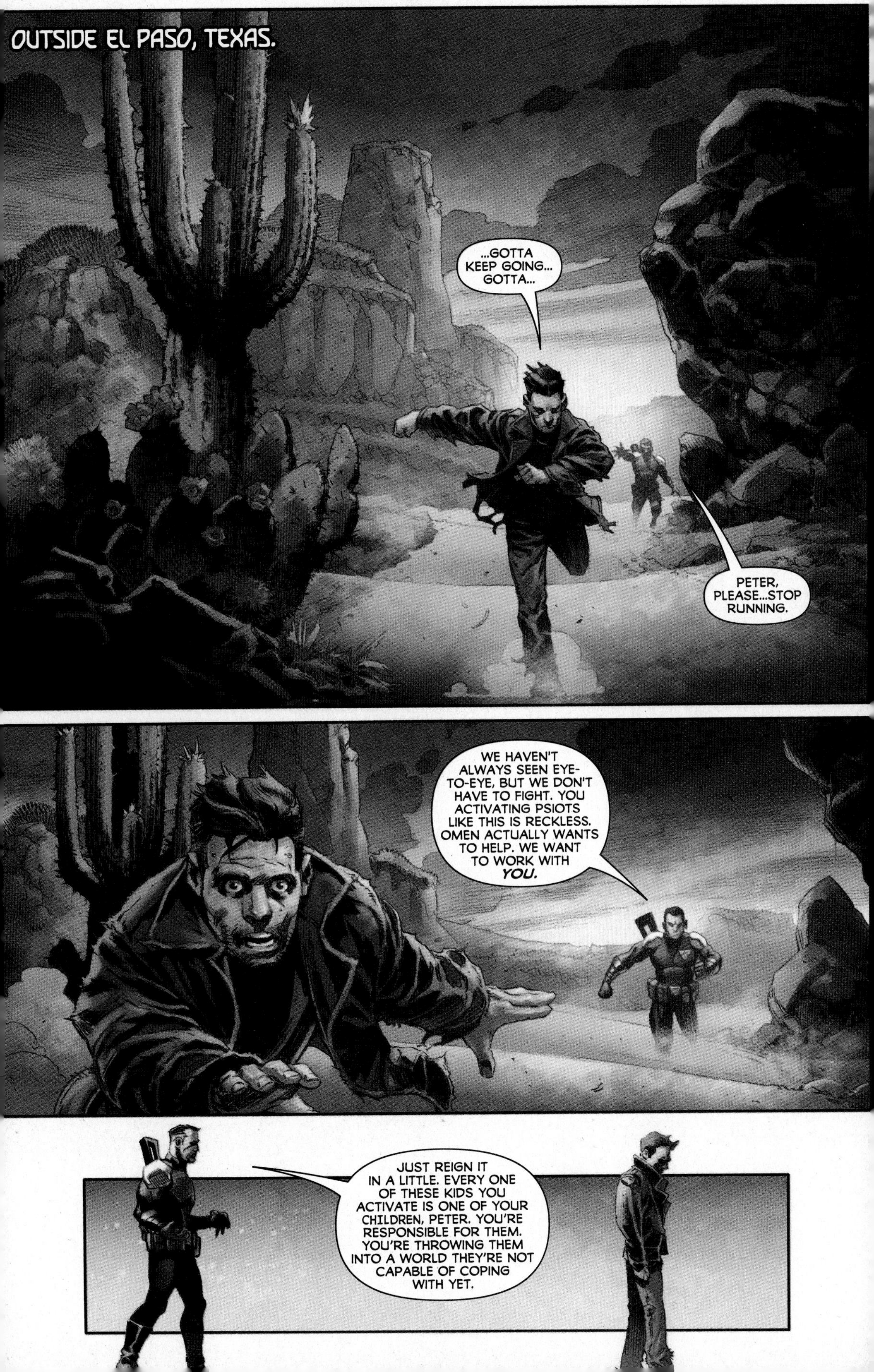
OUTSIDE EL PASO, TEXAS.
...GOTTA KEEP GOING... GOTTA...
PETER, PLEASE...STOP RUNNING.
WE HAVEN'T ALWAYS SEEN EYE-TO-EYE, BUT WE DON'T HAVE TO FIGHT. YOU ACTIVATING PSIOTS LIKE THIS IS RECKLESS. OMEN ACTUALLY WANTS TO HELP. WE WANT TO WORK WITH *YOU.*
JUST REIGN IT IN A LITTLE. EVERY ONE OF THESE KIDS YOU ACTIVATE IS ONE OF YOUR CHILDREN, PETER. YOU'RE RESPONSIBLE FOR THEM. YOU'RE THROWING THEM INTO A WORLD THEY'RE NOT CAPABLE OF COPING WITH YET.

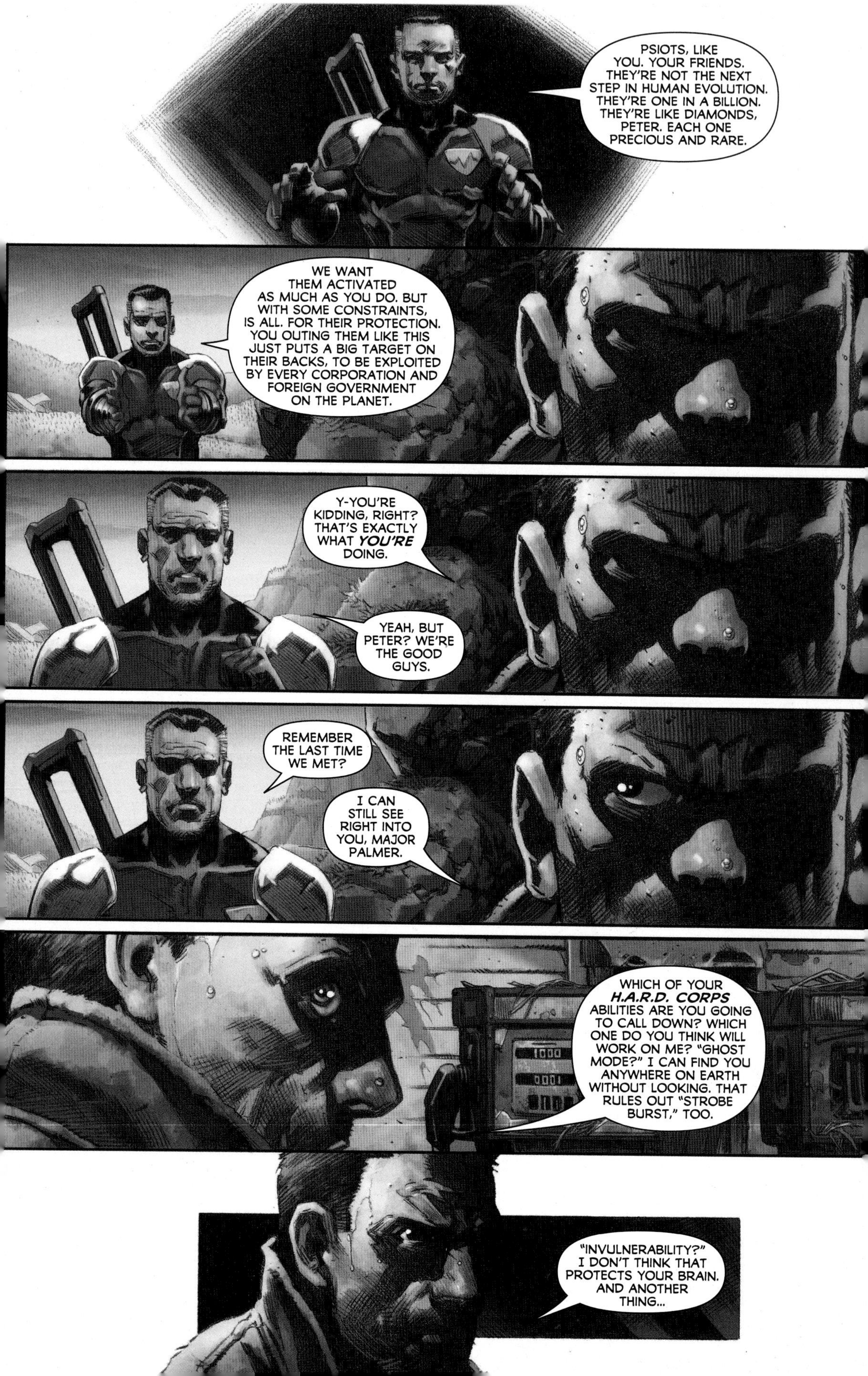
PSIOTS, LIKE YOU. YOUR FRIENDS. THEY'RE NOT THE NEXT STEP IN HUMAN EVOLUTION. THEY'RE ONE IN A BILLION. THEY'RE LIKE DIAMONDS, PETER. EACH ONE PRECIOUS AND RARE.
WE WANT THEM ACTIVATED AS MUCH AS YOU DO. BUT WITH SOME CONSTRAINTS, IS ALL. FOR THEIR PROTECTION. YOU OUTING THEM LIKE THIS JUST PUTS A BIG TARGET ON THEIR BACKS, TO BE EXPLOITED BY EVERY CORPORATION AND FOREIGN GOVERNMENT ON THE PLANET.
Y-YOU'RE KIDDING, RIGHT? THAT'S EXACTLY WHAT ***YOU'RE*** DOING.
YEAH, BUT PETER? WE'RE THE GOOD GUYS.
REMEMBER THE LAST TIME WE MET?
I CAN STILL SEE RIGHT INTO YOU, MAJOR PALMER.
WHICH OF YOUR ***H.A.R.D. CORPS*** ABILITIES ARE YOU GOING TO CALL DOWN? WHICH ONE DO YOU THINK WILL WORK ON ME? "GHOST MODE?" I CAN FIND YOU ANYWHERE ON EARTH WITHOUT LOOKING. THAT RULES OUT "STROBE BURST," TOO.
"INVULNERABILITY?" I DON'T THINK THAT PROTECTS YOUR BRAIN. AND ANOTHER THING...

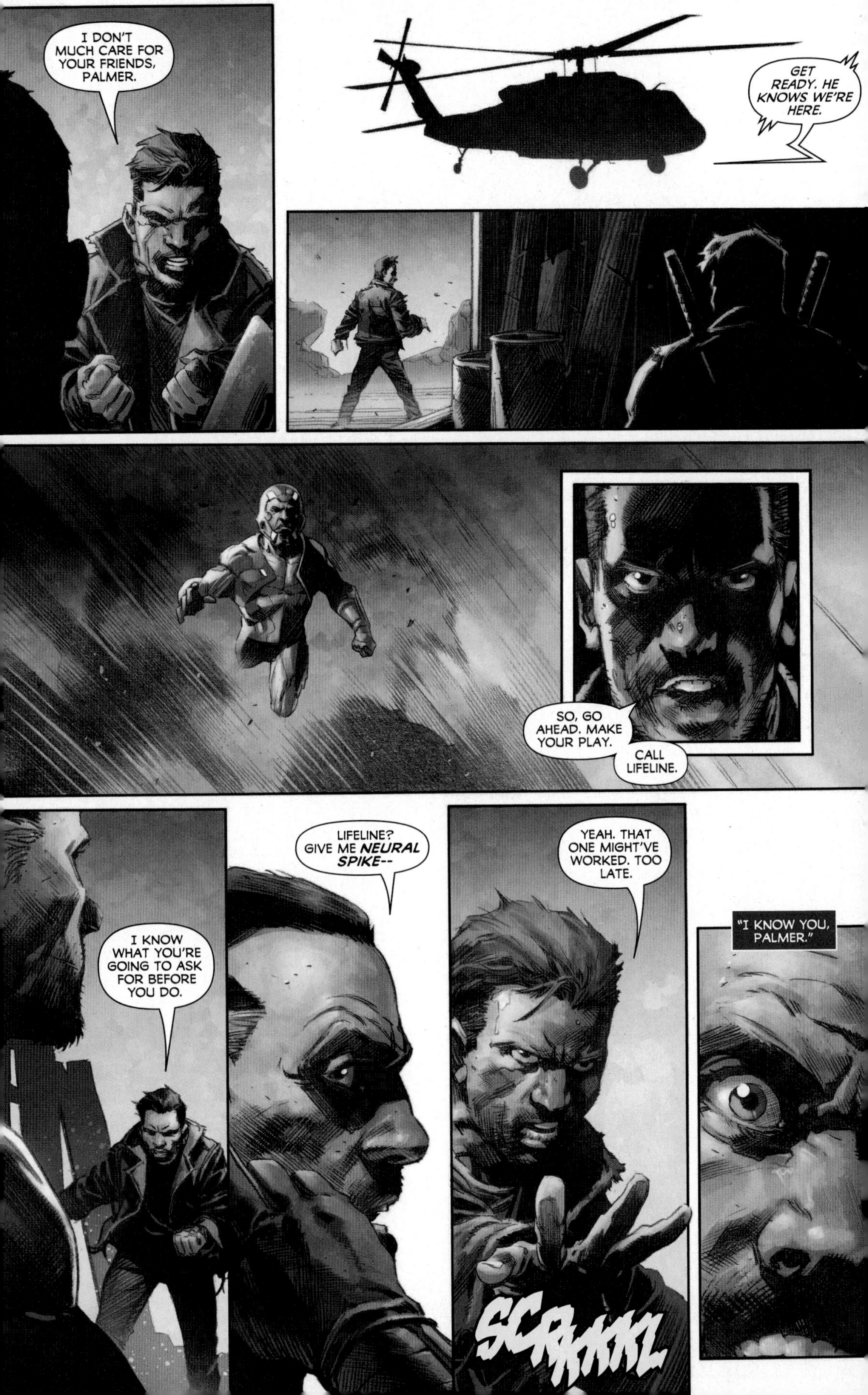
I DON'T MUCH CARE FOR YOUR FRIENDS, PALMER.
GET READY. HE KNOWS WE'RE HERE.
SO, GO AHEAD. MAKE YOUR PLAY.
CALL LIFELINE.
I KNOW WHAT YOU'RE GOING TO ASK FOR BEFORE YOU DO.
LIFELINE? GIVE ME *NEURAL SPIKE*--
YEAH. THAT ONE MIGHT'VE WORKED. TOO LATE.
SCRKKKL
"I KNOW YOU, PALMER."

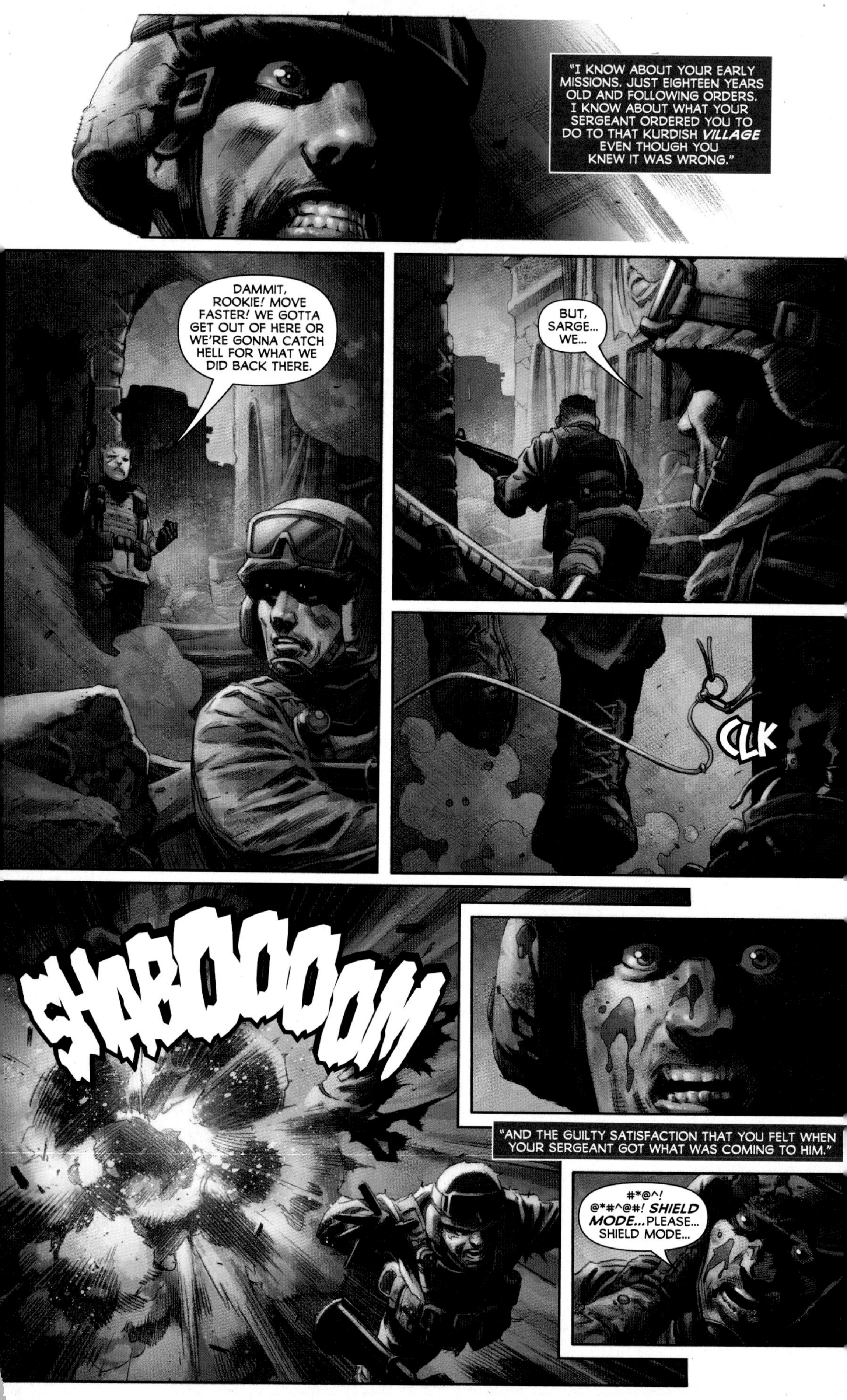
"I KNOW ABOUT YOUR EARLY MISSIONS. JUST EIGHTEEN YEARS OLD AND FOLLOWING ORDERS. I KNOW ABOUT WHAT YOUR SERGEANT ORDERED YOU TO DO TO THAT KURDISH *VILLAGE* EVEN THOUGH YOU KNEW IT WAS WRONG."
DAMMIT, ROOKIE! MOVE FASTER! WE GOTTA GET OUT OF HERE OR WE'RE GONNA CATCH HELL FOR WHAT WE DID BACK THERE.
BUT, SARGE... WE...
CLK
SHABOOOOOM
"AND THE GUILTY SATISFACTION THAT YOU FELT WHEN YOUR SERGEANT GOT WHAT WAS COMING TO HIM."
#*@^! @*#^@#! *SHIELD MODE...* PLEASE... SHIELD MODE...

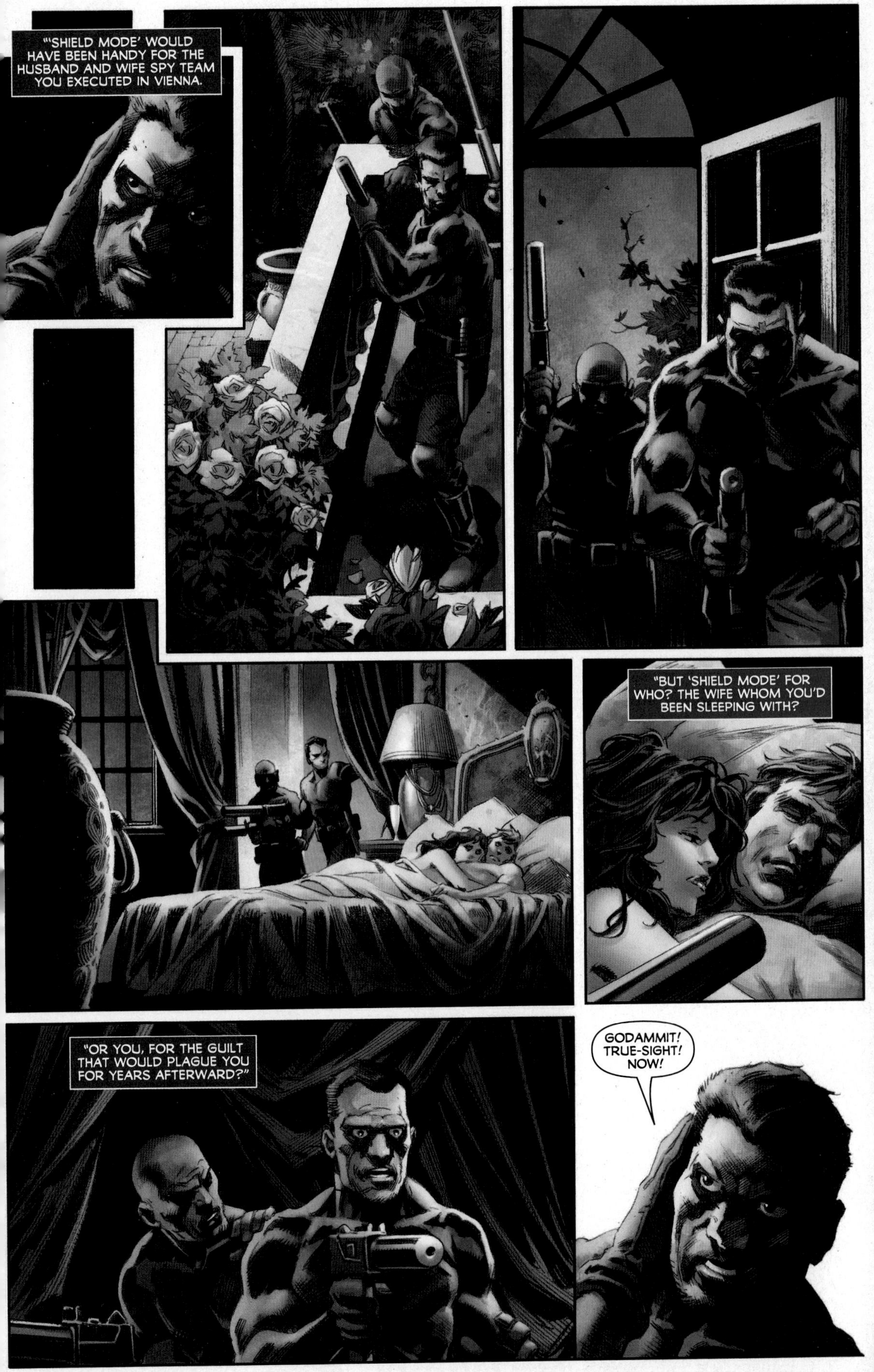
"'SHIELD MODE' WOULD HAVE BEEN HANDY FOR THE HUSBAND AND WIFE SPY TEAM YOU EXECUTED IN VIENNA.
"BUT 'SHIELD MODE' FOR WHO? THE WIFE WHOM YOU'D BEEN SLEEPING WITH?
"OR YOU, FOR THE GUILT THAT WOULD PLAGUE YOU FOR YEARS AFTERWARD?"
GODAMMIT! TRUE-SIGHT! NOW!

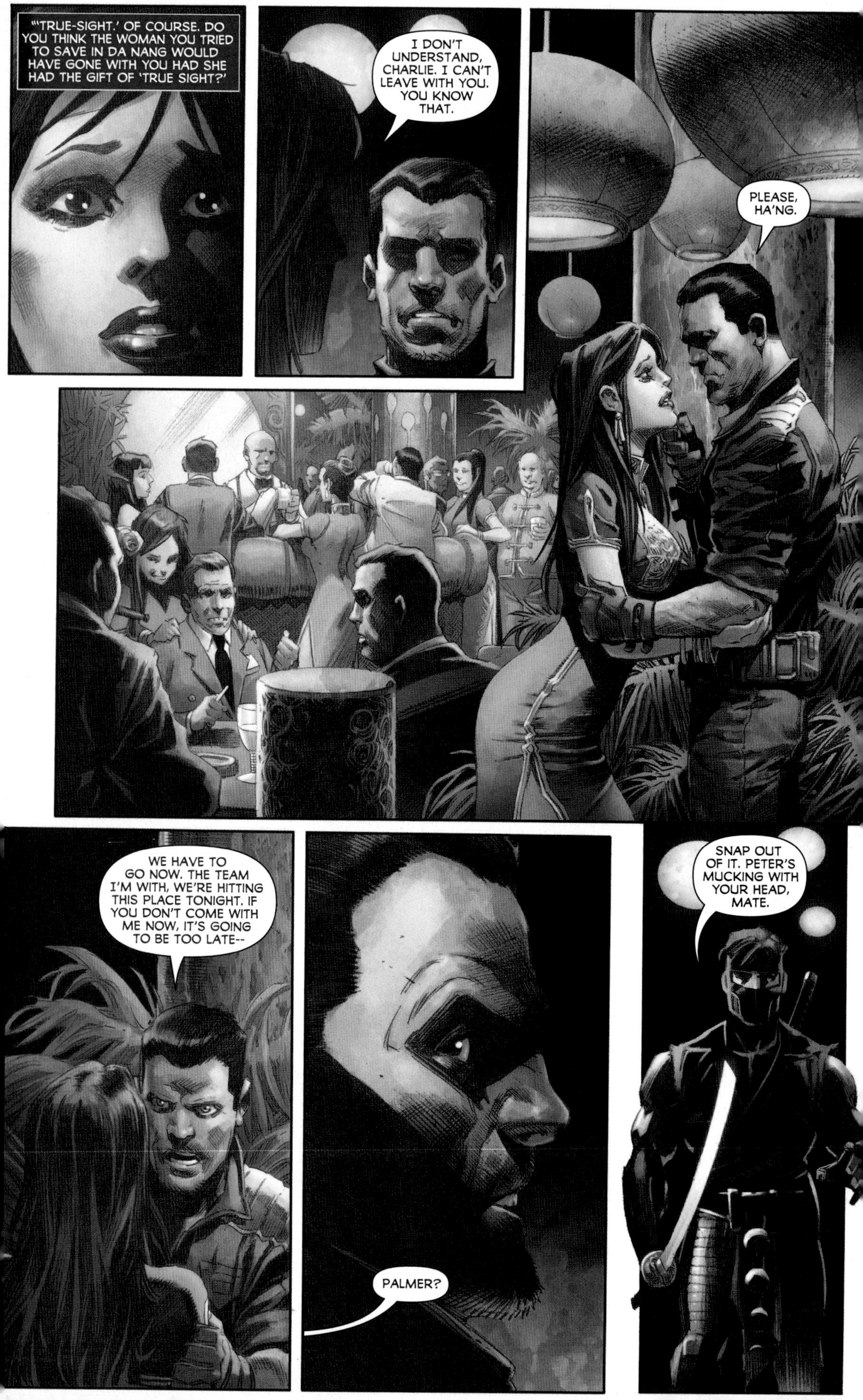
"'TRUE-SIGHT.' OF COURSE. DO YOU THINK THE WOMAN YOU TRIED TO SAVE IN DA NANG WOULD HAVE GONE WITH YOU HAD SHE HAD THE GIFT OF 'TRUE SIGHT?'
I DON'T UNDERSTAND, CHARLIE. I CAN'T LEAVE WITH YOU. YOU KNOW THAT.
PLEASE, HA'NG.
WE HAVE TO GO NOW. THE TEAM I'M WITH, WE'RE HITTING THIS PLACE TONIGHT. IF YOU DON'T COME WITH ME NOW, IT'S GOING TO BE TOO LATE--
PALMER?
SNAP OUT OF IT. PETER'S MUCKING WITH YOUR HEAD, MATE.

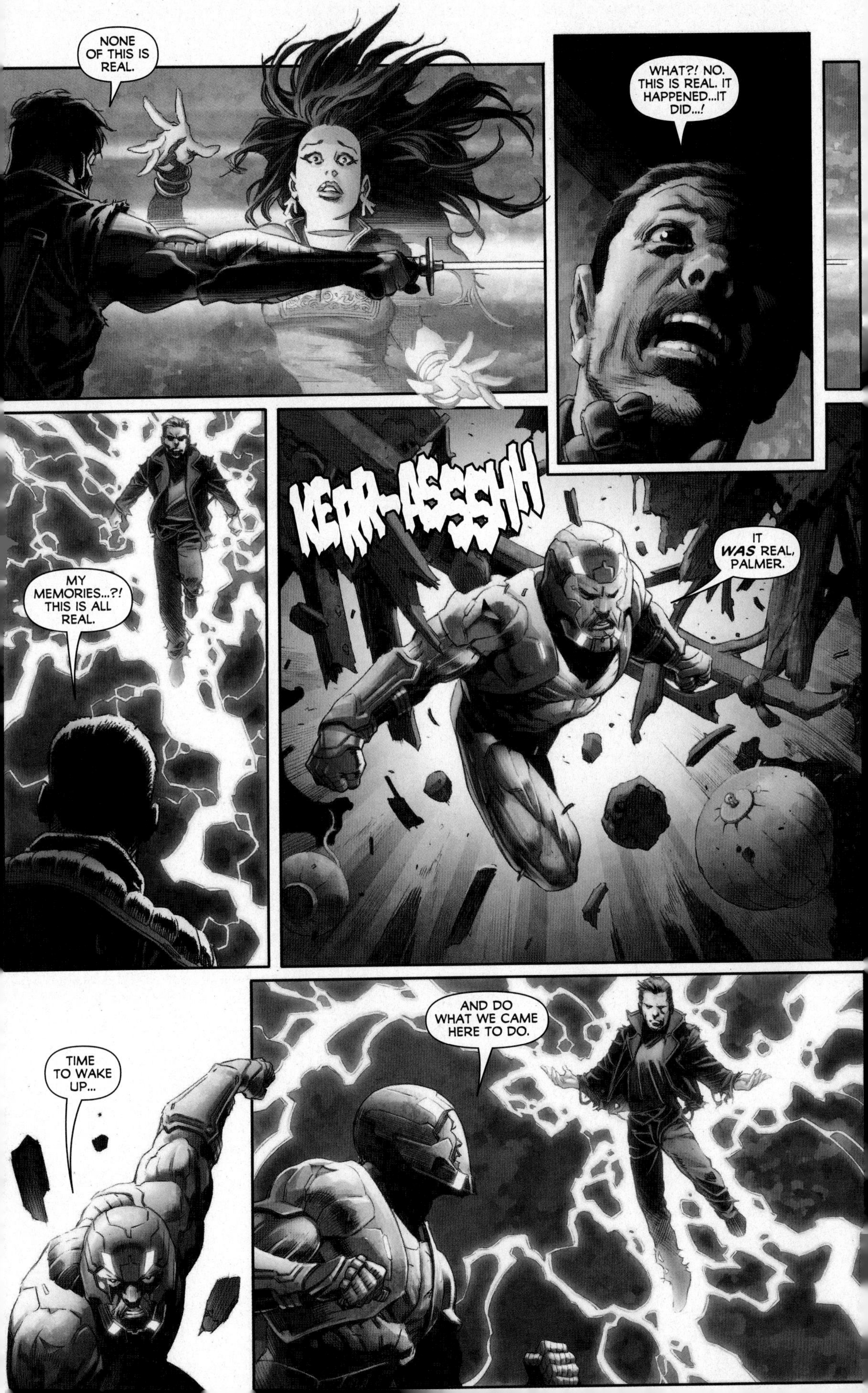
NONE OF THIS IS REAL.
WHAT?! NO. THIS IS REAL. IT HAPPENED...IT DID...!
MY MEMORIES...?! THIS IS ALL REAL.
KERR-ASSSHH
IT WAS REAL, PALMER.
TIME TO WAKE UP...
AND DO WHAT WE CAME HERE TO DO.

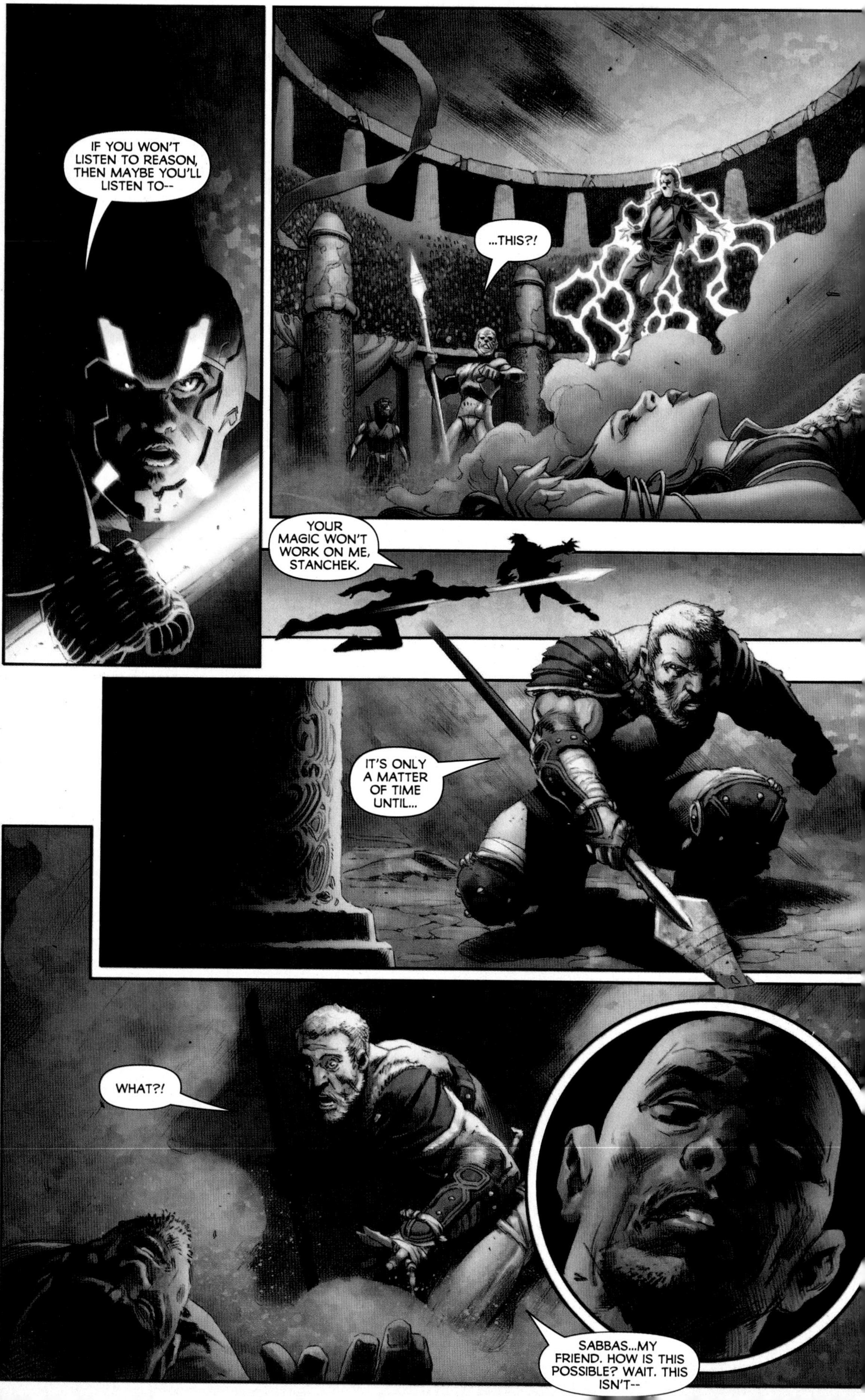
IF YOU WON'T LISTEN TO REASON, THEN MAYBE YOU'LL LISTEN TO--
...THIS?!
YOUR MAGIC WON'T WORK ON ME, STANCHEK.
IT'S ONLY A MATTER OF TIME UNTIL...
WHAT?!
SABBAS...MY FRIEND. HOW IS THIS POSSIBLE? WAIT. THIS ISN'T--

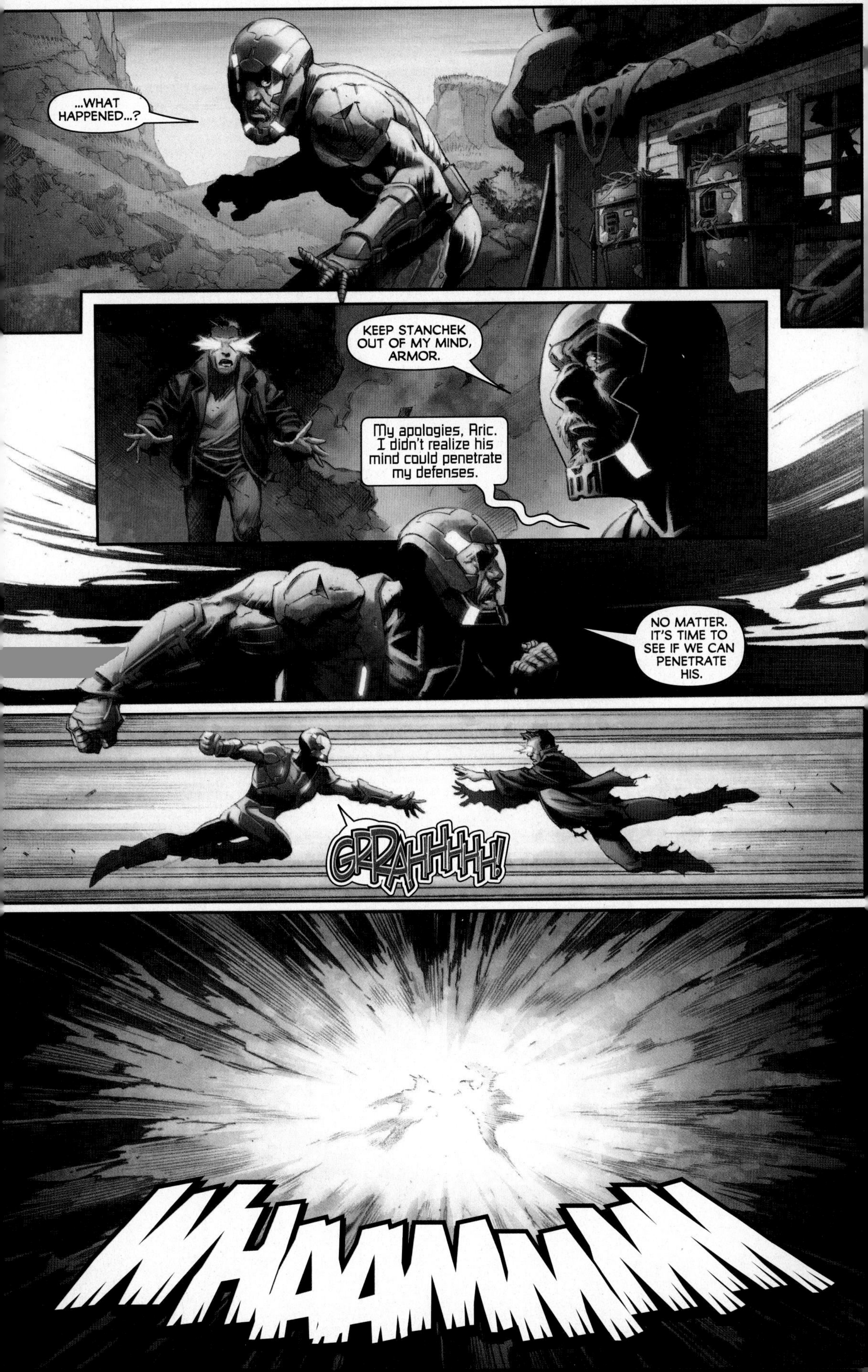
...WHAT HAPPENED...?
KEEP STANCHEK OUT OF MY MIND, ARMOR.
My apologies, Aric. I didn't realize his mind could penetrate my defenses.
NO MATTER. IT'S TIME TO SEE IF WE CAN PENETRATE HIS.
GRRAHHHHH!
WHAAMMMM

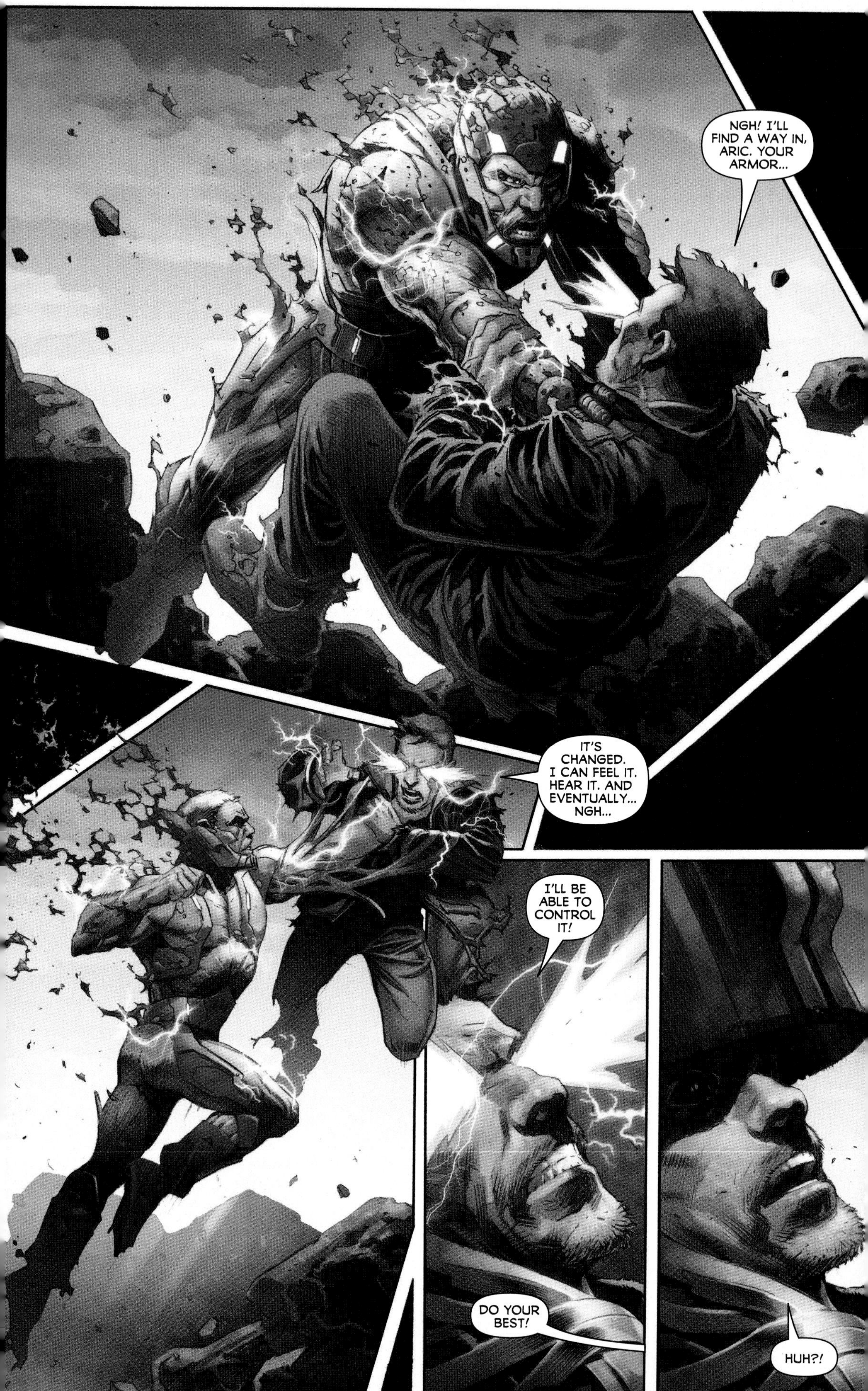
NGH! I'LL FIND A WAY IN, ARIC. YOUR ARMOR...
IT'S CHANGED. I CAN FEEL IT. HEAR IT. AND EVENTUALLY... NGH...
I'LL BE ABLE TO CONTROL IT!
DO YOUR BEST!
HUH?!

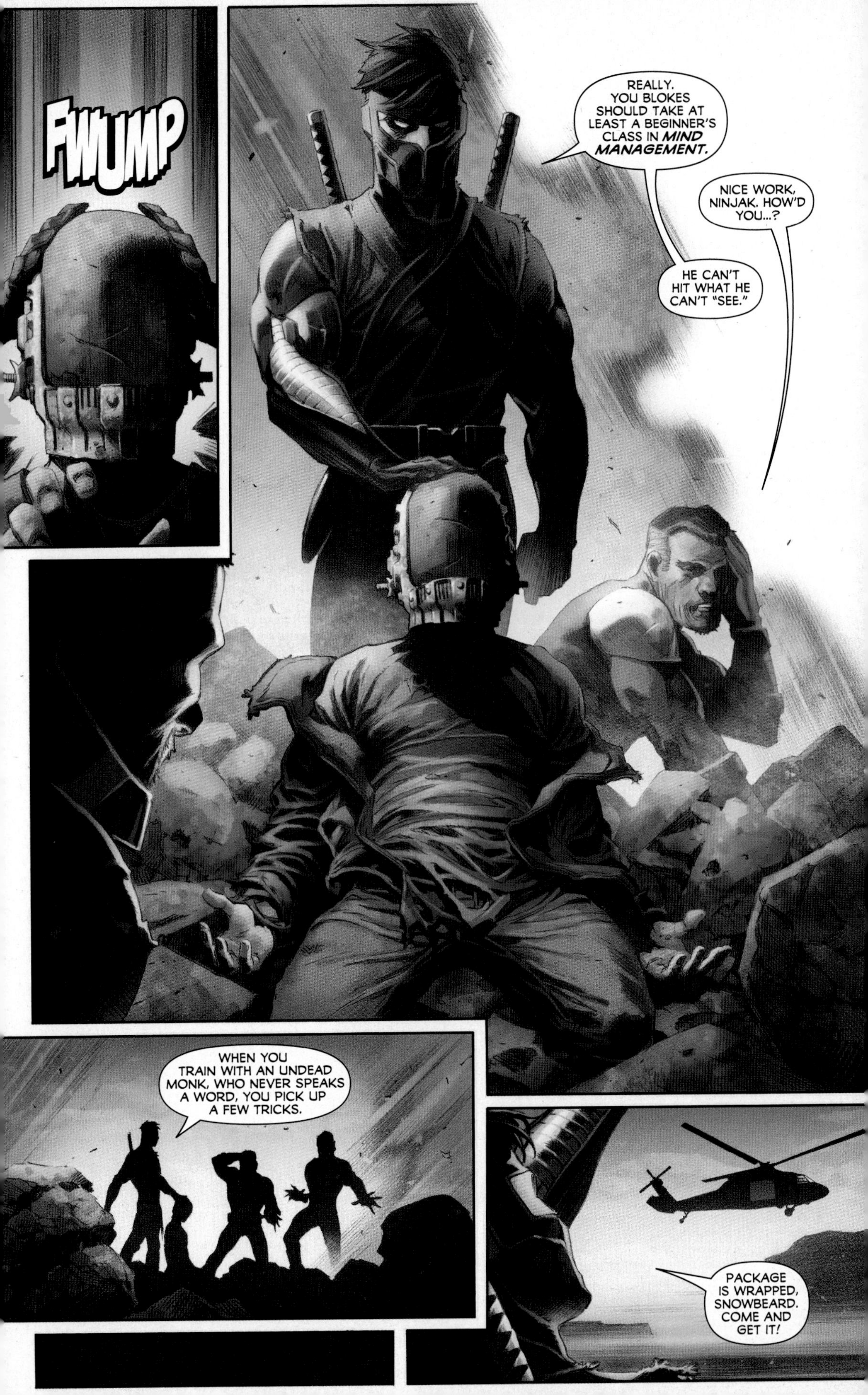

FWUMP
REALLY. YOU BLOKES SHOULD TAKE AT LEAST A BEGINNER'S CLASS IN *MIND MANAGEMENT*.
NICE WORK, NINJAK. HOW'D YOU...?
HE CAN'T HIT WHAT HE CAN'T "SEE."
WHEN YOU TRAIN WITH AN UNDEAD MONK, WHO NEVER SPEAKS A WORD, YOU PICK UP A FEW TRICKS.
PACKAGE IS WRAPPED, SNOWBEARD. COME AND GET IT!

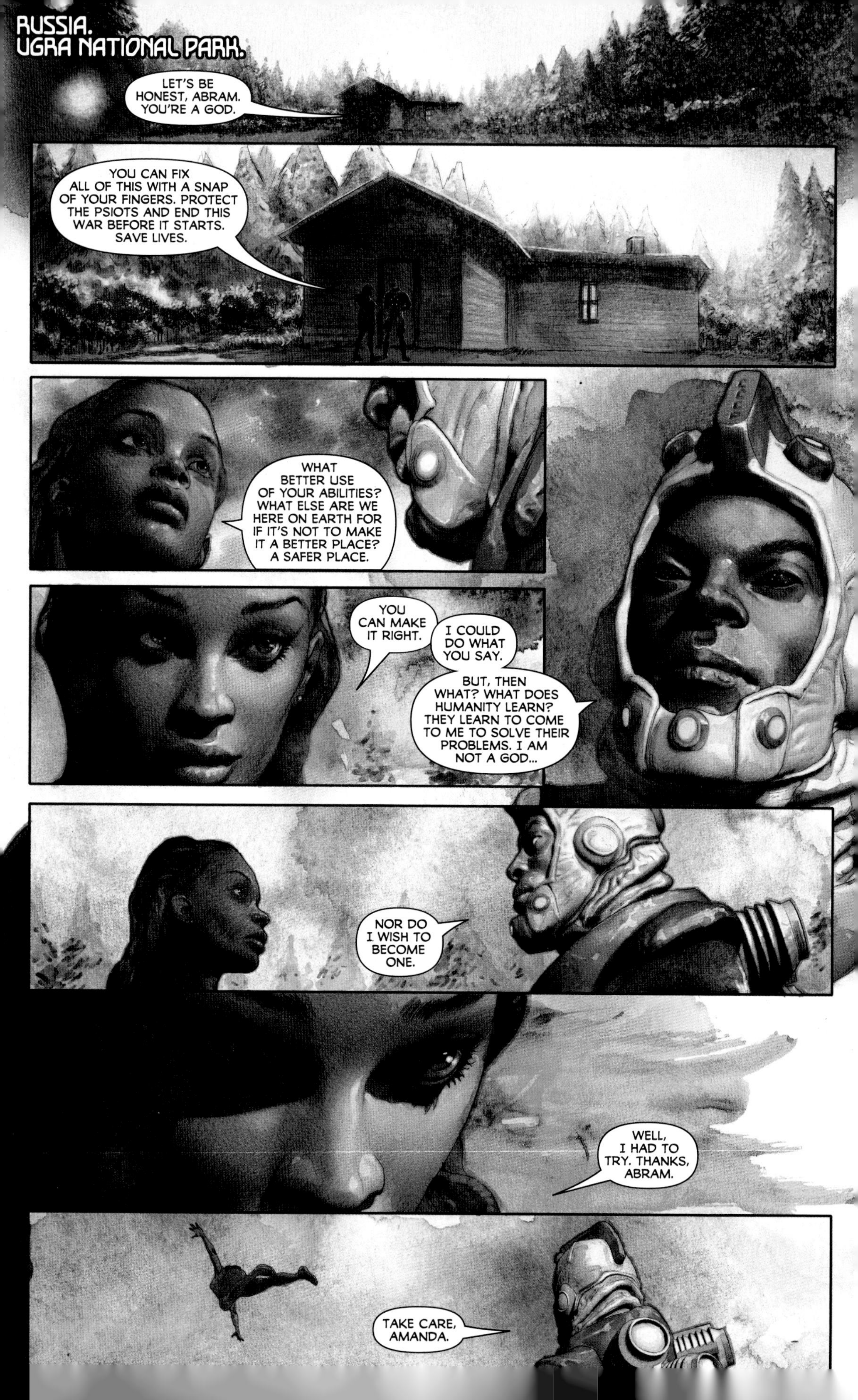
RUSSIA.
UGRA NATIONAL PARK.
LET'S BE HONEST, ABRAM. YOU'RE A GOD.
YOU CAN FIX ALL OF THIS WITH A SNAP OF YOUR FINGERS. PROTECT THE PSIOTS AND END THIS WAR BEFORE IT STARTS. SAVE LIVES.
WHAT BETTER USE OF YOUR ABILITIES? WHAT ELSE ARE WE HERE ON EARTH FOR IF IT'S NOT TO MAKE IT A BETTER PLACE? A SAFER PLACE.
YOU CAN MAKE IT RIGHT.
I COULD DO WHAT YOU SAY.
BUT, THEN WHAT? WHAT DOES HUMANITY LEARN? THEY LEARN TO COME TO ME TO SOLVE THEIR PROBLEMS. I AM NOT A GOD...
NOR DO I WISH TO BECOME ONE.
WELL, I HAD TO TRY. THANKS, ABRAM.
TAKE CARE, AMANDA.

I'M IN POSITION. APPROACHING TARGET AT 105 KNOTS.

STAY THE COURSE AND TIME THE IMPACT. YOU'LL BE FINE.

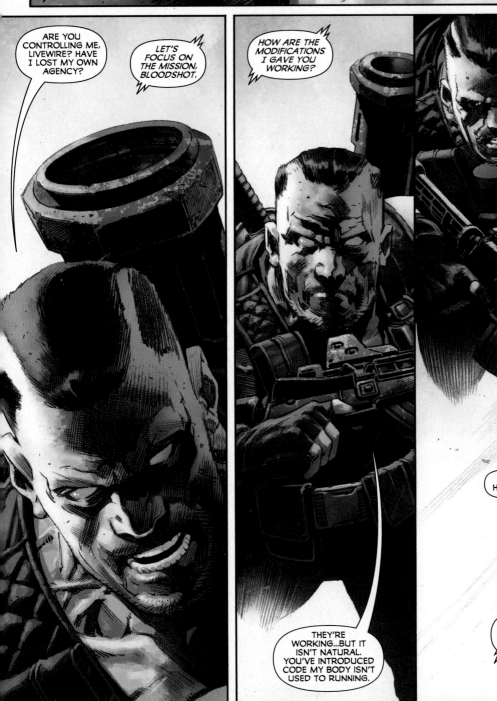

ARE YOU CONTROLLING ME, LIVEWIRE? HAVE I LOST MY OWN AGENCY?

LET'S FOCUS ON THE MISSION, BLOODSHOT.

HOW ARE THE MODIFICATIONS I GAVE YOU WORKING?

THEY'RE WORKING...BUT IT ISN'T NATURAL. YOU'VE INTRODUCED CODE MY BODY ISN'T USED TO RUNNING.

IT HURTS.

I WASN'T AWARE YOU COULD FEEL PAIN.

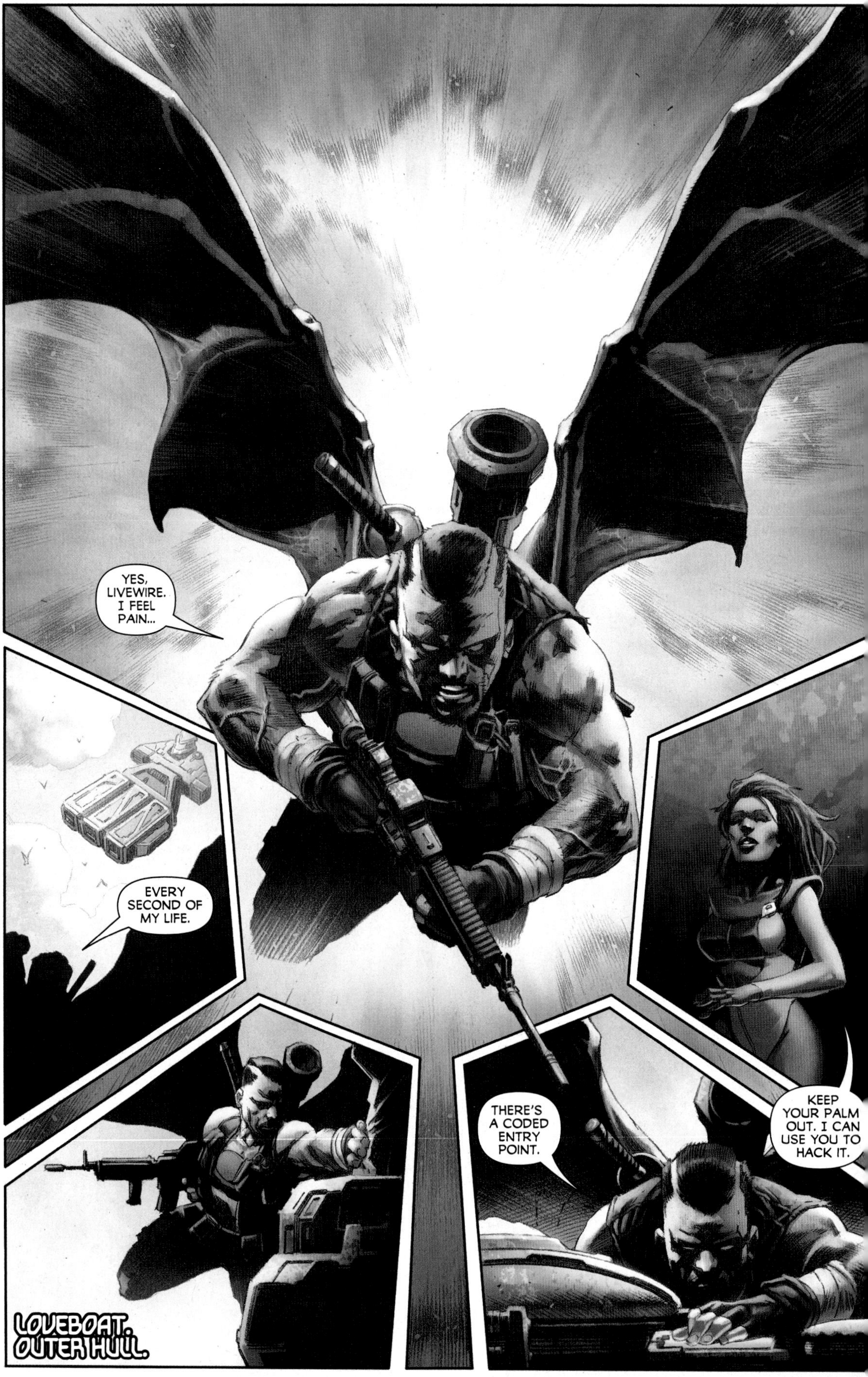
YES, LIVEWIRE. I FEEL PAIN...
EVERY SECOND OF MY LIFE.
LOVEBOAT. OUTER HULL.
THERE'S A CODED ENTRY POINT.
KEEP YOUR PALM OUT. I CAN USE YOU TO HACK IT.

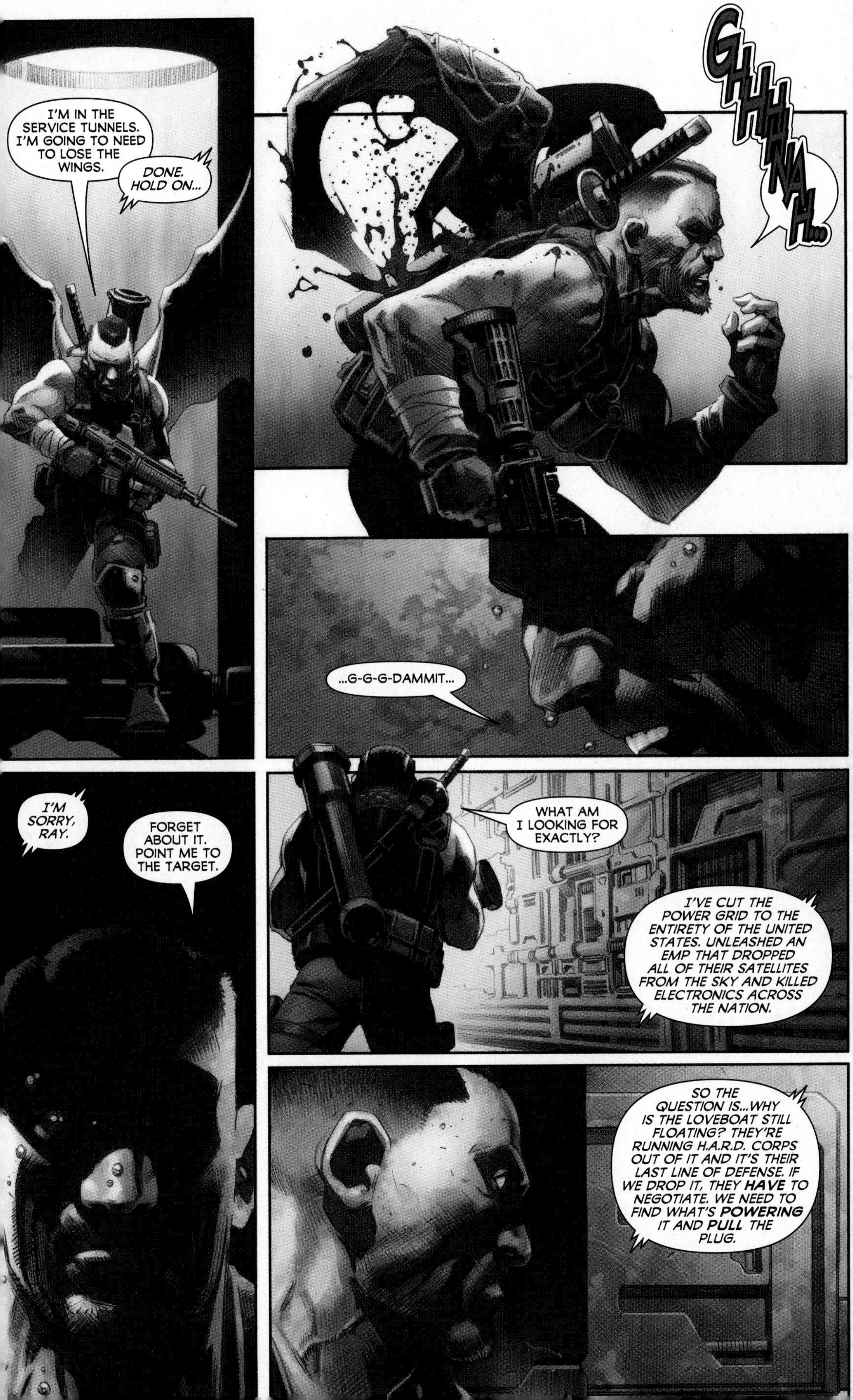

I'M IN THE SERVICE TUNNELS. I'M GOING TO NEED TO LOSE THE WINGS.
DONE. HOLD ON...
GHHHHNAHH...
...G-G-G-DAMMIT...
I'M SORRY, RAY.
FORGET ABOUT IT. POINT ME TO THE TARGET.
WHAT AM I LOOKING FOR EXACTLY?
I'VE CUT THE POWER GRID TO THE ENTIRETY OF THE UNITED STATES. UNLEASHED AN EMP THAT DROPPED ALL OF THEIR SATELLITES FROM THE SKY AND KILLED ELECTRONICS ACROSS THE NATION.
SO THE QUESTION IS...WHY IS THE LOVEBOAT STILL FLOATING? THEY'RE RUNNING H.A.R.D. CORPS OUT OF IT AND IT'S THEIR LAST LINE OF DEFENSE. IF WE DROP IT, THEY **HAVE** TO NEGOTIATE. WE NEED TO FIND WHAT'S **POWERING** IT AND **PULL** THE PLUG.

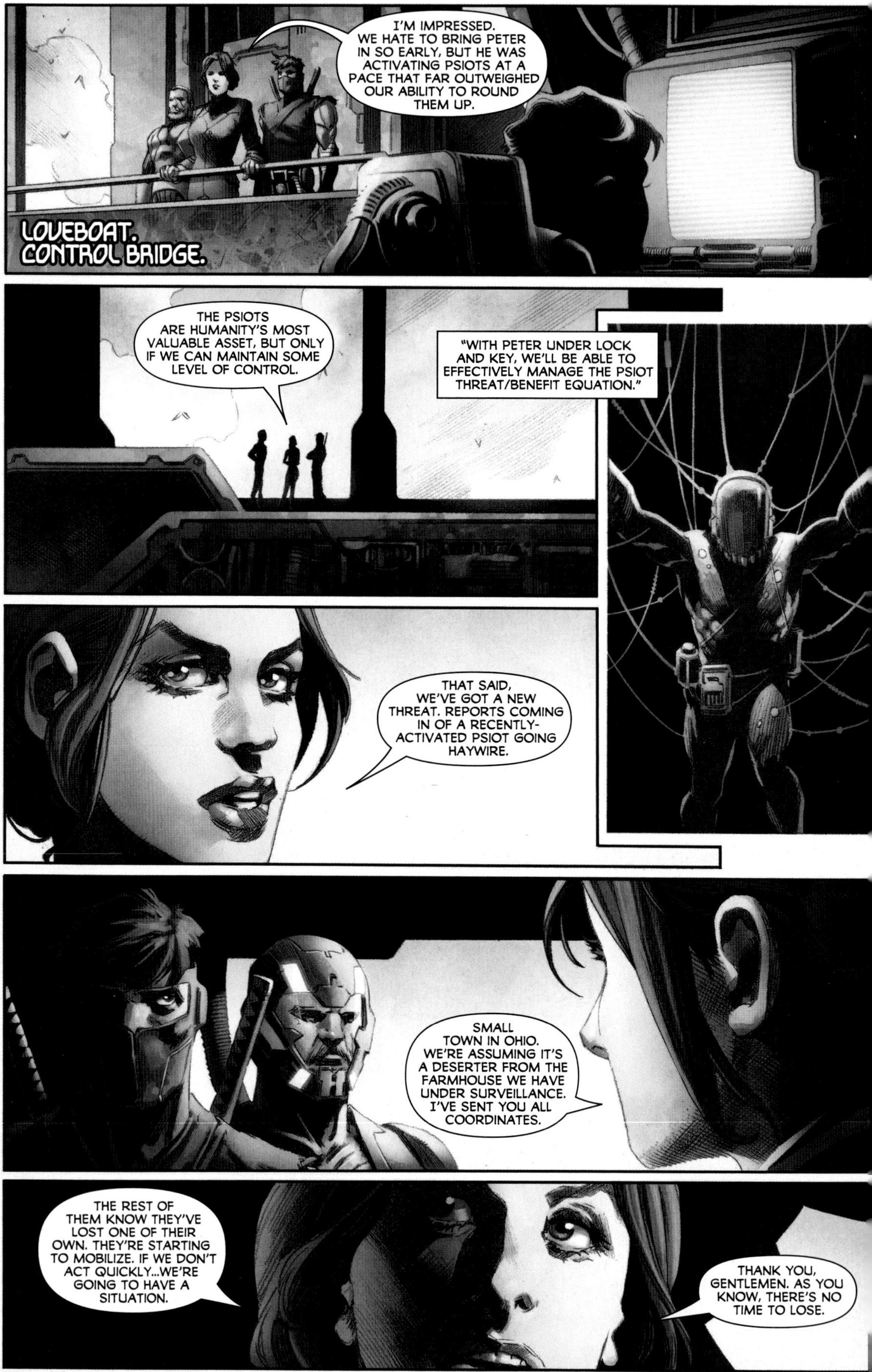
I'M IMPRESSED. WE HATE TO BRING PETER IN SO EARLY, BUT HE WAS ACTIVATING PSIOTS AT A PACE THAT FAR OUTWEIGHED OUR ABILITY TO ROUND THEM UP.
LOVEBOAT. CONTROL BRIDGE.
THE PSIOTS ARE HUMANITY'S MOST VALUABLE ASSET, BUT ONLY IF WE CAN MAINTAIN SOME LEVEL OF CONTROL.
"WITH PETER UNDER LOCK AND KEY, WE'LL BE ABLE TO EFFECTIVELY MANAGE THE PSIOT THREAT/BENEFIT EQUATION."
THAT SAID, WE'VE GOT A NEW THREAT. REPORTS COMING IN OF A RECENTLY-ACTIVATED PSIOT GOING HAYWIRE.
SMALL TOWN IN OHIO. WE'RE ASSUMING IT'S A DESERTER FROM THE FARMHOUSE WE HAVE UNDER SURVEILLANCE. I'VE SENT YOU ALL COORDINATES.
THE REST OF THEM KNOW THEY'VE LOST ONE OF THEIR OWN. THEY'RE STARTING TO MOBILIZE. IF WE DON'T ACT QUICKLY...WE'RE GOING TO HAVE A SITUATION.
THANK YOU, GENTLEMEN. AS YOU KNOW, THERE'S NO TIME TO LOSE.

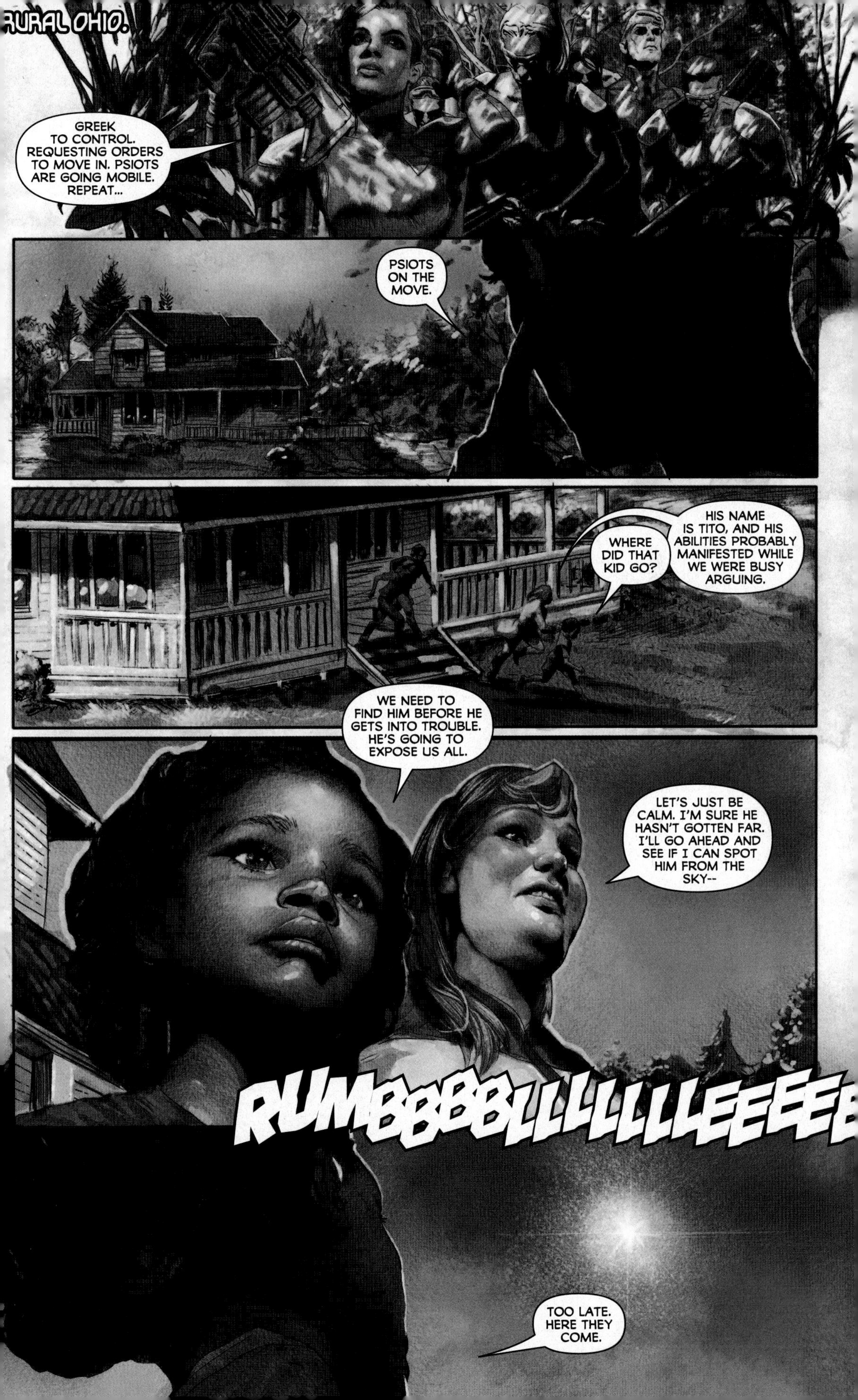
RURAL OHIO.
GREEK TO CONTROL. REQUESTING ORDERS TO MOVE IN. PSIOTS ARE GOING MOBILE. REPEAT...
PSIOTS ON THE MOVE.
WHERE DID THAT KID GO?
HIS NAME IS TITO, AND HIS ABILITIES PROBABLY MANIFESTED WHILE WE WERE BUSY ARGUING.
WE NEED TO FIND HIM BEFORE HE GETS INTO TROUBLE. HE'S GOING TO EXPOSE US ALL.
LET'S JUST BE CALM. I'M SURE HE HASN'T GOTTEN FAR. I'LL GO AHEAD AND SEE IF I CAN SPOT HIM FROM THE SKY--
RUMBBBBLLLLLLLLEEEEE
TOO LATE. HERE THEY COME.

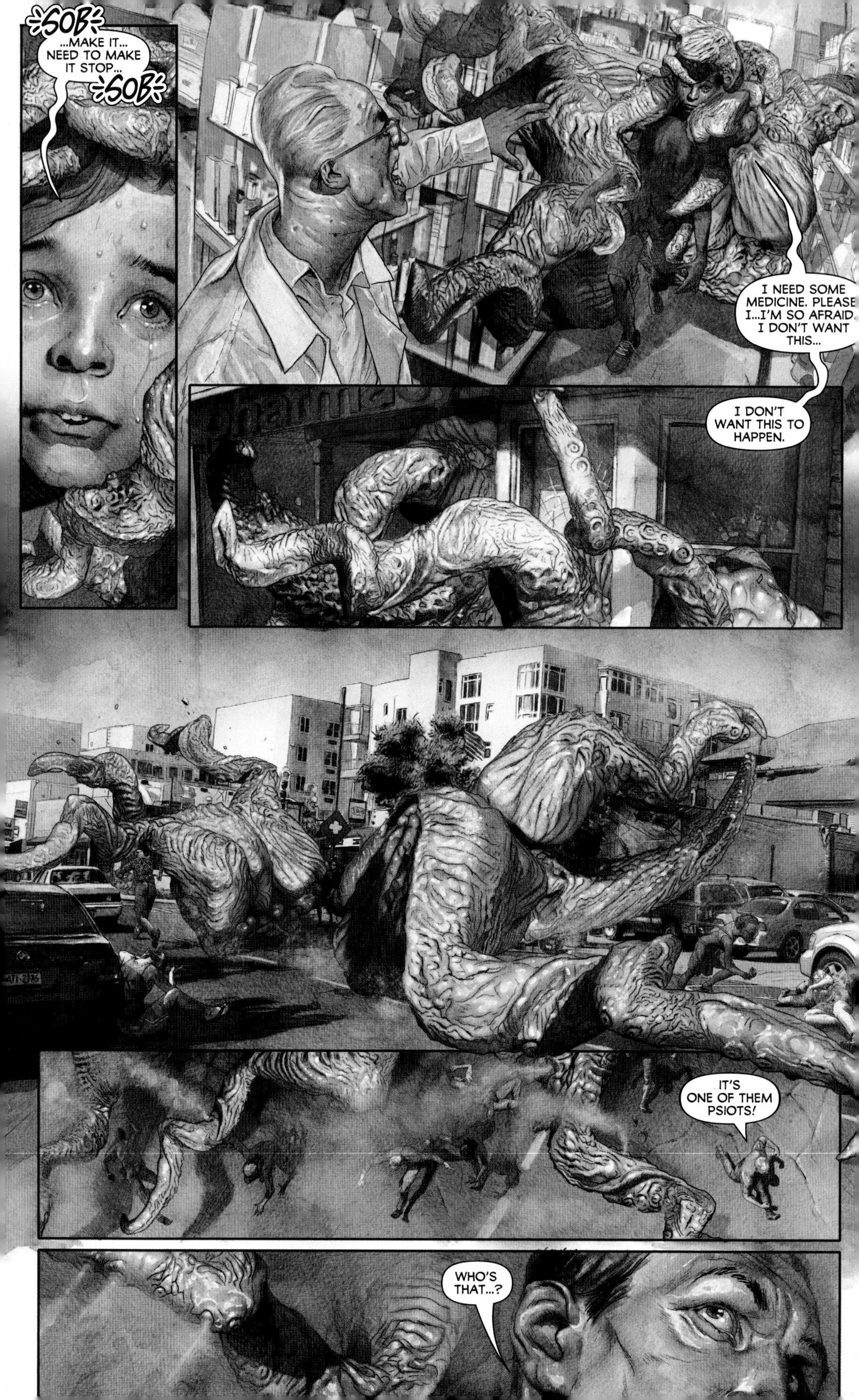
SOB
...MAKE IT... NEED TO MAKE IT STOP...
SOB
I NEED SOME MEDICINE. PLEASE I...I'M SO AFRAID. I DON'T WANT THIS...
I DON'T WANT THIS TO HAPPEN.
IT'S ONE OF THEM PSIOTS!
WHO'S THAT...?

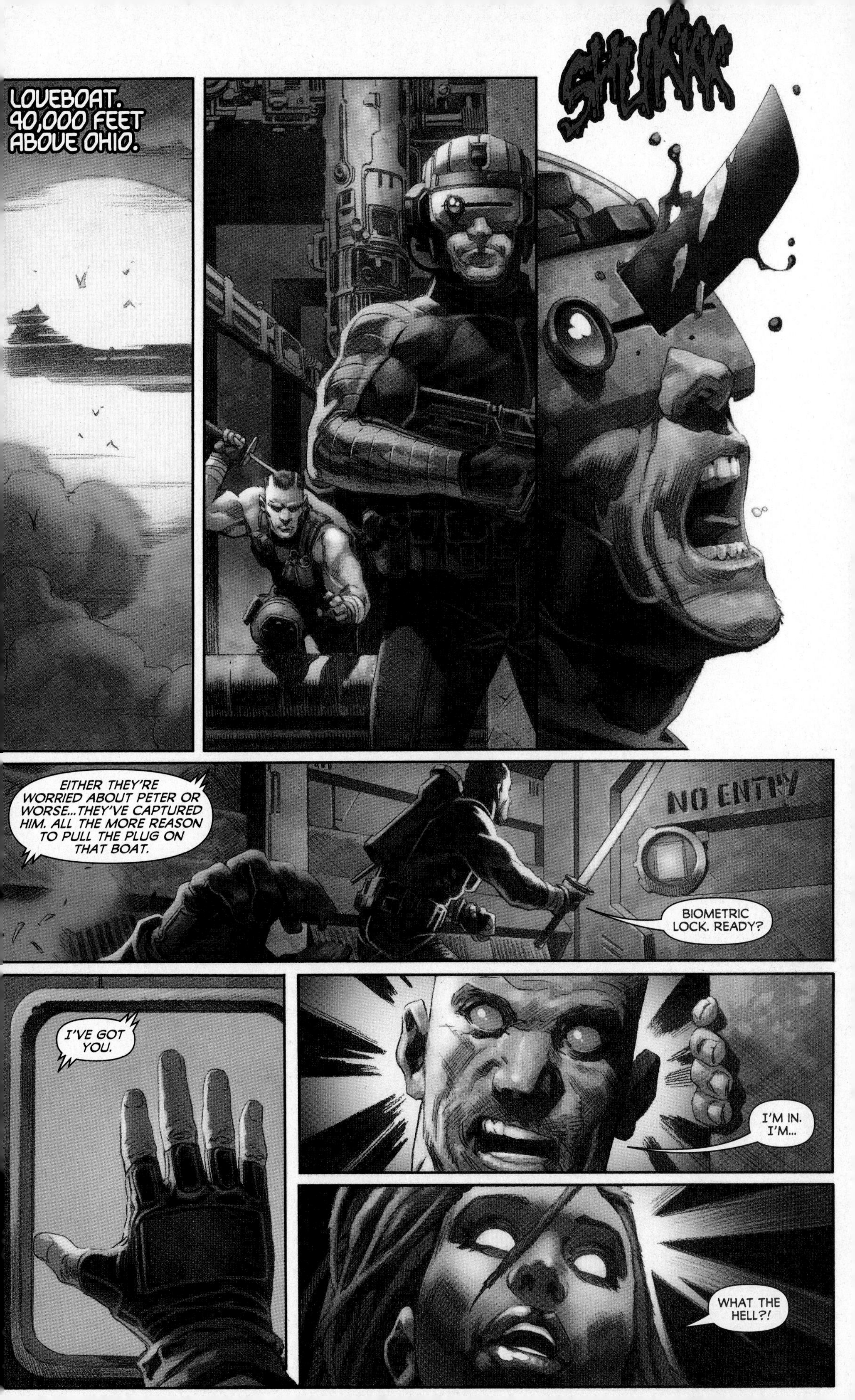
LOVEBOAT.
40,000 FEET ABOVE OHIO.
SHLIKKK
EITHER THEY'RE WORRIED ABOUT PETER OR WORSE...THEY'VE CAPTURED HIM. ALL THE MORE REASON TO PULL THE PLUG ON THAT BOAT.
NO ENTRY
BIOMETRIC LOCK. READY?
I'VE GOT YOU.
I'M IN. I'M...
WHAT THE HELL?!

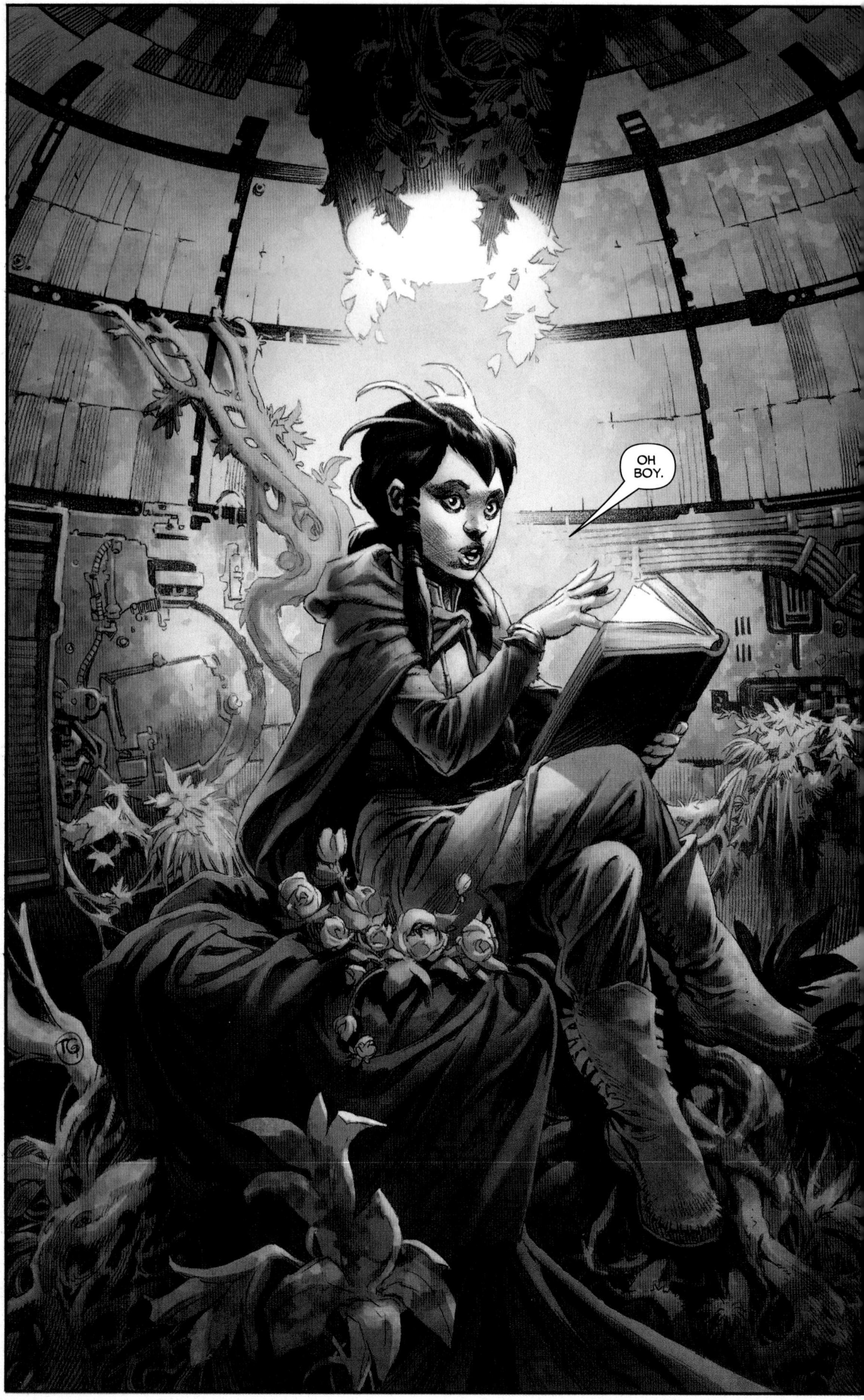
OH BOY.

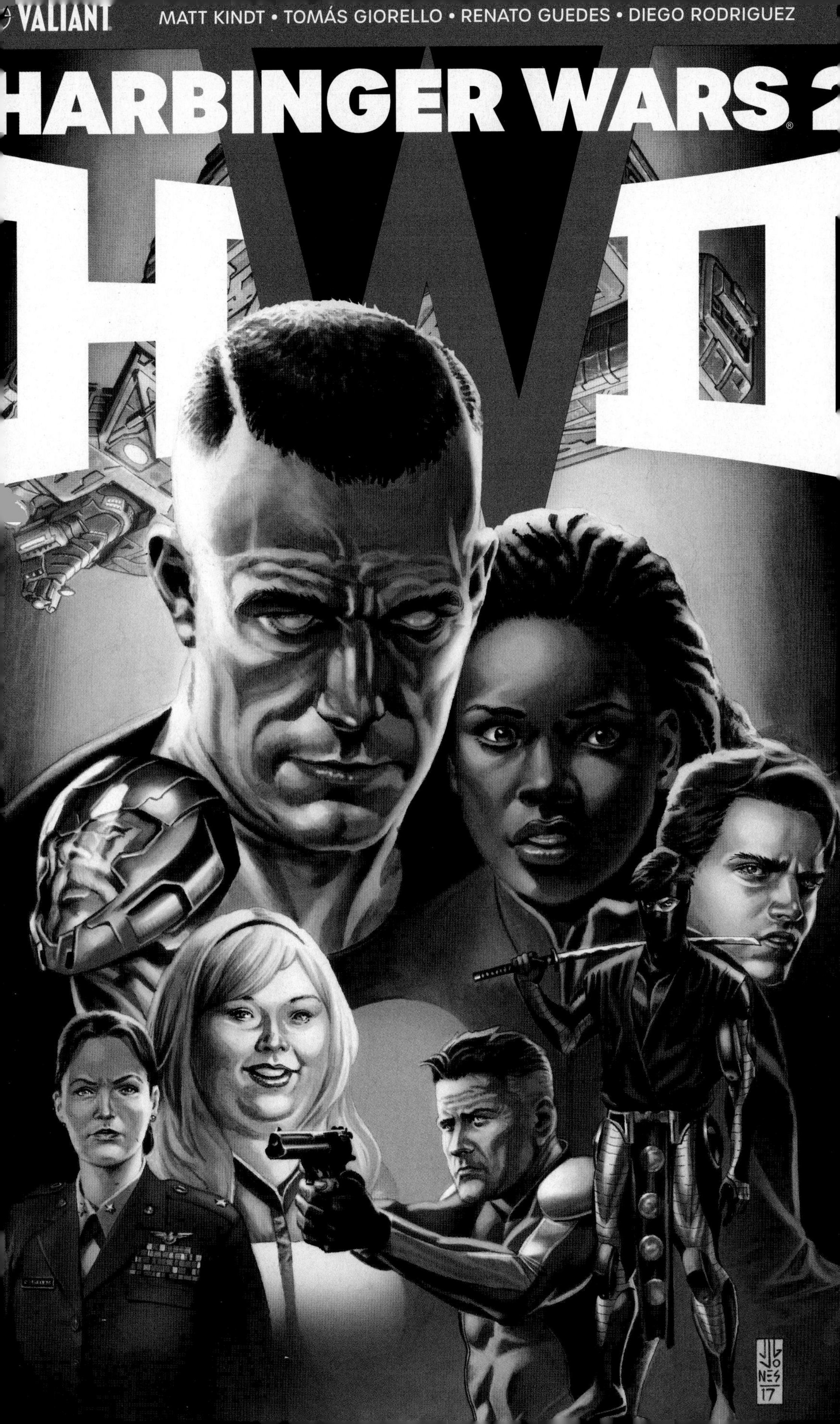
VALIANT
MATT KINDT • TOMÁS GIORELLO • RENATO GUEDES • DIEGO RODRIGUEZ
HARBINGER WARS 2
HWII

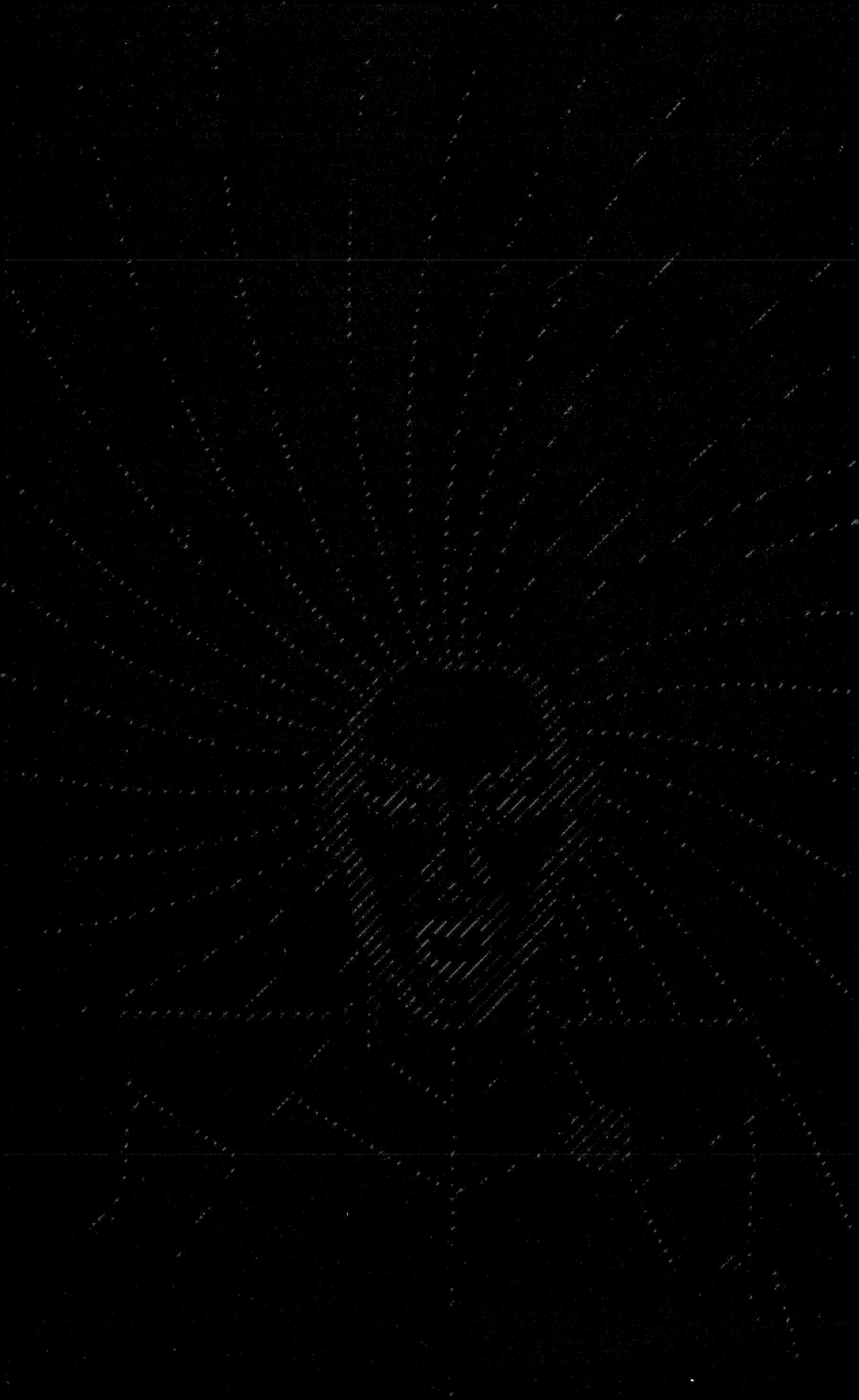

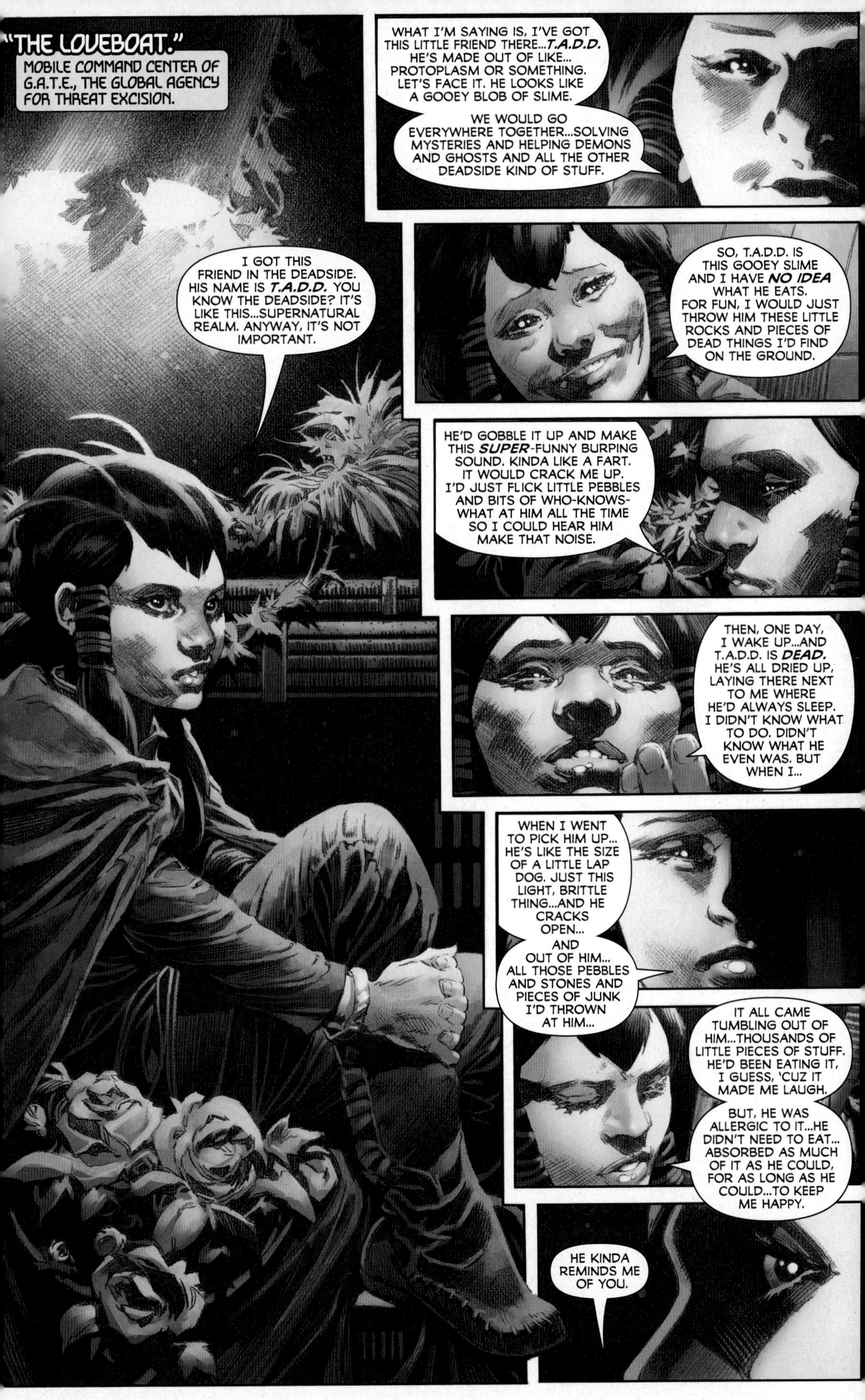
"THE LOVEBOAT."
MOBILE COMMAND CENTER OF G.A.T.E., THE GLOBAL AGENCY FOR THREAT EXCISION.
I GOT THIS FRIEND IN THE DEADSIDE. HIS NAME IS T.A.D.D. YOU KNOW THE DEADSIDE? IT'S LIKE THIS...SUPERNATURAL REALM. ANYWAY, IT'S NOT IMPORTANT.
WHAT I'M SAYING IS, I'VE GOT THIS LITTLE FRIEND THERE...T.A.D.D. HE'S MADE OUT OF LIKE... PROTOPLASM OR SOMETHING. LET'S FACE IT. HE LOOKS LIKE A GOOEY BLOB OF SLIME.
WE WOULD GO EVERYWHERE TOGETHER...SOLVING MYSTERIES AND HELPING DEMONS AND GHOSTS AND ALL THE OTHER DEADSIDE KIND OF STUFF.
SO, T.A.D.D. IS THIS GOOEY SLIME AND I HAVE NO IDEA WHAT HE EATS. FOR FUN, I WOULD JUST THROW HIM THESE LITTLE ROCKS AND PIECES OF DEAD THINGS I'D FIND ON THE GROUND.
HE'D GOBBLE IT UP AND MAKE THIS SUPER-FUNNY BURPING SOUND. KINDA LIKE A FART. IT WOULD CRACK ME UP. I'D JUST FLICK LITTLE PEBBLES AND BITS OF WHO-KNOWS-WHAT AT HIM ALL THE TIME SO I COULD HEAR HIM MAKE THAT NOISE.
THEN, ONE DAY, I WAKE UP...AND T.A.D.D. IS DEAD. HE'S ALL DRIED UP, LAYING THERE NEXT TO ME WHERE HE'D ALWAYS SLEEP. I DIDN'T KNOW WHAT TO DO. DIDN'T KNOW WHAT HE EVEN WAS. BUT WHEN I...
WHEN I WENT TO PICK HIM UP... HE'S LIKE THE SIZE OF A LITTLE LAP DOG. JUST THIS LIGHT, BRITTLE THING...AND HE CRACKS OPEN...
AND OUT OF HIM... ALL THOSE PEBBLES AND STONES AND PIECES OF JUNK I'D THROWN AT HIM...
IT ALL CAME TUMBLING OUT OF HIM...THOUSANDS OF LITTLE PIECES OF STUFF. HE'D BEEN EATING IT, I GUESS, 'CUZ IT MADE ME LAUGH.
BUT, HE WAS ALLERGIC TO IT...HE DIDN'T NEED TO EAT... ABSORBED AS MUCH OF IT AS HE COULD, FOR AS LONG AS HE COULD...TO KEEP ME HAPPY.
HE KINDA REMINDS ME OF YOU.

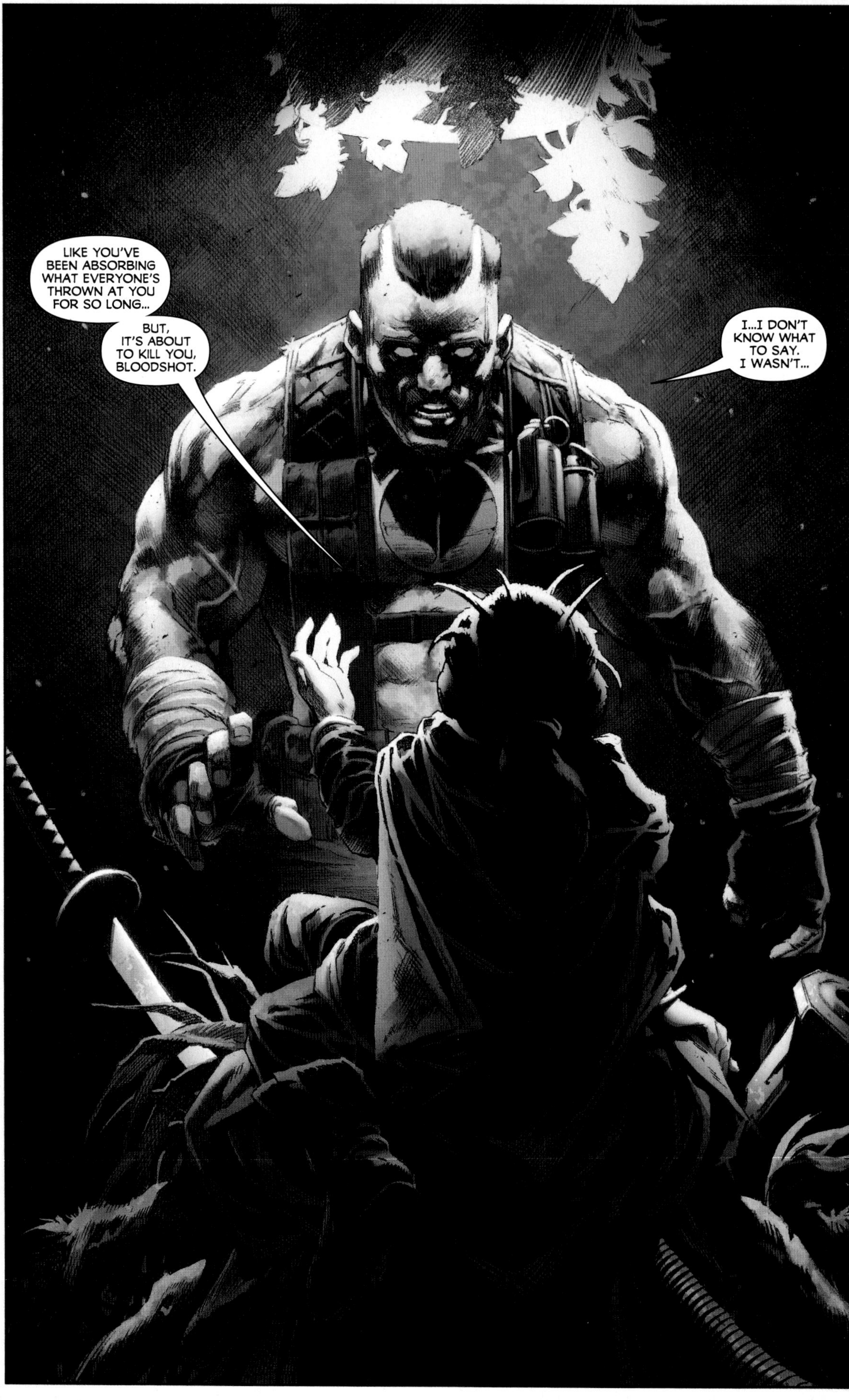
LIKE YOU'VE BEEN ABSORBING WHAT EVERYONE'S THROWN AT YOU FOR SO LONG...
BUT, IT'S ABOUT TO KILL YOU, BLOODSHOT.
I...I DON'T KNOW WHAT TO SAY. I WASN'T...

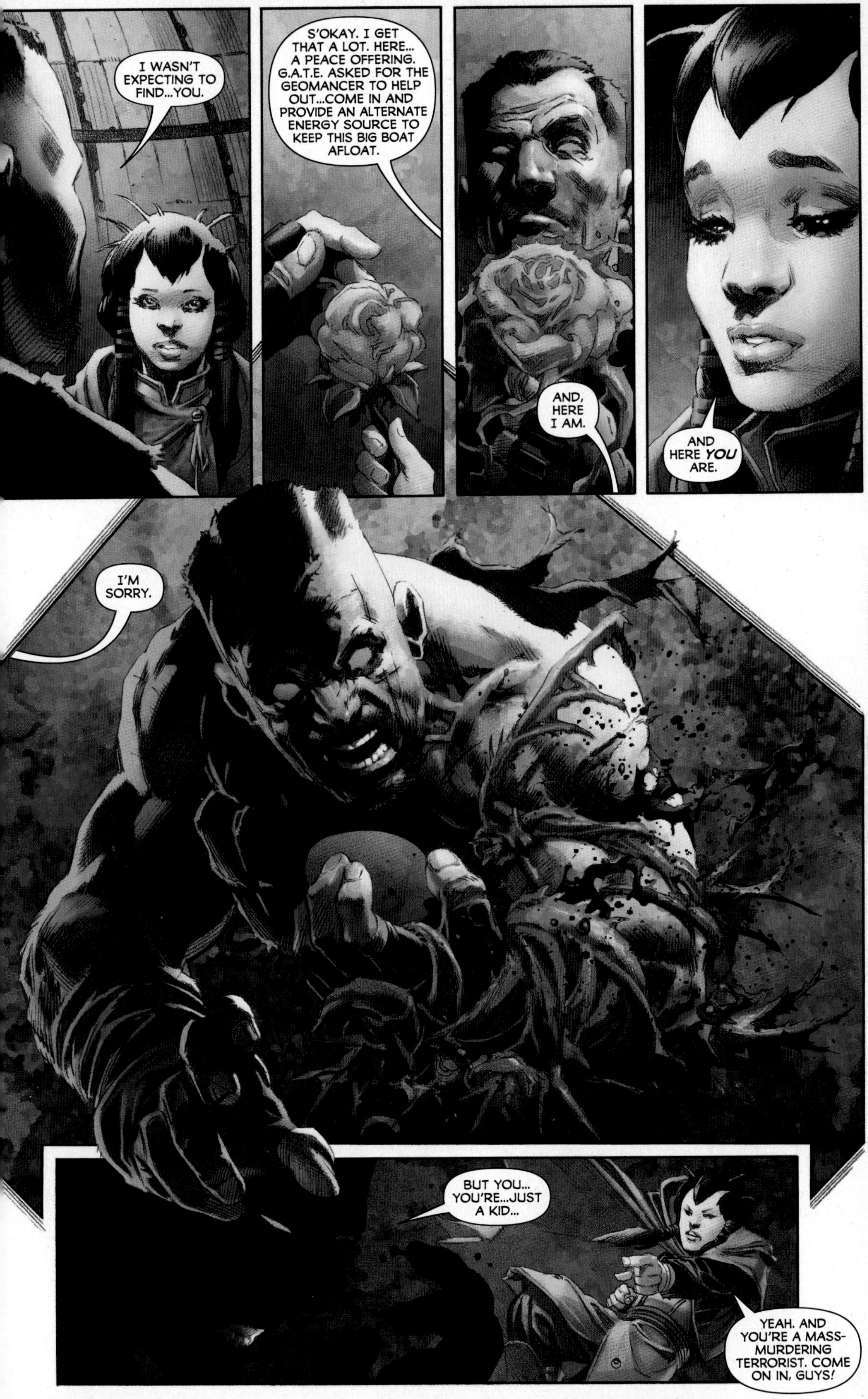
I WASN'T EXPECTING TO FIND...YOU.
S'OKAY. I GET THAT A LOT. HERE... A PEACE OFFERING. G.A.T.E. ASKED FOR THE GEOMANCER TO HELP OUT...COME IN AND PROVIDE AN ALTERNATE ENERGY SOURCE TO KEEP THIS BIG BOAT AFLOAT.
AND, HERE I AM.
AND HERE *YOU* ARE.
I'M SORRY.
BUT YOU... YOU'RE...JUST A KID...
YEAH. AND YOU'RE A MASS-MURDERING TERRORIST. COME ON IN, GUYS!

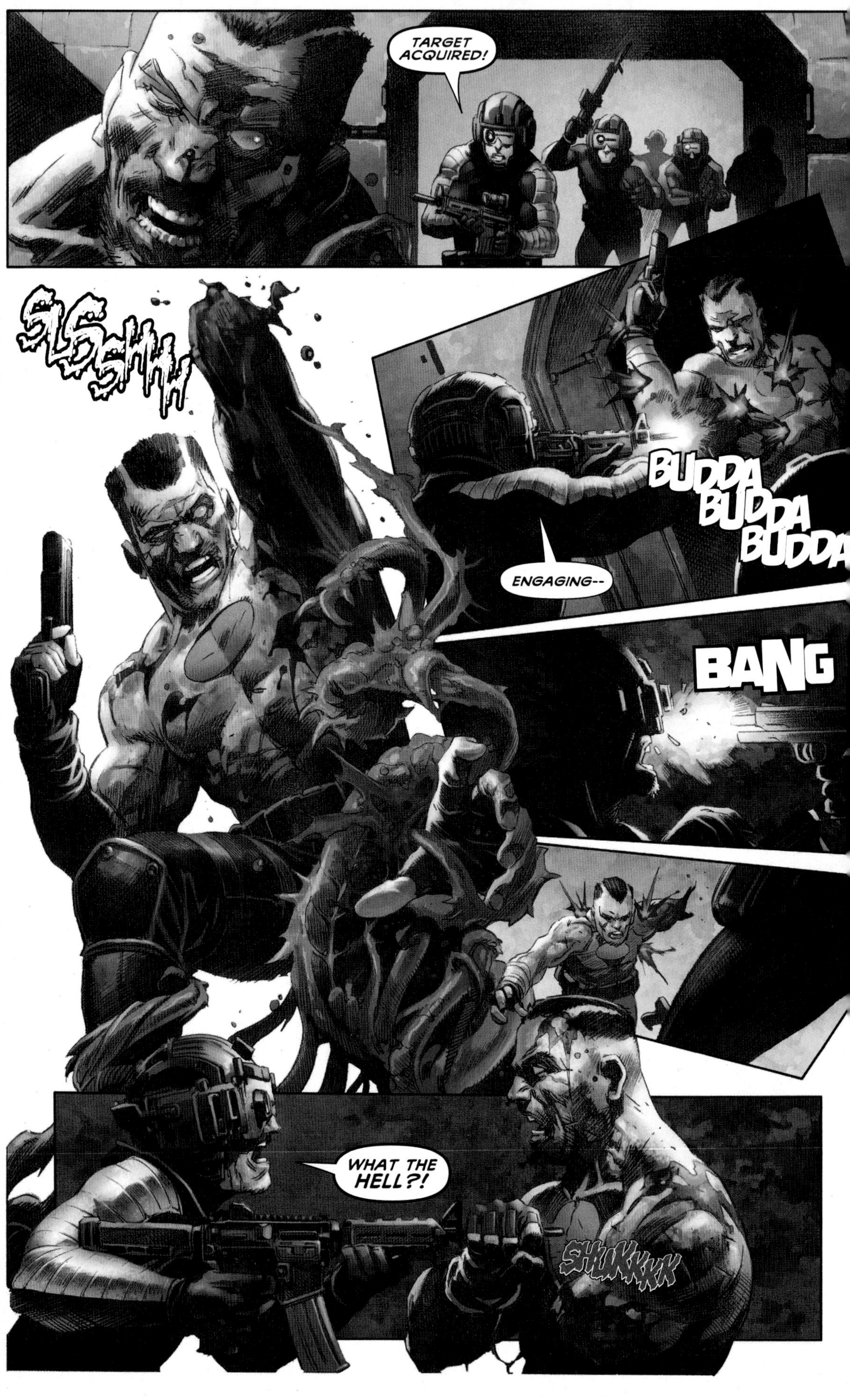
TARGET ACQUIRED!
SLSHHH
BUDDA BUDDA BUDDA
ENGAGING--
BANG
WHAT THE HELL?!
SHUKKKK

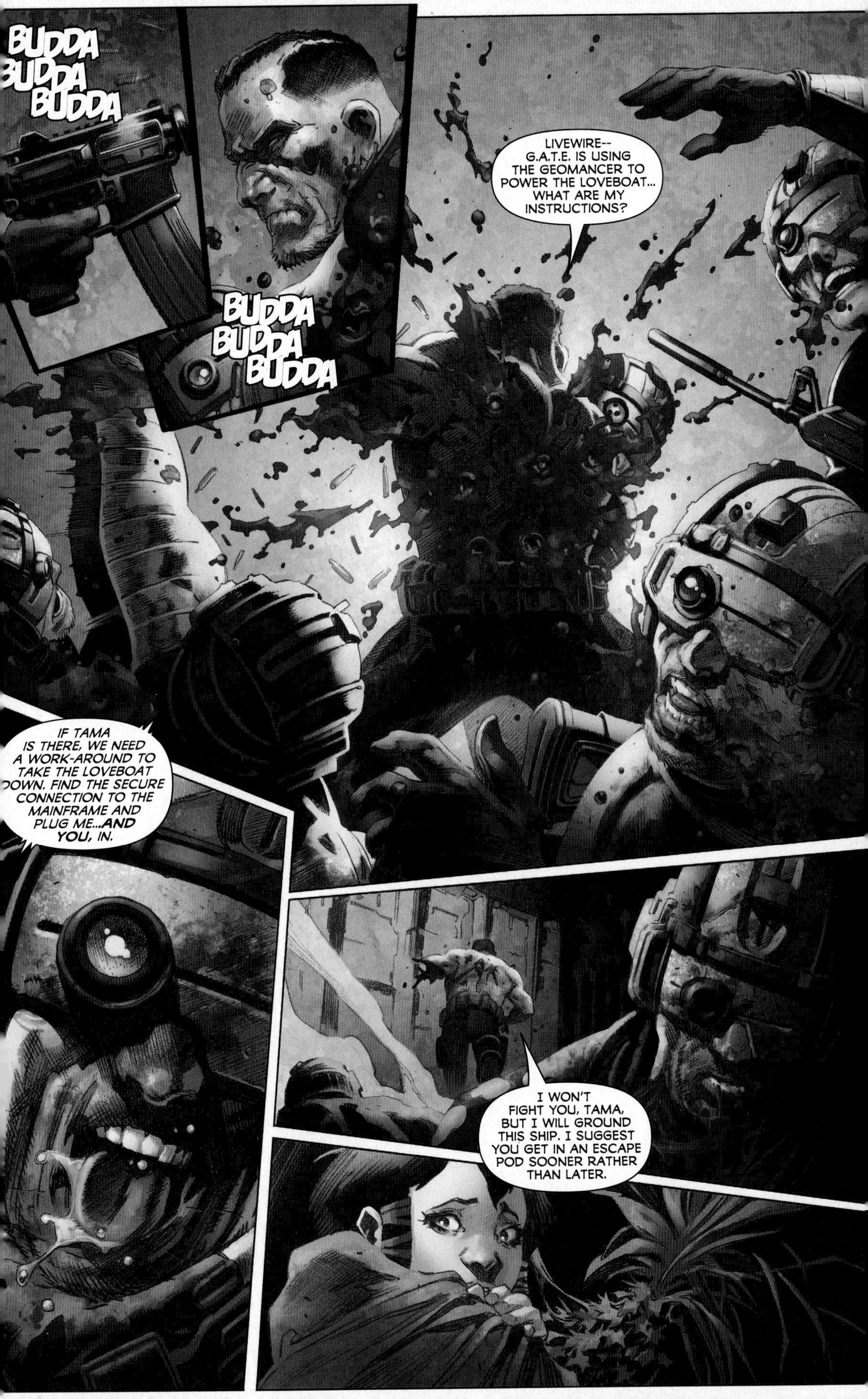
BUDDA BUDDA BUDDA
BUDDA BUDDA BUDDA
LIVEWIRE-- G.A.T.E. IS USING THE GEOMANCER TO POWER THE LOVEBOAT... WHAT ARE MY INSTRUCTIONS?
IF TAMA IS THERE, WE NEED A WORK-AROUND TO TAKE THE LOVEBOAT DOWN. FIND THE SECURE CONNECTION TO THE MAINFRAME AND PLUG ME...**AND YOU,** IN.
I WON'T FIGHT YOU, TAMA, BUT I WILL GROUND THIS SHIP. I SUGGEST YOU GET IN AN ESCAPE POD SOONER RATHER THAN LATER.

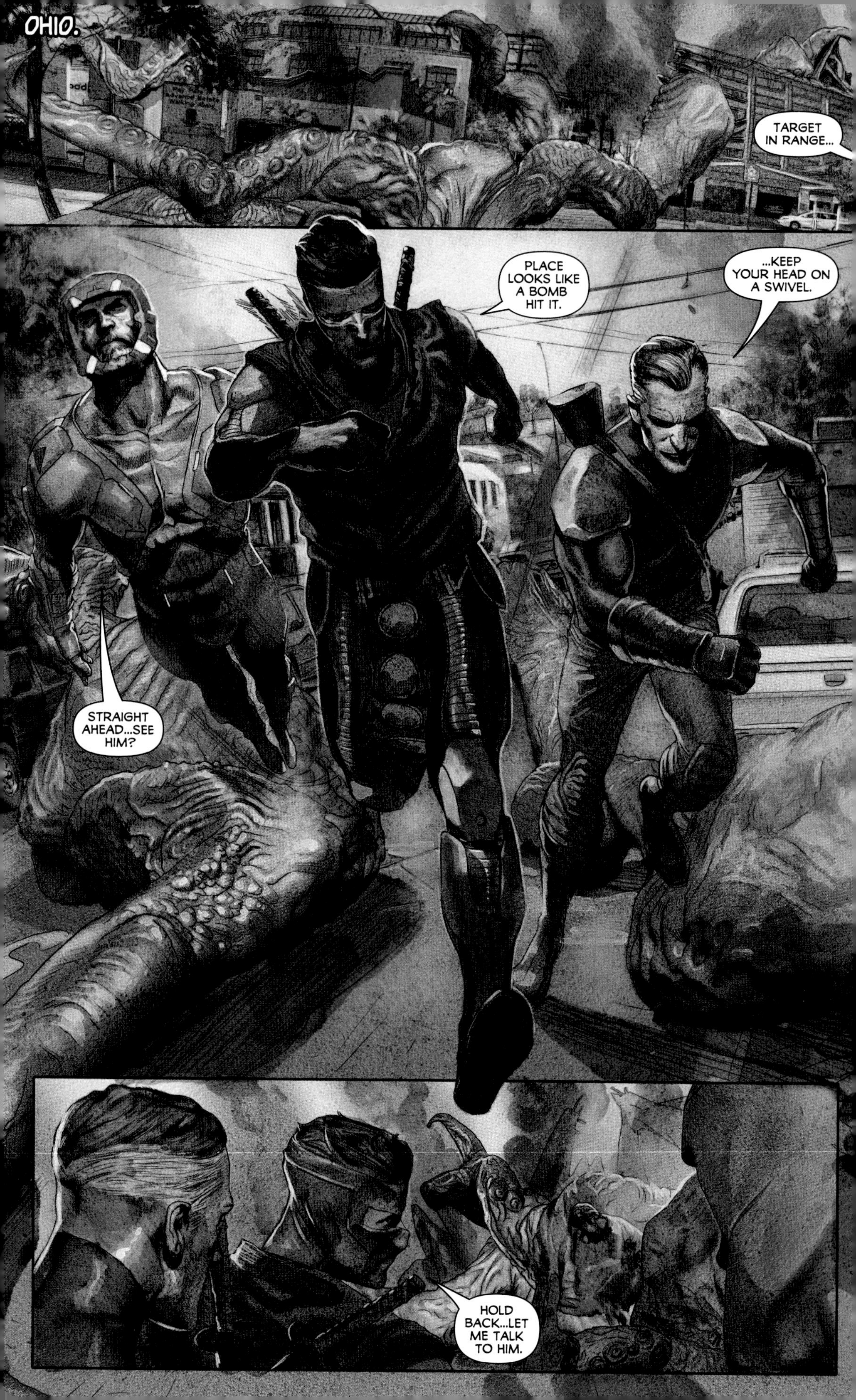
OHIO.
TARGET IN RANGE...
PLACE LOOKS LIKE A BOMB HIT IT.
...KEEP YOUR HEAD ON A SWIVEL.
STRAIGHT AHEAD...SEE HIM?
HOLD BACK...LET ME TALK TO HIM.

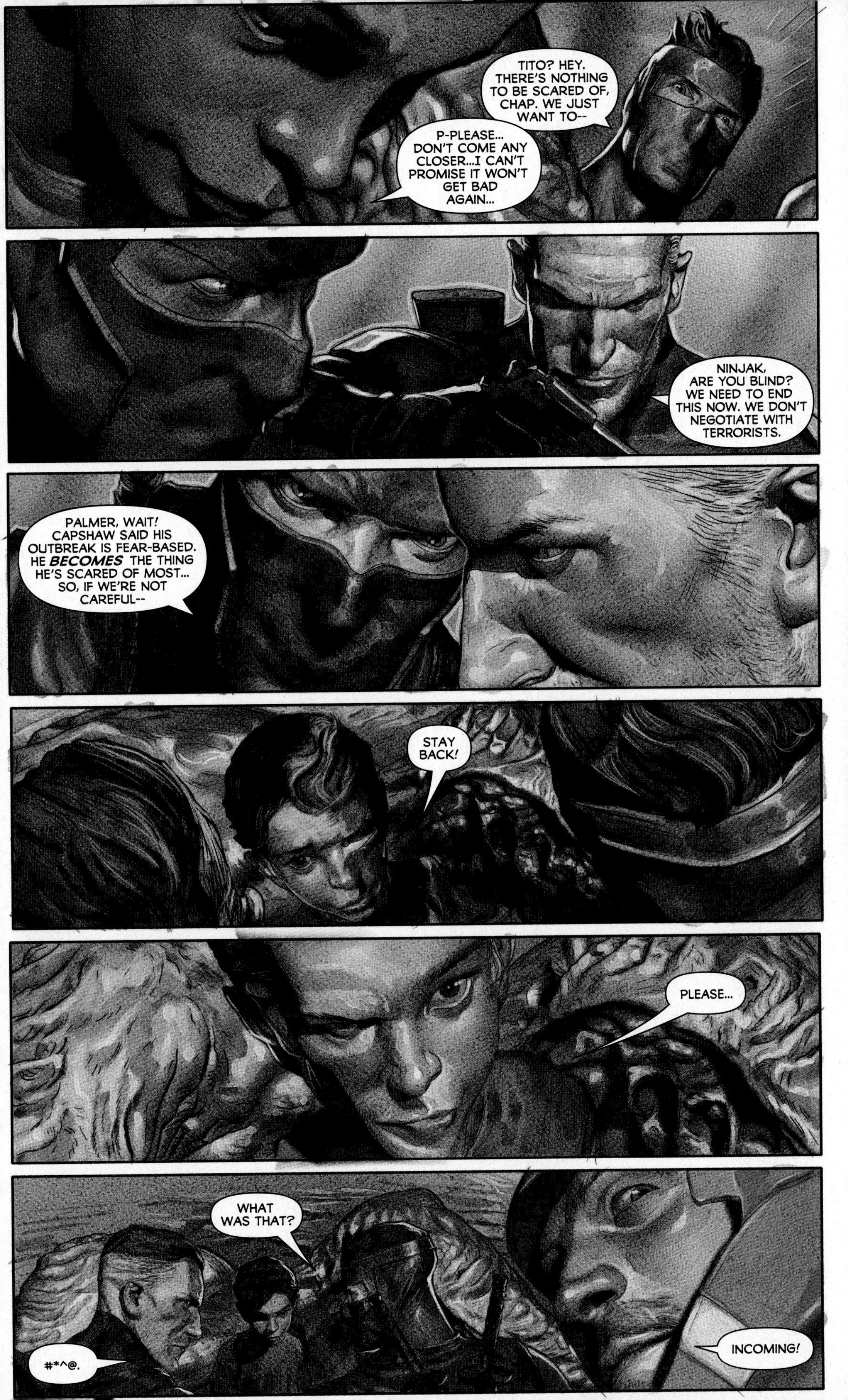
TITO? HEY. THERE'S NOTHING TO BE SCARED OF, CHAP. WE JUST WANT TO--
P-PLEASE... DON'T COME ANY CLOSER...I CAN'T PROMISE IT WON'T GET BAD AGAIN...
NINJAK, ARE YOU BLIND? WE NEED TO END THIS NOW. WE DON'T NEGOTIATE WITH TERRORISTS.
PALMER, WAIT! CAPSHAW SAID HIS OUTBREAK IS FEAR-BASED. HE BECOMES THE THING HE'S SCARED OF MOST... SO, IF WE'RE NOT CAREFUL--
STAY BACK!
PLEASE...
WHAT WAS THAT?
#*^@.
INCOMING!

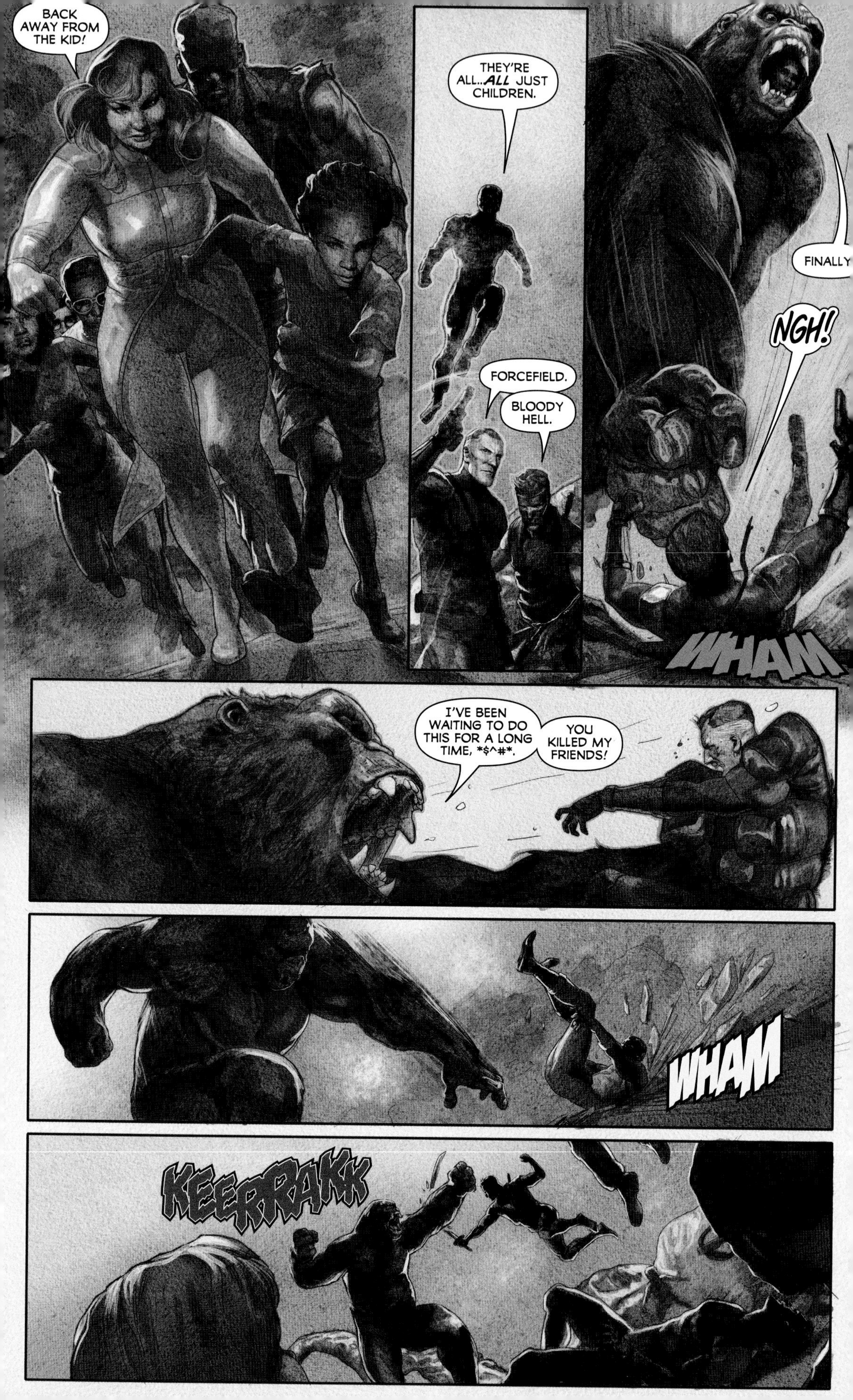
BACK AWAY FROM THE KID!
THEY'RE ALL...ALL JUST CHILDREN.
FORCEFIELD.
BLOODY HELL.
FINALLY
NGH!
WHAM
I'VE BEEN WAITING TO DO THIS FOR A LONG TIME, *$^#*.
YOU KILLED MY FRIENDS!
WHAM
KEERRAKK

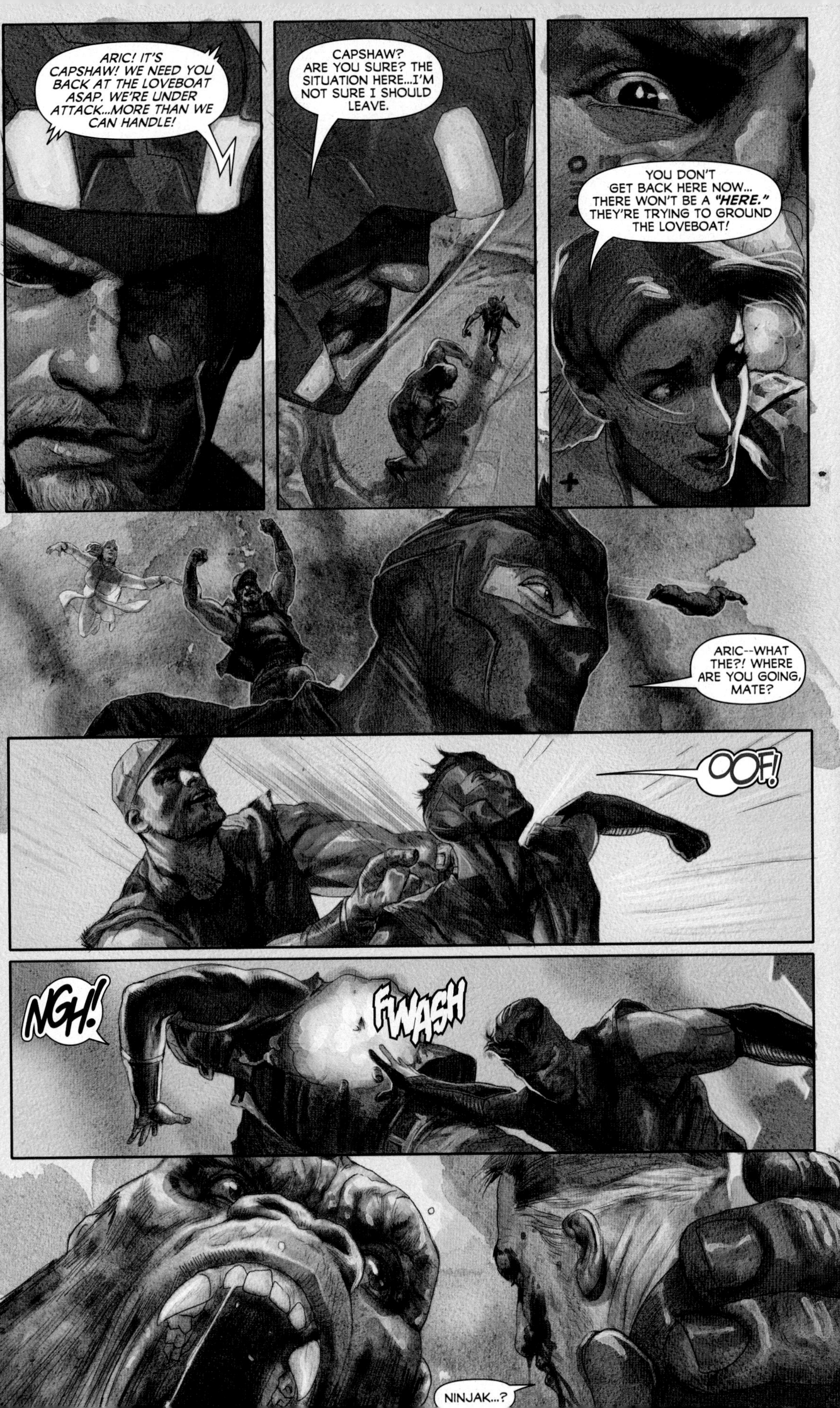
ARIC! IT'S CAPSHAW! WE NEED YOU BACK AT THE LOVEBOAT ASAP. WE'RE UNDER ATTACK...MORE THAN WE CAN HANDLE!
CAPSHAW? ARE YOU SURE? THE SITUATION HERE...I'M NOT SURE I SHOULD LEAVE.
YOU DON'T GET BACK HERE NOW... THERE WON'T BE A "HERE." THEY'RE TRYING TO GROUND THE LOVEBOAT!
ARIC--WHAT THE?! WHERE ARE YOU GOING, MATE?
OOF!
NGH!
FWASH
NINJAK...?

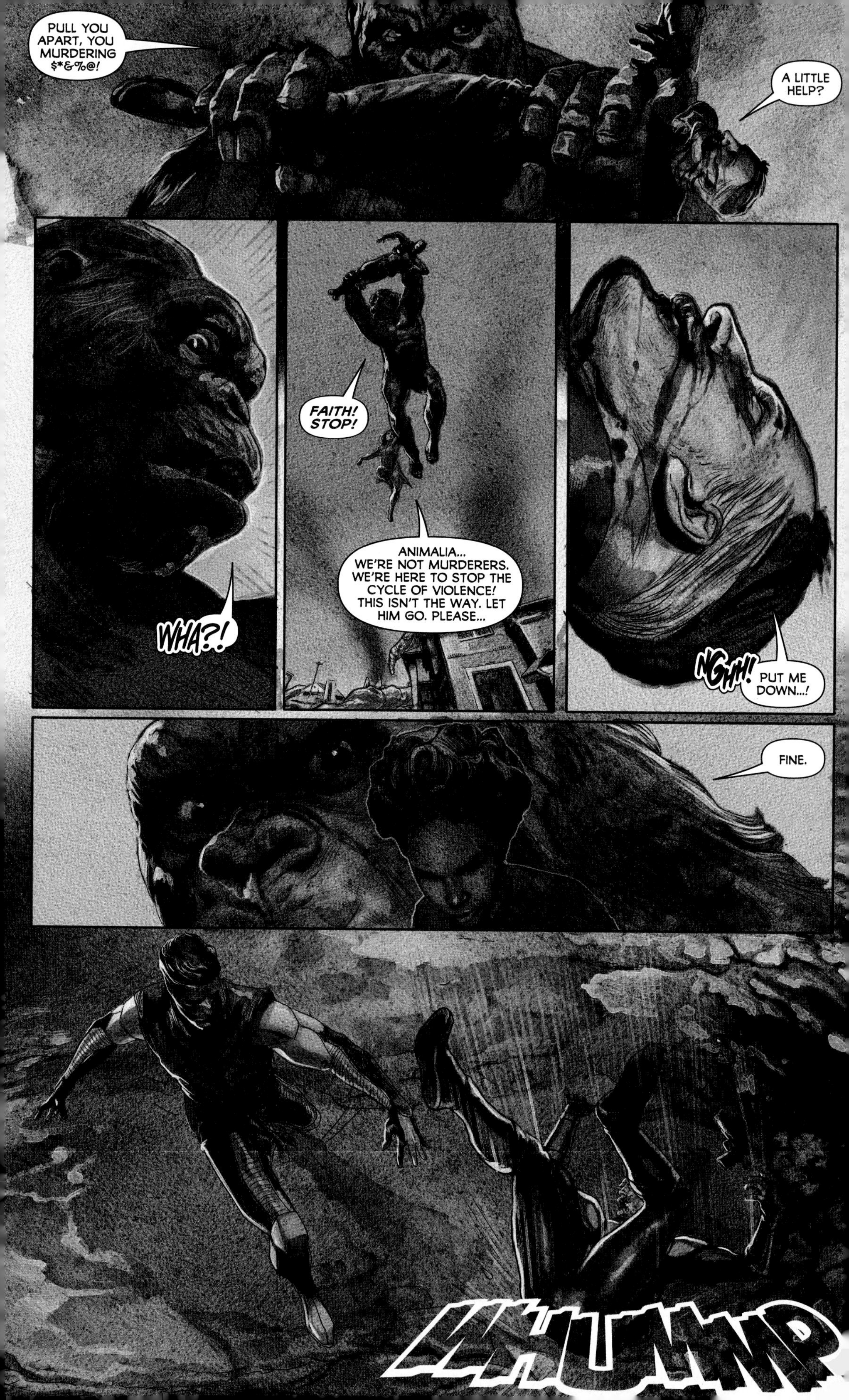
PULL YOU APART, YOU MURDERING $*&%@!
A LITTLE HELP?
WHA?!
FAITH! STOP!
ANIMALIA... WE'RE NOT MURDERERS. WE'RE HERE TO STOP THE CYCLE OF VIOLENCE! THIS ISN'T THE WAY. LET HIM GO. PLEASE...
NGHH!
PUT ME DOWN...!
FINE.
WHUMMP

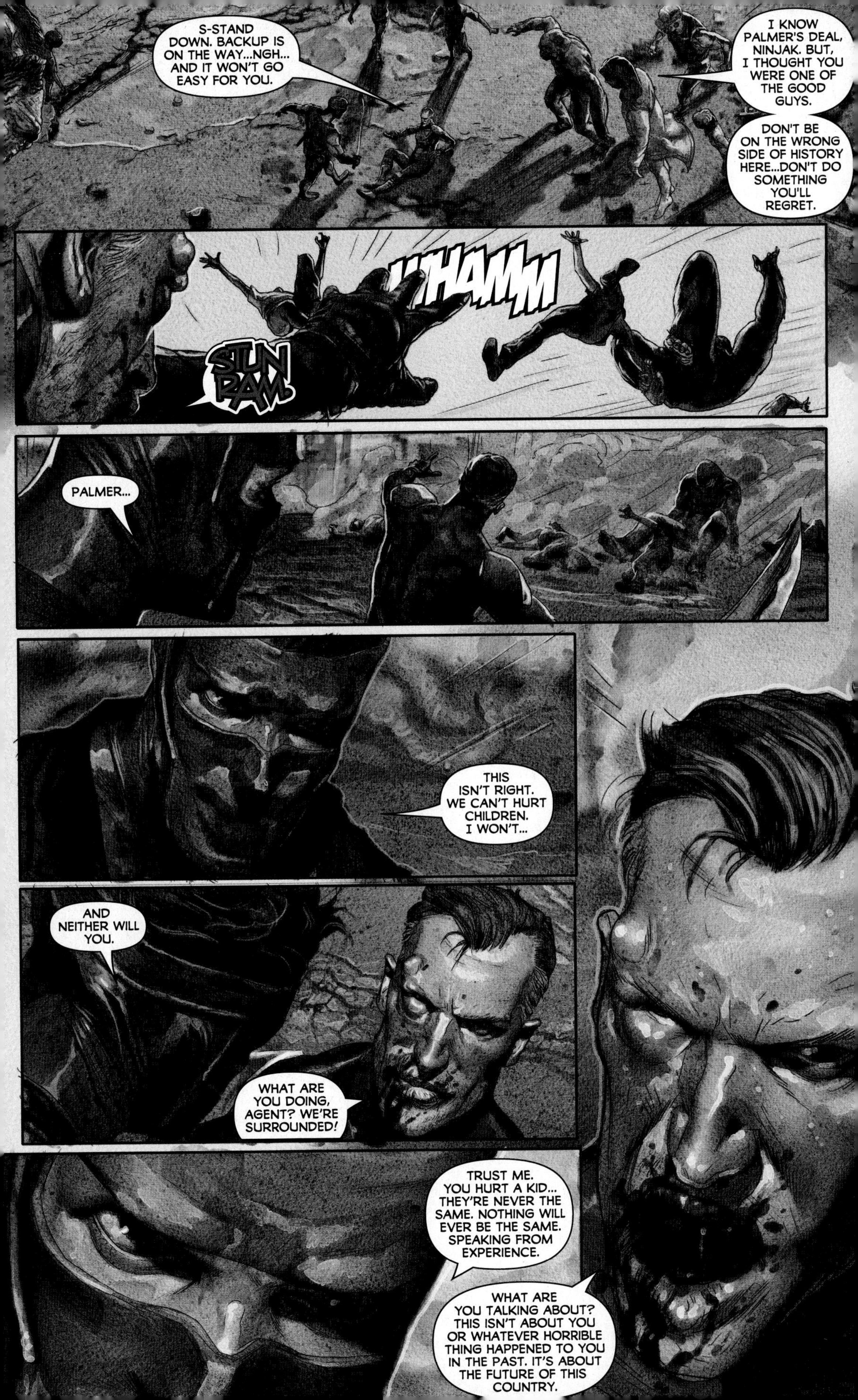
S-STAND DOWN. BACKUP IS ON THE WAY...NGH... AND IT WON'T GO EASY FOR YOU.
I KNOW PALMER'S DEAL, NINJAK. BUT, I THOUGHT YOU WERE ONE OF THE GOOD GUYS.
DON'T BE ON THE WRONG SIDE OF HISTORY HERE...DON'T DO SOMETHING YOU'LL REGRET.
STUN RAM.
WHAMM
PALMER...
THIS ISN'T RIGHT. WE CAN'T HURT CHILDREN. I WON'T...
AND NEITHER WILL YOU.
WHAT ARE YOU DOING, AGENT? WE'RE SURROUNDED!
TRUST ME. YOU HURT A KID... THEY'RE NEVER THE SAME. NOTHING WILL EVER BE THE SAME. SPEAKING FROM EXPERIENCE.
WHAT ARE YOU TALKING ABOUT? THIS ISN'T ABOUT YOU OR WHATEVER HORRIBLE THING HAPPENED TO YOU IN THE PAST. IT'S ABOUT THE FUTURE OF THIS COUNTRY.

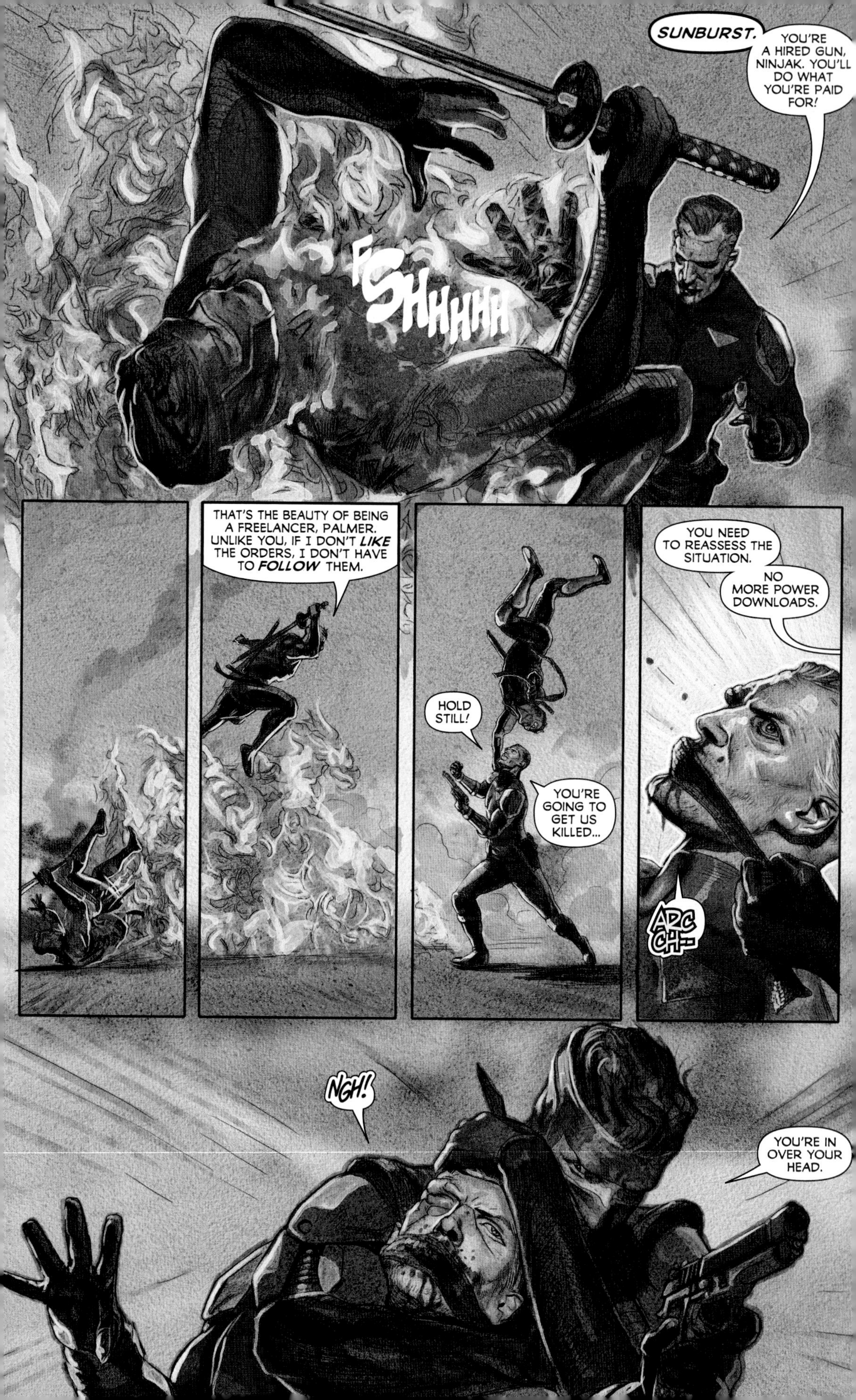
SUNBURST.
YOU'RE A HIRED GUN, NINJAK. YOU'LL DO WHAT YOU'RE PAID FOR!
FSHHHHH
THAT'S THE BEAUTY OF BEING A FREELANCER, PALMER. UNLIKE YOU, IF I DON'T LIKE THE ORDERS, I DON'T HAVE TO FOLLOW THEM.
HOLD STILL!
YOU'RE GOING TO GET US KILLED...
YOU NEED TO REASSESS THE SITUATION.
NO MORE POWER DOWNLOADS.
ADC CHF--
NGH!
YOU'RE IN OVER YOUR HEAD.

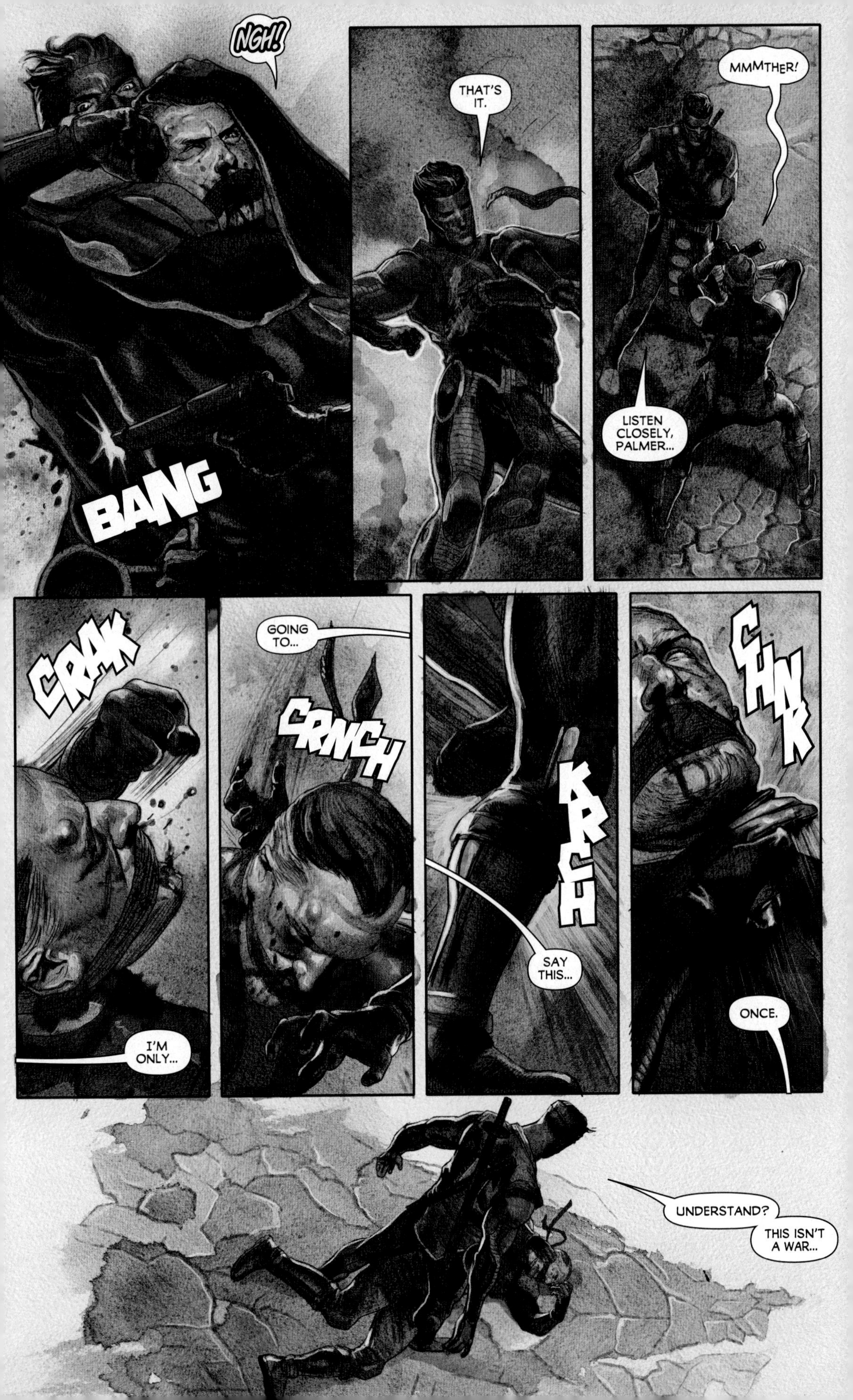
NGH!
BANG
THAT'S IT.
MMMTHER!
LISTEN CLOSELY, PALMER...
CRAK
I'M ONLY...
GOING TO...
CRNCH
KRCH
SAY THIS...
CHNK
ONCE.
UNDERSTAND?
THIS ISN'T A WAR...

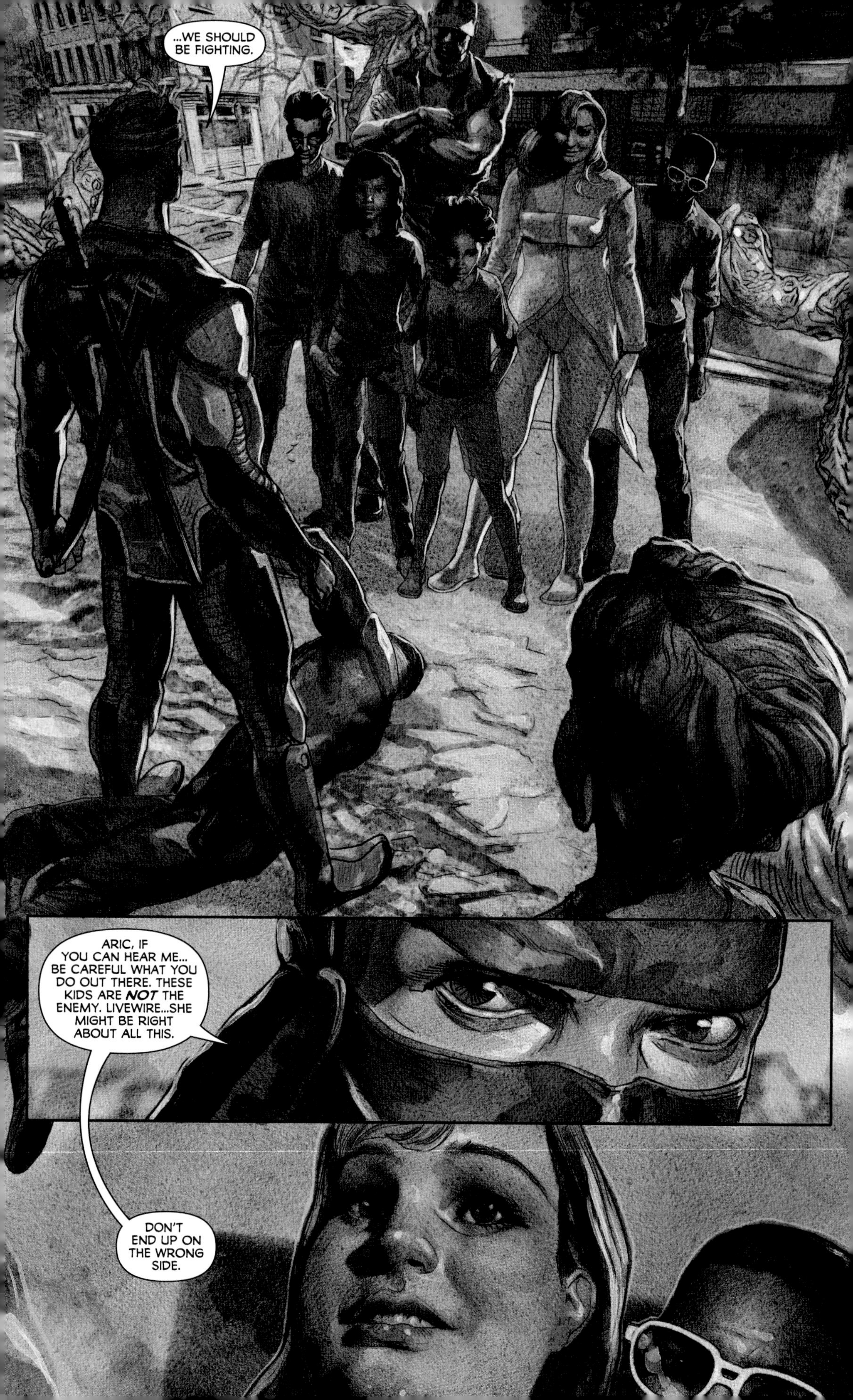
...WE SHOULD BE FIGHTING.
ARIC, IF YOU CAN HEAR ME... BE CAREFUL WHAT YOU DO OUT THERE. THESE KIDS ARE *NOT* THE ENEMY. LIVEWIRE...SHE MIGHT BE RIGHT ABOUT ALL THIS.
DON'T END UP ON THE WRONG SIDE.

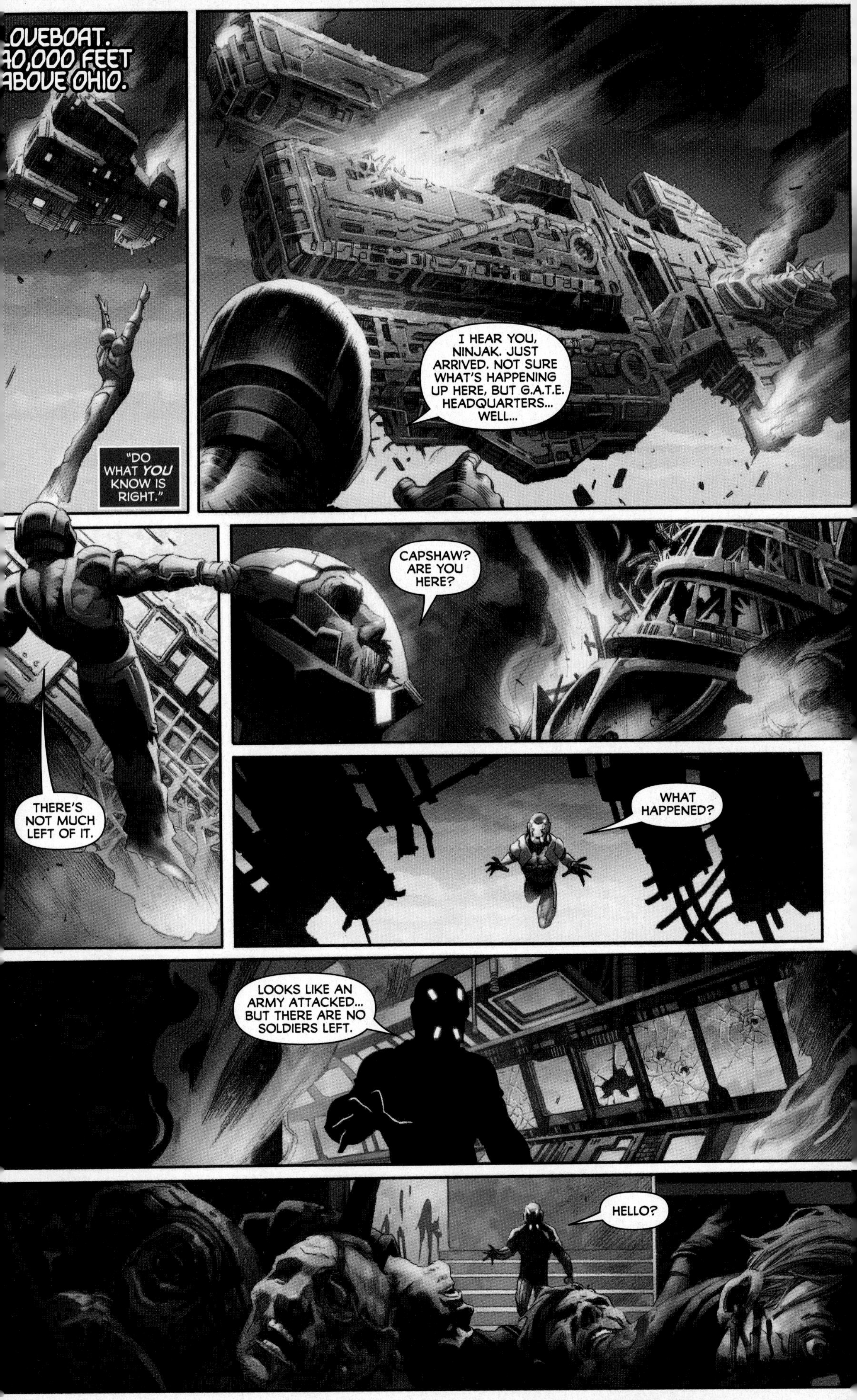
LOVEBOAT.
40,000 FEET
ABOVE OHIO.
"DO WHAT YOU KNOW IS RIGHT."
I HEAR YOU, NINJAK. JUST ARRIVED. NOT SURE WHAT'S HAPPENING UP HERE, BUT G.A.T.E. HEADQUARTERS... WELL...
THERE'S NOT MUCH LEFT OF IT.
CAPSHAW? ARE YOU HERE?
WHAT HAPPENED?
LOOKS LIKE AN ARMY ATTACKED... BUT THERE ARE NO SOLDIERS LEFT.
HELLO?

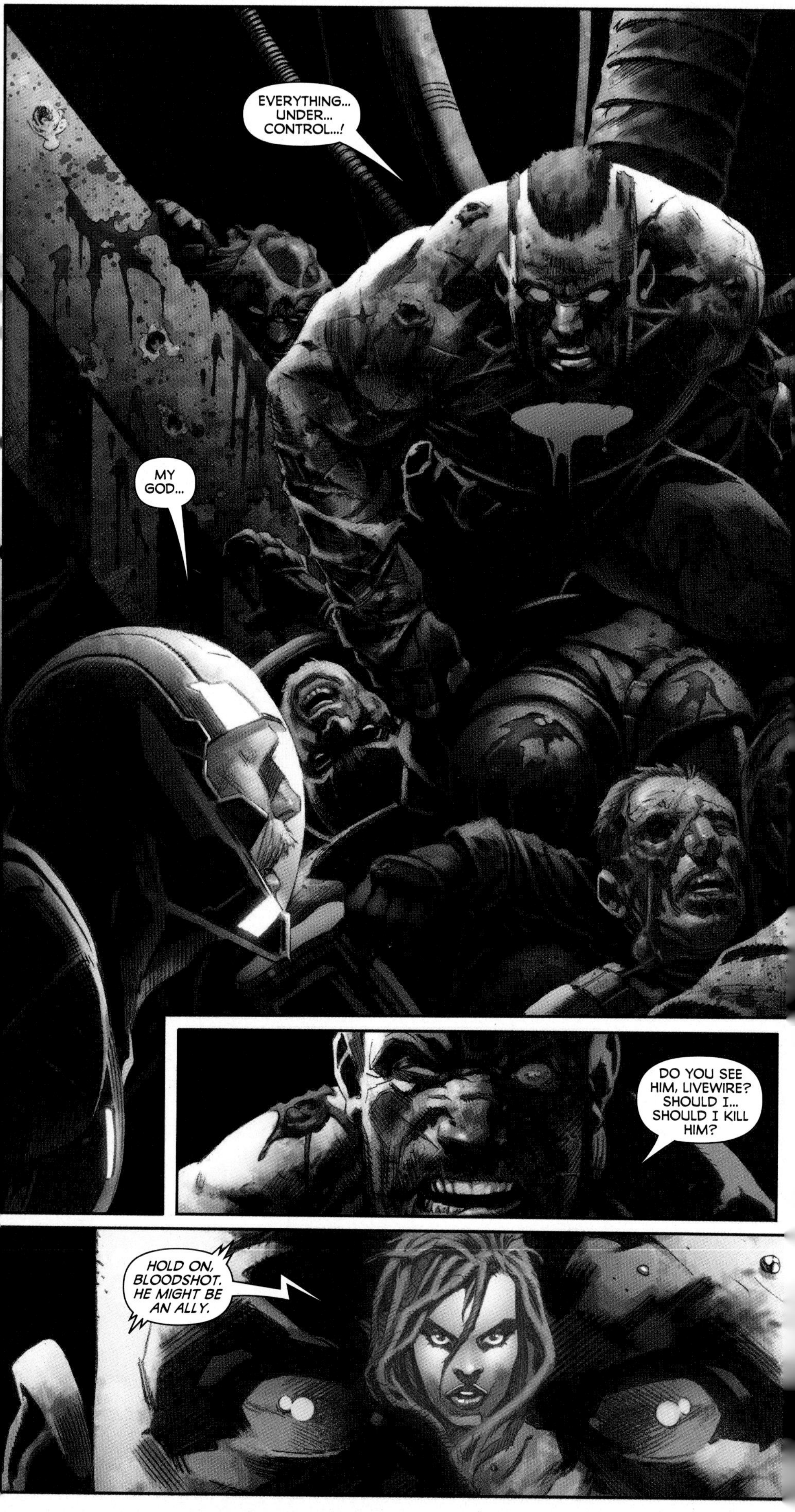
EVERYTHING... UNDER... CONTROL...!
MY GOD...
DO YOU SEE HIM, LIVEWIRE? SHOULD I... SHOULD I KILL HIM?
HOLD ON, BLOODSHOT. HE MIGHT BE AN ALLY.

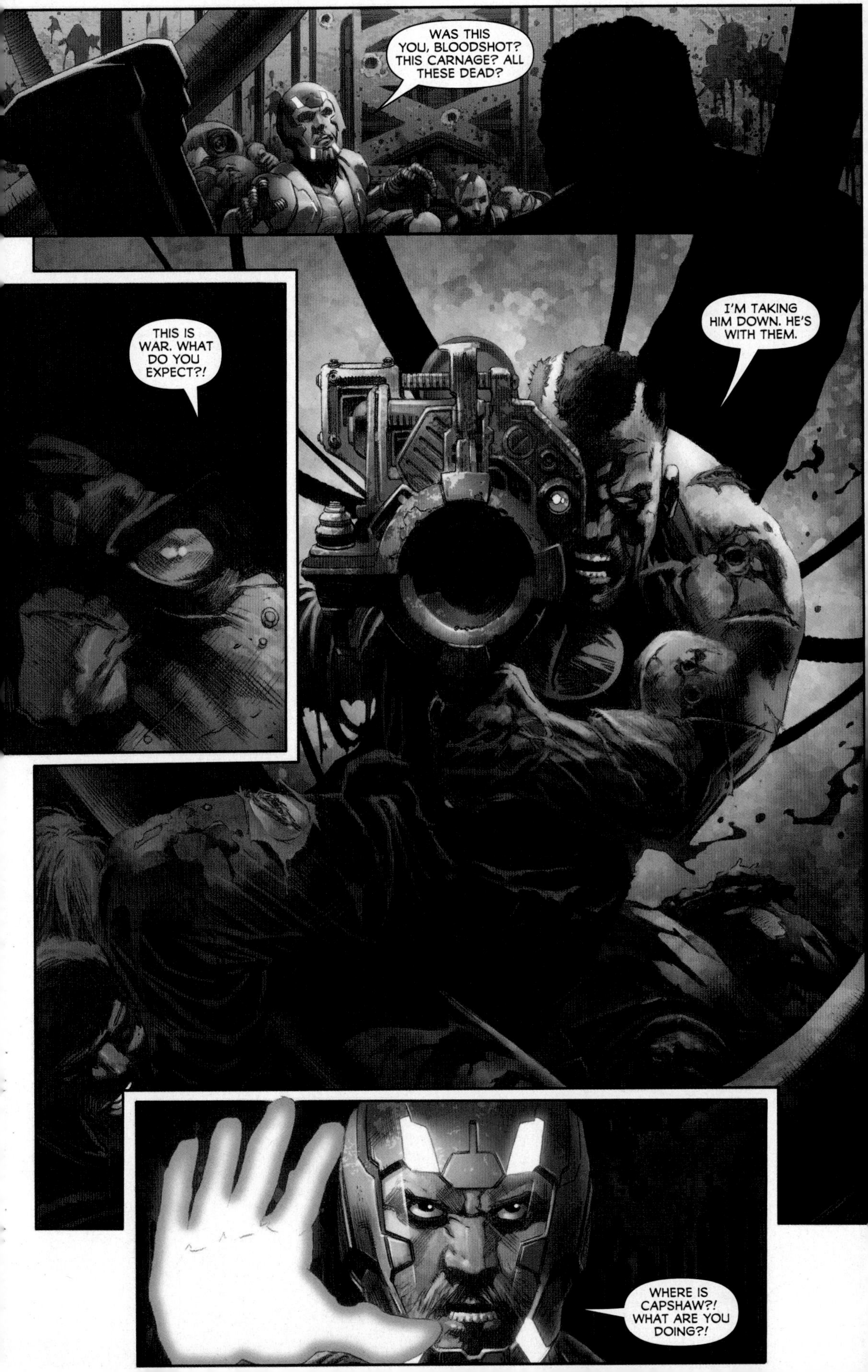
WAS THIS YOU, BLOODSHOT? THIS CARNAGE? ALL THESE DEAD?
THIS IS WAR. WHAT DO YOU EXPECT?!
I'M TAKING HIM DOWN. HE'S WITH THEM.
WHERE IS CAPSHAW?! WHAT ARE YOU DOING?!

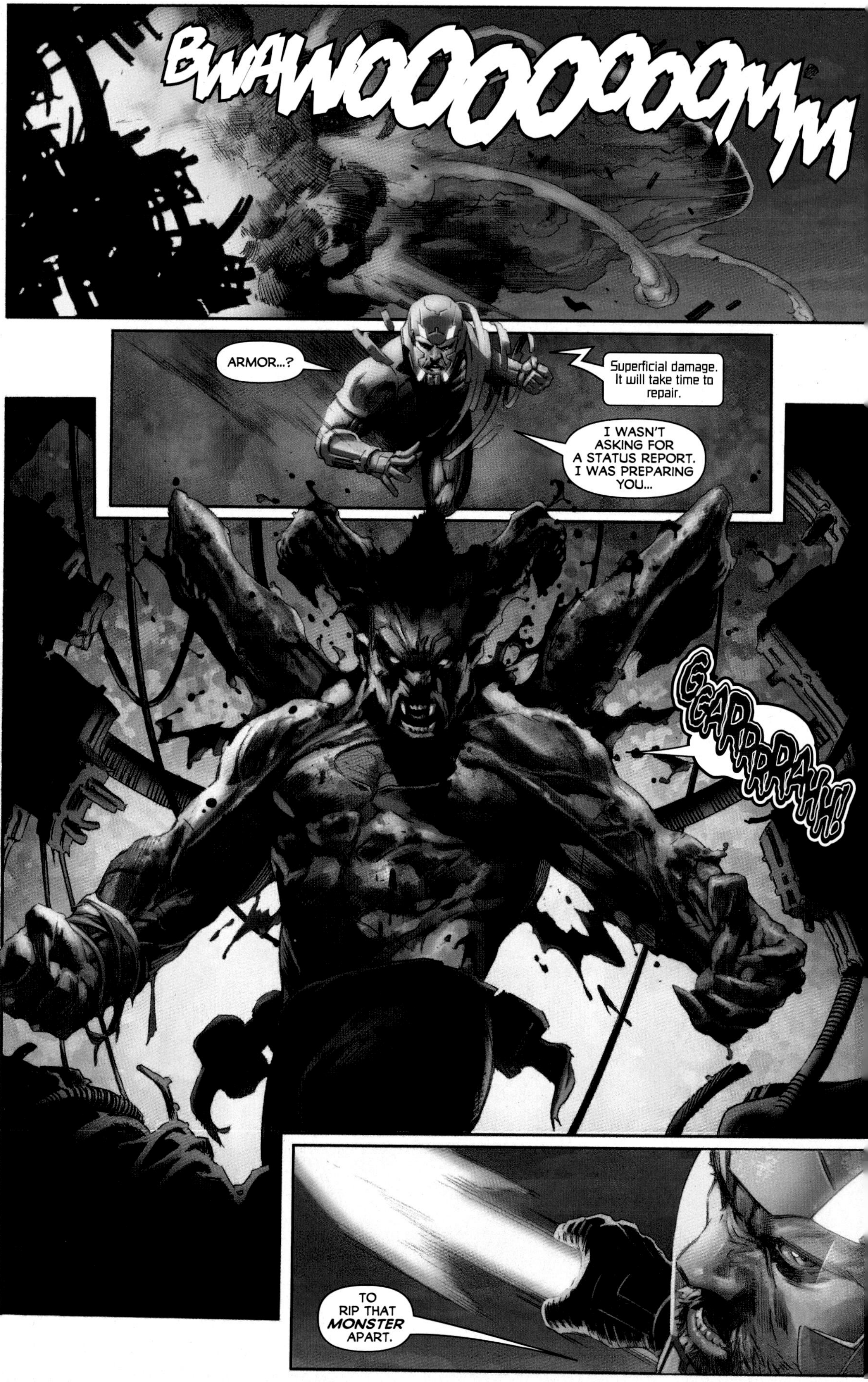
BWAWOOOOOOOOMMM
ARMOR...?
Superficial damage. It will take time to repair.
I WASN'T ASKING FOR A STATUS REPORT. I WAS PREPARING YOU...
GGARRRRAHH!
TO RIP THAT *MONSTER* APART.

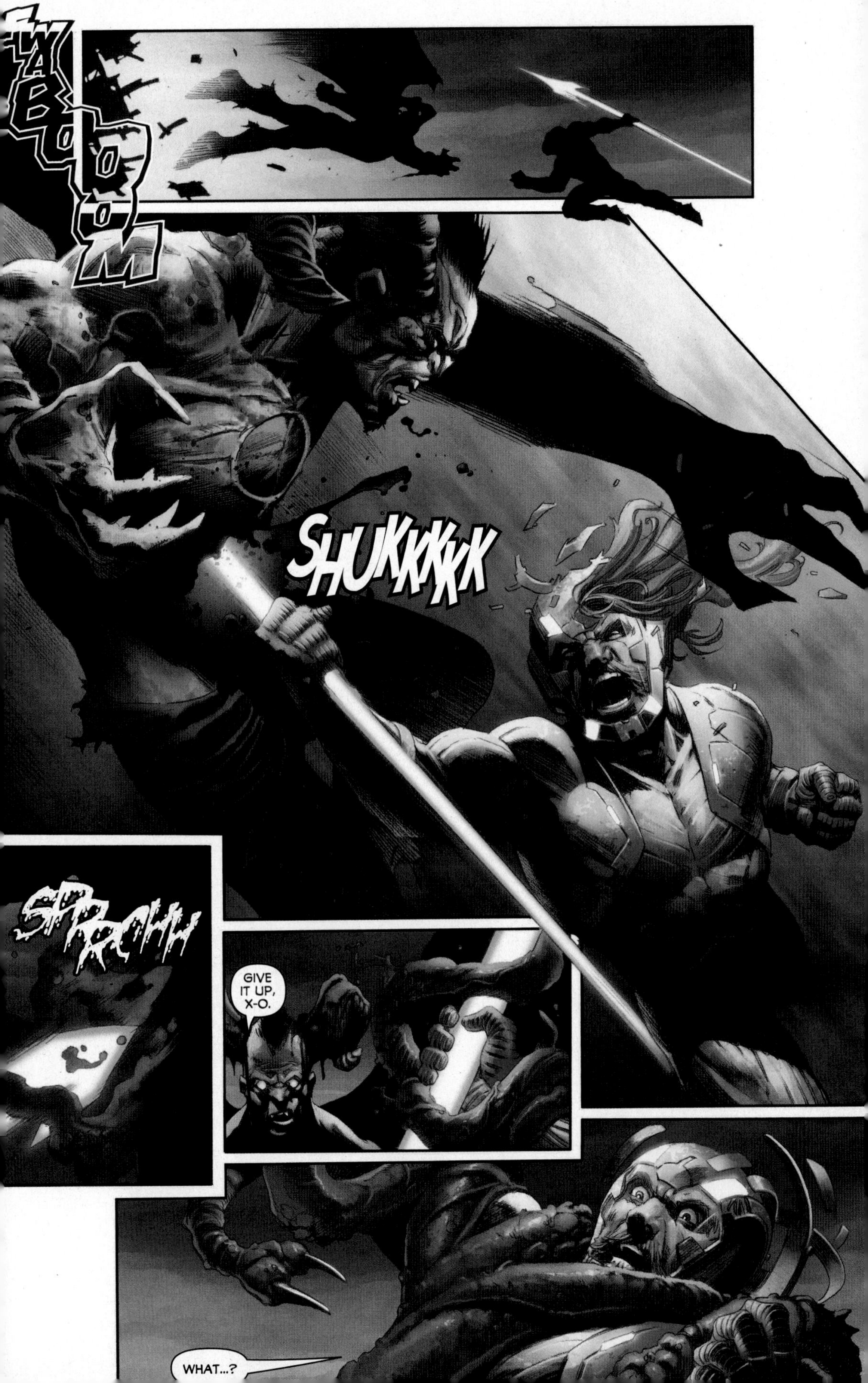
FWABOOOOM
SHUKKKKK
SPROCHH
GIVE IT UP, X-O.
WHAT...?

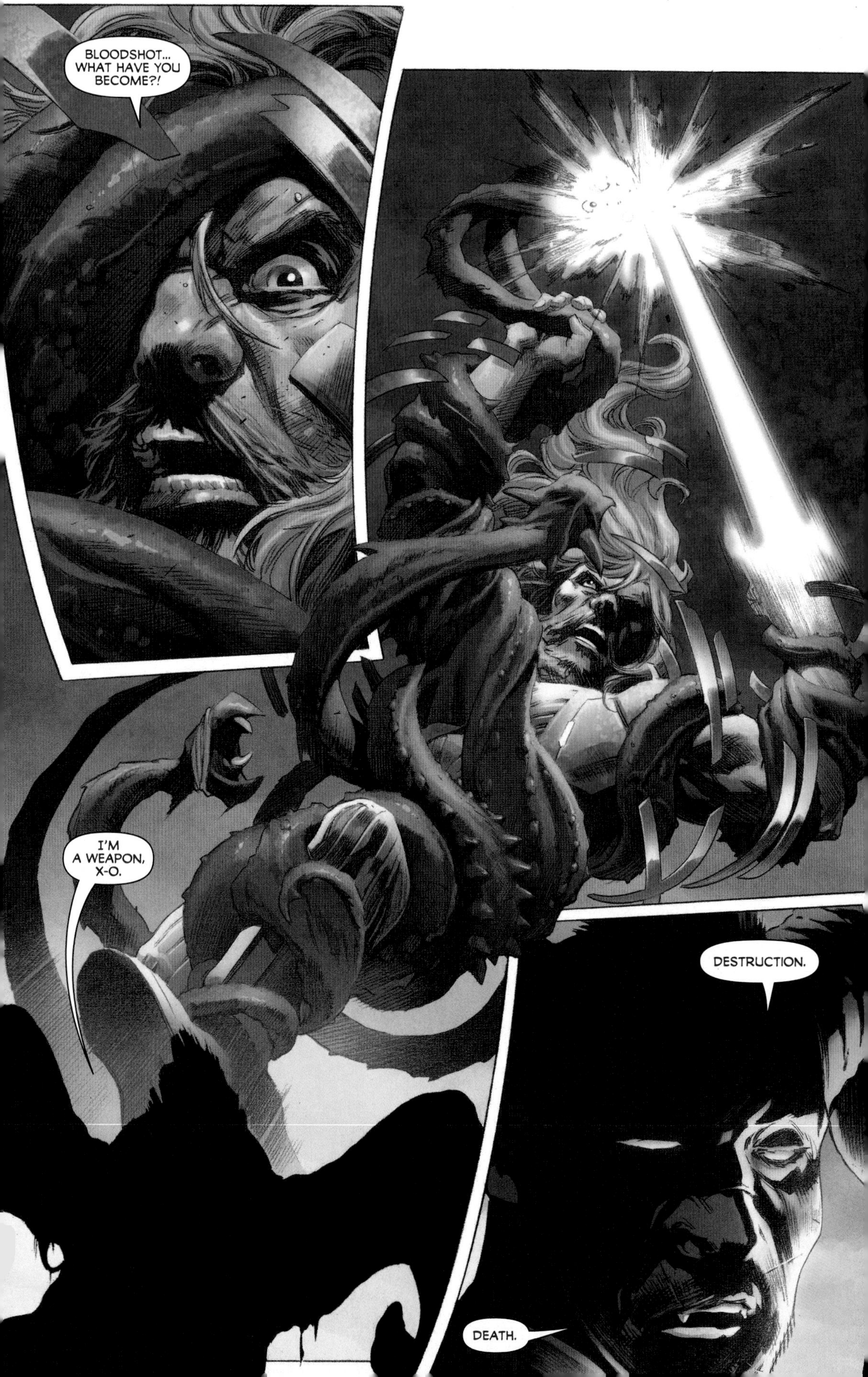
BLOODSHOT... WHAT HAVE YOU BECOME?!
I'M A WEAPON, X-O.
DESTRUCTION.
DEATH.

LIVEWIRE?

YOU GOT MY PERMISSION. MAKE IT HAPPEN.

REPROGRAMMING YOUR NANITES NOW. THIS WILL HURT...

I CAN HANDLE IT...

GRAHHHHH!

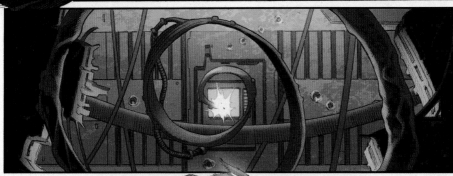

EXCELLENT WORK, BLOODSHOT. I'VE CONNECTED TO THE CONTROL CENTER. YOUR JOB IS DONE...

WE'RE TEARING IT ALL DOWN.
DON'T DO THIS!
THERE'S NO REASON TO--!
WHAT CHOICE DO I HAVE?
WHAT CHOICE...
"...DO ANY OF US HAVE?"

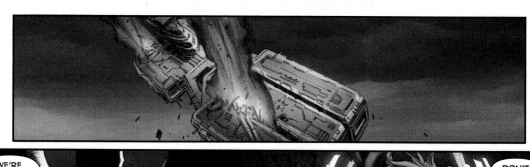

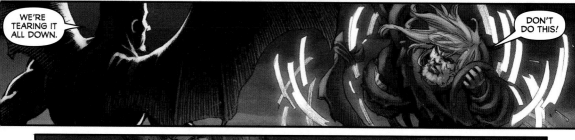

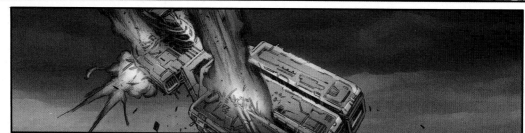

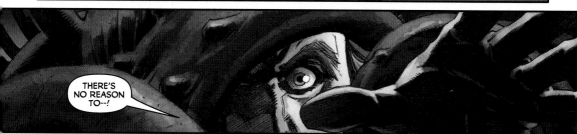

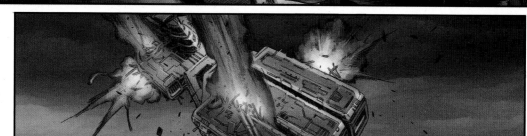

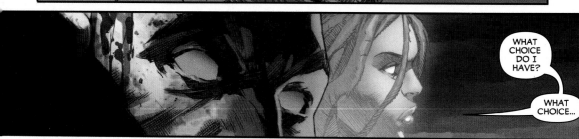

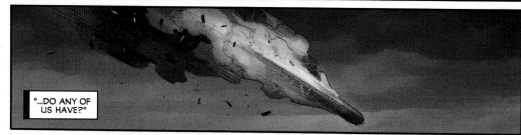

VALIANT

MATT KINDT • TOMÁS GIORELLO • RENATO GUEDES • DIEGO RODRIGUEZ

4

HARBINGER WARS 2

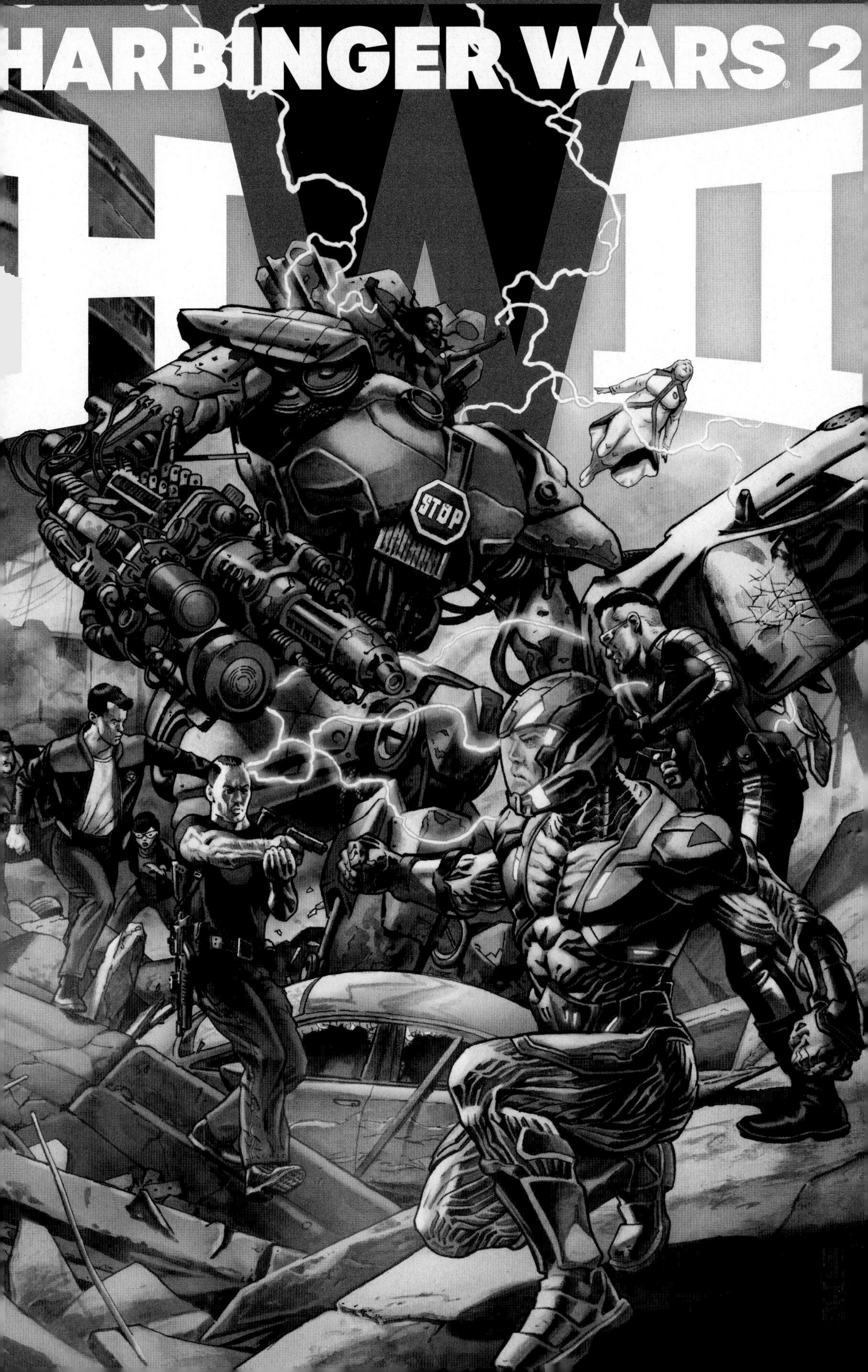
STOP

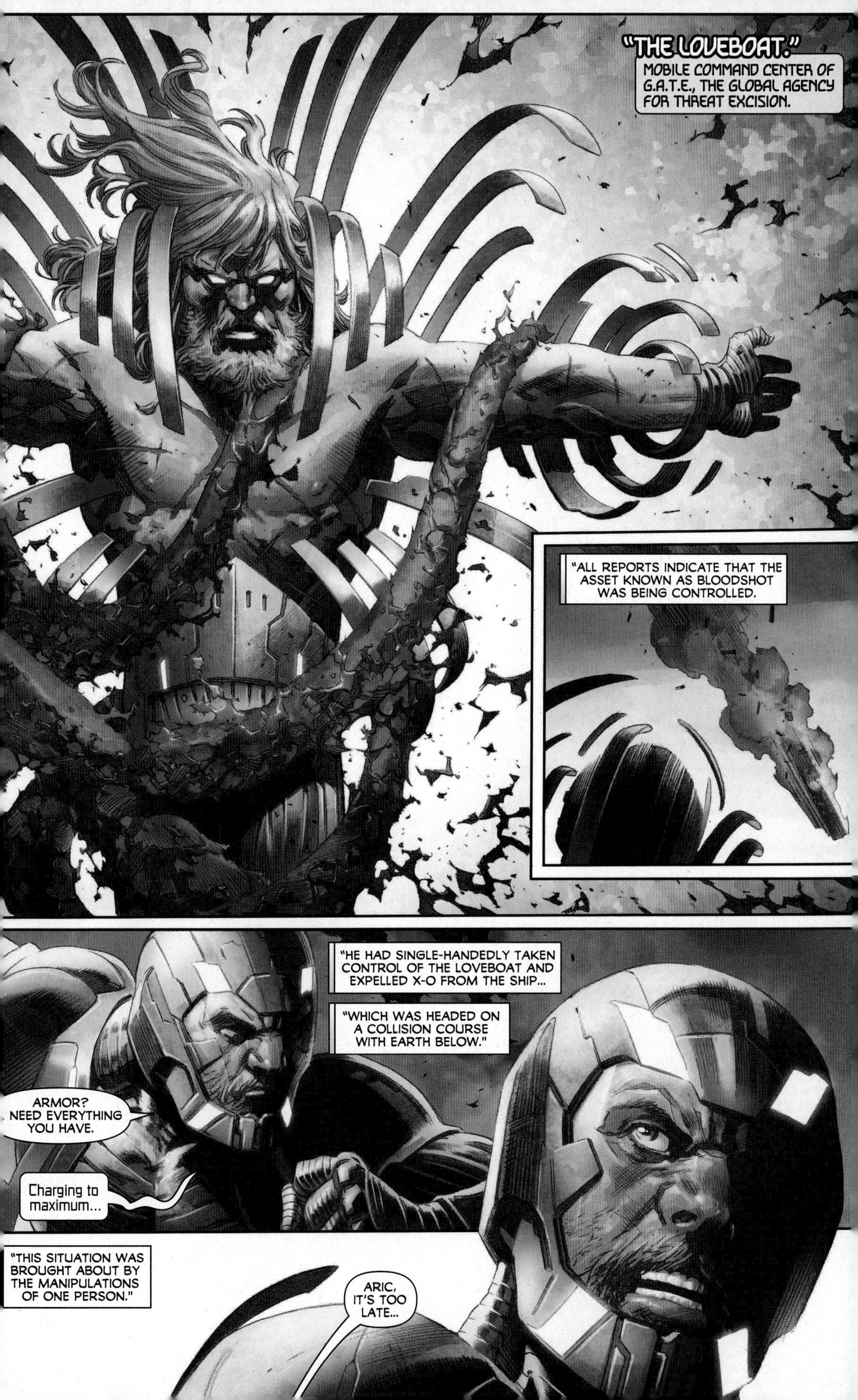
"THE LOVEBOAT."
MOBILE COMMAND CENTER OF G.A.T.E., THE GLOBAL AGENCY FOR THREAT EXCISION.
"ALL REPORTS INDICATE THAT THE ASSET KNOWN AS BLOODSHOT WAS BEING CONTROLLED.
"HE HAD SINGLE-HANDEDLY TAKEN CONTROL OF THE LOVEBOAT AND EXPELLED X-O FROM THE SHIP...
"WHICH WAS HEADED ON A COLLISION COURSE WITH EARTH BELOW."
ARMOR? NEED EVERYTHING YOU HAVE.
Charging to maximum...
"THIS SITUATION WAS BROUGHT ABOUT BY THE MANIPULATIONS OF ONE PERSON."
ARIC, IT'S TOO LATE...

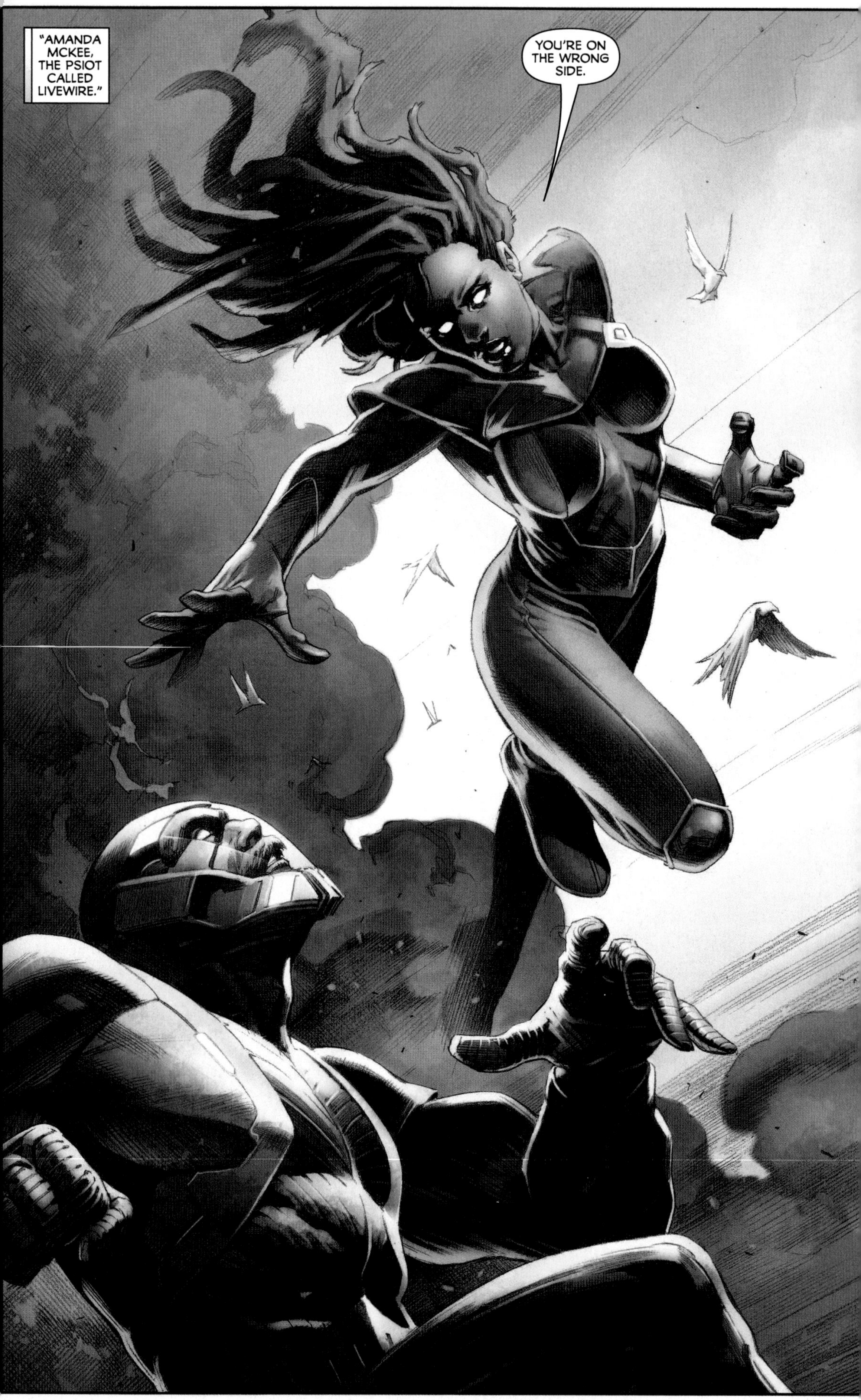
"AMANDA MCKEE, THE PSIOT CALLED LIVEWIRE."
YOU'RE ON THE WRONG SIDE.

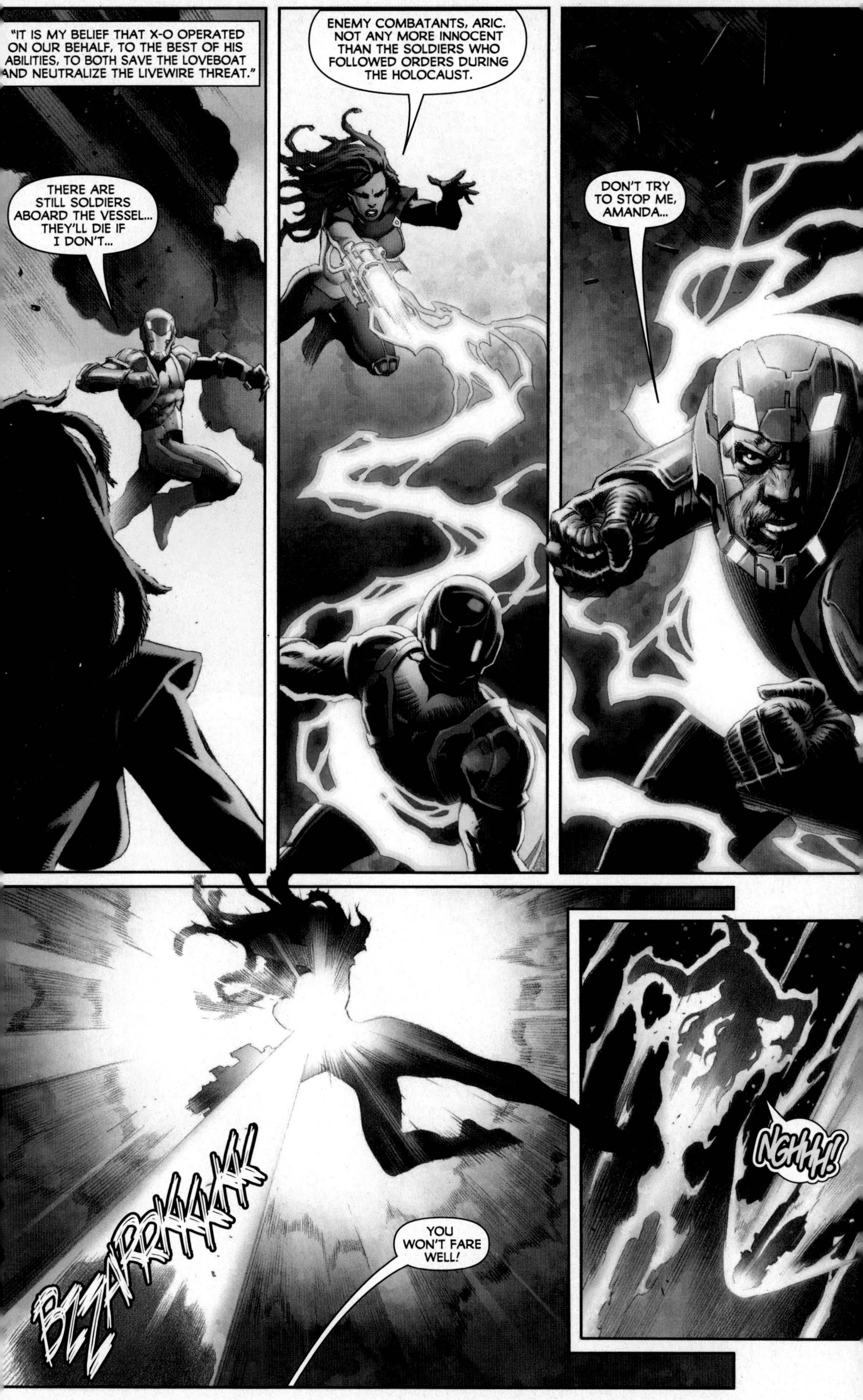
"IT IS MY BELIEF THAT X-O OPERATED ON OUR BEHALF, TO THE BEST OF HIS ABILITIES, TO BOTH SAVE THE LOVEBOAT AND NEUTRALIZE THE LIVEWIRE THREAT."
THERE ARE STILL SOLDIERS ABOARD THE VESSEL... THEY'LL DIE IF I DON'T...
ENEMY COMBATANTS, ARIC. NOT ANY MORE INNOCENT THAN THE SOLDIERS WHO FOLLOWED ORDERS DURING THE HOLOCAUST.
DON'T TRY TO STOP ME, AMANDA...
BZZARRKAAAK
YOU WON'T FARE WELL!
NGHHH!

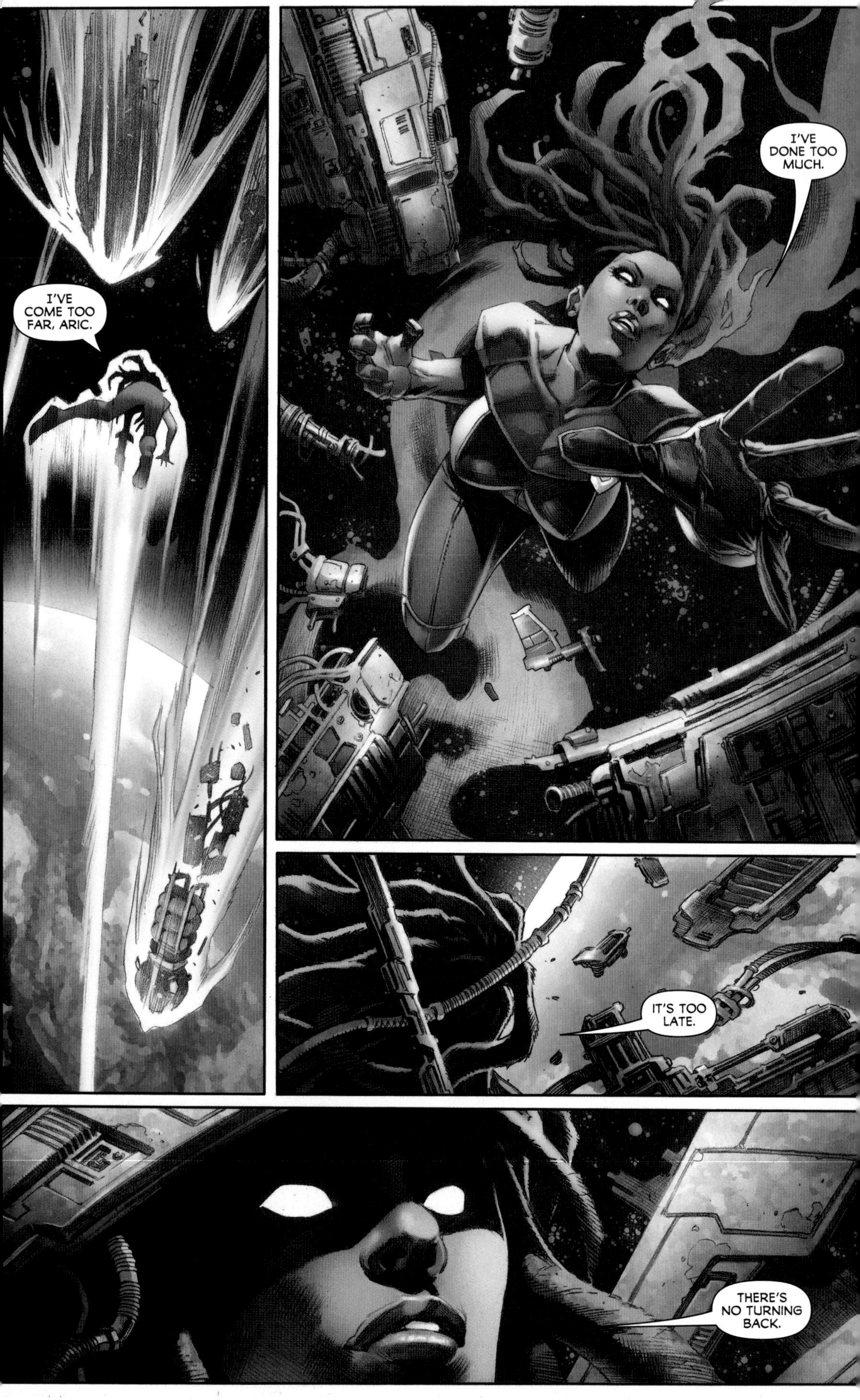
I'VE COME TOO FAR, ARIC.
I'VE DONE TOO MUCH.
IT'S TOO LATE.
THERE'S NO TURNING BACK.

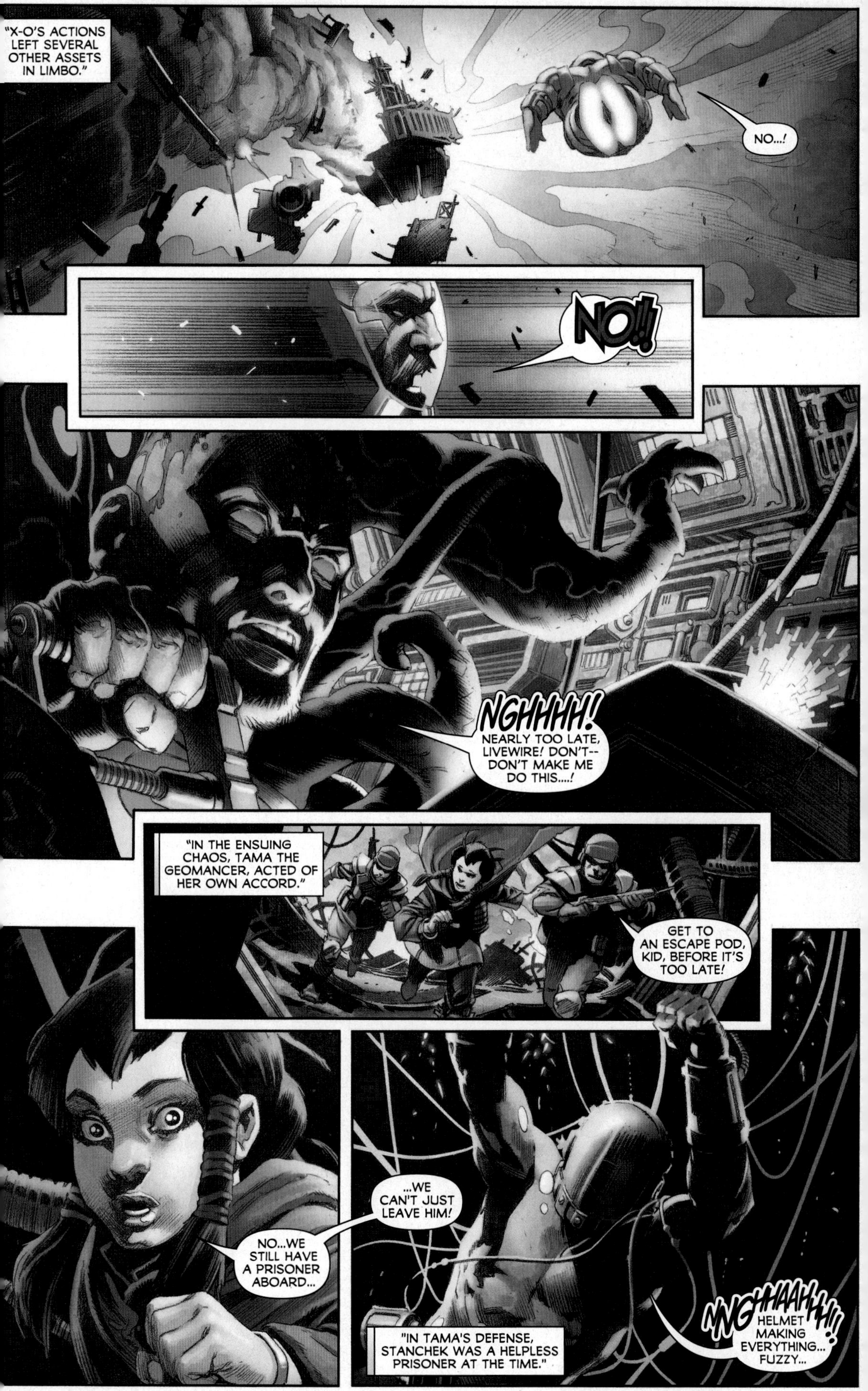
"X-O'S ACTIONS LEFT SEVERAL OTHER ASSETS IN LIMBO."
NO...!
NO!!!
NGHHHH!
NEARLY TOO LATE, LIVEWIRE! DON'T-- DON'T MAKE ME DO THIS....!
"IN THE ENSUING CHAOS, TAMA THE GEOMANCER, ACTED OF HER OWN ACCORD."
GET TO AN ESCAPE POD, KID, BEFORE IT'S TOO LATE!
NO...WE STILL HAVE A PRISONER ABOARD...
...WE CAN'T JUST LEAVE HIM!
"IN TAMA'S DEFENSE, STANCHEK WAS A HELPLESS PRISONER AT THE TIME."
NNGHHAAHHH!!
HELMET MAKING EVERYTHING... FUZZY...

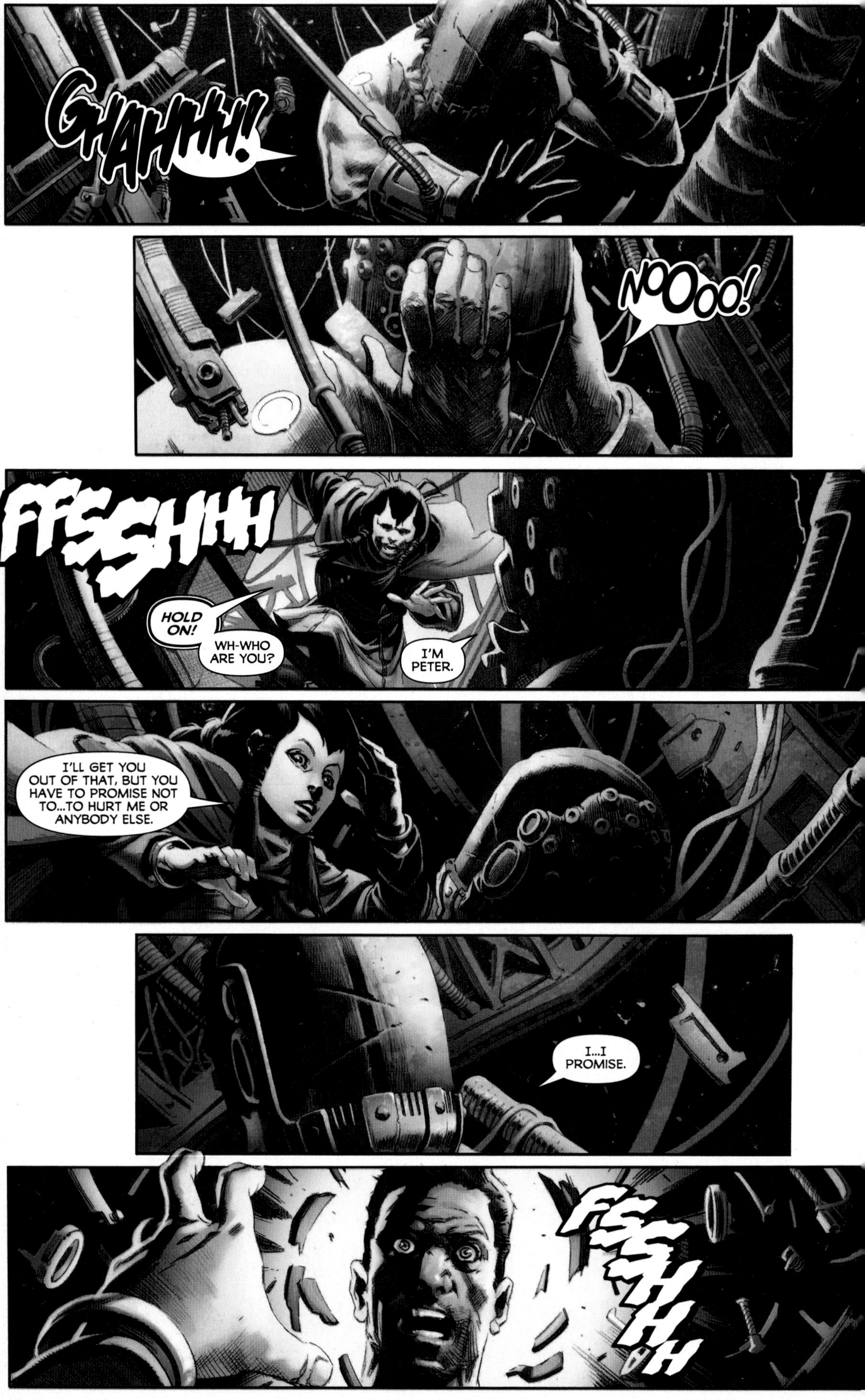
GHAHHH!
NOOOO!
FFSSHHH
HOLD ON!
WH-WHO ARE YOU?
I'M PETER.
I'LL GET YOU OUT OF THAT, BUT YOU HAVE TO PROMISE NOT TO...TO HURT ME OR ANYBODY ELSE.
I...I PROMISE.
FSSHHH

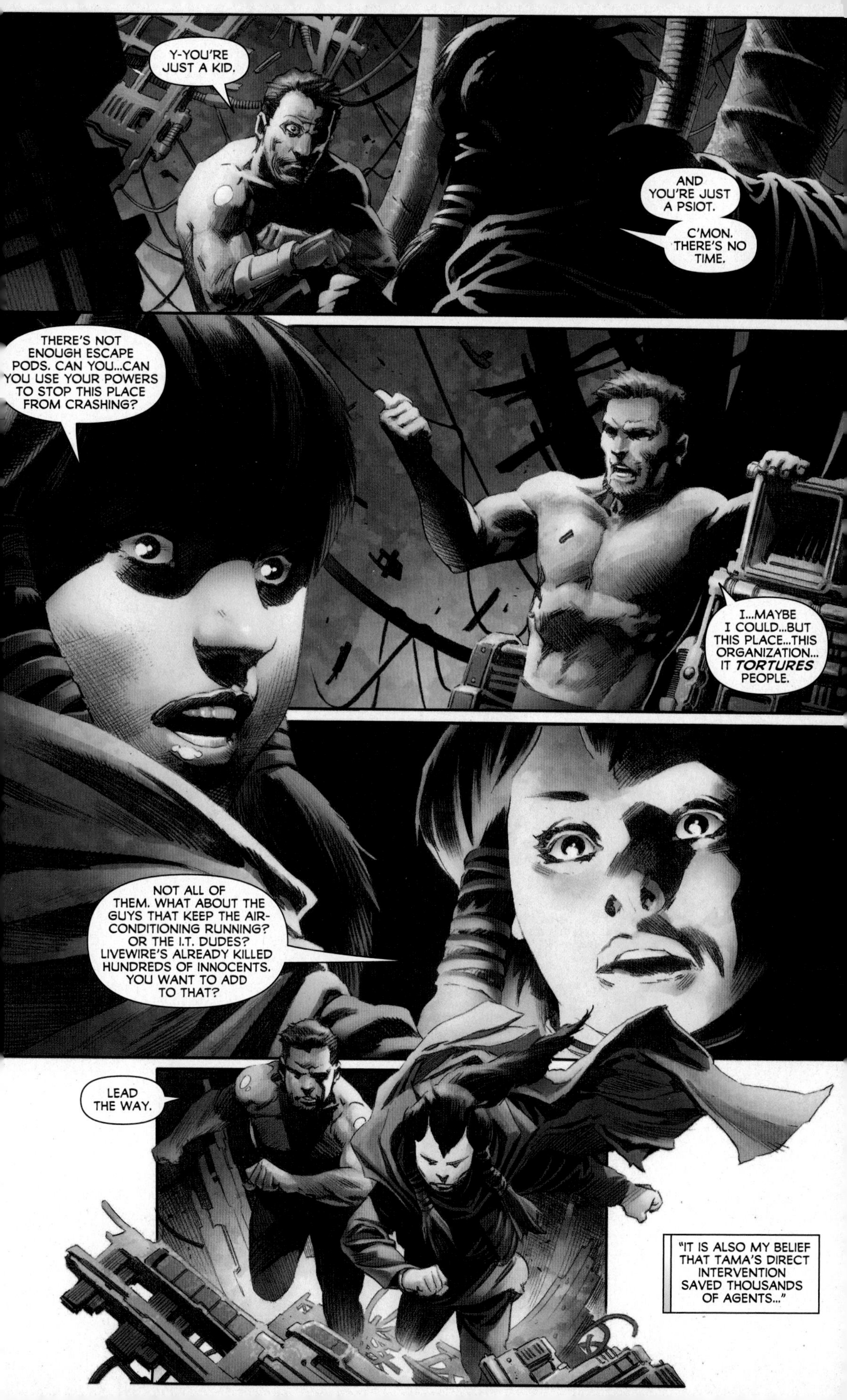
Y-YOU'RE JUST A KID.
AND YOU'RE JUST A PSIOT.
C'MON. THERE'S NO TIME.
THERE'S NOT ENOUGH ESCAPE PODS. CAN YOU...CAN YOU USE YOUR POWERS TO STOP THIS PLACE FROM CRASHING?
I...MAYBE I COULD...BUT THIS PLACE...THIS ORGANIZATION... IT *TORTURES* PEOPLE.
NOT ALL OF THEM. WHAT ABOUT THE GUYS THAT KEEP THE AIR-CONDITIONING RUNNING? OR THE I.T. DUDES? LIVEWIRE'S ALREADY KILLED HUNDREDS OF INNOCENTS. YOU WANT TO ADD TO THAT?
LEAD THE WAY.
"IT IS ALSO MY BELIEF THAT TAMA'S DIRECT INTERVENTION SAVED THOUSANDS OF AGENTS..."

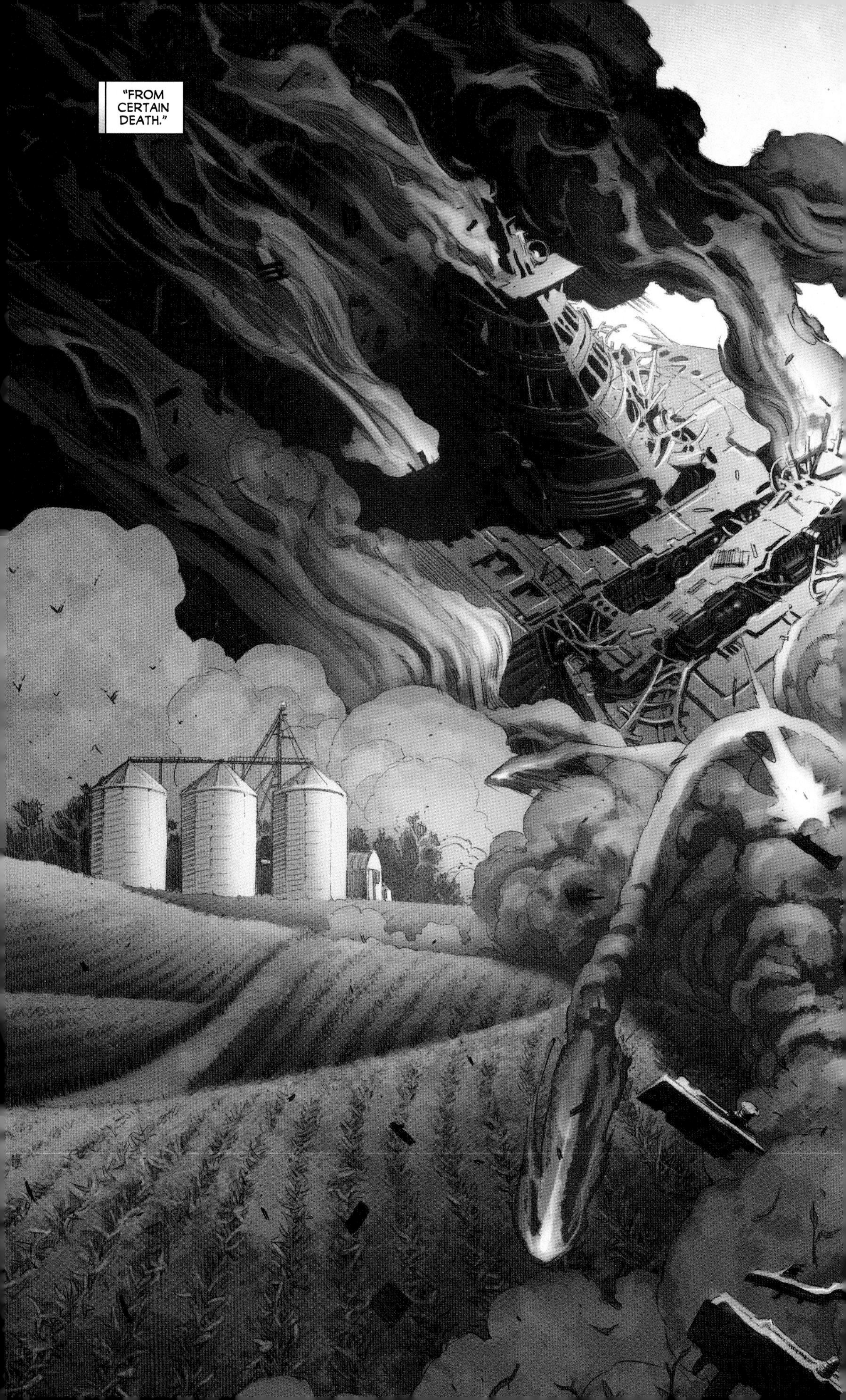
"FROM CERTAIN DEATH."

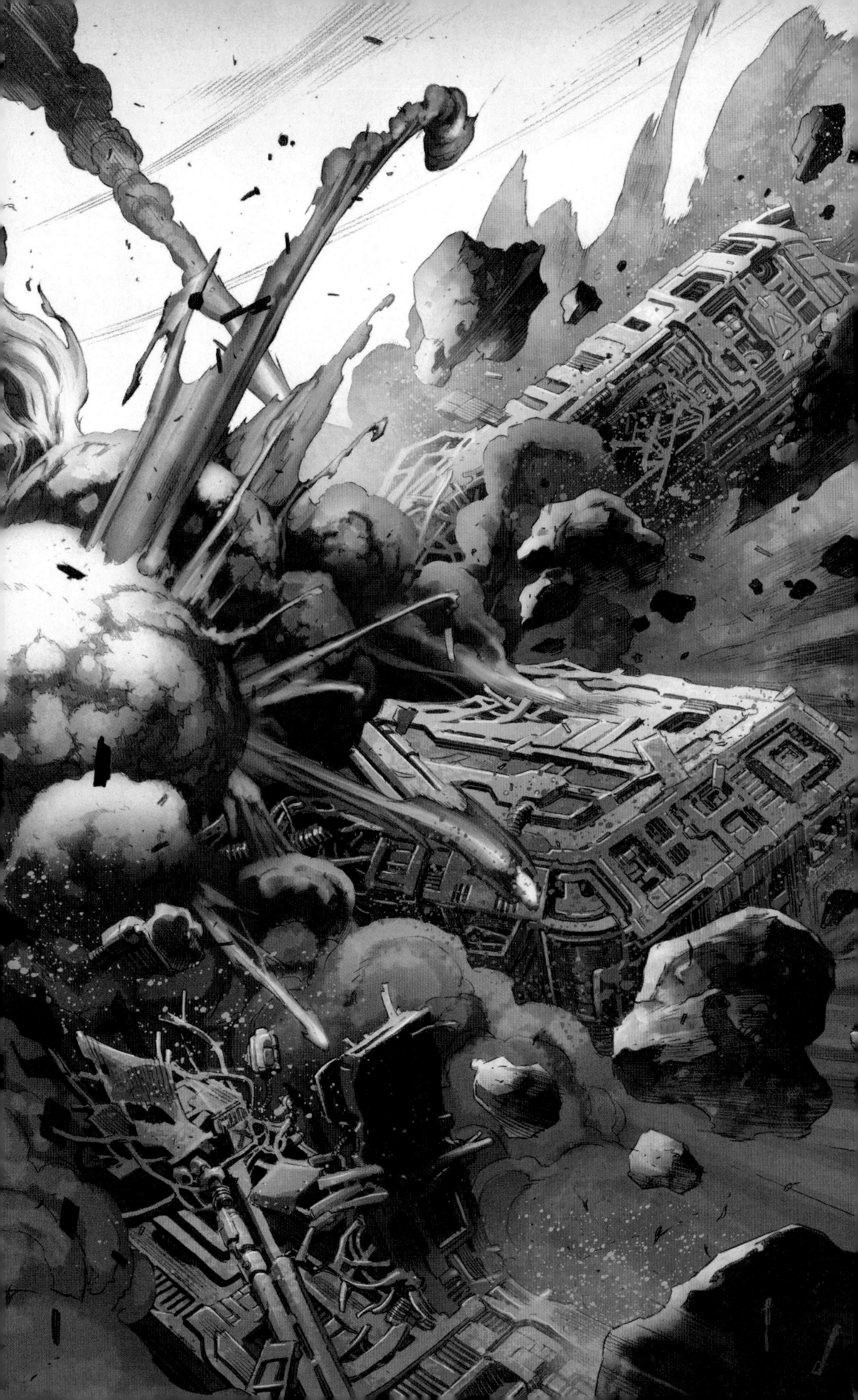

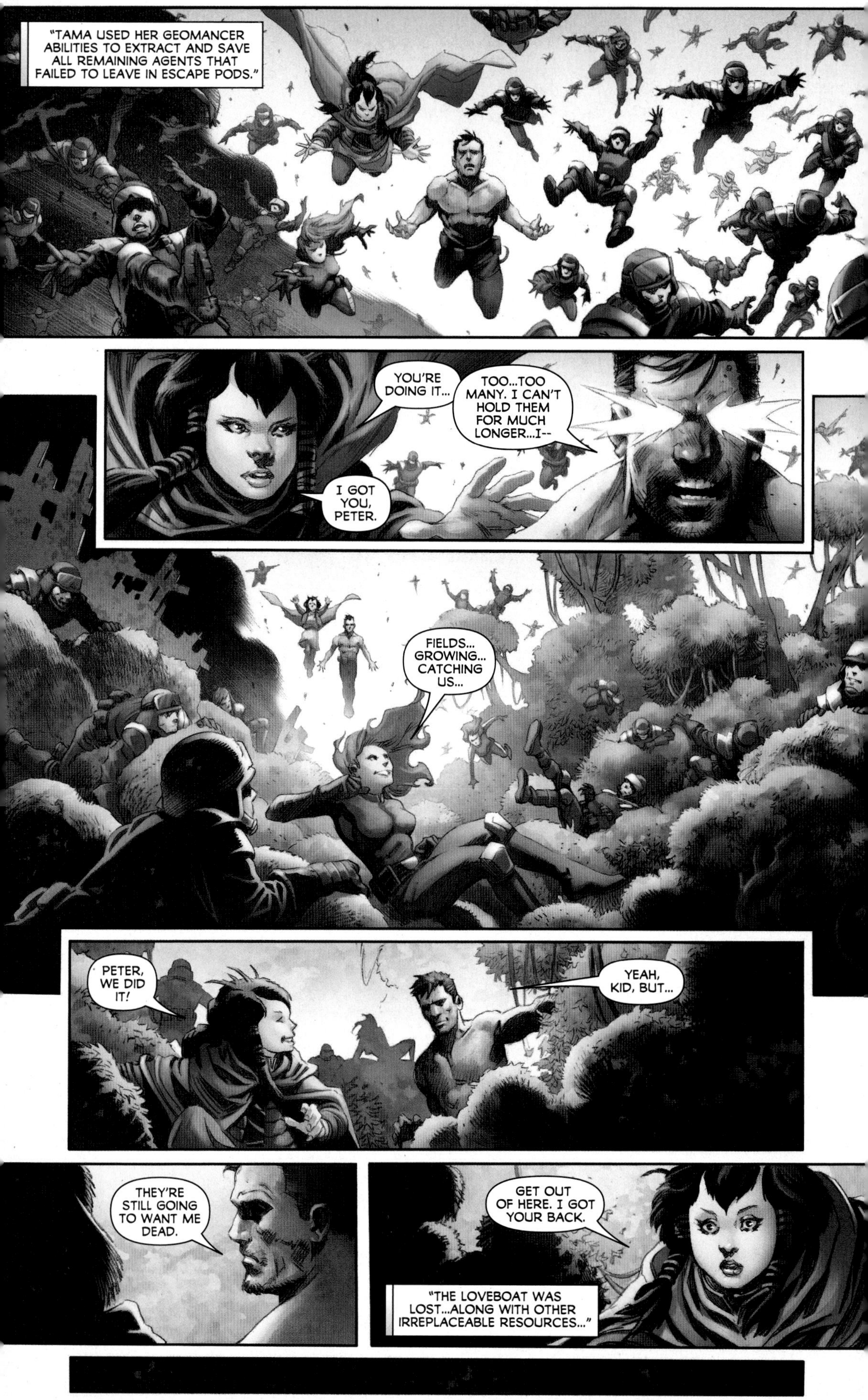
"TAMA USED HER GEOMANCER ABILITIES TO EXTRACT AND SAVE ALL REMAINING AGENTS THAT FAILED TO LEAVE IN ESCAPE PODS."
YOU'RE DOING IT...
TOO...TOO MANY. I CAN'T HOLD THEM FOR MUCH LONGER...I--
I GOT YOU, PETER.
FIELDS... GROWING... CATCHING US...
PETER, WE DID IT!
YEAH, KID, BUT...
THEY'RE STILL GOING TO WANT ME DEAD.
GET OUT OF HERE. I GOT YOUR BACK.
"THE LOVEBOAT WAS LOST...ALONG WITH OTHER IRREPLACEABLE RESOURCES..."

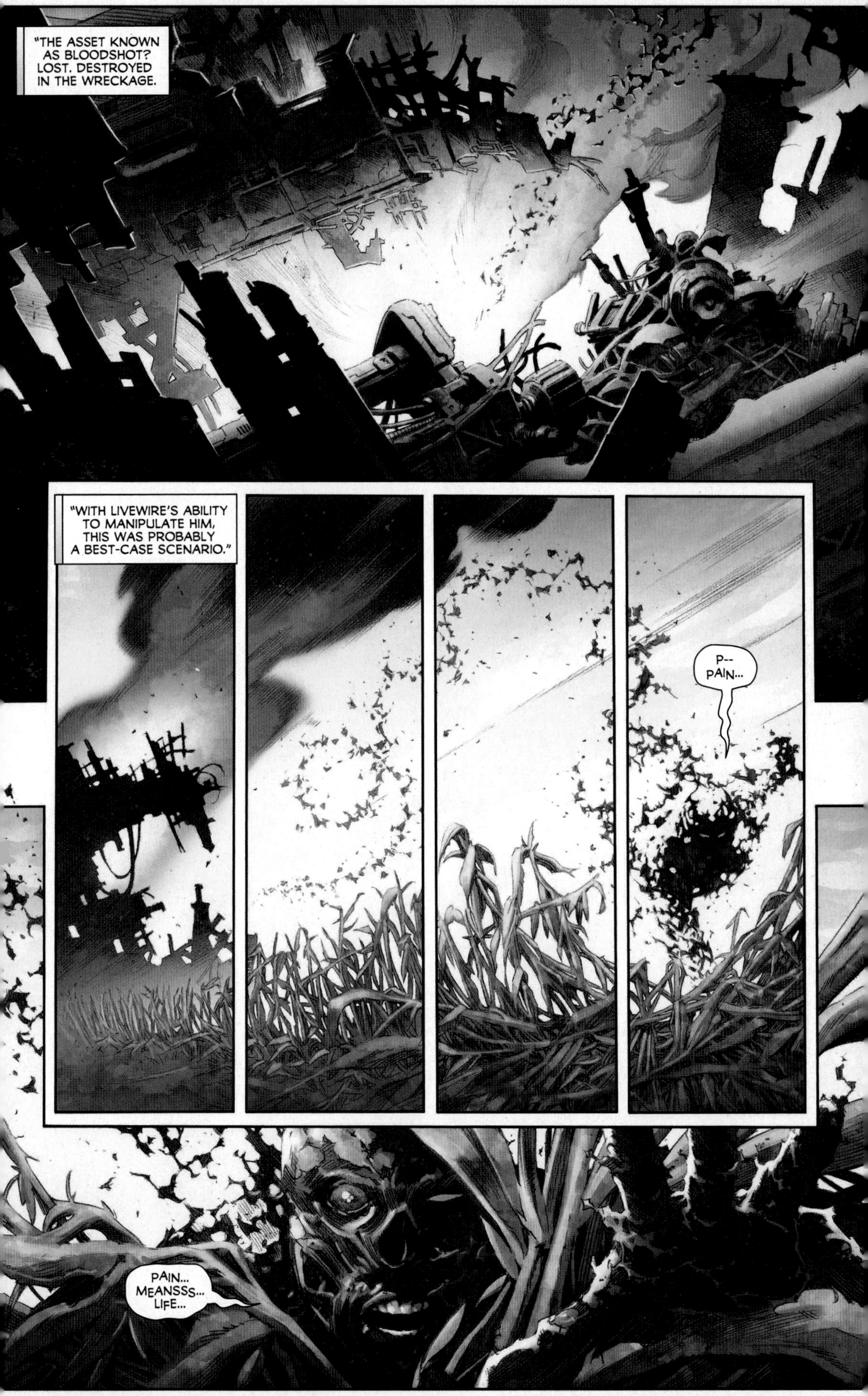
"THE ASSET KNOWN AS BLOODSHOT? LOST. DESTROYED IN THE WRECKAGE.
"WITH LIVEWIRE'S ABILITY TO MANIPULATE HIM, THIS WAS PROBABLY A BEST-CASE SCENARIO."
P-- PAIN...
PAIN... MEANSSS... LIFE...

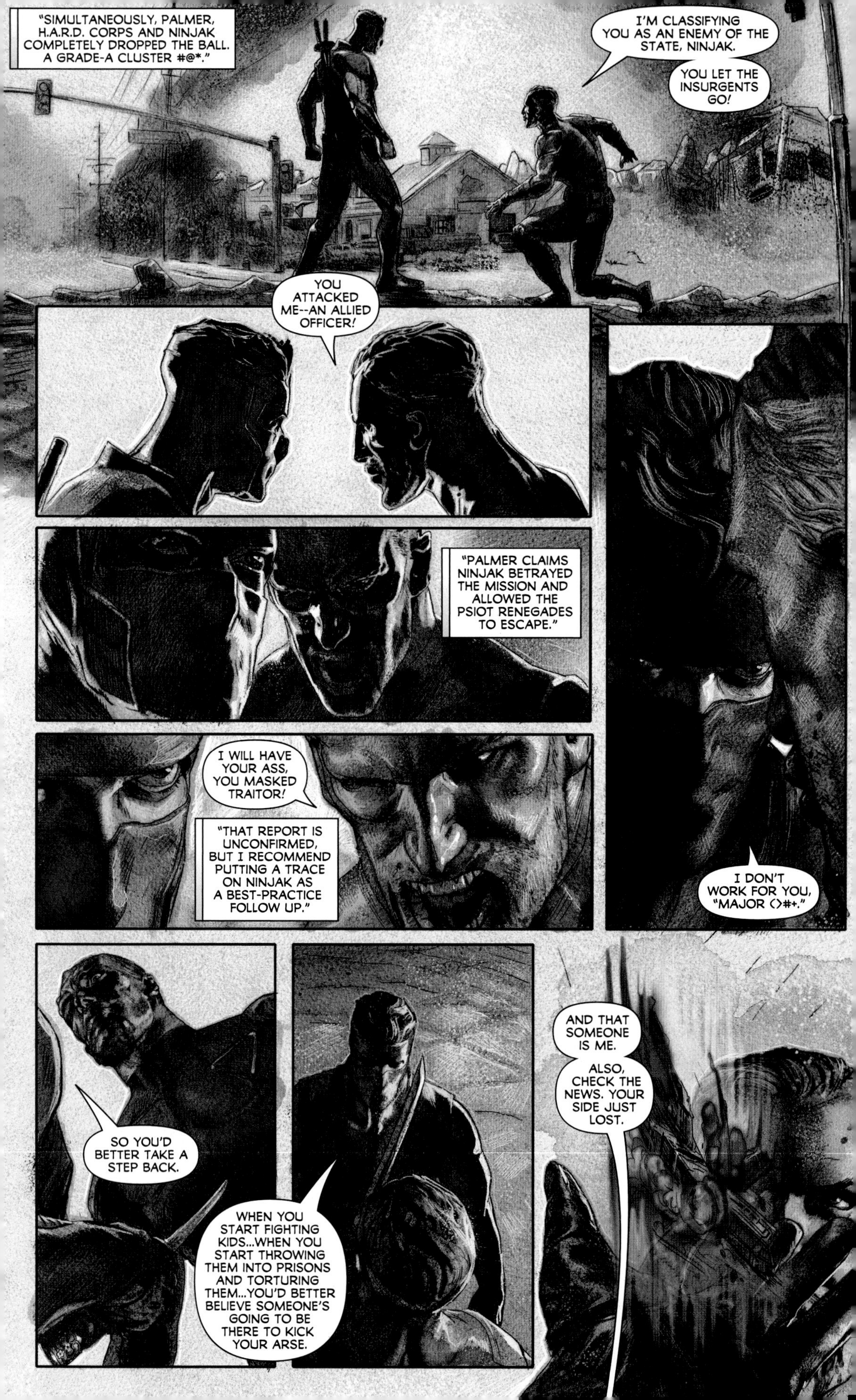
"SIMULTANEOUSLY, PALMER, H.A.R.D. CORPS AND NINJAK COMPLETELY DROPPED THE BALL. A GRADE-A CLUSTER #@*."
I'M CLASSIFYING YOU AS AN ENEMY OF THE STATE, NINJAK.
YOU LET THE INSURGENTS GO!
YOU ATTACKED ME--AN ALLIED OFFICER!
"PALMER CLAIMS NINJAK BETRAYED THE MISSION AND ALLOWED THE PSIOT RENEGADES TO ESCAPE."
I WILL HAVE YOUR ASS, YOU MASKED TRAITOR!
"THAT REPORT IS UNCONFIRMED, BUT I RECOMMEND PUTTING A TRACE ON NINJAK AS A BEST-PRACTICE FOLLOW UP."
I DON'T WORK FOR YOU, "MAJOR <>#+."
WHEN YOU START FIGHTING KIDS...WHEN YOU START THROWING THEM INTO PRISONS AND TORTURING THEM...YOU'D BETTER BELIEVE SOMEONE'S GOING TO BE THERE TO KICK YOUR ARSE.
SO YOU'D BETTER TAKE A STEP BACK.
AND THAT SOMEONE IS ME.
ALSO, CHECK THE NEWS. YOUR SIDE JUST LOST.

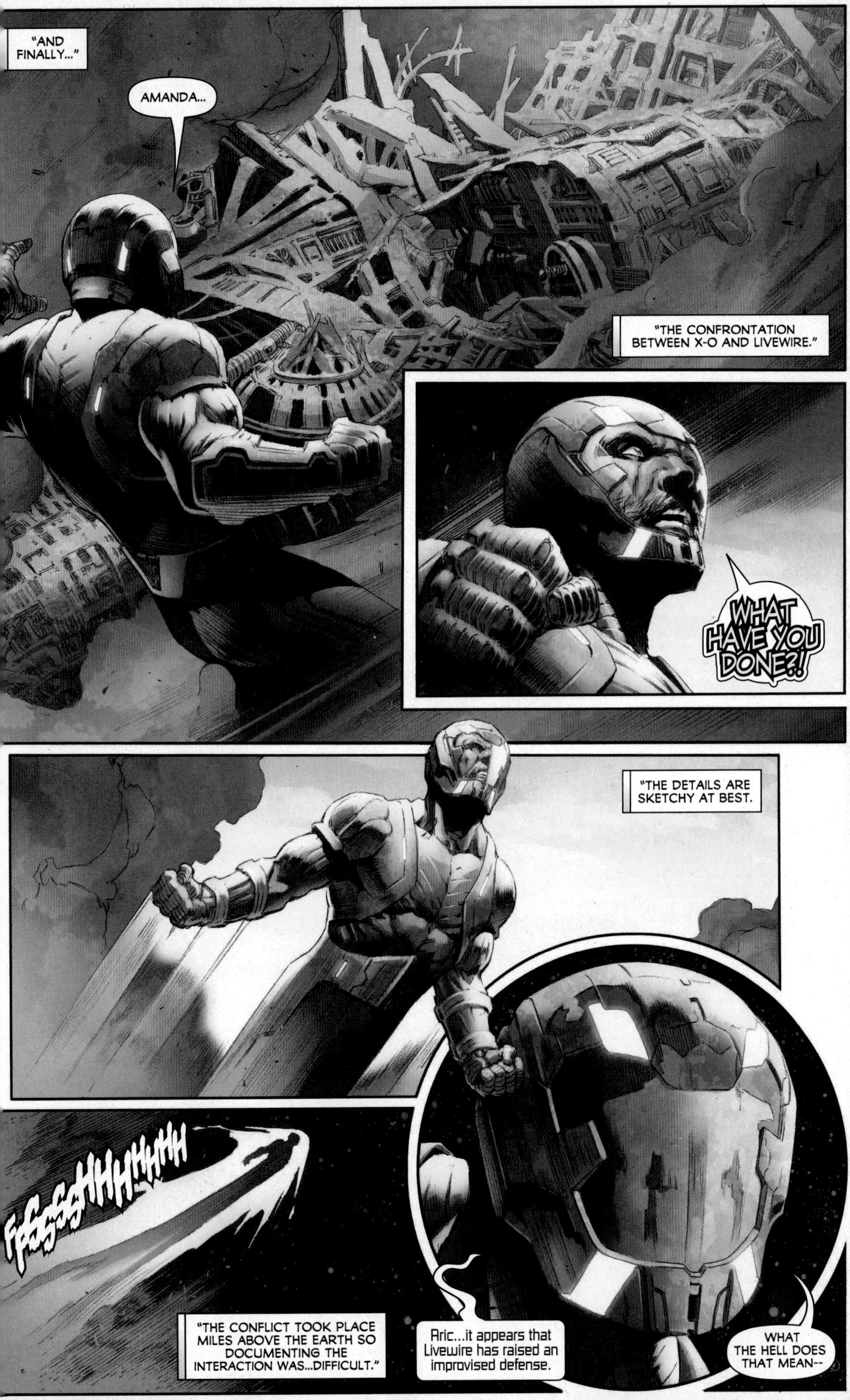
"AND FINALLY..."
AMANDA...
"THE CONFRONTATION BETWEEN X-O AND LIVEWIRE."
WHAT HAVE YOU DONE?!
"THE DETAILS ARE SKETCHY AT BEST.
FFSSSSHHHHHHHH
"THE CONFLICT TOOK PLACE MILES ABOVE THE EARTH SO DOCUMENTING THE INTERACTION WAS...DIFFICULT."
Aric...it appears that Livewire has raised an improvised defense.
WHAT THE HELL DOES THAT MEAN--

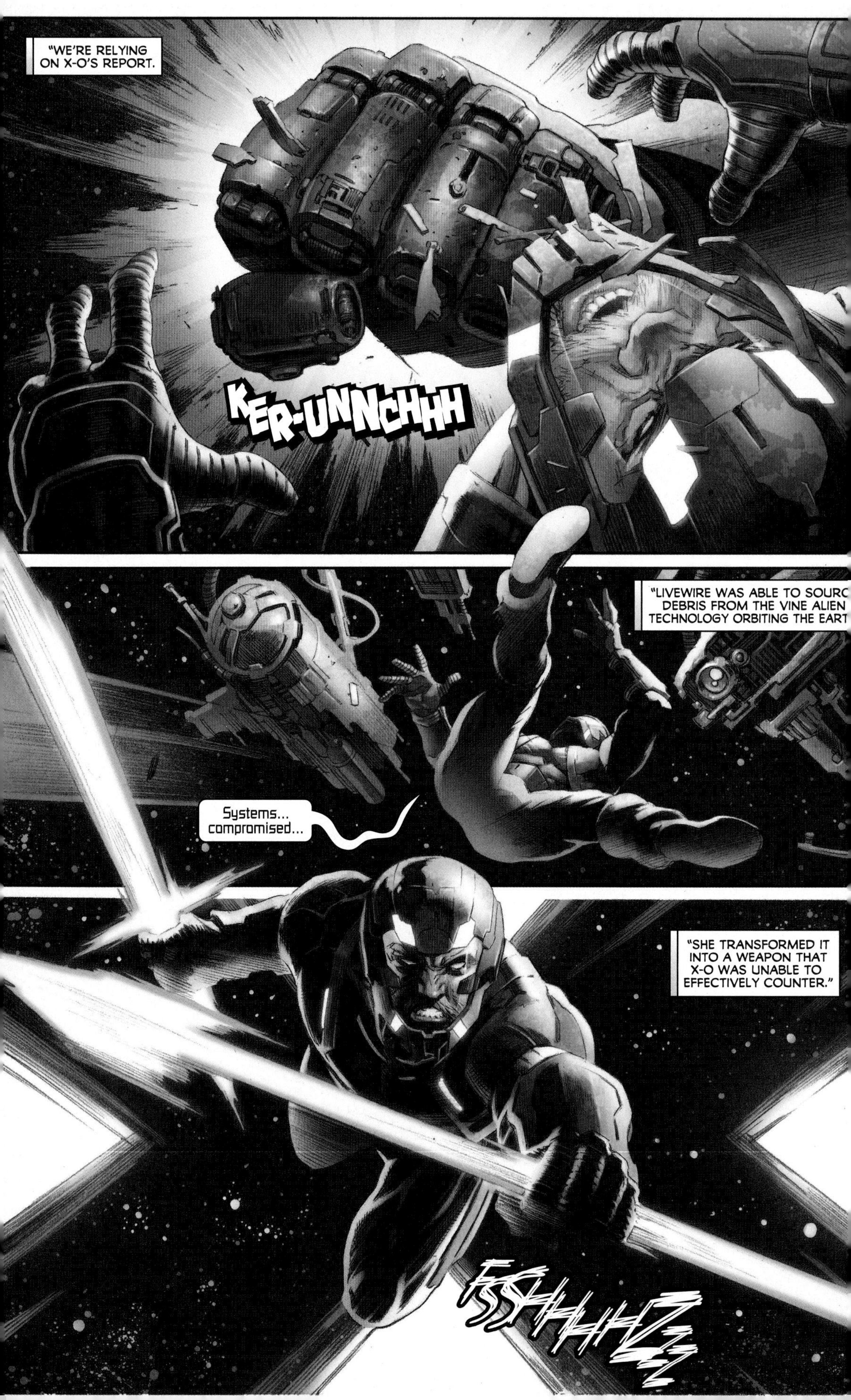
"WE'RE RELYING ON X-O'S REPORT.
KER-UNNCHHH
"LIVEWIRE WAS ABLE TO SOURC DEBRIS FROM THE VINE ALIEN TECHNOLOGY ORBITING THE EART
Systems... compromised...
"SHE TRANSFORMED IT INTO A WEAPON THAT X-O WAS UNABLE TO EFFECTIVELY COUNTER."
FSSHHHHZZZ

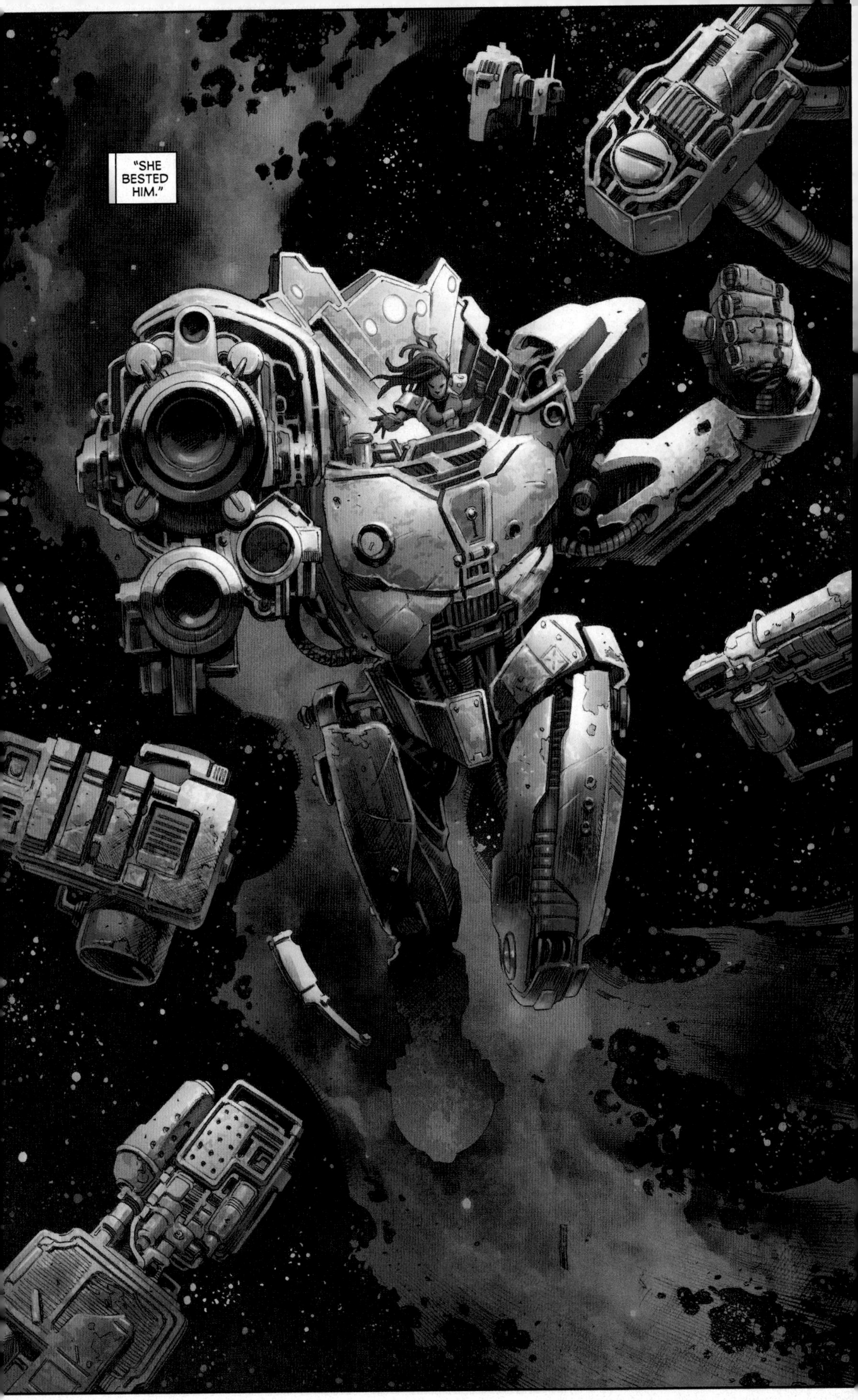
"SHE BESTED HIM."

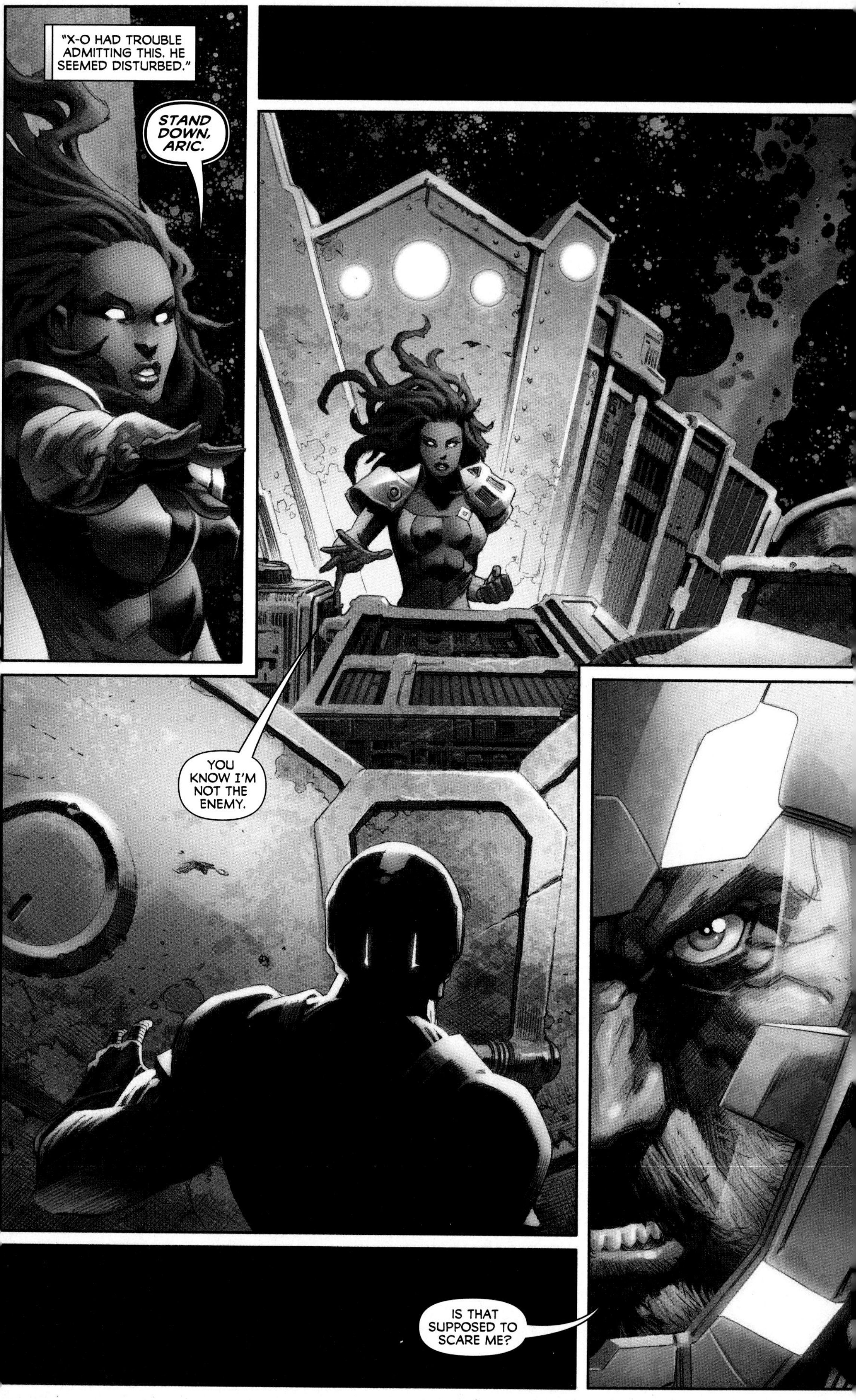
"X-O HAD TROUBLE ADMITTING THIS. HE SEEMED DISTURBED."
STAND DOWN, ARIC.
YOU KNOW I'M NOT THE ENEMY.
IS THAT SUPPOSED TO SCARE ME?

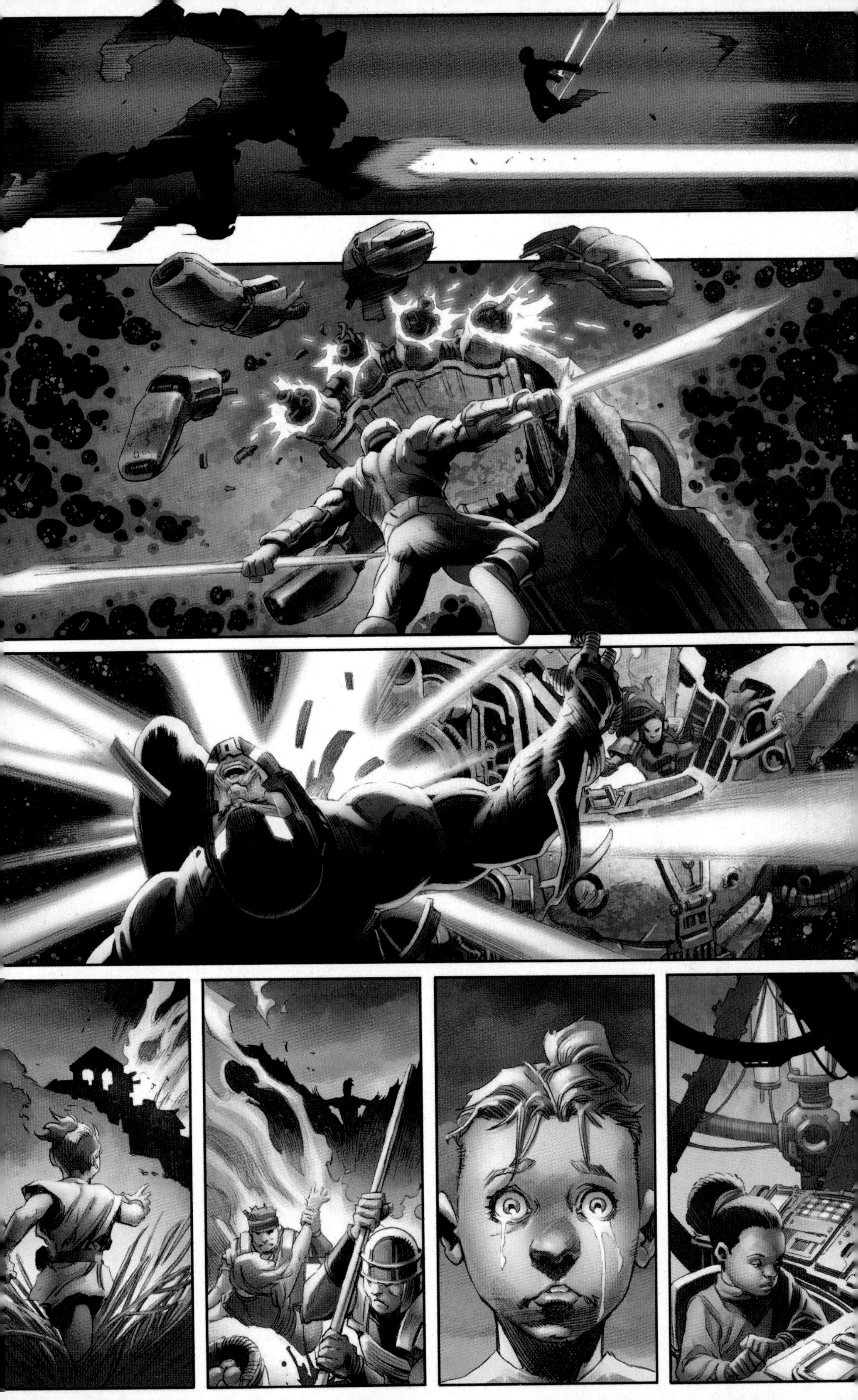

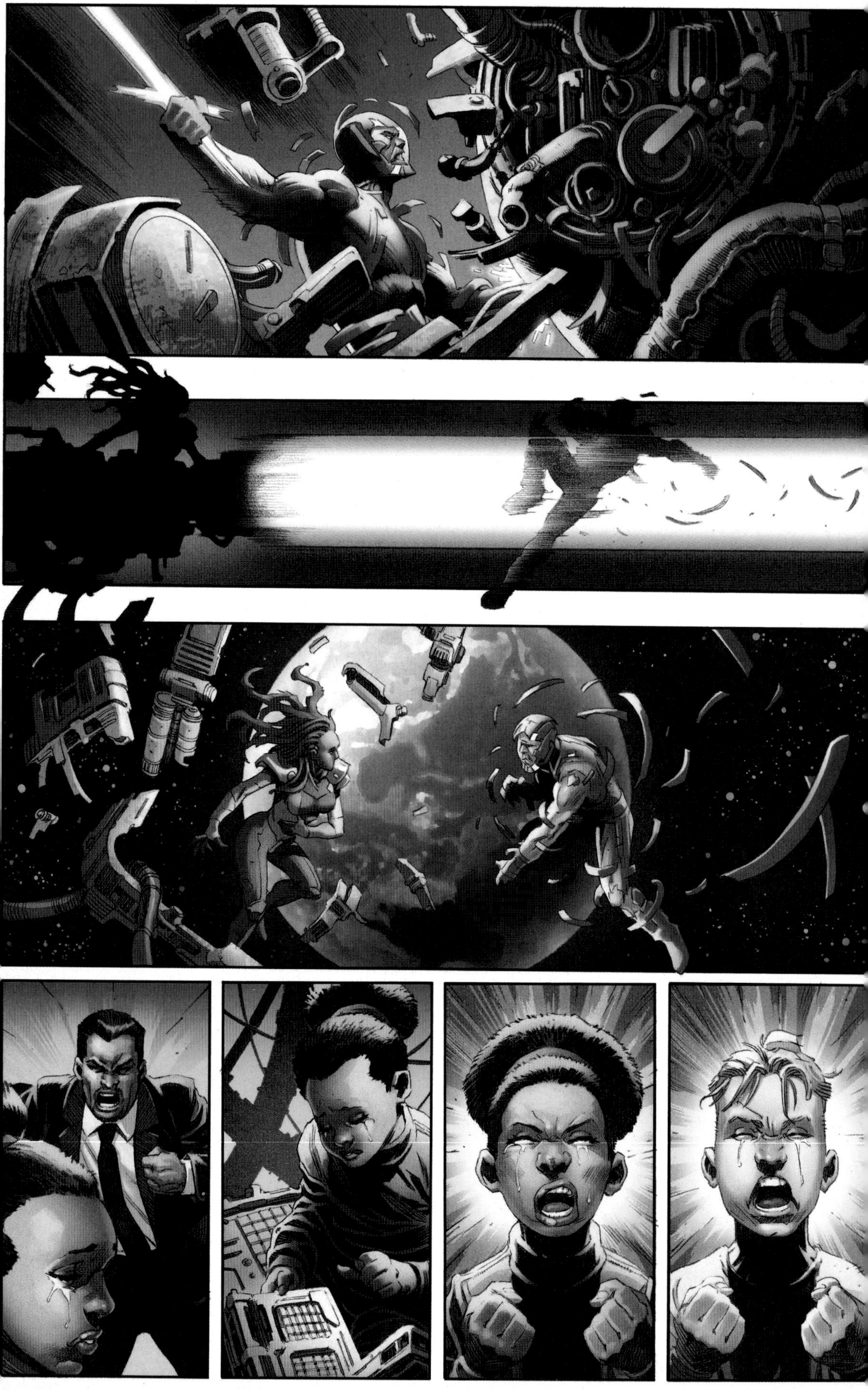

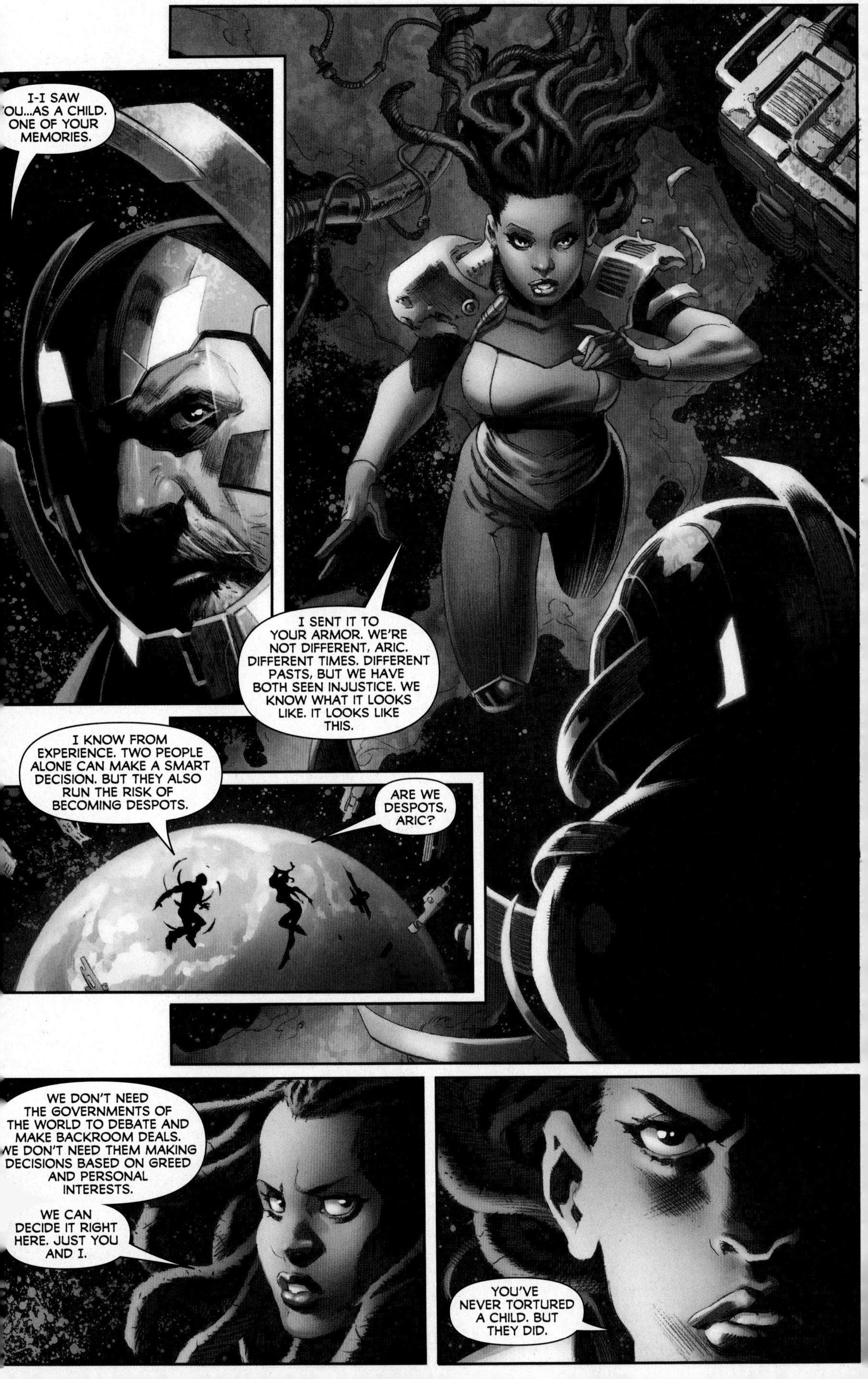
I-I SAW OU...AS A CHILD. ONE OF YOUR MEMORIES.
I SENT IT TO YOUR ARMOR. WE'RE NOT DIFFERENT, ARIC. DIFFERENT TIMES. DIFFERENT PASTS, BUT WE HAVE BOTH SEEN INJUSTICE. WE KNOW WHAT IT LOOKS LIKE. IT LOOKS LIKE THIS.
I KNOW FROM EXPERIENCE. TWO PEOPLE ALONE CAN MAKE A SMART DECISION. BUT THEY ALSO RUN THE RISK OF BECOMING DESPOTS.
ARE WE DESPOTS, ARIC?
WE DON'T NEED THE GOVERNMENTS OF THE WORLD TO DEBATE AND MAKE BACKROOM DEALS. WE DON'T NEED THEM MAKING DECISIONS BASED ON GREED AND PERSONAL INTERESTS.
WE CAN DECIDE IT RIGHT HERE. JUST YOU AND I.
YOU'VE NEVER TORTURED A CHILD. BUT THEY DID.

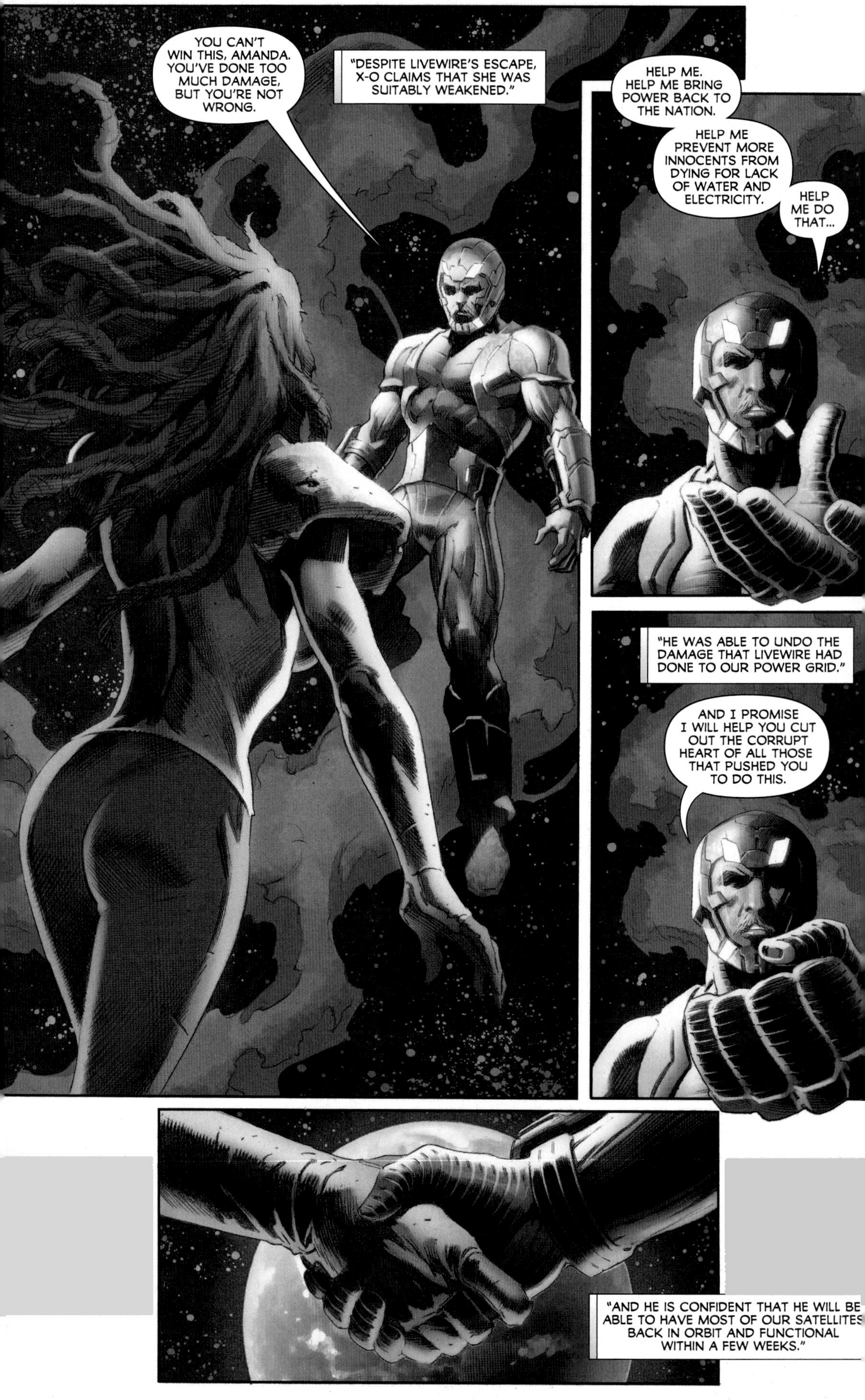
"DESPITE LIVEWIRE'S ESCAPE, X-O CLAIMS THAT SHE WAS SUITABLY WEAKENED."
YOU CAN'T WIN THIS, AMANDA. YOU'VE DONE TOO MUCH DAMAGE, BUT YOU'RE NOT WRONG.
HELP ME. HELP ME BRING POWER BACK TO THE NATION.
HELP ME PREVENT MORE INNOCENTS FROM DYING FOR LACK OF WATER AND ELECTRICITY.
HELP ME DO THAT...
"HE WAS ABLE TO UNDO THE DAMAGE THAT LIVEWIRE HAD DONE TO OUR POWER GRID."
AND I PROMISE I WILL HELP YOU CUT OUT THE CORRUPT HEART OF ALL THOSE THAT PUSHED YOU TO DO THIS.
"AND HE IS CONFIDENT THAT HE WILL BE ABLE TO HAVE MOST OF OUR SATELLITES BACK IN ORBIT AND FUNCTIONAL WITHIN A FEW WEEKS."

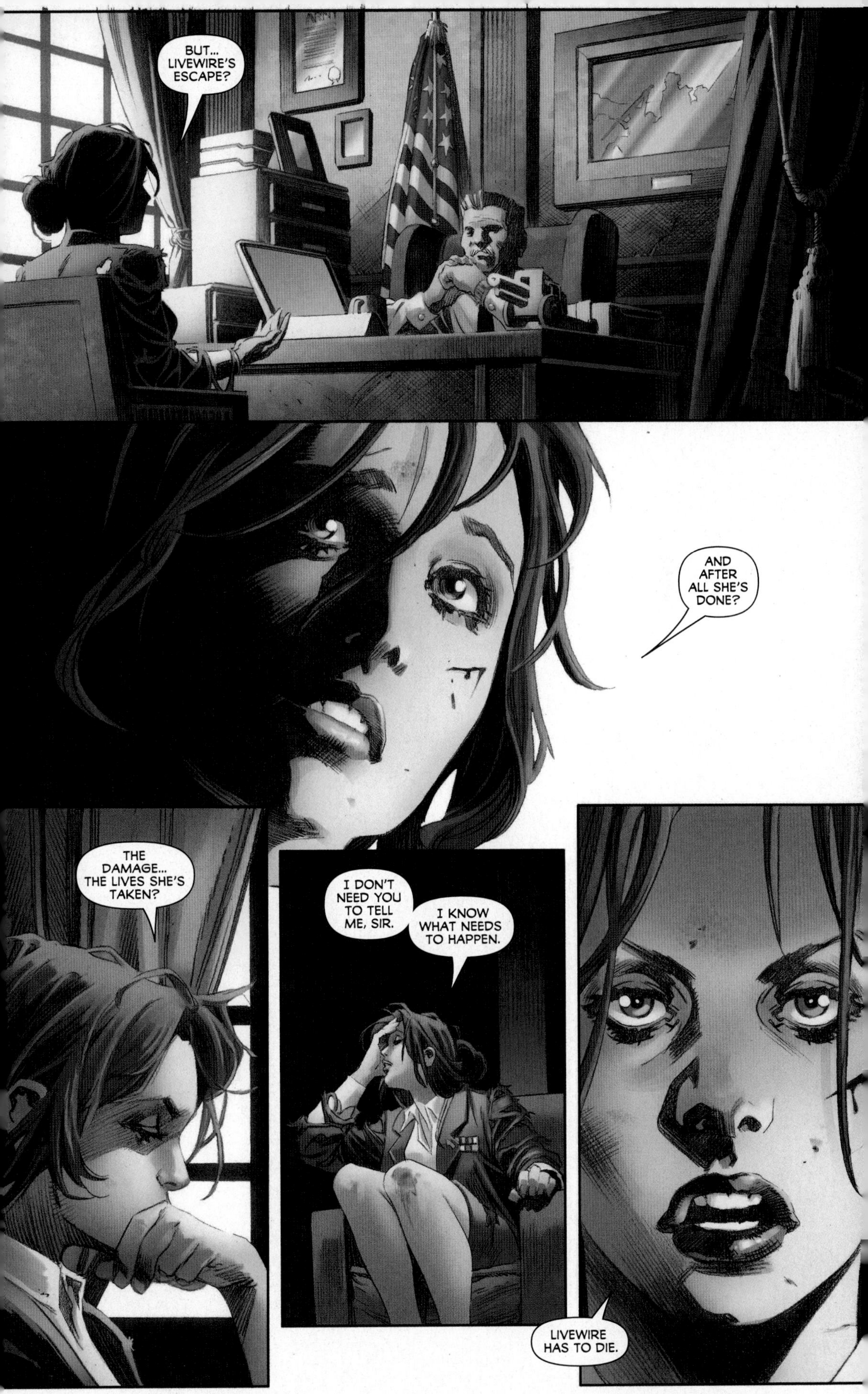
BUT... LIVEWIRE'S ESCAPE?
AND AFTER ALL SHE'S DONE?
THE DAMAGE... THE LIVES SHE'S TAKEN?
I DON'T NEED YOU TO TELL ME, SIR.
I KNOW WHAT NEEDS TO HAPPEN.
LIVEWIRE HAS TO DIE.

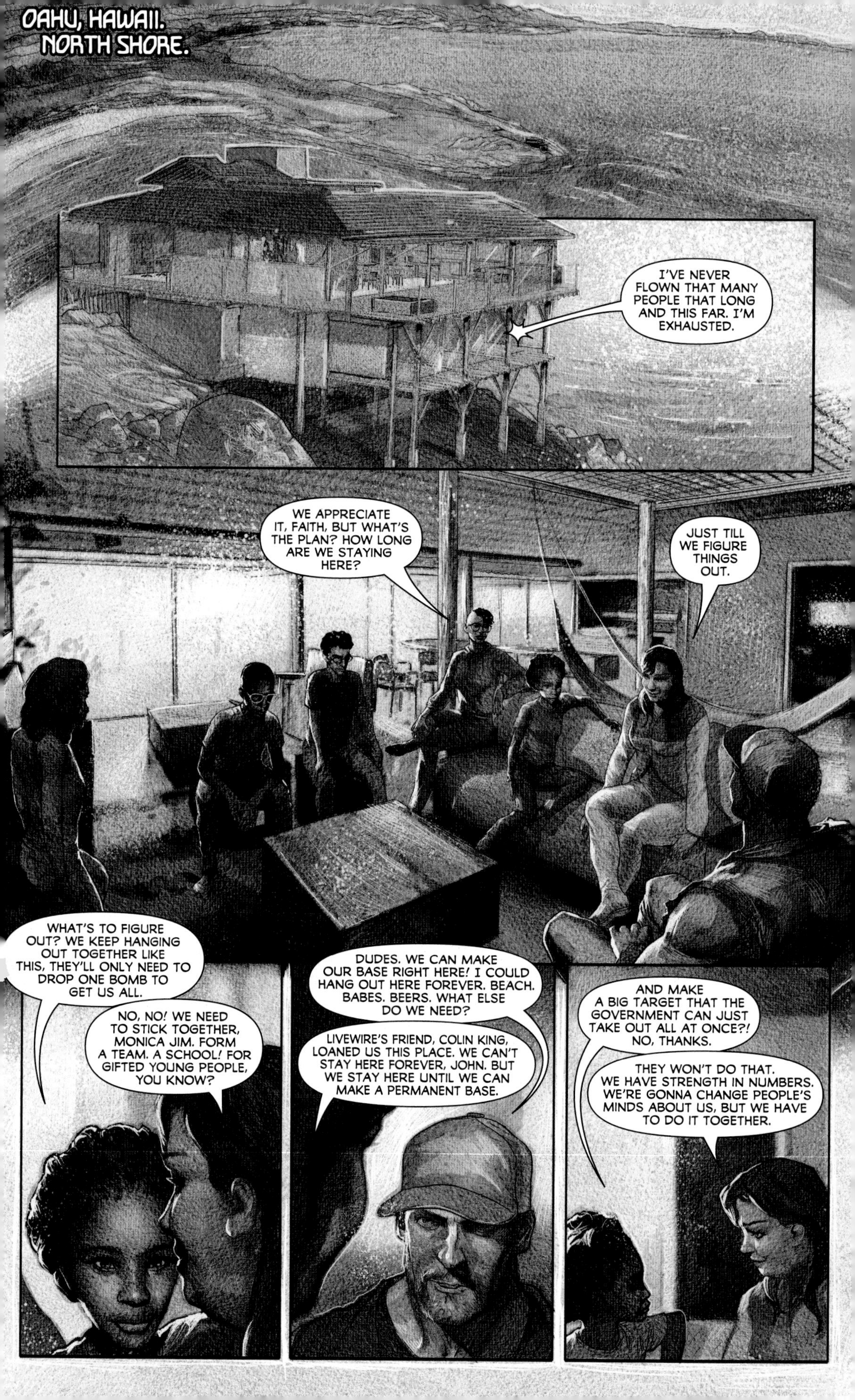
OAHU, HAWAII. NORTH SHORE.
I'VE NEVER FLOWN THAT MANY PEOPLE THAT LONG AND THIS FAR. I'M EXHAUSTED.
WE APPRECIATE IT, FAITH, BUT WHAT'S THE PLAN? HOW LONG ARE WE STAYING HERE?
JUST TILL WE FIGURE THINGS OUT.
WHAT'S TO FIGURE OUT? WE KEEP HANGING OUT TOGETHER LIKE THIS, THEY'LL ONLY NEED TO DROP ONE BOMB TO GET US ALL.
NO, NO! WE NEED TO STICK TOGETHER, MONICA JIM. FORM A TEAM. A SCHOOL! FOR GIFTED YOUNG PEOPLE, YOU KNOW?
DUDES. WE CAN MAKE OUR BASE RIGHT HERE! I COULD HANG OUT HERE FOREVER. BEACH. BABES. BEERS. WHAT ELSE DO WE NEED?
LIVEWIRE'S FRIEND, COLIN KING, LOANED US THIS PLACE. WE CAN'T STAY HERE FOREVER, JOHN. BUT WE STAY HERE UNTIL WE CAN MAKE A PERMANENT BASE.
AND MAKE A BIG TARGET THAT THE GOVERNMENT CAN JUST TAKE OUT ALL AT ONCE?! NO, THANKS.
THEY WON'T DO THAT. WE HAVE STRENGTH IN NUMBERS. WE'RE GONNA CHANGE PEOPLE'S MINDS ABOUT US, BUT WE HAVE TO DO IT TOGETHER.

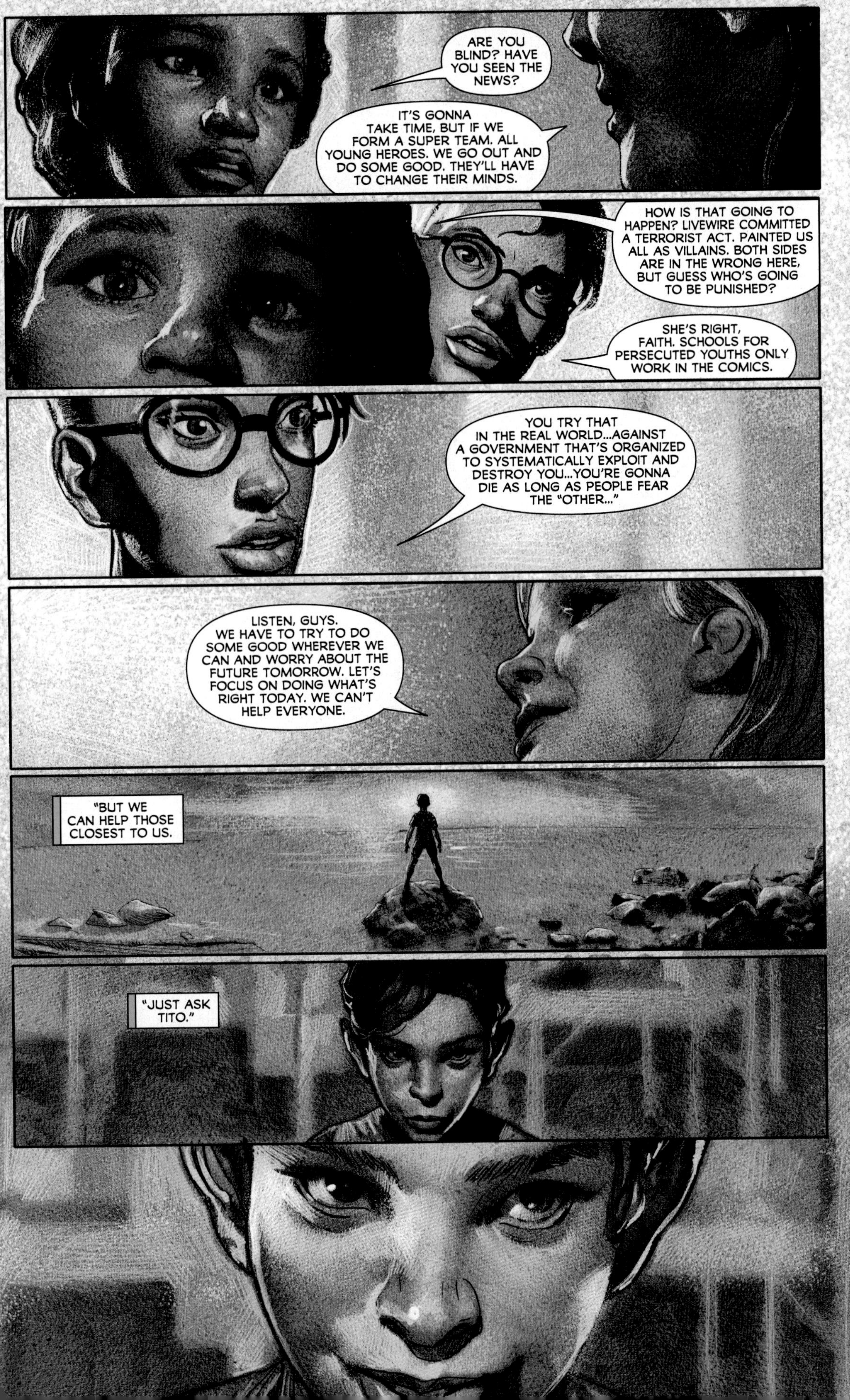
ARE YOU BLIND? HAVE YOU SEEN THE NEWS?
IT'S GONNA TAKE TIME, BUT IF WE FORM A SUPER TEAM. ALL YOUNG HEROES. WE GO OUT AND DO SOME GOOD. THEY'LL HAVE TO CHANGE THEIR MINDS.
HOW IS THAT GOING TO HAPPEN? LIVEWIRE COMMITTED A TERRORIST ACT. PAINTED US ALL AS VILLAINS. BOTH SIDES ARE IN THE WRONG HERE, BUT GUESS WHO'S GOING TO BE PUNISHED?
SHE'S RIGHT, FAITH. SCHOOLS FOR PERSECUTED YOUTHS ONLY WORK IN THE COMICS.
YOU TRY THAT IN THE REAL WORLD...AGAINST A GOVERNMENT THAT'S ORGANIZED TO SYSTEMATICALLY EXPLOIT AND DESTROY YOU...YOU'RE GONNA DIE AS LONG AS PEOPLE FEAR THE "OTHER..."
LISTEN, GUYS. WE HAVE TO TRY TO DO SOME GOOD WHEREVER WE CAN AND WORRY ABOUT THE FUTURE TOMORROW. LET'S FOCUS ON DOING WHAT'S RIGHT TODAY. WE CAN'T HELP EVERYONE.
"BUT WE CAN HELP THOSE CLOSEST TO US.
"JUST ASK TITO."

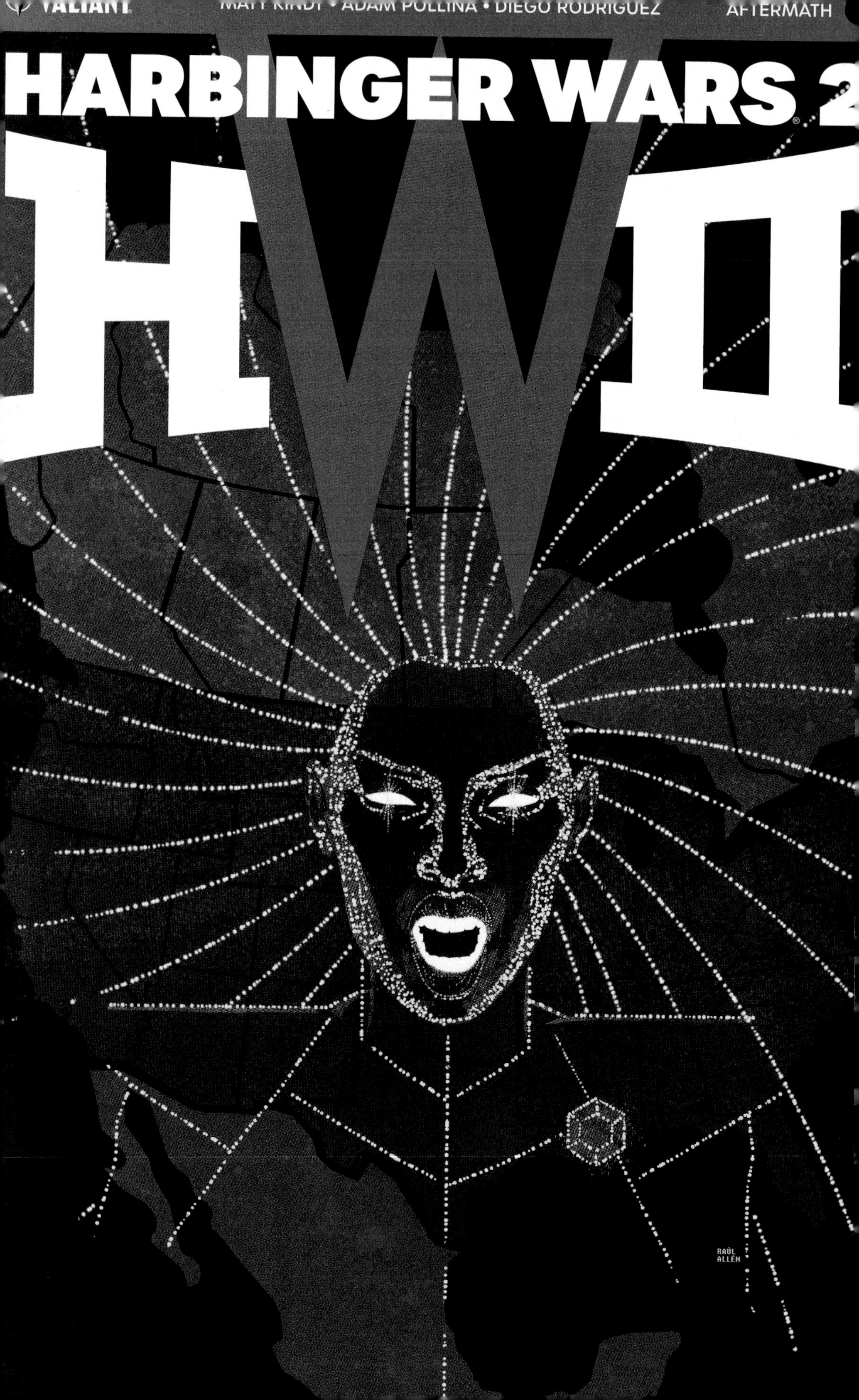
VALIANT
MATT KINDT • ADAM POLLINA • DIEGO RODRIGUEZ
AFTERMATH
HARBINGER WARS 2®
HWII
RAÚL
ALLÉN

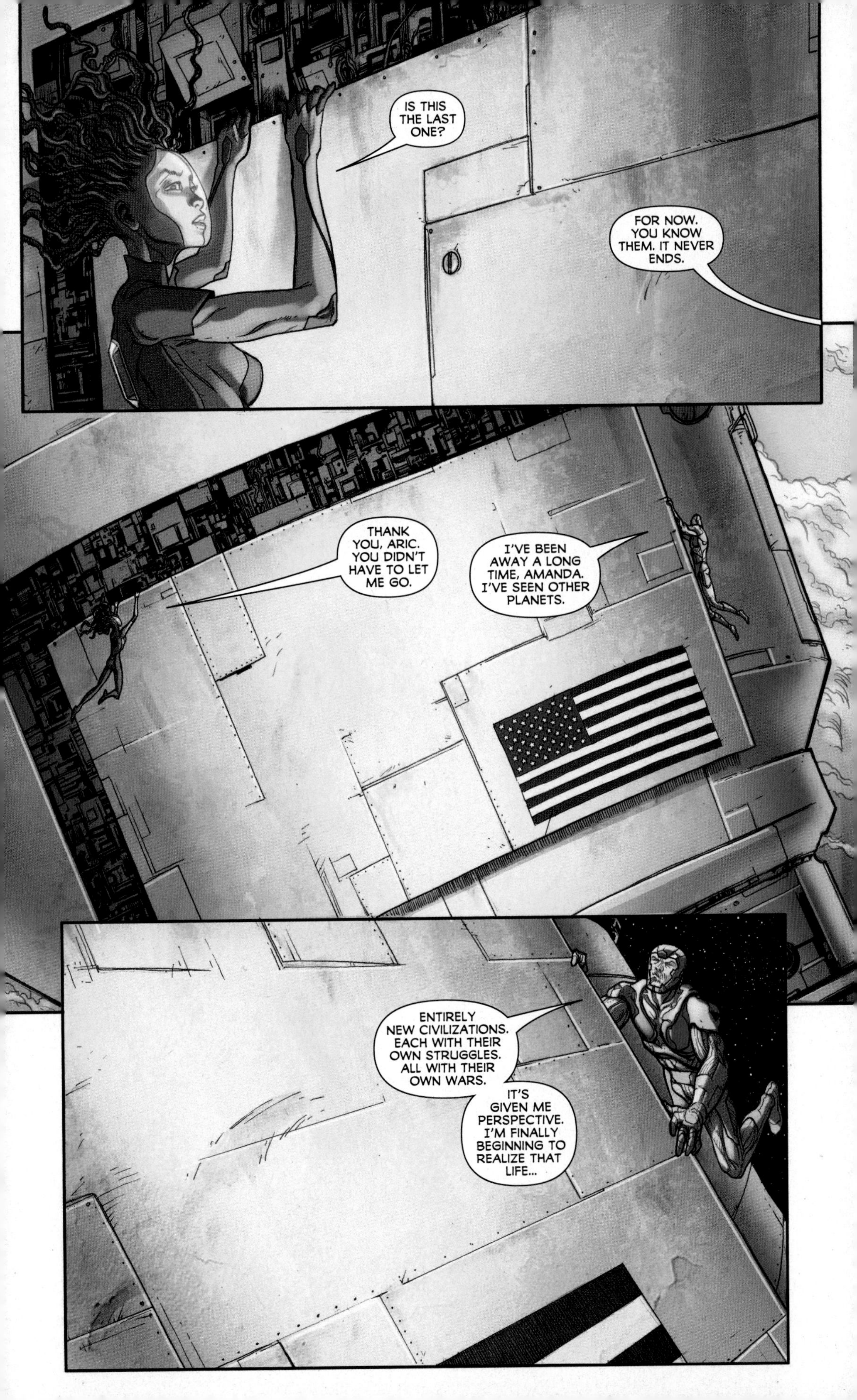
IS THIS THE LAST ONE?
FOR NOW. YOU KNOW THEM. IT NEVER ENDS.
THANK YOU, ARIC. YOU DIDN'T HAVE TO LET ME GO.
I'VE BEEN AWAY A LONG TIME, AMANDA. I'VE SEEN OTHER PLANETS.
ENTIRELY NEW CIVILIZATIONS. EACH WITH THEIR OWN STRUGGLES. ALL WITH THEIR OWN WARS.
IT'S GIVEN ME PERSPECTIVE. I'M FINALLY BEGINNING TO REALIZE THAT LIFE...

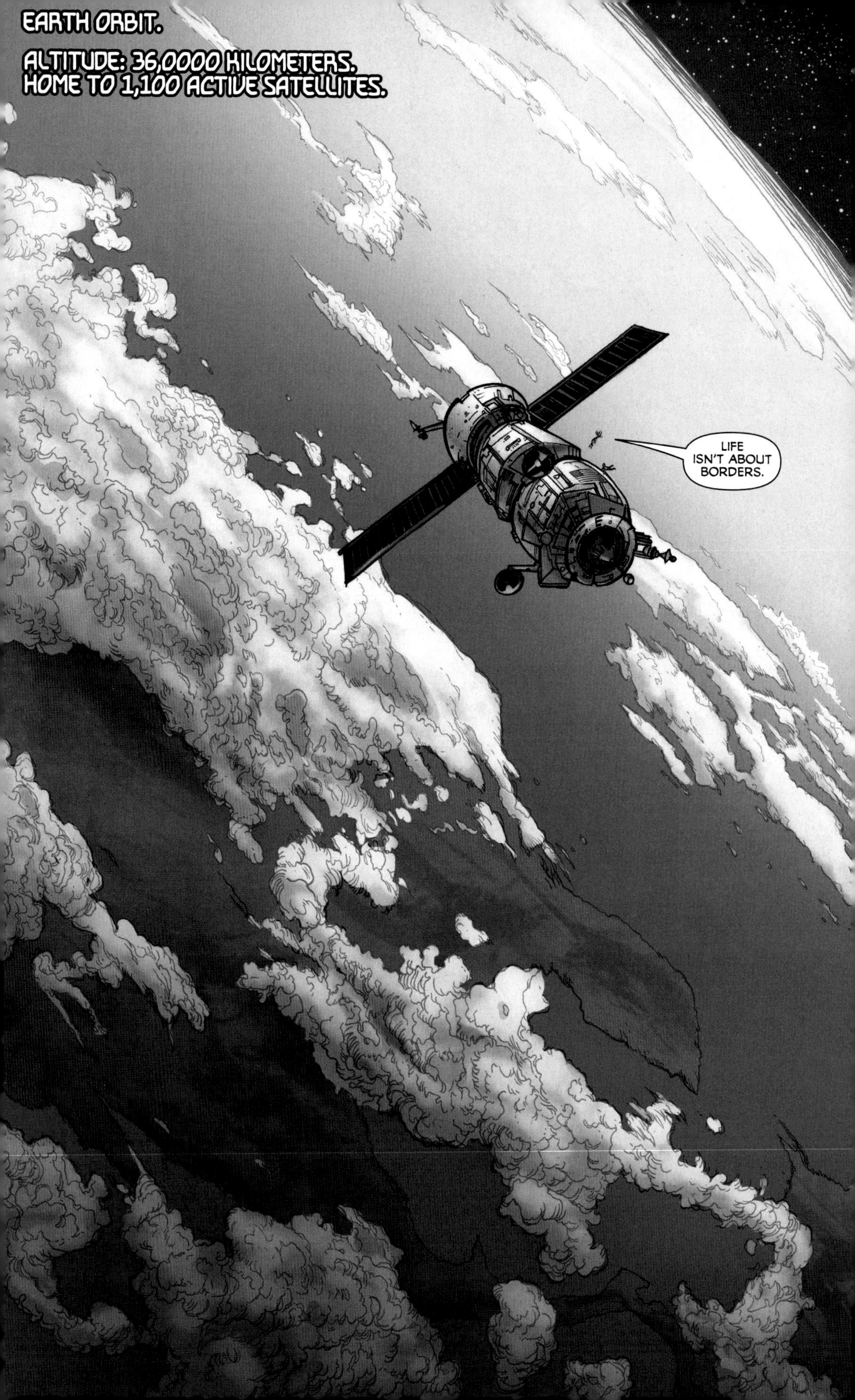
EARTH ORBIT.
ALTITUDE: 36,0000 KILOMETERS. HOME TO 1,100 ACTIVE SATELLITES.
LIFE ISN'T ABOUT BORDERS.

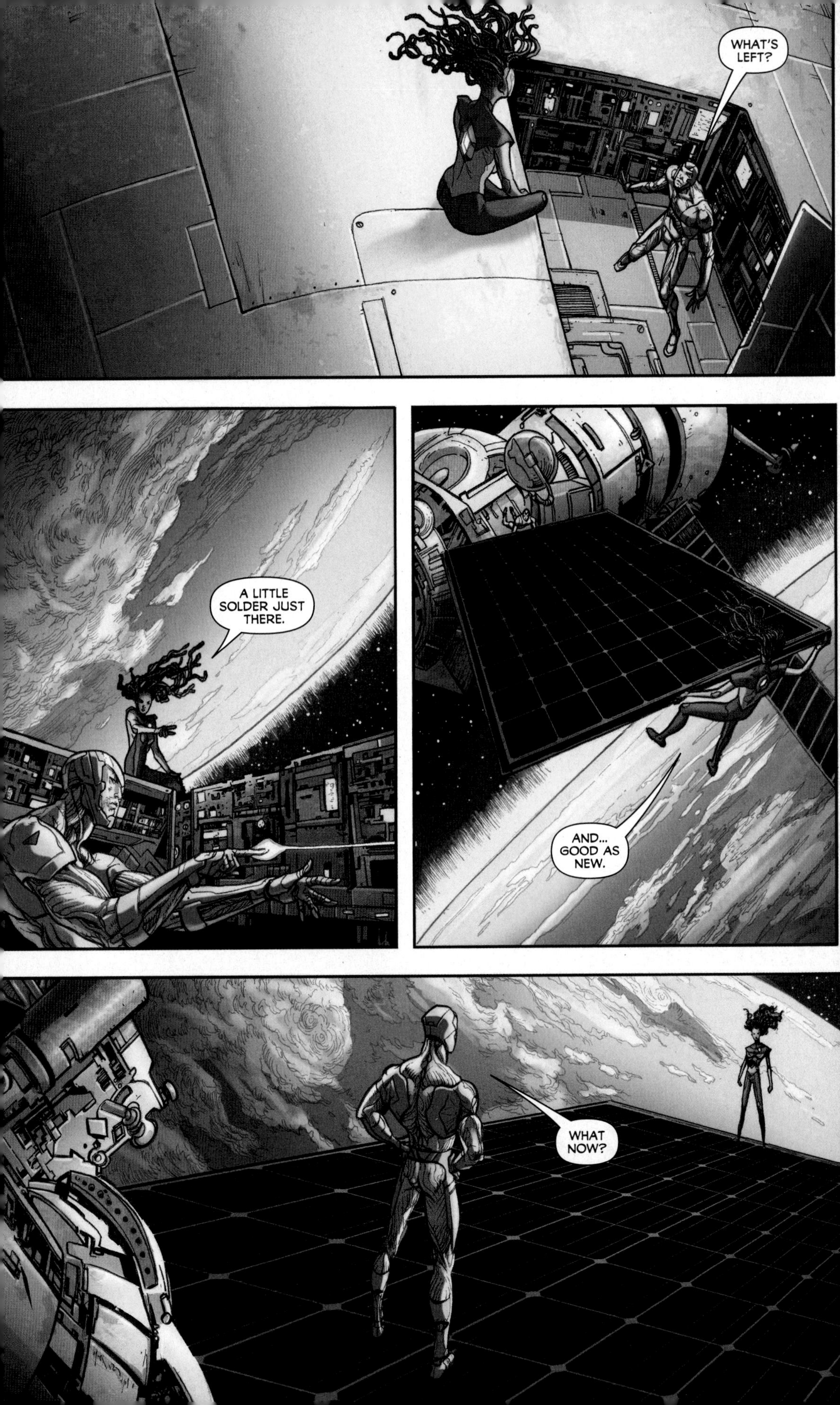
WHAT'S LEFT?
A LITTLE SOLDER JUST THERE.
AND... GOOD AS NEW.
WHAT NOW?

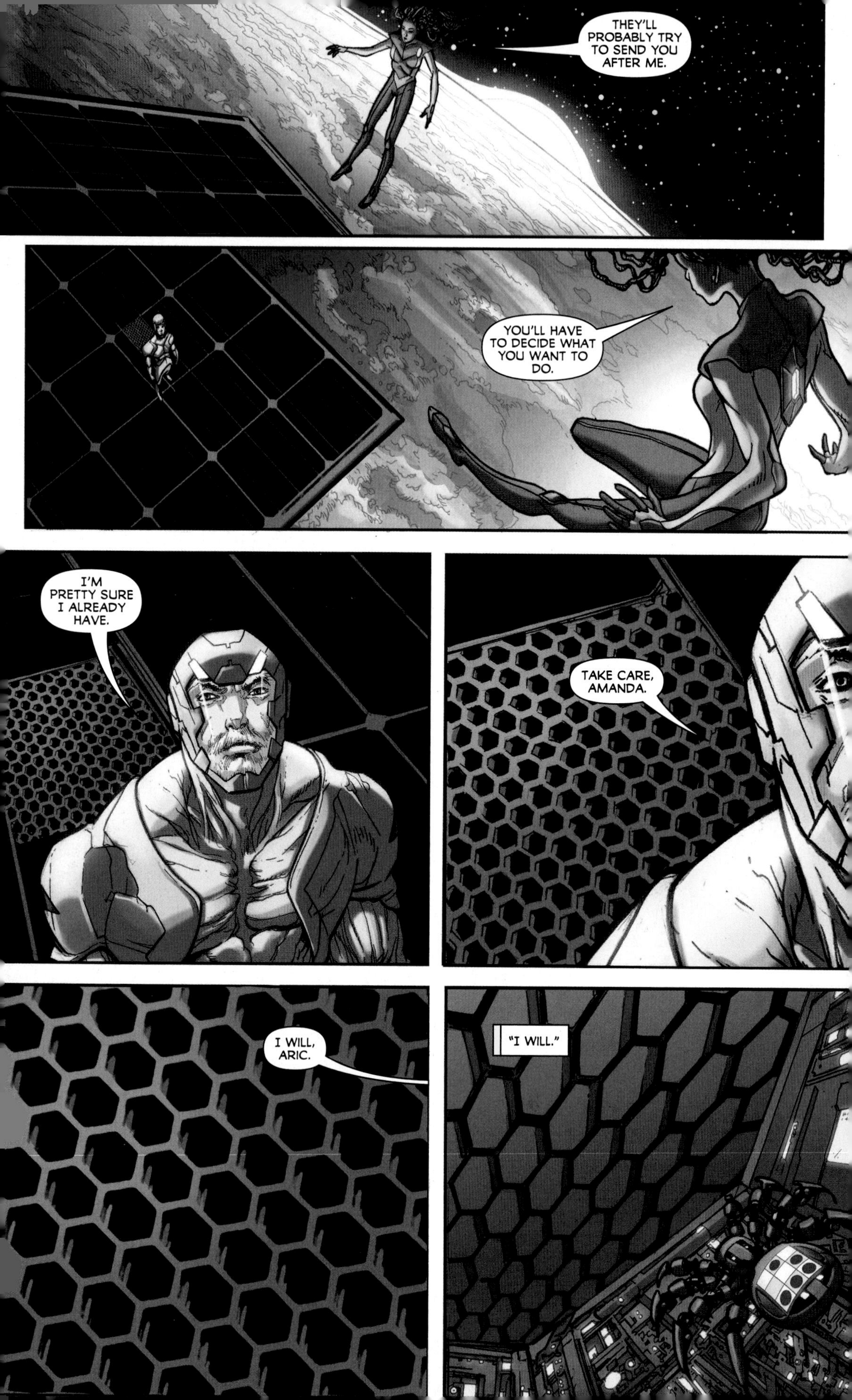
THEY'LL PROBABLY TRY TO SEND YOU AFTER ME.
YOU'LL HAVE TO DECIDE WHAT YOU WANT TO DO.
I'M PRETTY SURE I ALREADY HAVE.
TAKE CARE, AMANDA.
I WILL, ARIC.
"I WILL."

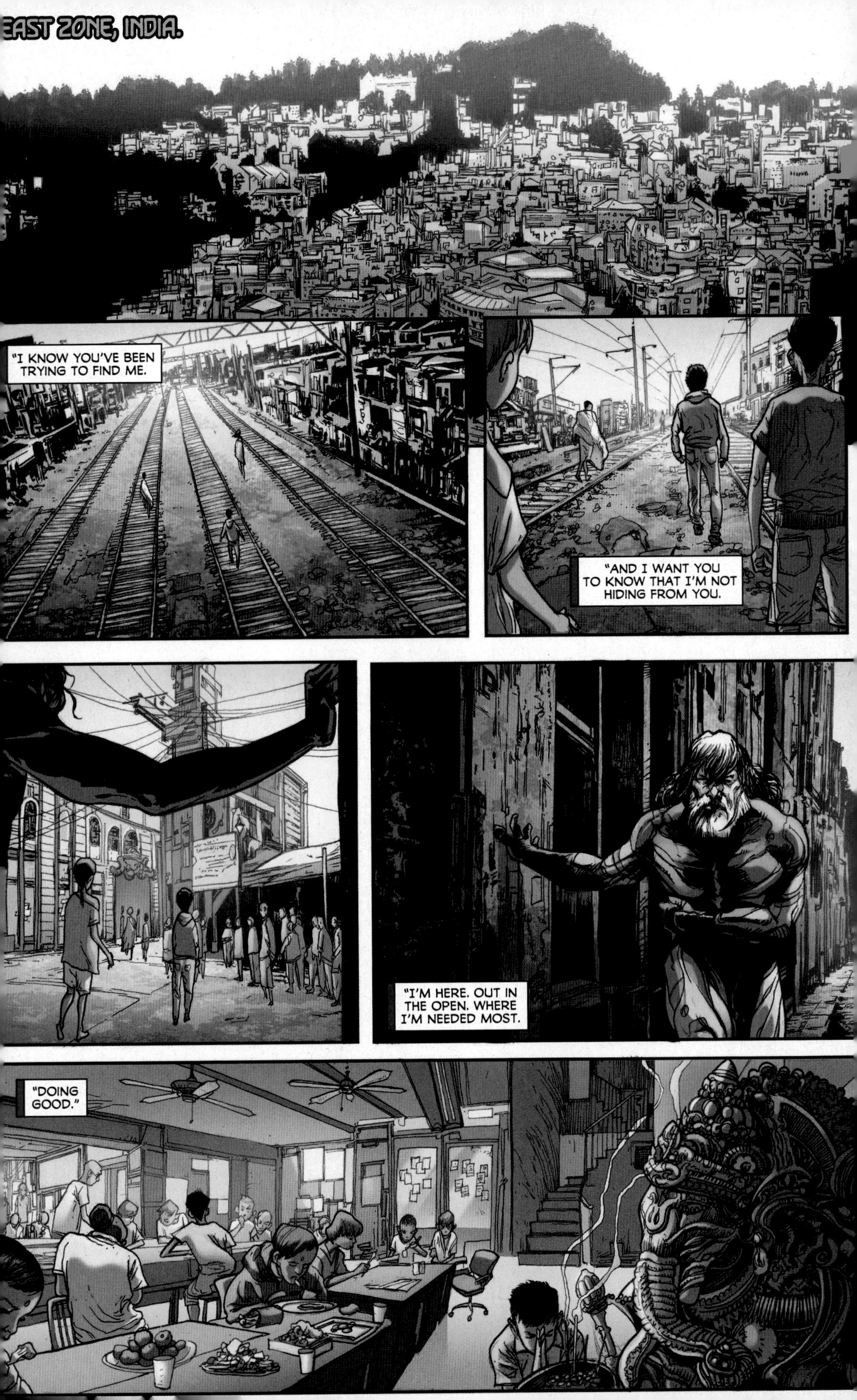
EAST ZONE, INDIA.
"I KNOW YOU'VE BEEN TRYING TO FIND ME.
"AND I WANT YOU TO KNOW THAT I'M NOT HIDING FROM YOU.
"I'M HERE. OUT IN THE OPEN. WHERE I'M NEEDED MOST.
"DOING GOOD."

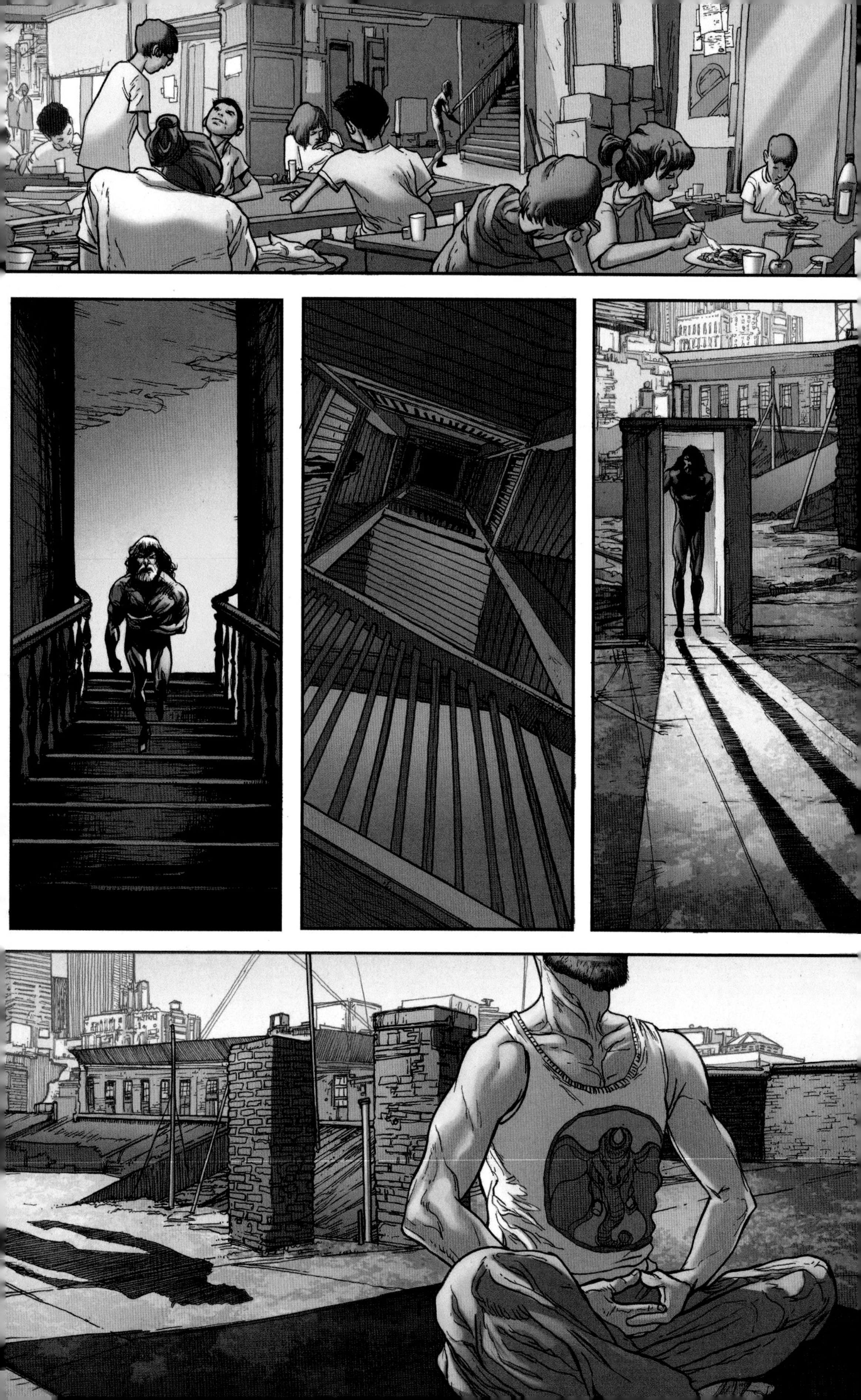

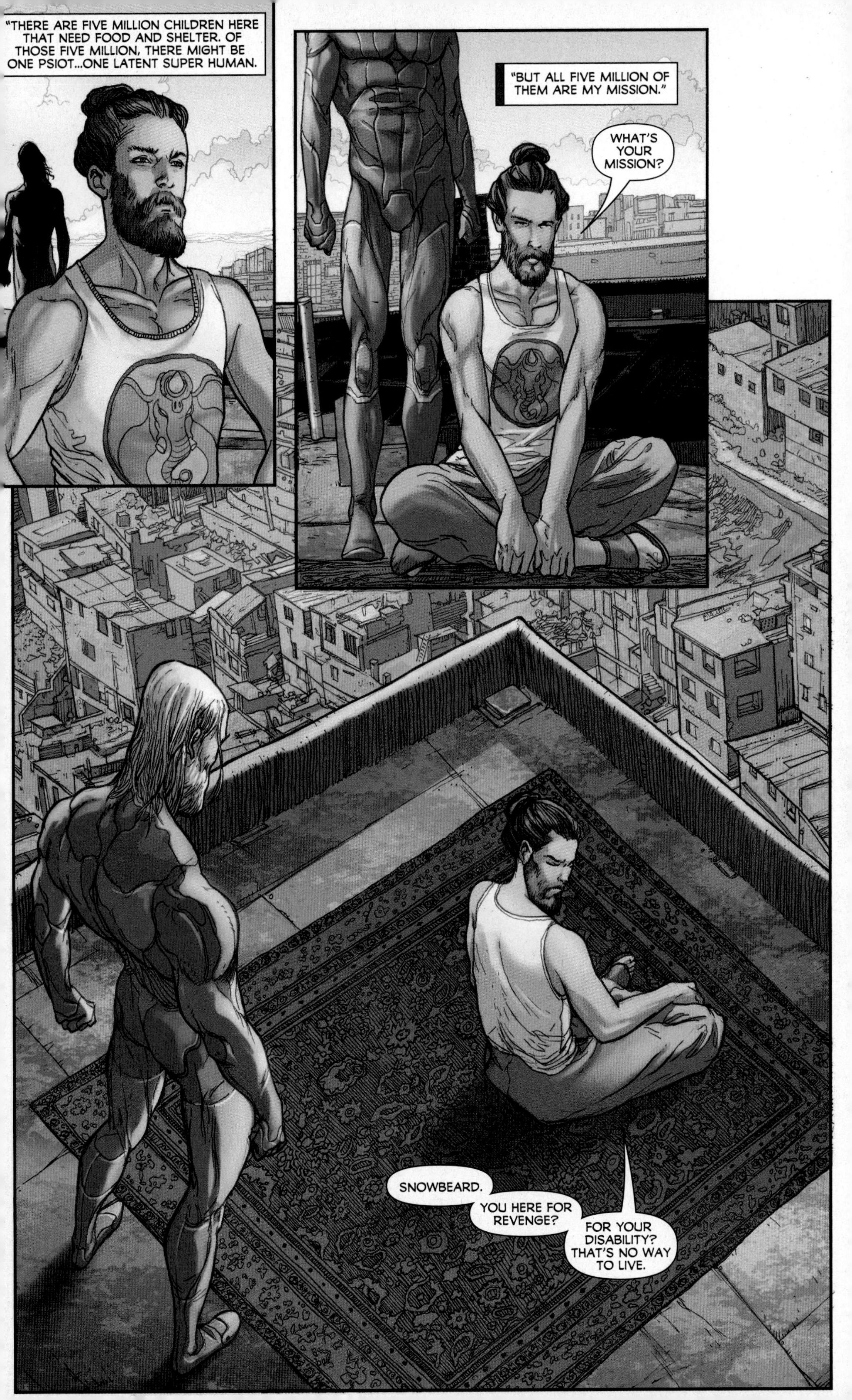
"THERE ARE FIVE MILLION CHILDREN HERE THAT NEED FOOD AND SHELTER. OF THOSE FIVE MILLION, THERE MIGHT BE ONE PSIOT...ONE LATENT SUPER HUMAN.
"BUT ALL FIVE MILLION OF THEM ARE MY MISSION."
WHAT'S YOUR MISSION?
SNOWBEARD.
YOU HERE FOR REVENGE?
FOR YOUR DISABILITY? THAT'S NO WAY TO LIVE.

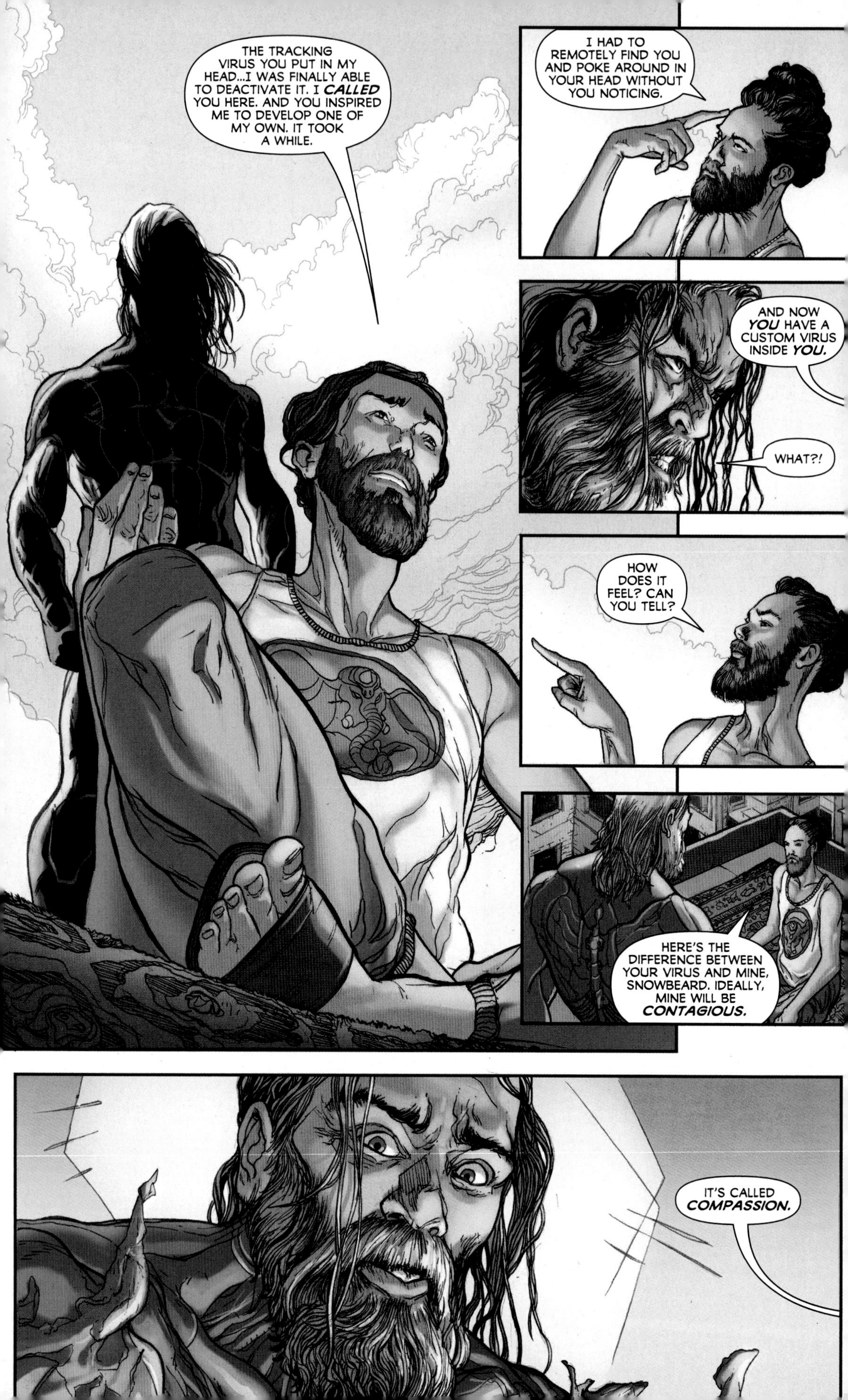
THE TRACKING VIRUS YOU PUT IN MY HEAD...I WAS FINALLY ABLE TO DEACTIVATE IT. I CALLED YOU HERE. AND YOU INSPIRED ME TO DEVELOP ONE OF MY OWN. IT TOOK A WHILE.
I HAD TO REMOTELY FIND YOU AND POKE AROUND IN YOUR HEAD WITHOUT YOU NOTICING.
AND NOW YOU HAVE A CUSTOM VIRUS INSIDE YOU.
WHAT?!
HOW DOES IT FEEL? CAN YOU TELL?
HERE'S THE DIFFERENCE BETWEEN YOUR VIRUS AND MINE, SNOWBEARD. IDEALLY, MINE WILL BE CONTAGIOUS.
IT'S CALLED COMPASSION.

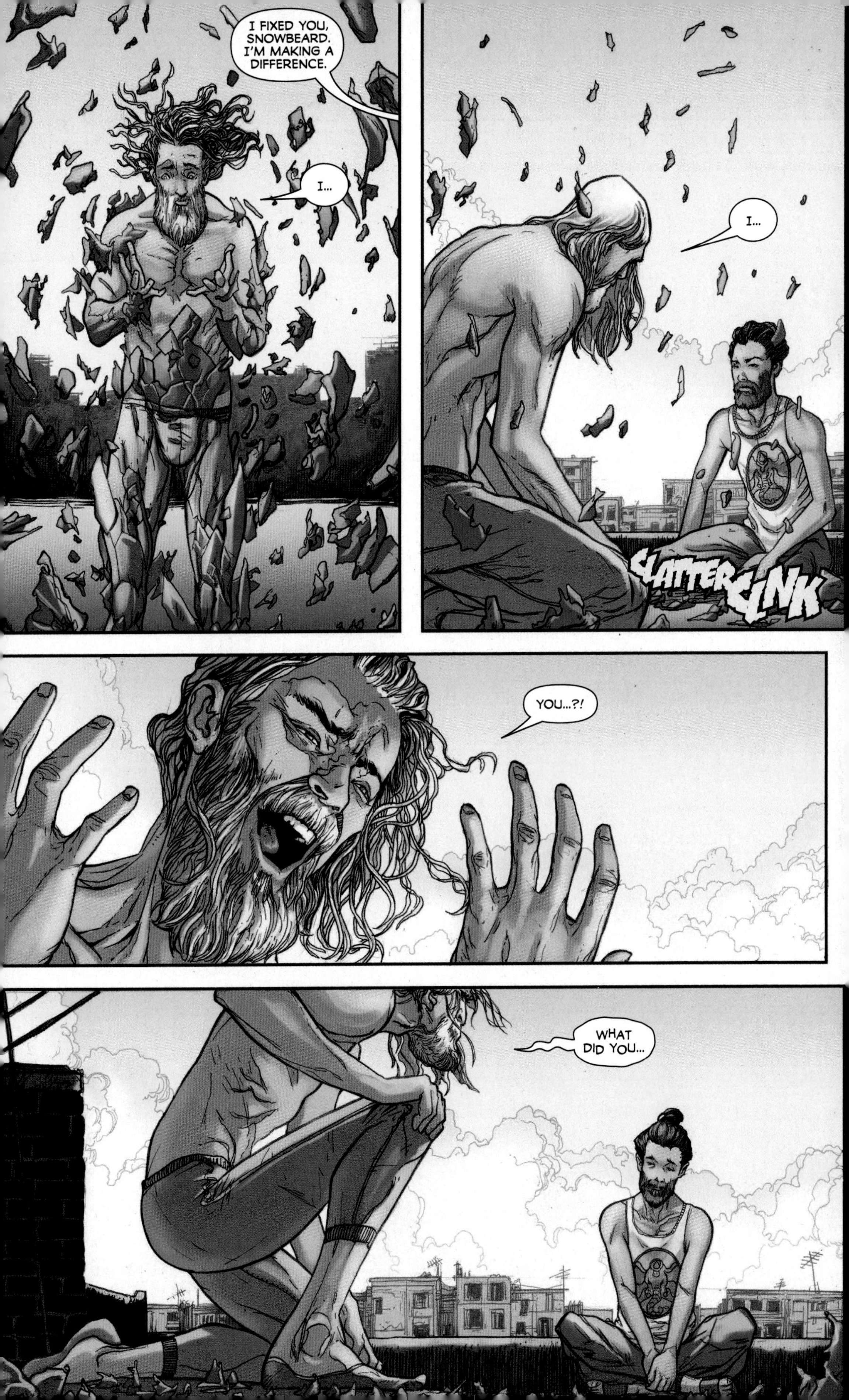
I FIXED YOU, SNOWBEARD. I'M MAKING A DIFFERENCE.
I...
I...
CLATTER CLINK
YOU...?!
WHAT DID YOU...

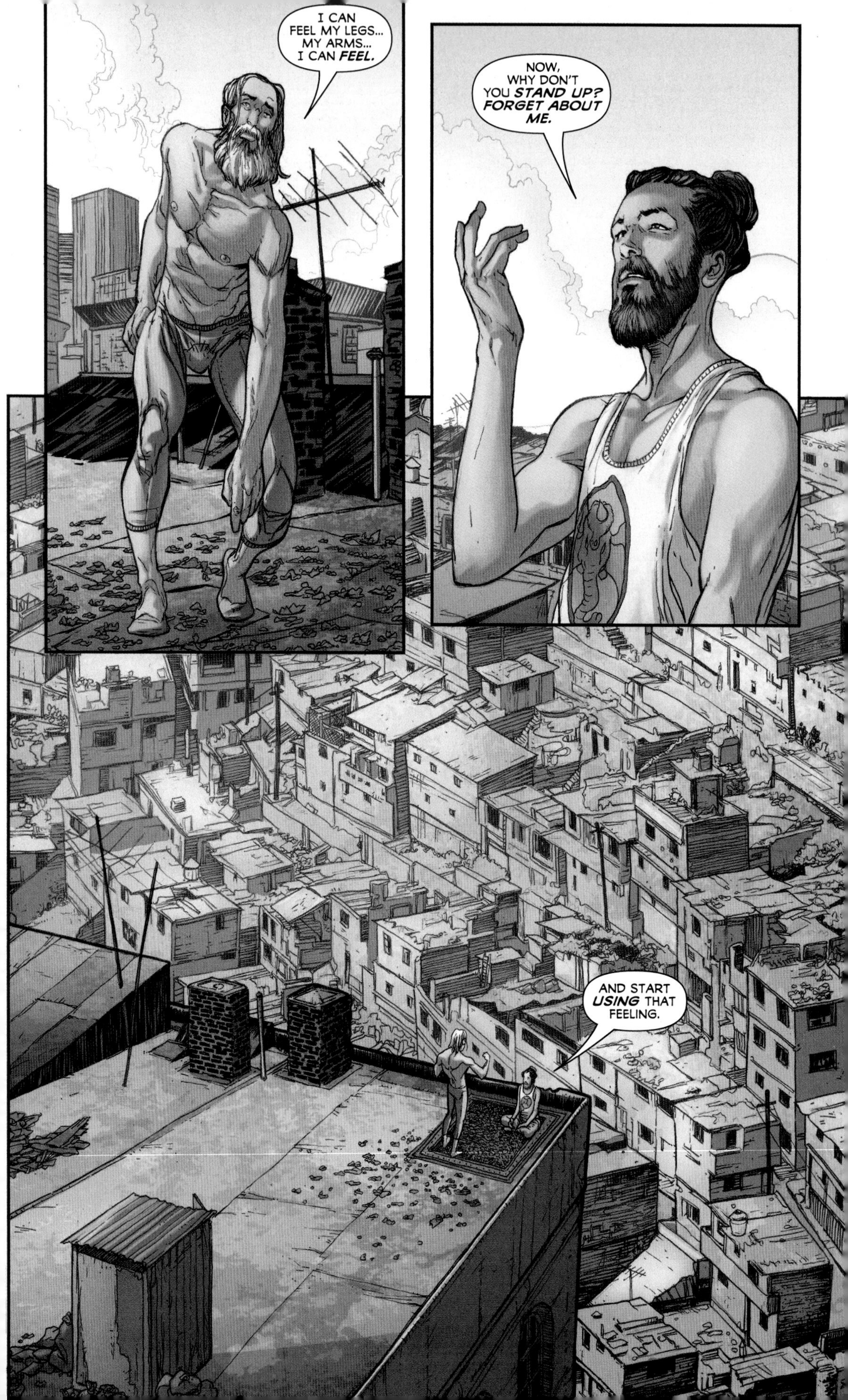
I CAN FEEL MY LEGS... MY ARMS... I CAN FEEL.
NOW, WHY DON'T YOU STAND UP? FORGET ABOUT ME.
AND START USING THAT FEELING.

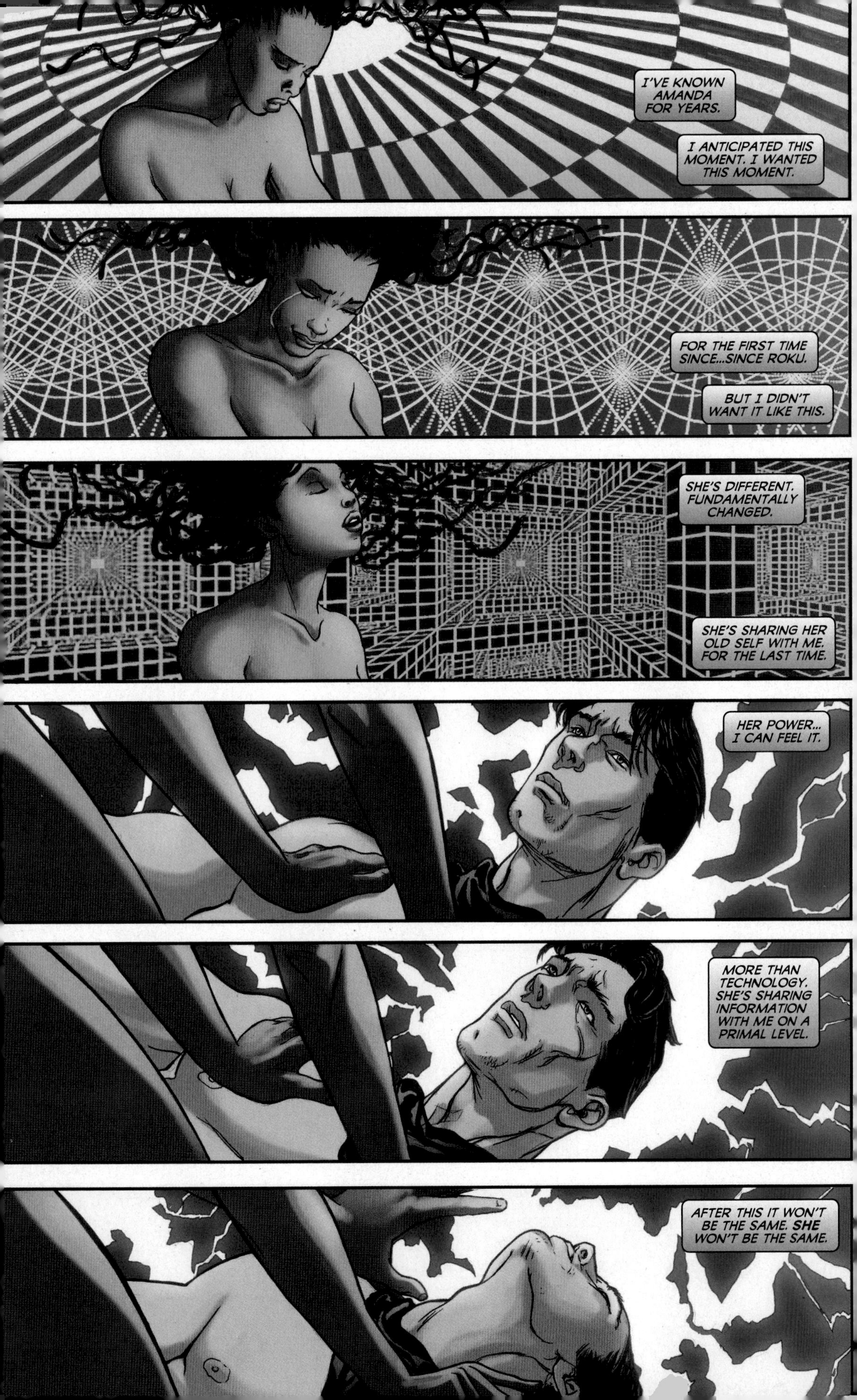
I'VE KNOWN AMANDA FOR YEARS.
I ANTICIPATED THIS MOMENT. I WANTED THIS MOMENT.
FOR THE FIRST TIME SINCE...SINCE ROKU.
BUT I DIDN'T WANT IT LIKE THIS.
SHE'S DIFFERENT. FUNDAMENTALLY CHANGED.
SHE'S SHARING HER OLD SELF WITH ME. FOR THE LAST TIME.
HER POWER... I CAN FEEL IT.
MORE THAN TECHNOLOGY. SHE'S SHARING INFORMATION WITH ME ON A PRIMAL LEVEL.
AFTER THIS IT WON'T BE THE SAME. **SHE** WON'T BE THE SAME.

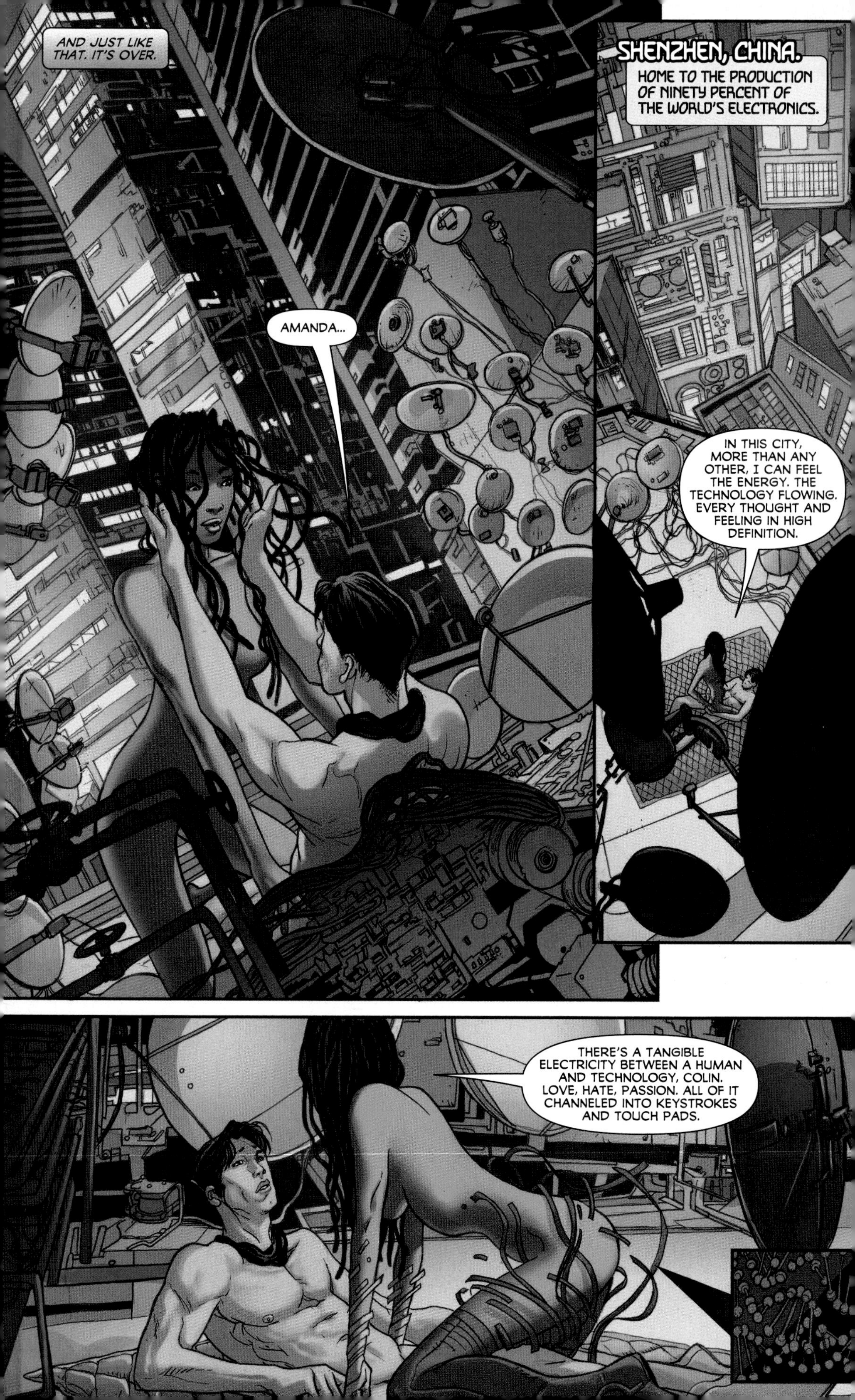
AND JUST LIKE THAT. IT'S OVER.
AMANDA...
SHENZHEN, CHINA.
HOME TO THE PRODUCTION OF NINETY PERCENT OF THE WORLD'S ELECTRONICS.
IN THIS CITY, MORE THAN ANY OTHER, I CAN FEEL THE ENERGY. THE TECHNOLOGY FLOWING. EVERY THOUGHT AND FEELING IN HIGH DEFINITION.
THERE'S A TANGIBLE ELECTRICITY BETWEEN A HUMAN AND TECHNOLOGY, COLIN. LOVE, HATE, PASSION. ALL OF IT CHANNELED INTO KEYSTROKES AND TOUCH PADS.

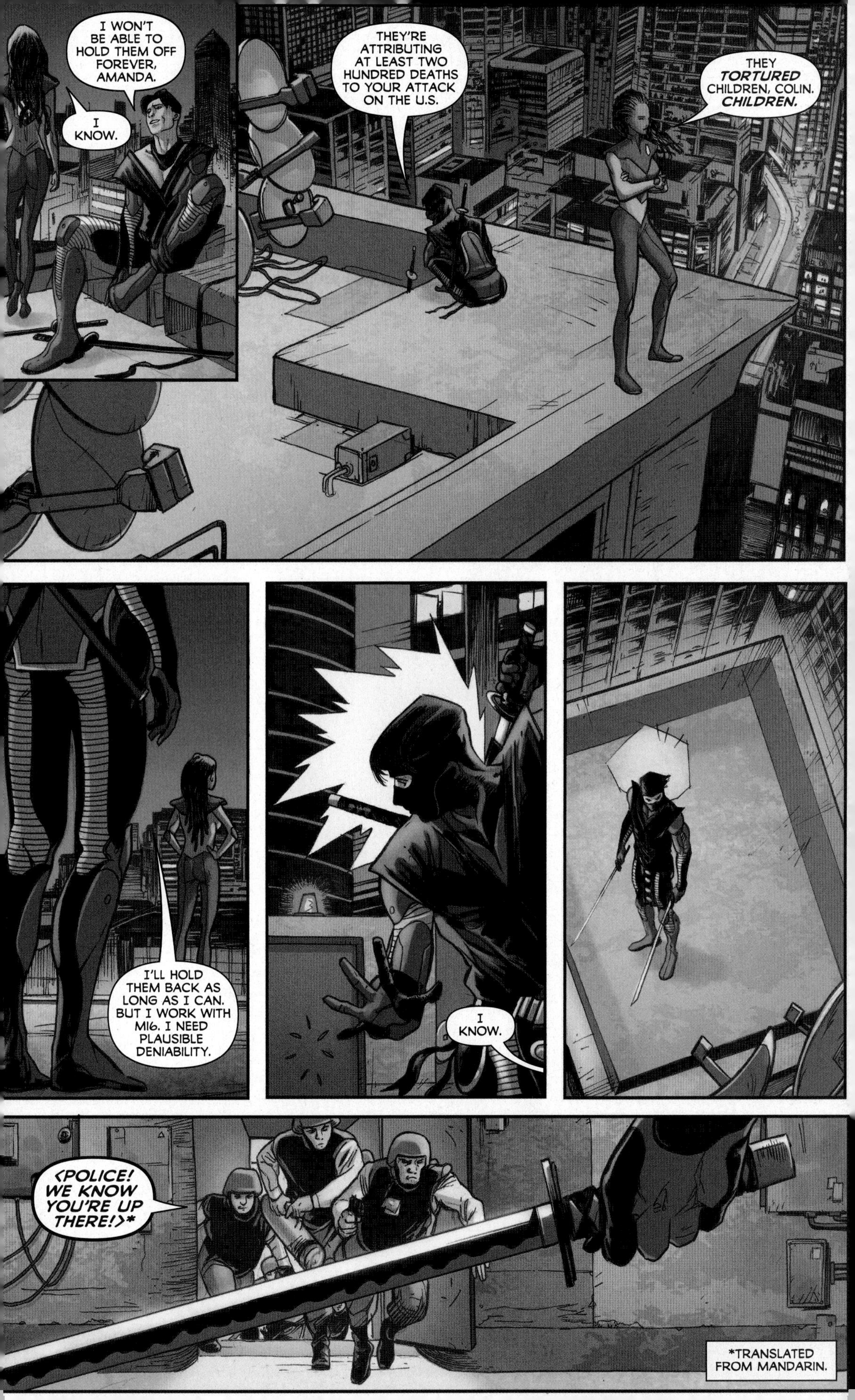
I WON'T BE ABLE TO HOLD THEM OFF FOREVER, AMANDA.
I KNOW.
THEY'RE ATTRIBUTING AT LEAST TWO HUNDRED DEATHS TO YOUR ATTACK ON THE U.S.
THEY TORTURED CHILDREN, COLIN. CHILDREN.
I'LL HOLD THEM BACK AS LONG AS I CAN. BUT I WORK WITH MI6. I NEED PLAUSIBLE DENIABILITY.
I KNOW.
<POLICE! WE KNOW YOU'RE UP THERE!>*
*TRANSLATED FROM MANDARIN.

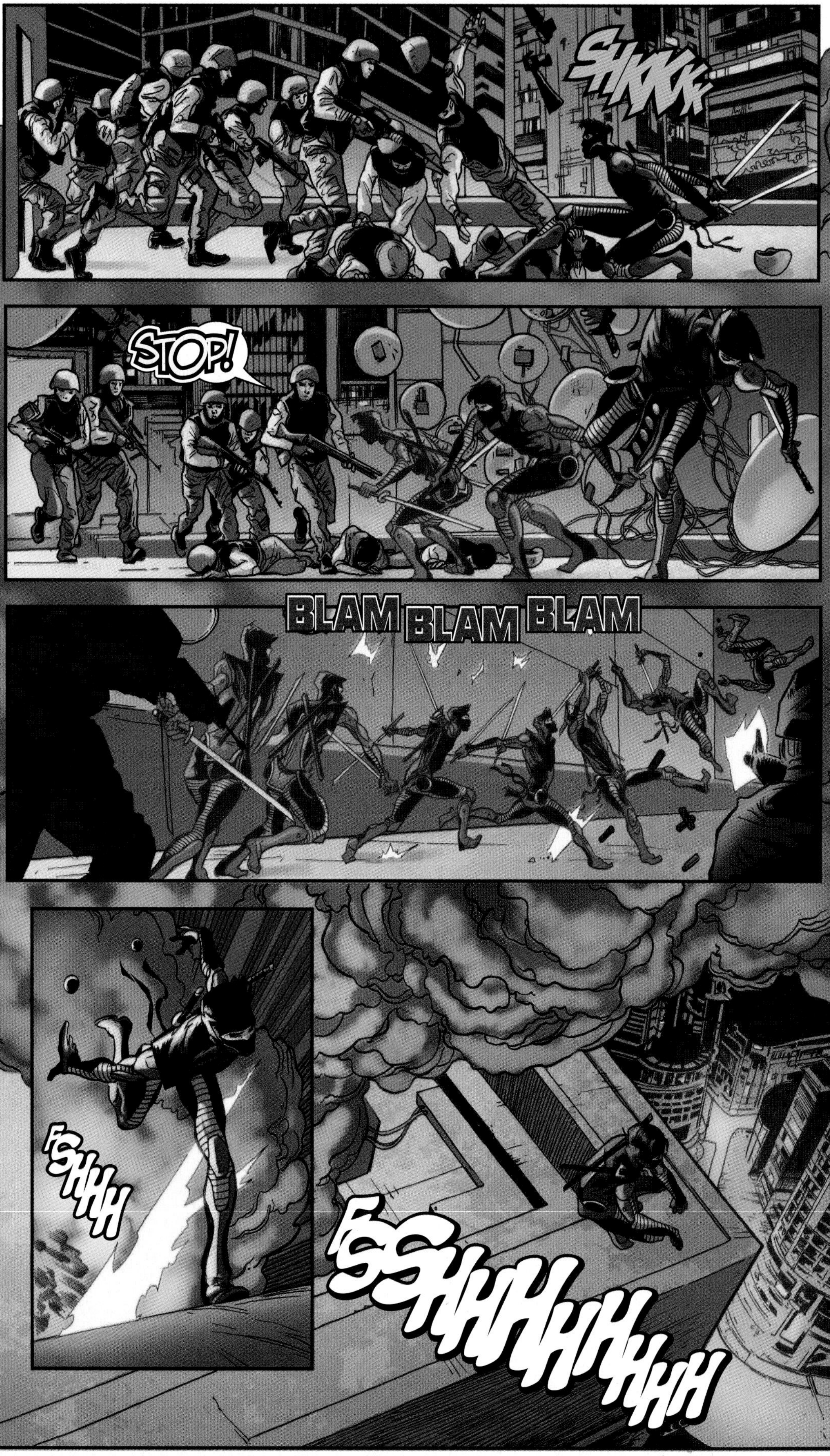
SHKKK
STOP!
BLAM BLAM BLAM
FSHHH
FSSHHHHHHHH

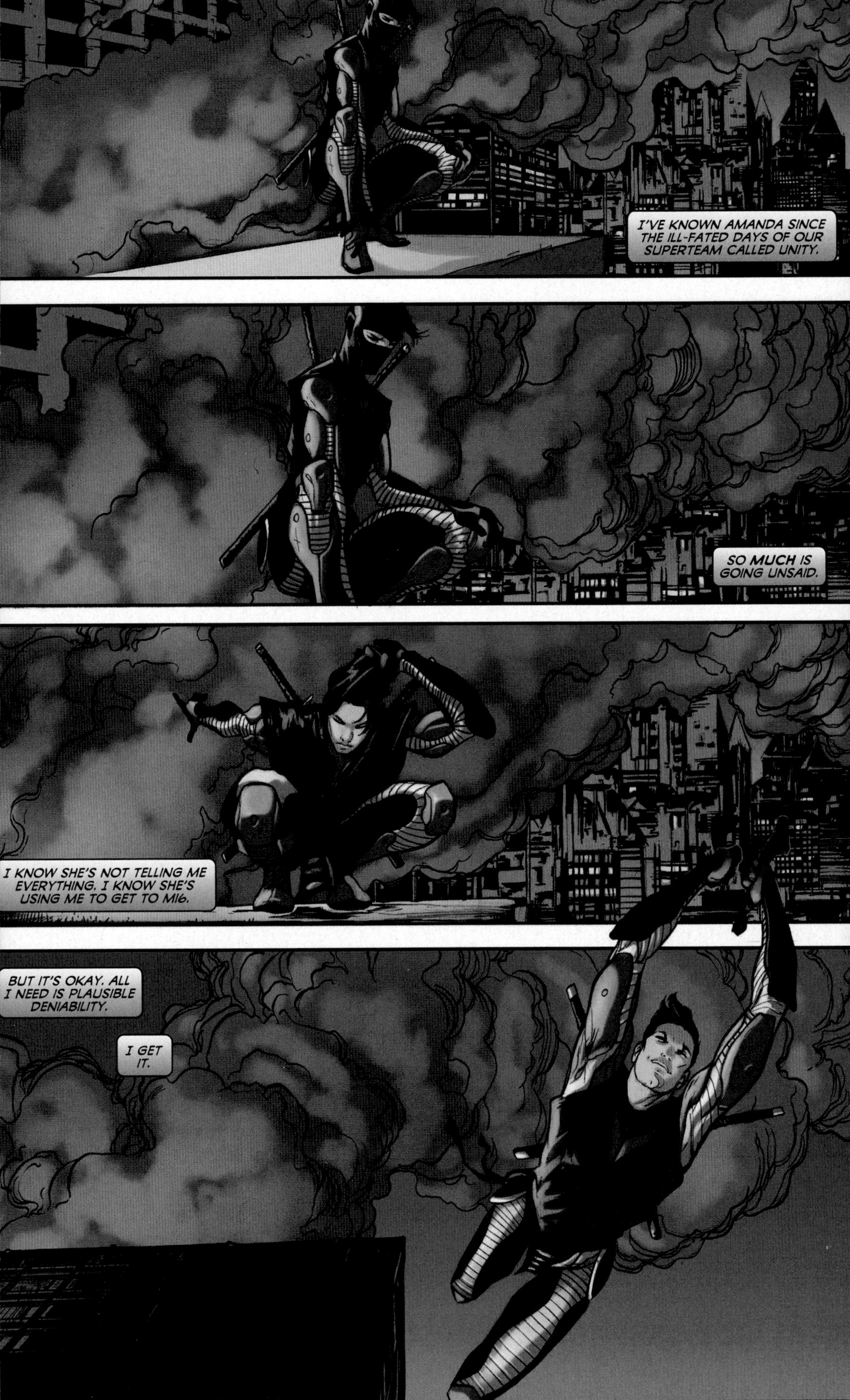
I'VE KNOWN AMANDA SINCE THE ILL-FATED DAYS OF OUR SUPERTEAM CALLED UNITY.
SO MUCH IS GOING UNSAID.
I KNOW SHE'S NOT TELLING ME EVERYTHING. I KNOW SHE'S USING ME TO GET TO MI6.
BUT IT'S OKAY. ALL I NEED IS PLAUSIBLE DENIABILITY.
I GET IT.

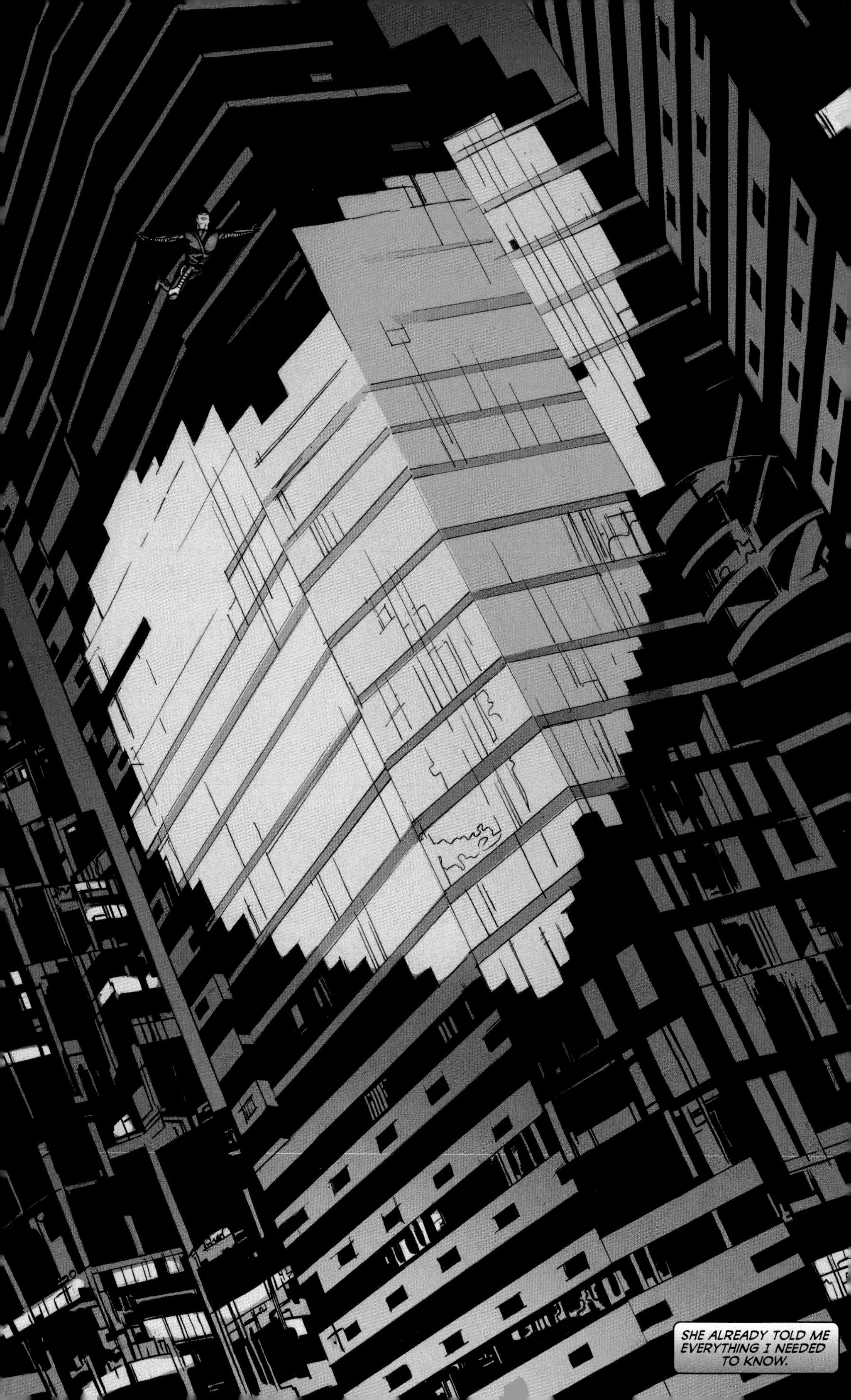
SHE ALREADY TOLD ME EVERYTHING I NEEDED TO KNOW.

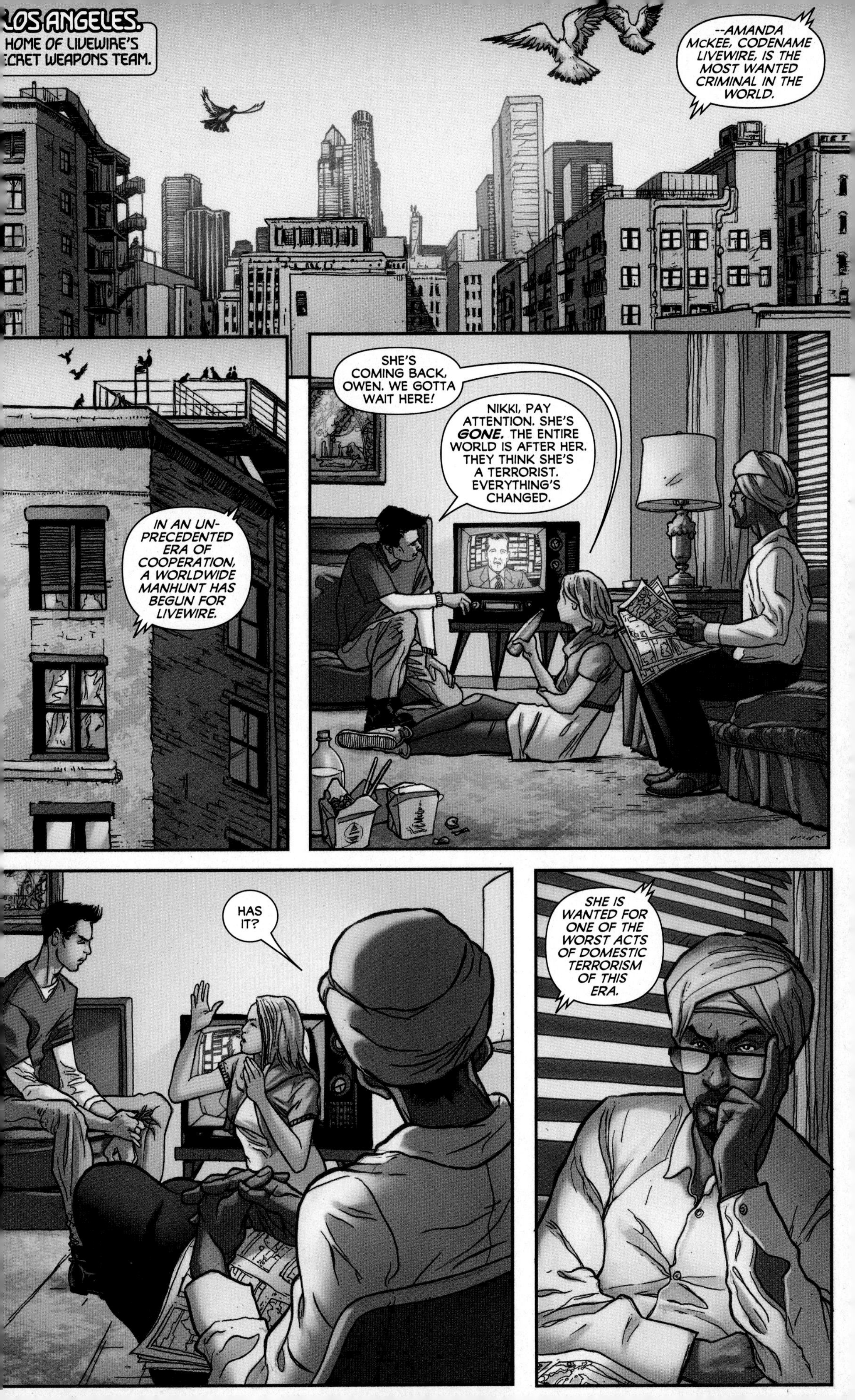
LOS ANGELES.
HOME OF LIVEWIRE'S SECRET WEAPONS TEAM.
--AMANDA McKEE, CODENAME LIVEWIRE, IS THE MOST WANTED CRIMINAL IN THE WORLD.
IN AN UN-PRECEDENTED ERA OF COOPERATION, A WORLDWIDE MANHUNT HAS BEGUN FOR LIVEWIRE.
SHE'S COMING BACK, OWEN. WE GOTTA WAIT HERE!
NIKKI, PAY ATTENTION. SHE'S GONE. THE ENTIRE WORLD IS AFTER HER. THEY THINK SHE'S A TERRORIST. EVERYTHING'S CHANGED.
HAS IT?
SHE IS WANTED FOR ONE OF THE WORST ACTS OF DOMESTIC TERRORISM OF THIS ERA.

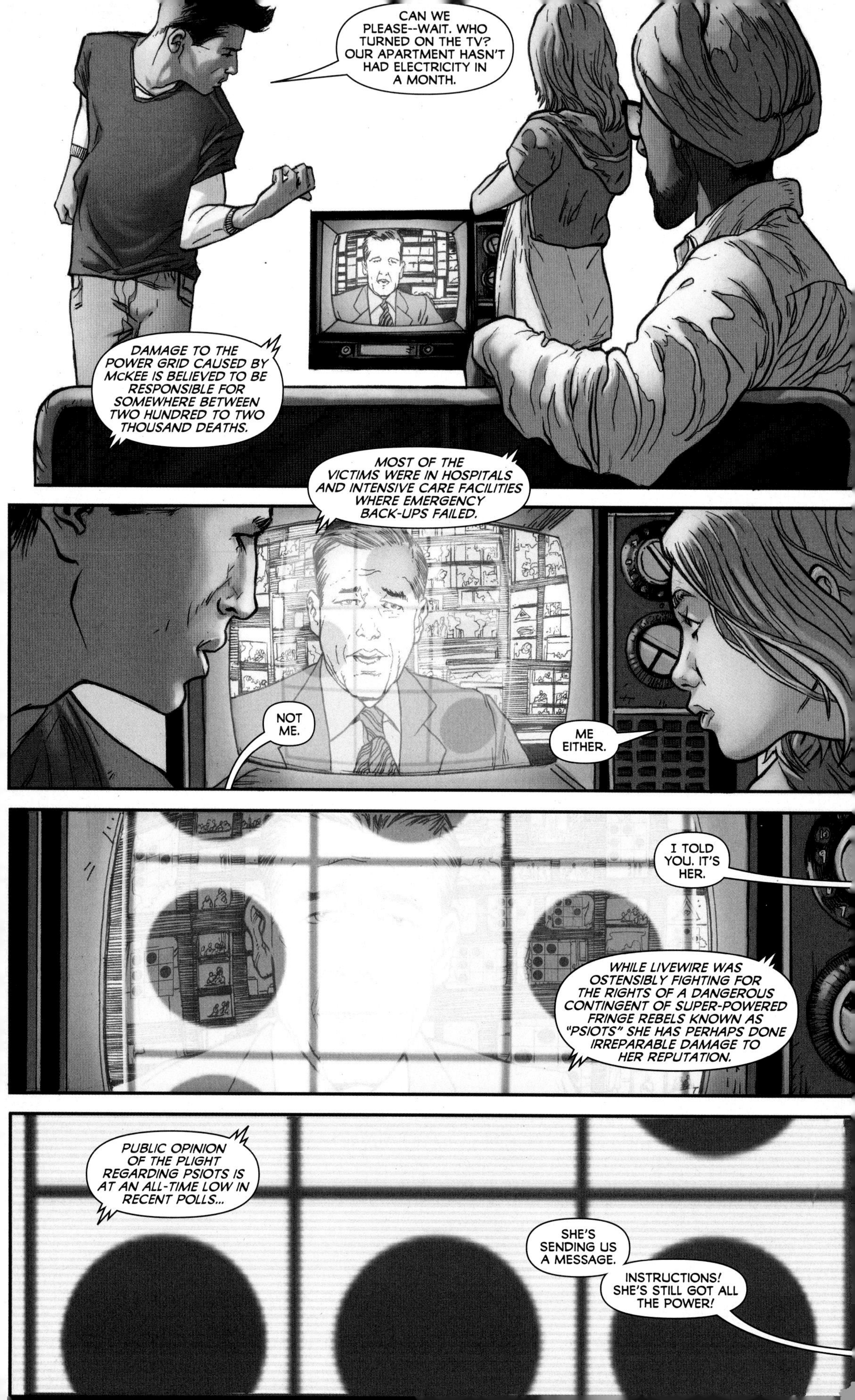
CAN WE PLEASE--WAIT. WHO TURNED ON THE TV? OUR APARTMENT HASN'T HAD ELECTRICITY IN A MONTH.
DAMAGE TO THE POWER GRID CAUSED BY McKEE IS BELIEVED TO BE RESPONSIBLE FOR SOMEWHERE BETWEEN TWO HUNDRED TO TWO THOUSAND DEATHS.
MOST OF THE VICTIMS WERE IN HOSPITALS AND INTENSIVE CARE FACILITIES WHERE EMERGENCY BACK-UPS FAILED.
NOT ME.
ME EITHER.
I TOLD YOU. IT'S HER.
WHILE LIVEWIRE WAS OSTENSIBLY FIGHTING FOR THE RIGHTS OF A DANGEROUS CONTINGENT OF SUPER-POWERED FRINGE REBELS KNOWN AS "PSIOTS" SHE HAS PERHAPS DONE IRREPARABLE DAMAGE TO HER REPUTATION.
PUBLIC OPINION OF THE PLIGHT REGARDING PSIOTS IS AT AN ALL-TIME LOW IN RECENT POLLS...
SHE'S SENDING US A MESSAGE.
INSTRUCTIONS! SHE'S STILL GOT ALL THE POWER!

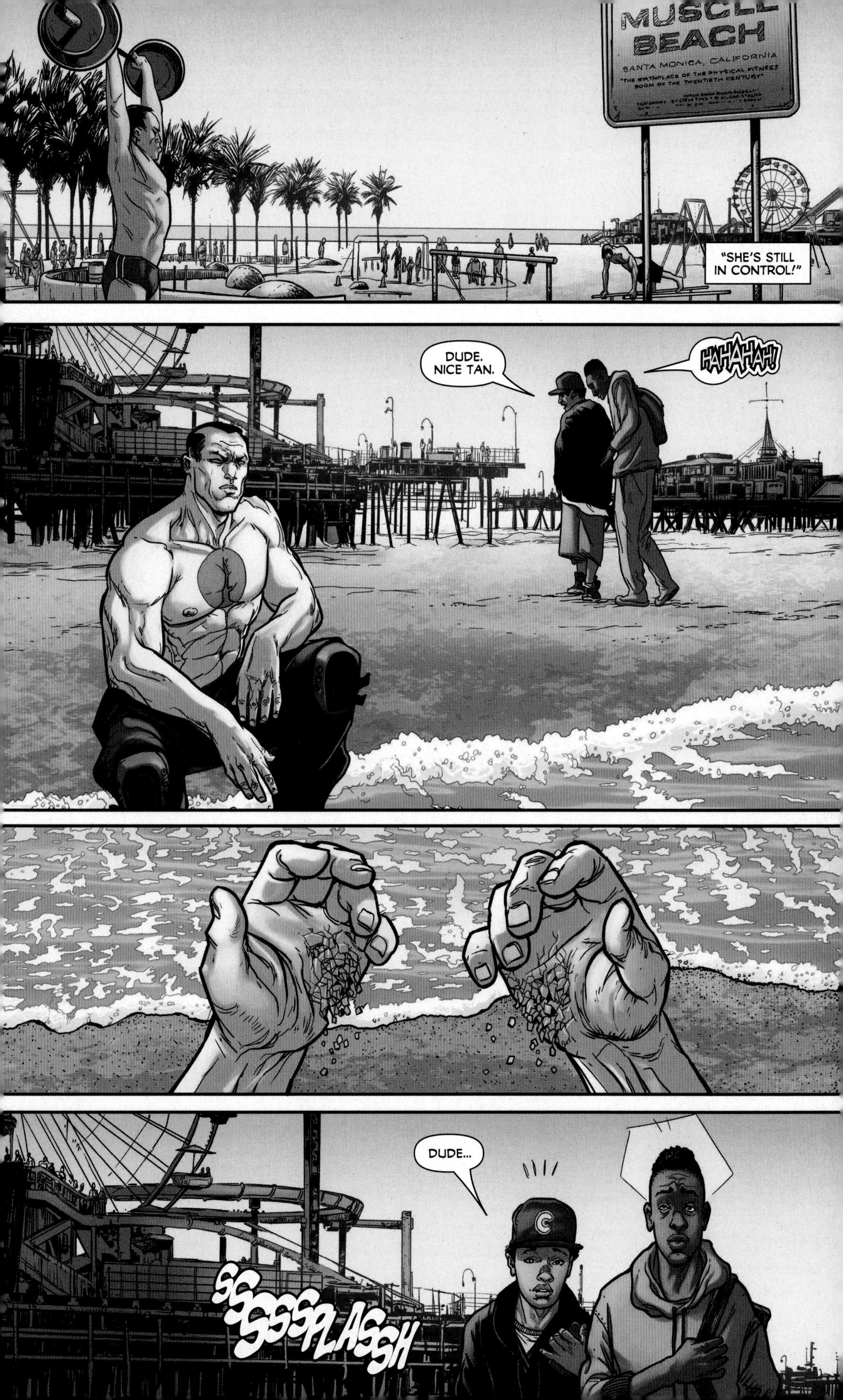

MUSCLE BEACH
SANTA MONICA, CALIFORNIA
"THE BIRTHPLACE OF THE PHYSICAL FITNESS BOOM OF THE TWENTIETH CENTURY"
"SHE'S STILL IN CONTROL!"
DUDE. NICE TAN.
HAHAHAH!
DUDE...
SSSSSPLASSH

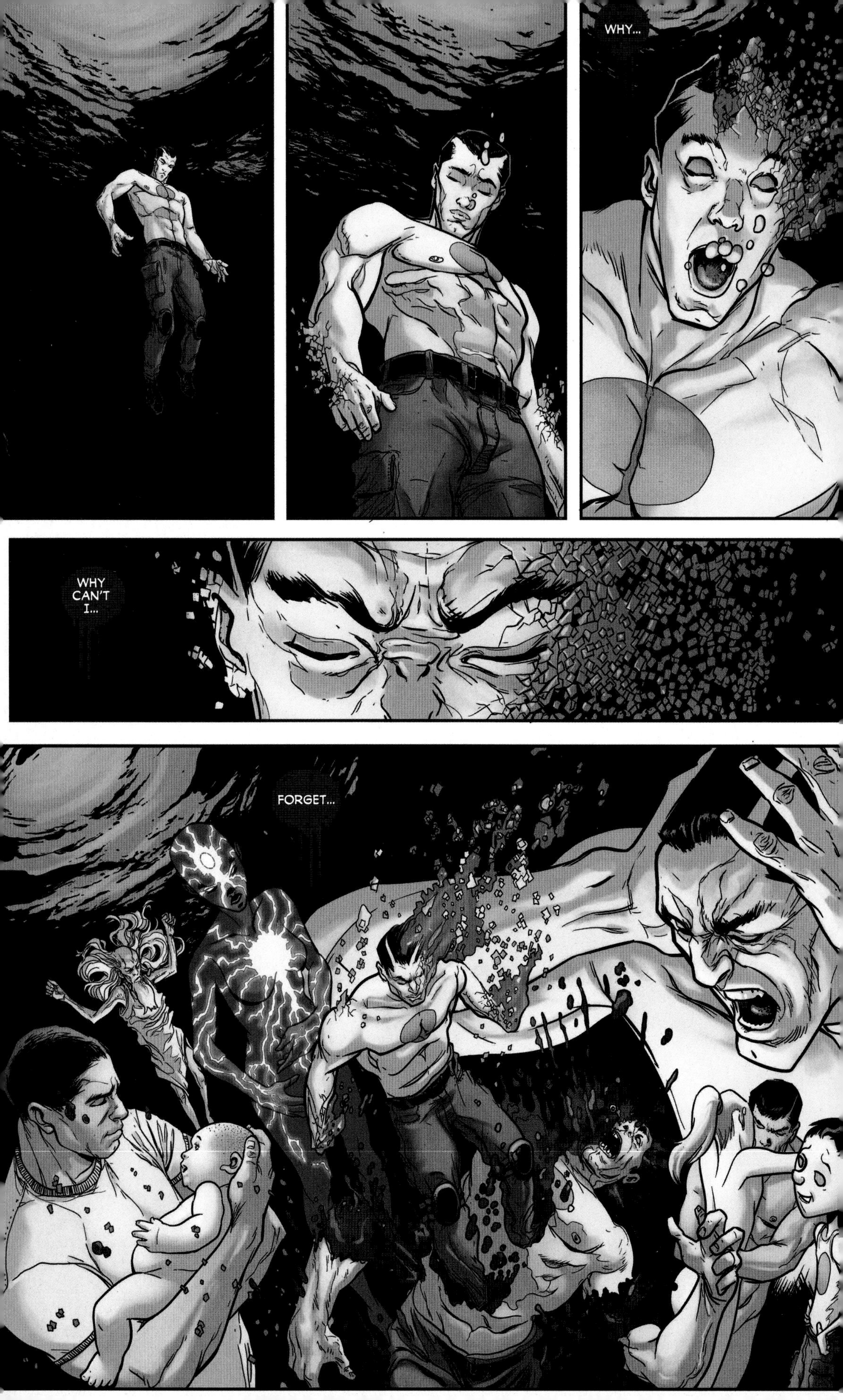
WHY...
WHY CAN'T I...
FORGET...

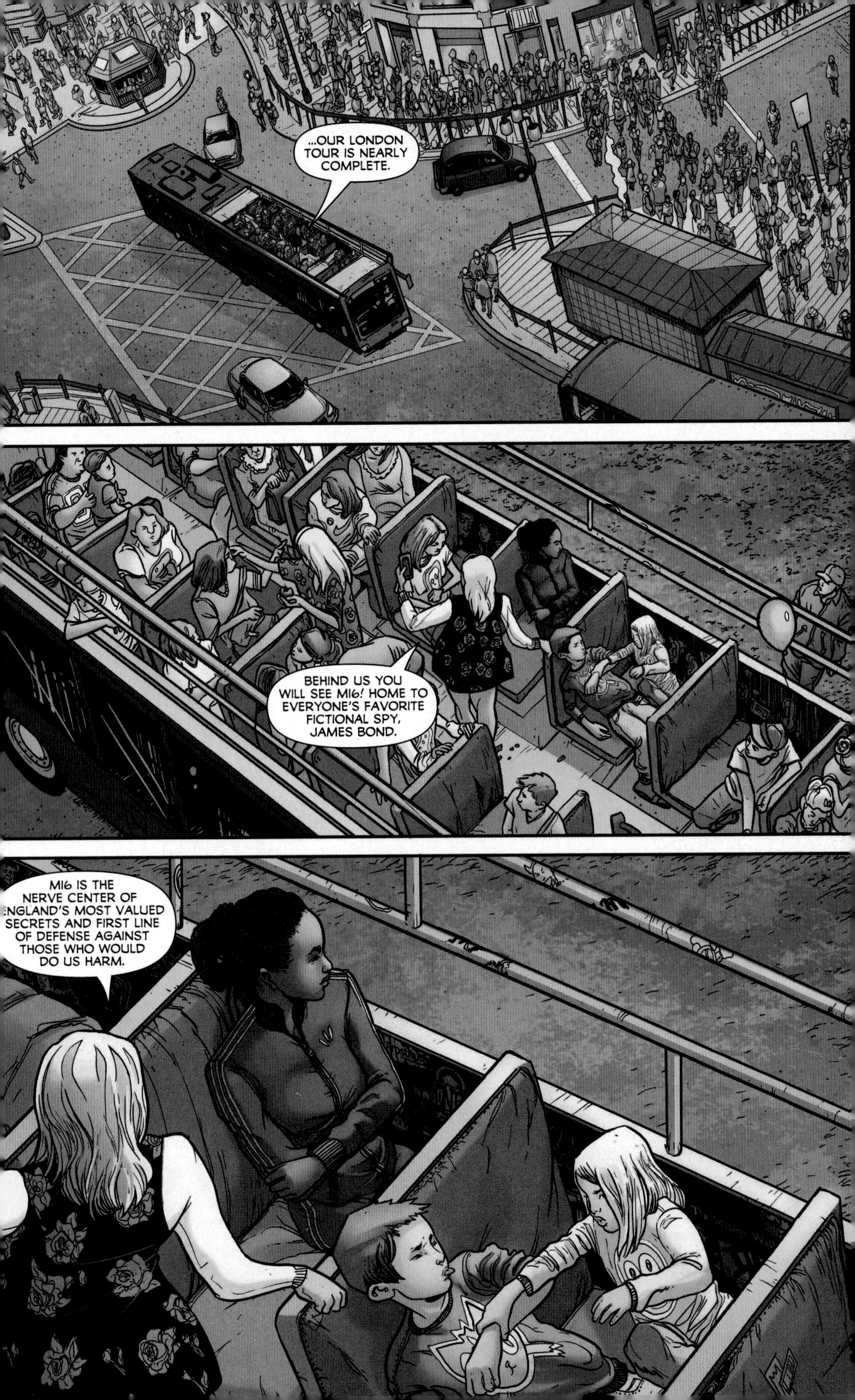
...OUR LONDON TOUR IS NEARLY COMPLETE.
BEHIND US YOU WILL SEE MI6! HOME TO EVERYONE'S FAVORITE FICTIONAL SPY, JAMES BOND.
MI6 IS THE NERVE CENTER OF ENGLAND'S MOST VALUED SECRETS AND FIRST LINE OF DEFENSE AGAINST THOSE WHO WOULD DO US HARM.

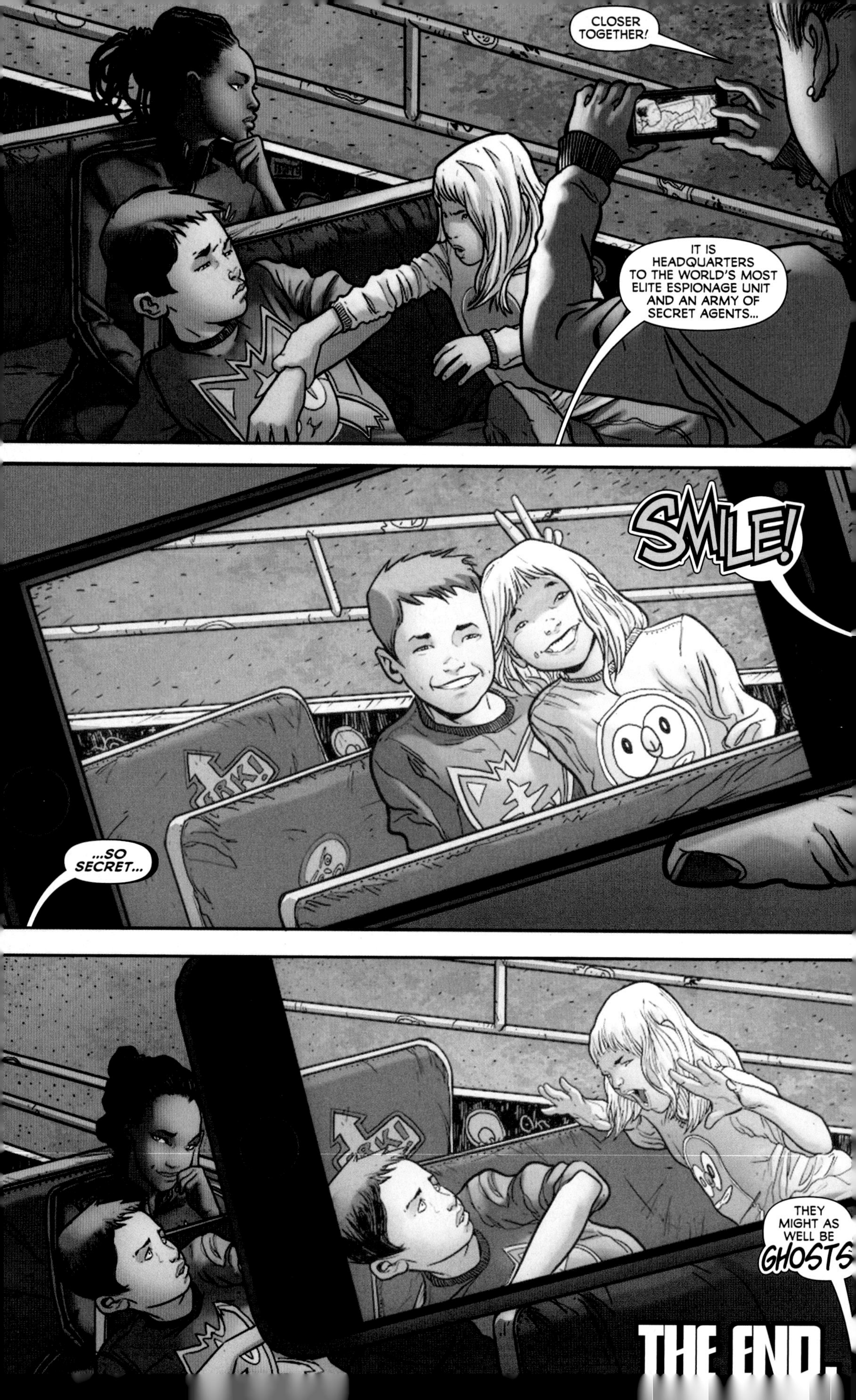
CLOSER TOGETHER!
IT IS HEADQUARTERS TO THE WORLD'S MOST ELITE ESPIONAGE UNIT AND AN ARMY OF SECRET AGENTS...
SMILE!
...SO SECRET...
THEY MIGHT AS WELL BE GHOSTS
THE END.

GALLERY

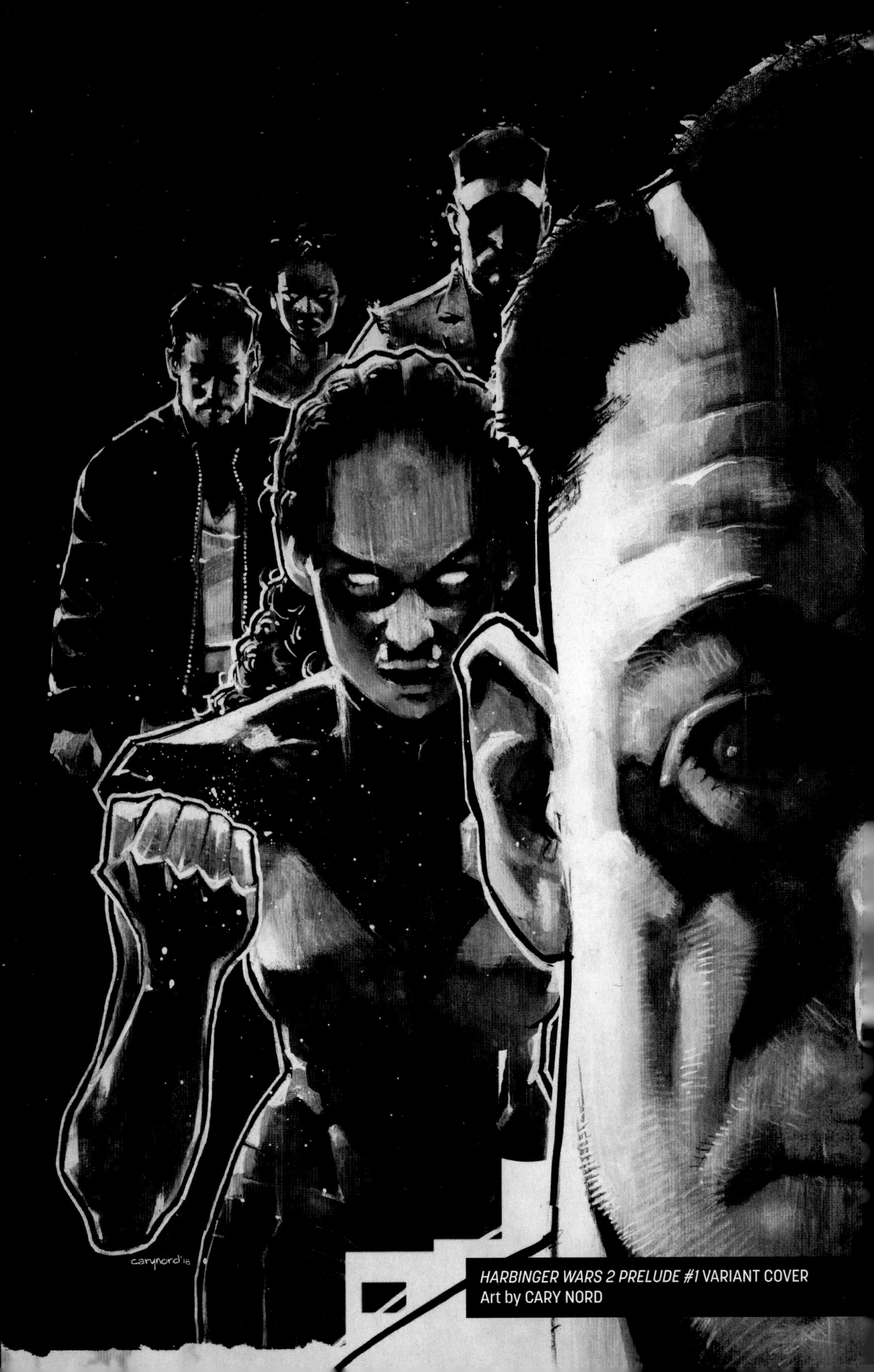
carynord'18

HARBINGER WARS 2 PRELUDE #1 VARIANT COVER
Art by CARY NORD

HARBINGER WARS 2 PRELUDE #1 PRE-ORDER EDITION COVER
Art by KHARI EVANS with ANDREW DALHOUSE

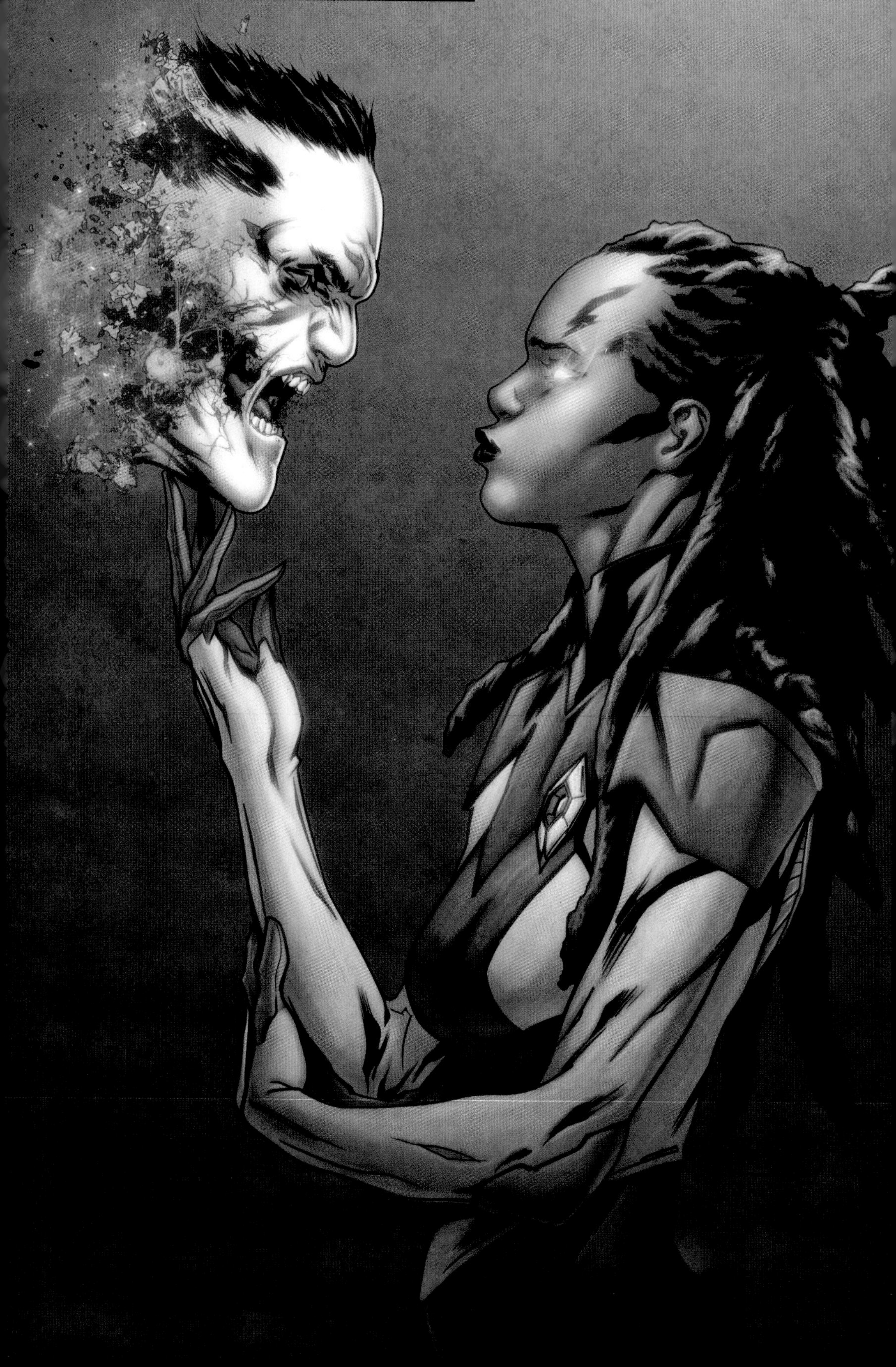

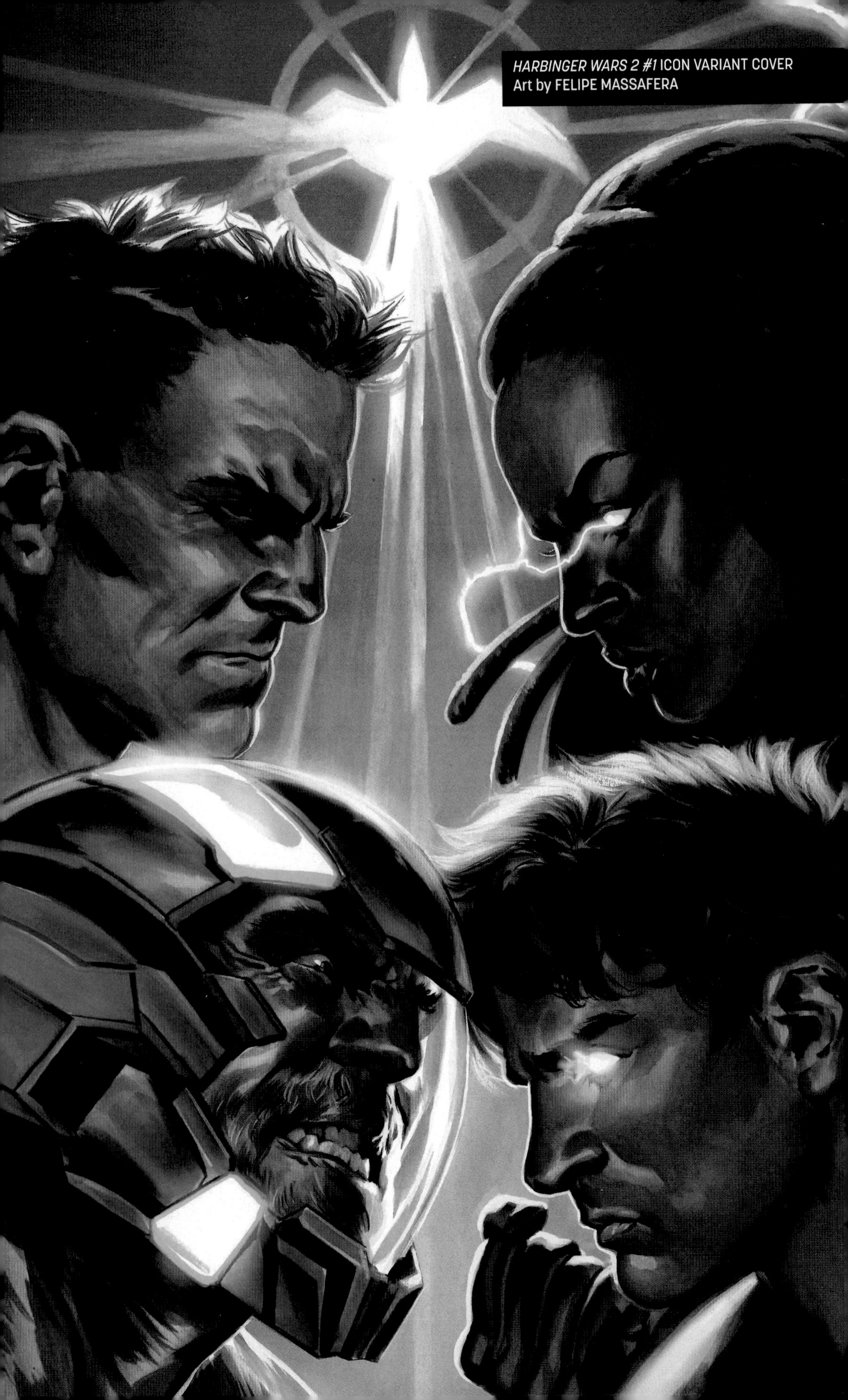

HARBINGER WARS 2 #1 ICON VARIANT COVER
Art by FELIPE MASSAFERA

HARBINGER WARS 2 #1 COVER B
Art by MICO SUAYAN with DAVID BARON

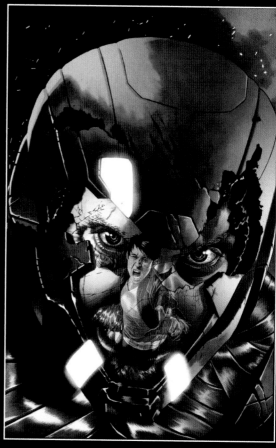

HARBINGER WARS 2 #2 COVER B
Art by MICO SUAYAN with DAVID BARON

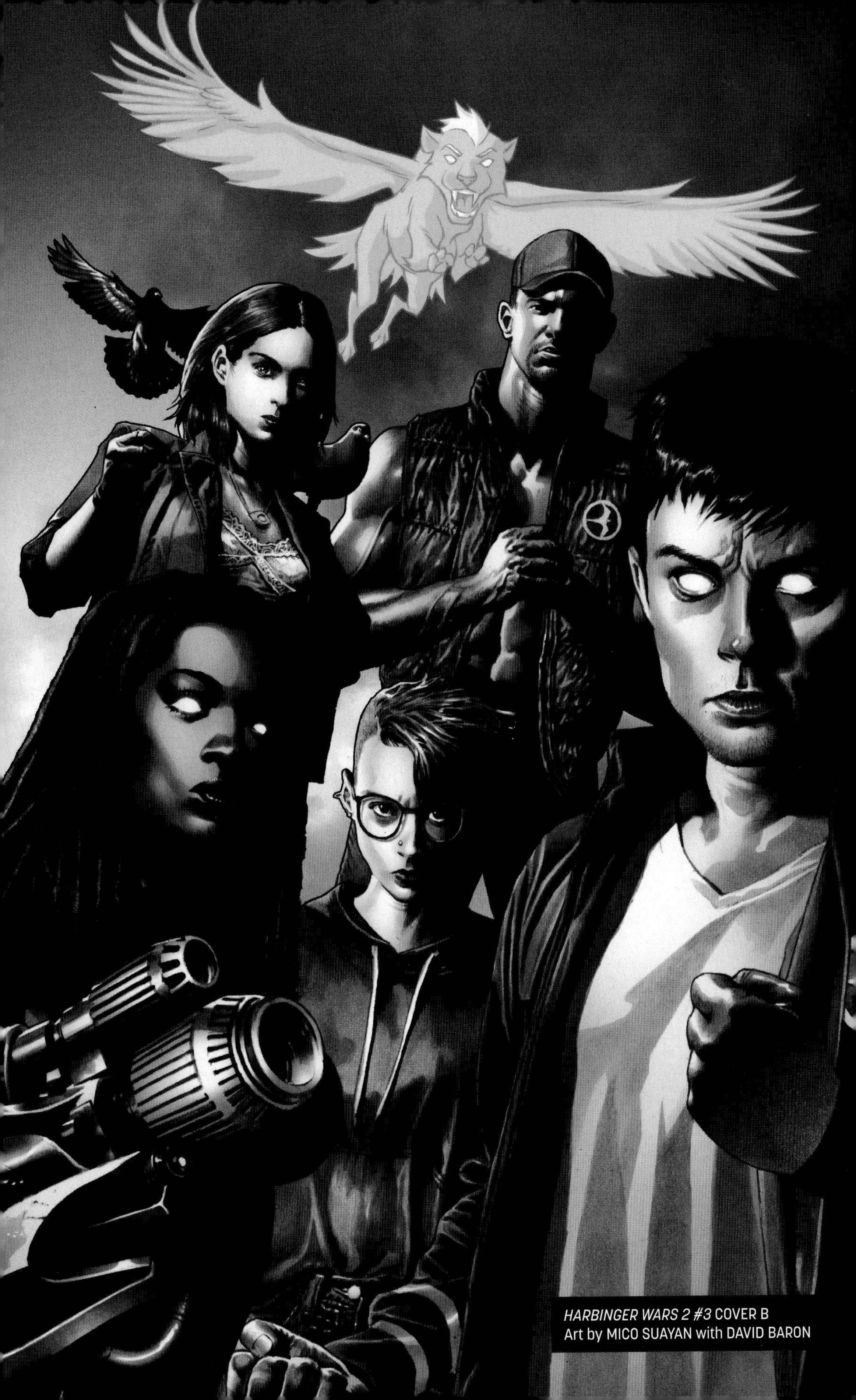

HARBINGER WARS 2 #3 COVER B
Art by MICO SUAYAN with DAVID BARON

HARBINGER WARS 2 #2 PRE-ORDER EDITION COVER
Art by TOMÁS GIORELLO with DIEGO RODRIGUEZ

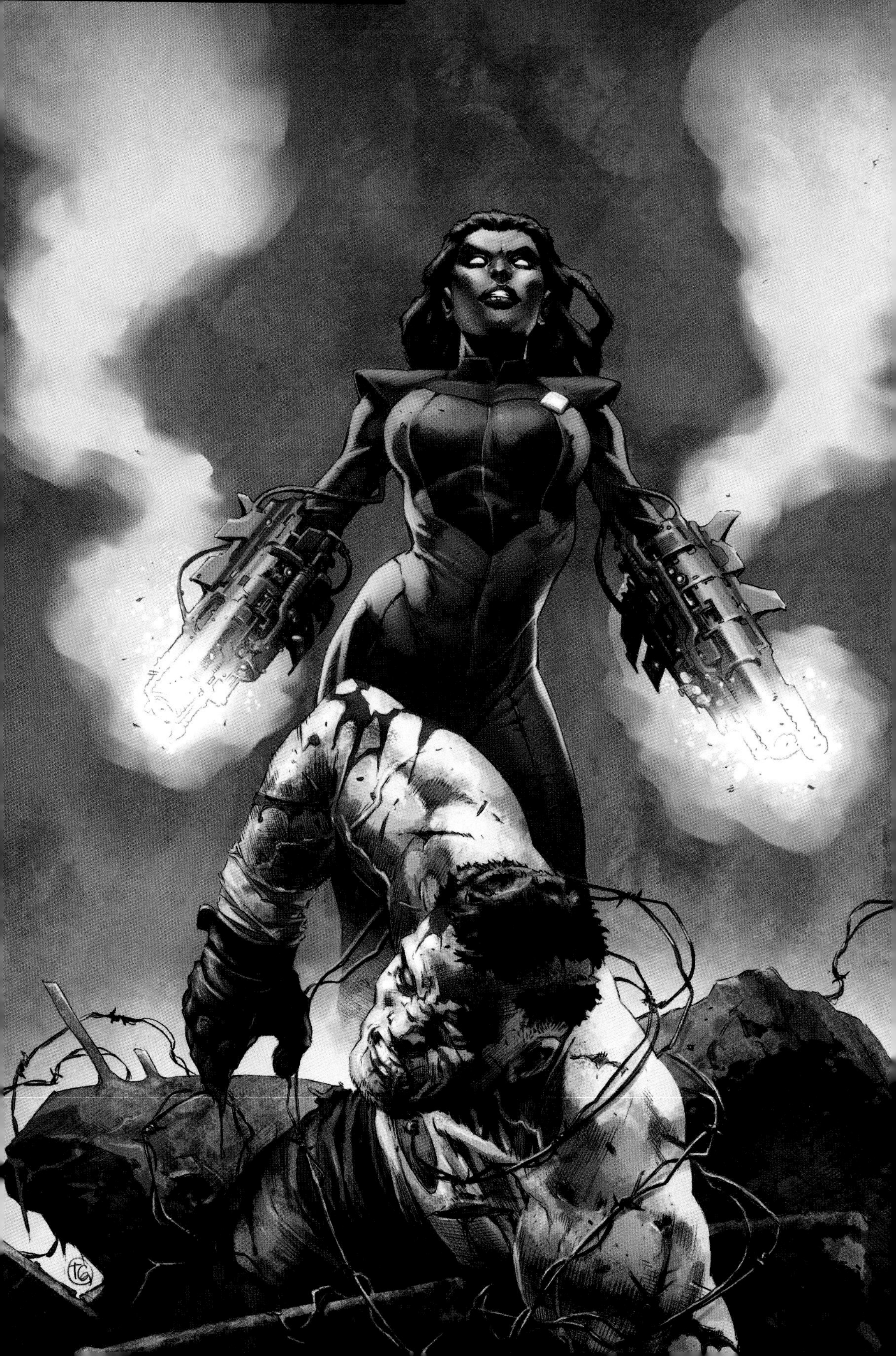

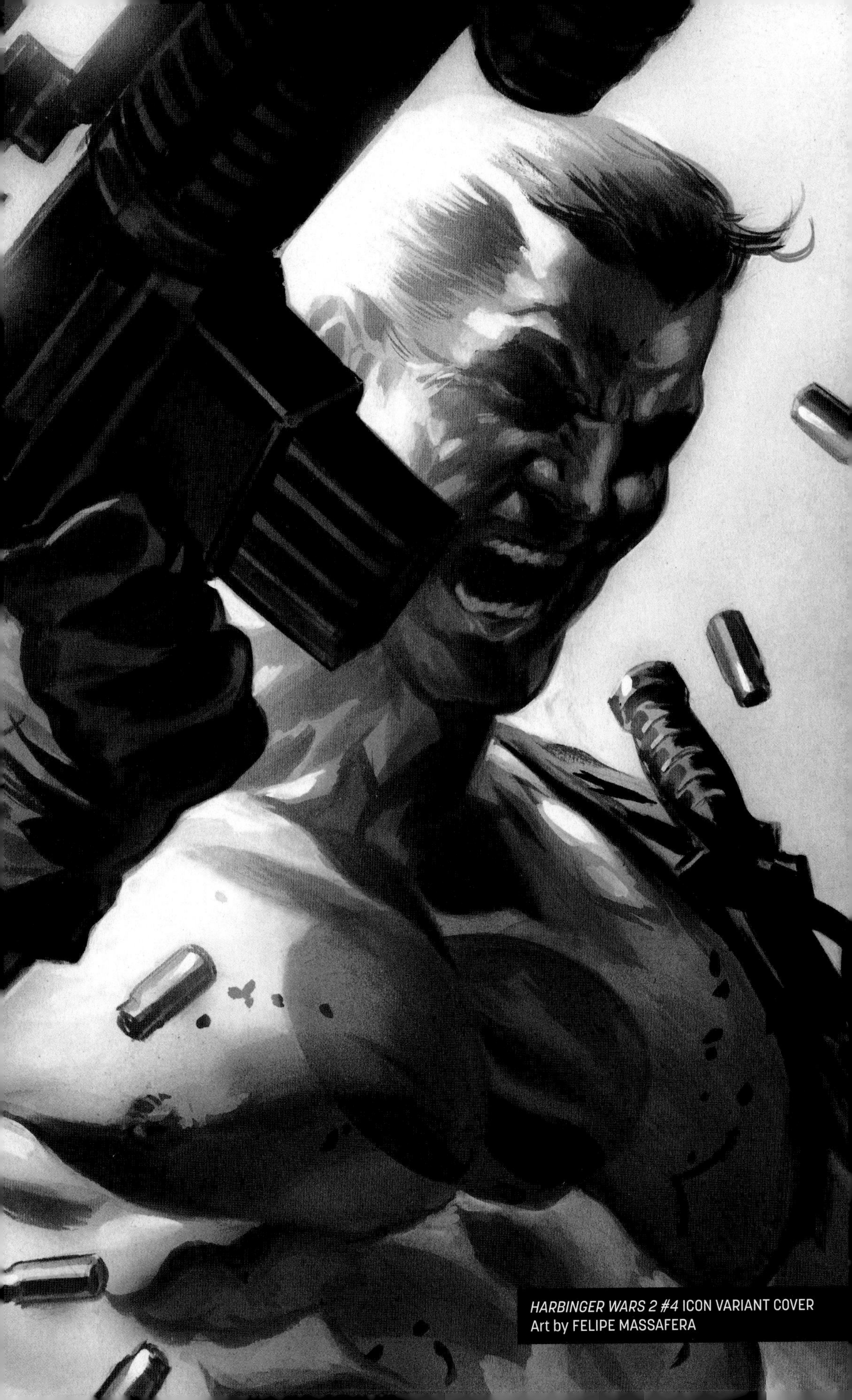

HARBINGER WARS 2 #4 ICON VARIANT COVER
Art by FELIPE MASSAFERA

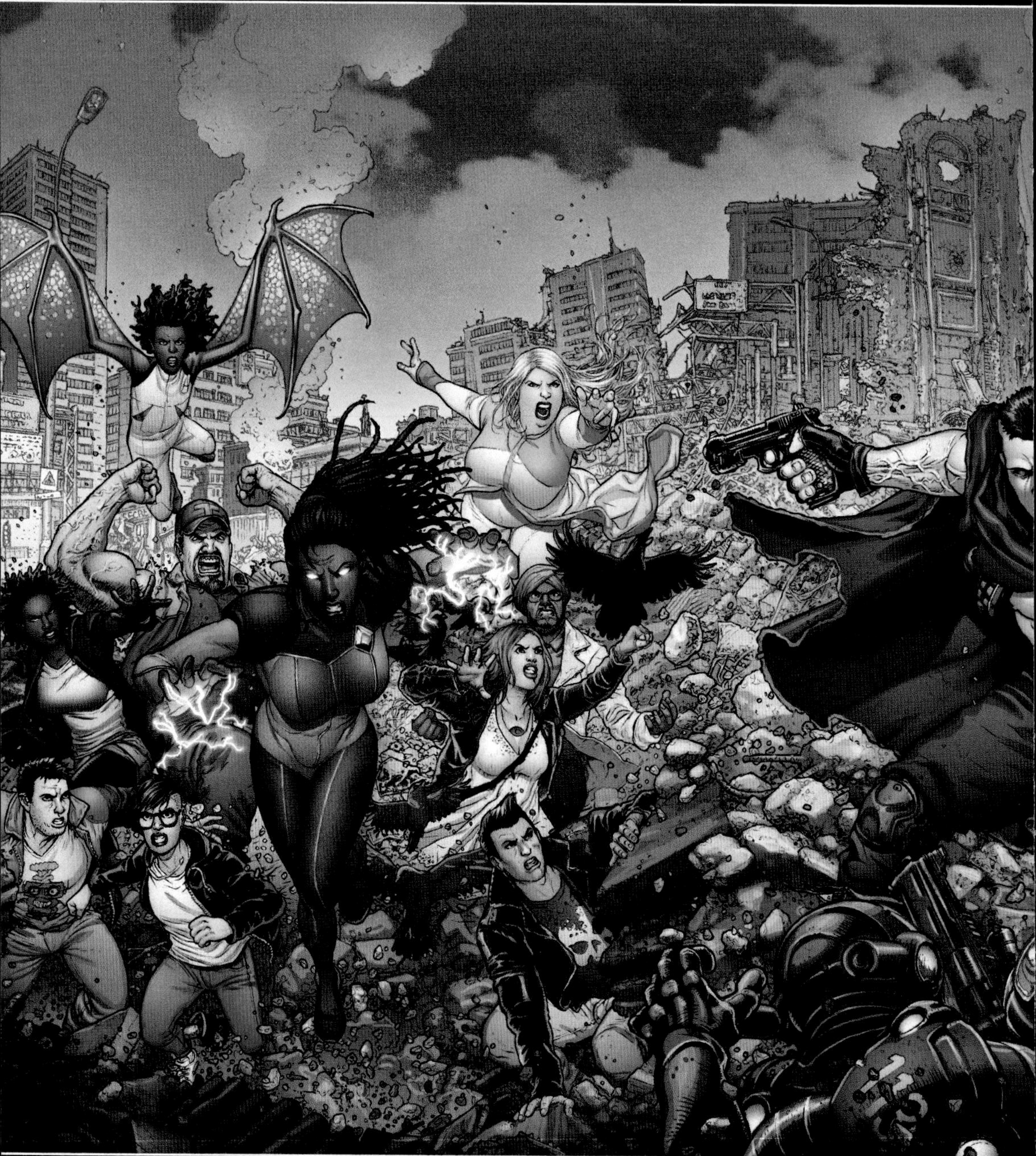

HARBINGER WARS 2 #1-4 INTERLOCKING VARIANT COVERS
Art by JUAN JOSÉ RYP with GABE ELTAEB

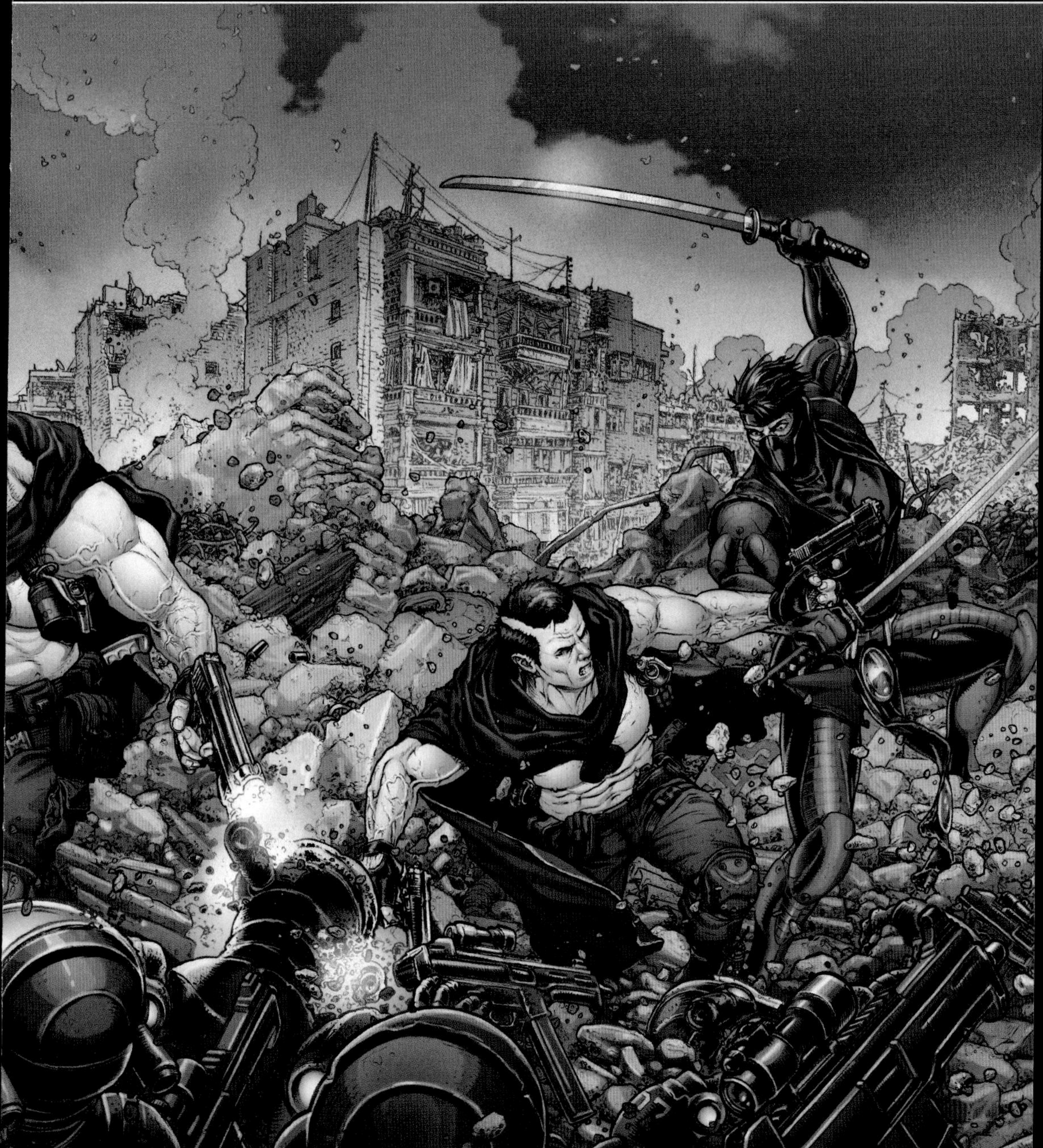

HARBINGER WARS 2 AFTERMATH #1 COVER B
Art by LEWIS LAROSA with DIEGO RODRIGUEZ

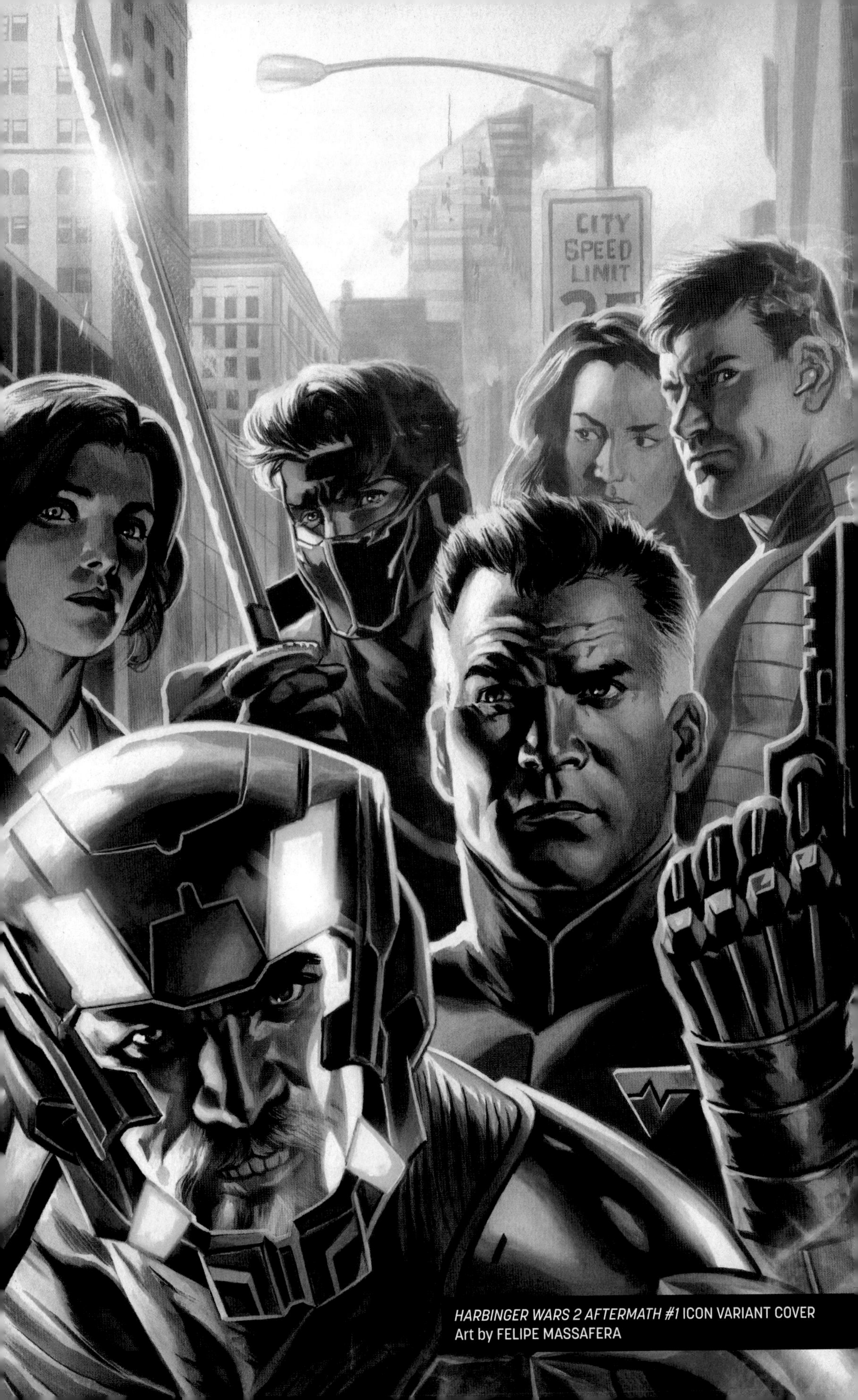
CITY
SPEED
LIMIT

HARBINGER WARS 2 AFTERMATH #1 ICON VARIANT COVER
Art by FELIPE MASSAFERA

HARBINGER WARS 2 #1, pages 3, 5, and (facing) 6
Art by TOMÁS GIORELLO

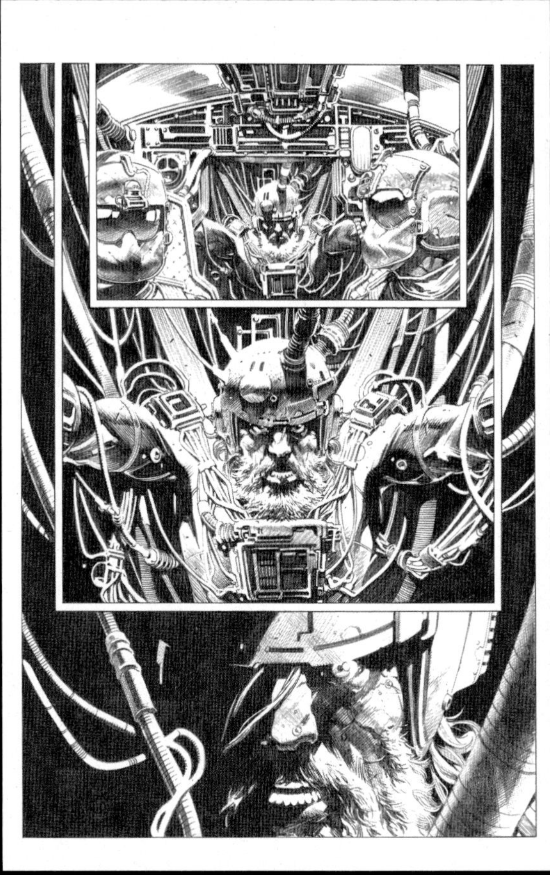

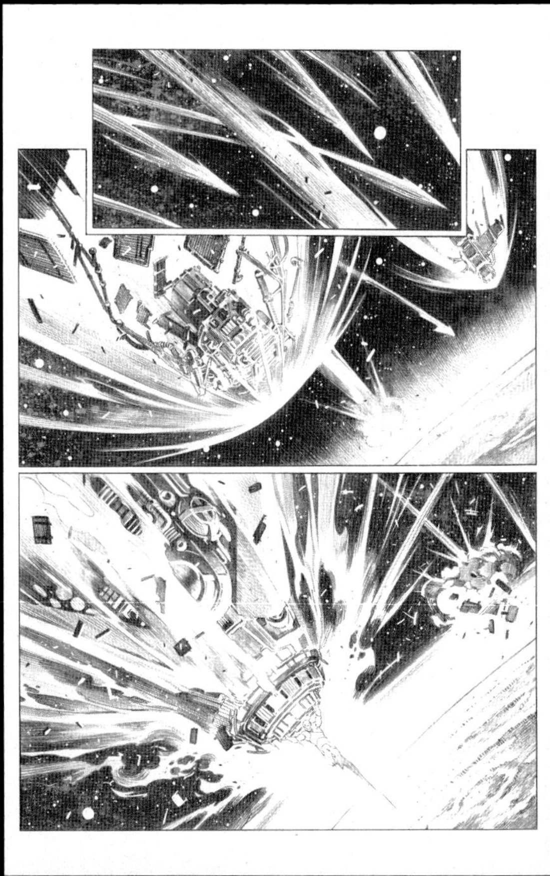

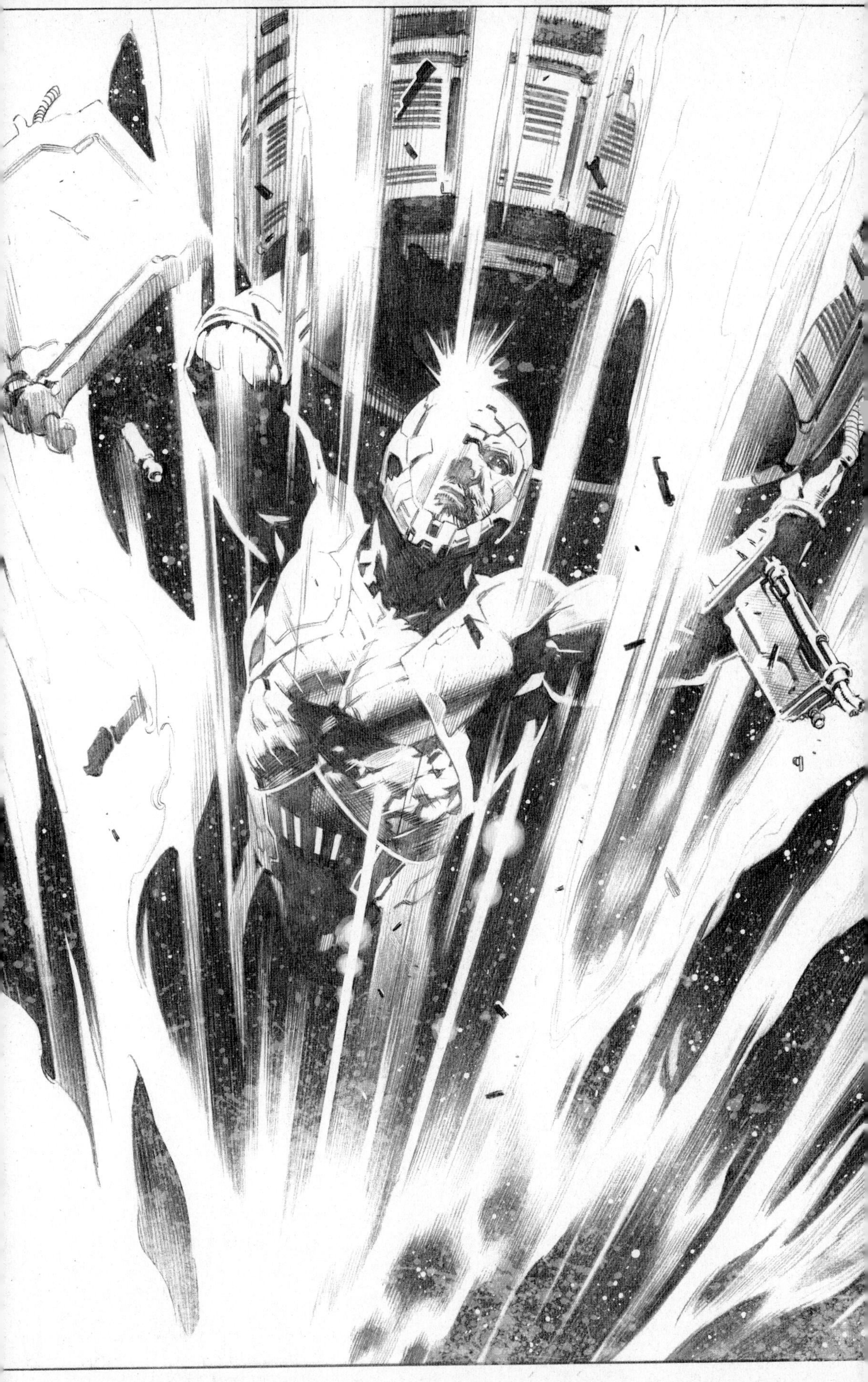

HARBINGER WARS 2 #2, pages 15, 16, and (facing) 22
Art by TOMÁS GIORELLO

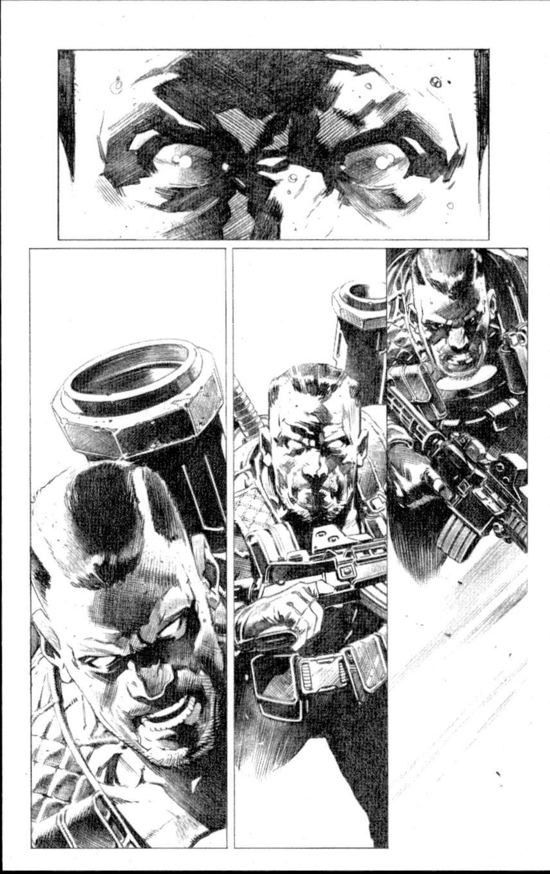

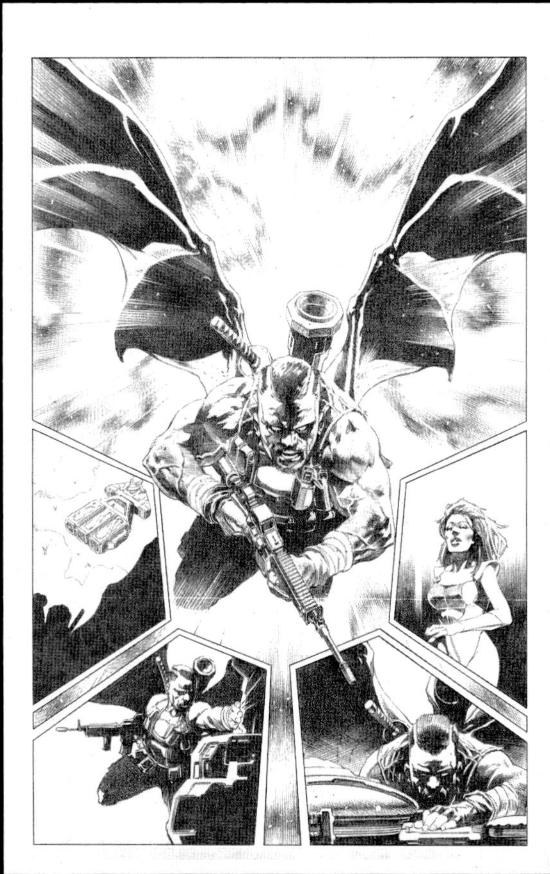

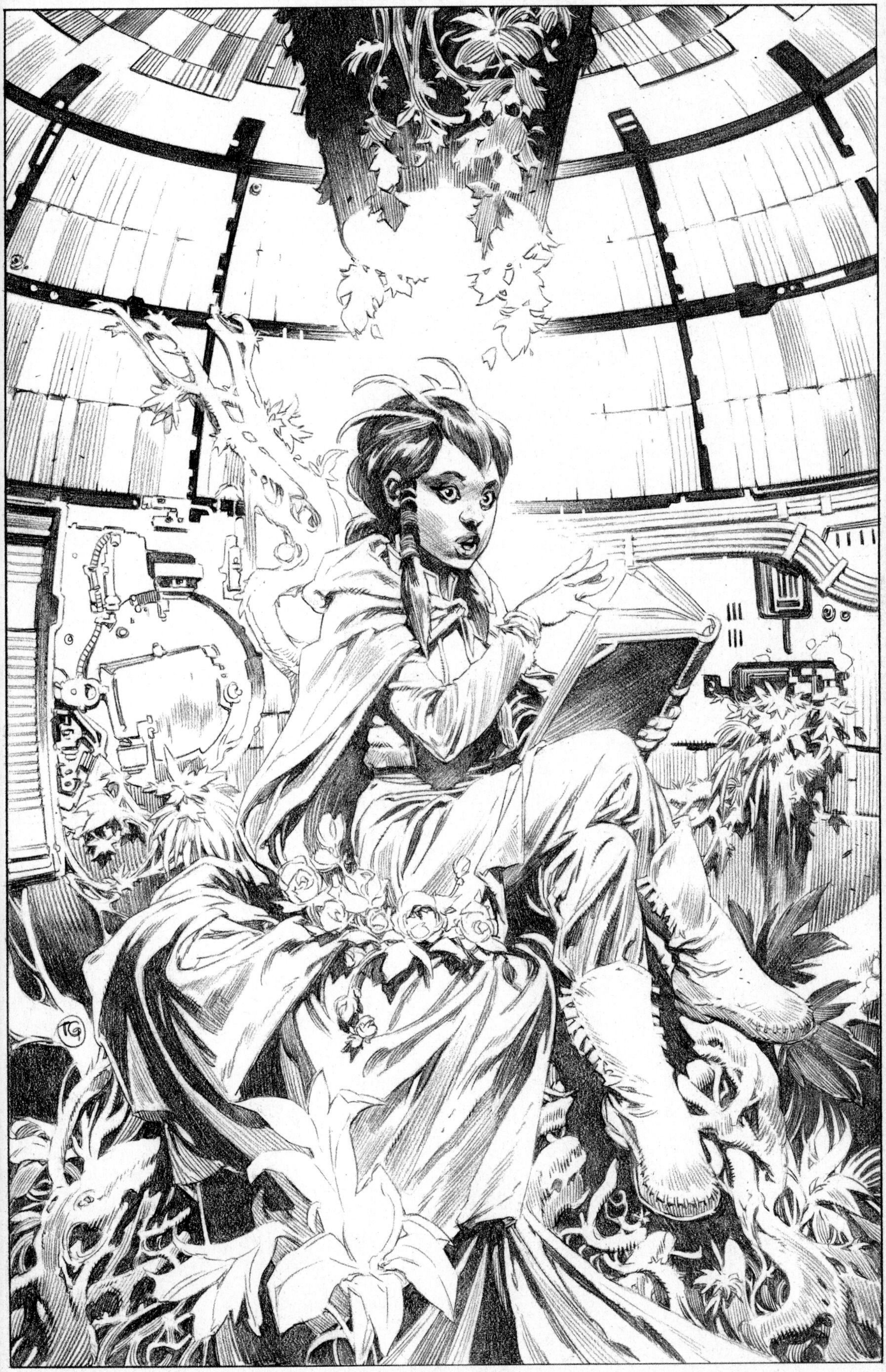

HARBINGER WARS 2 #3, pages 4, 5, and (facing) 16
Art by TOMÁS GIORELLO

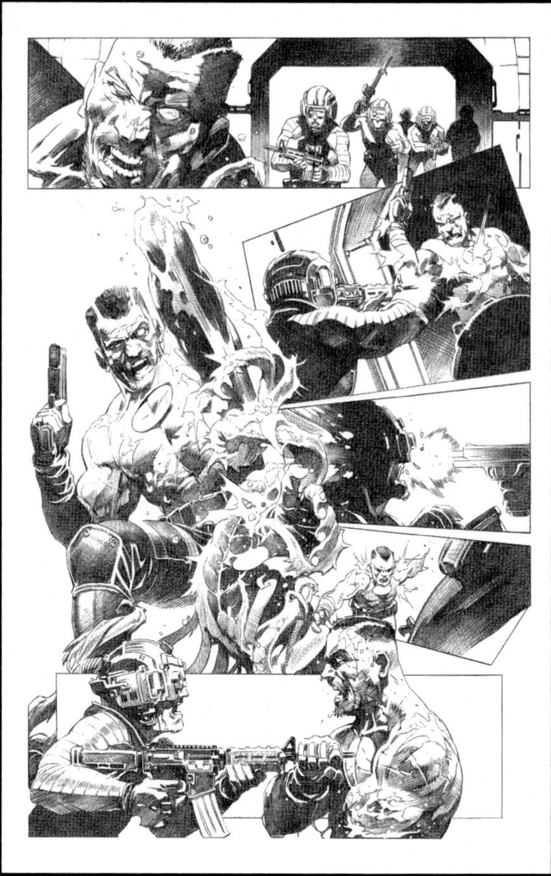

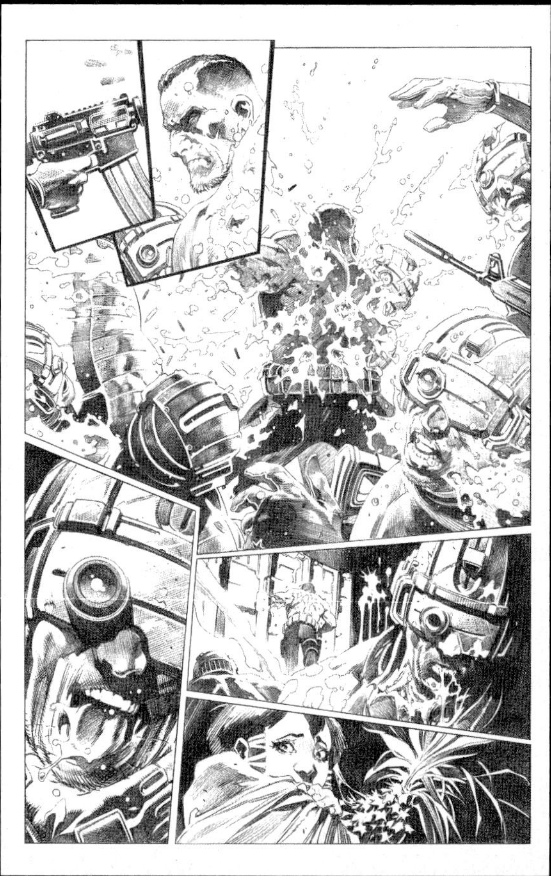

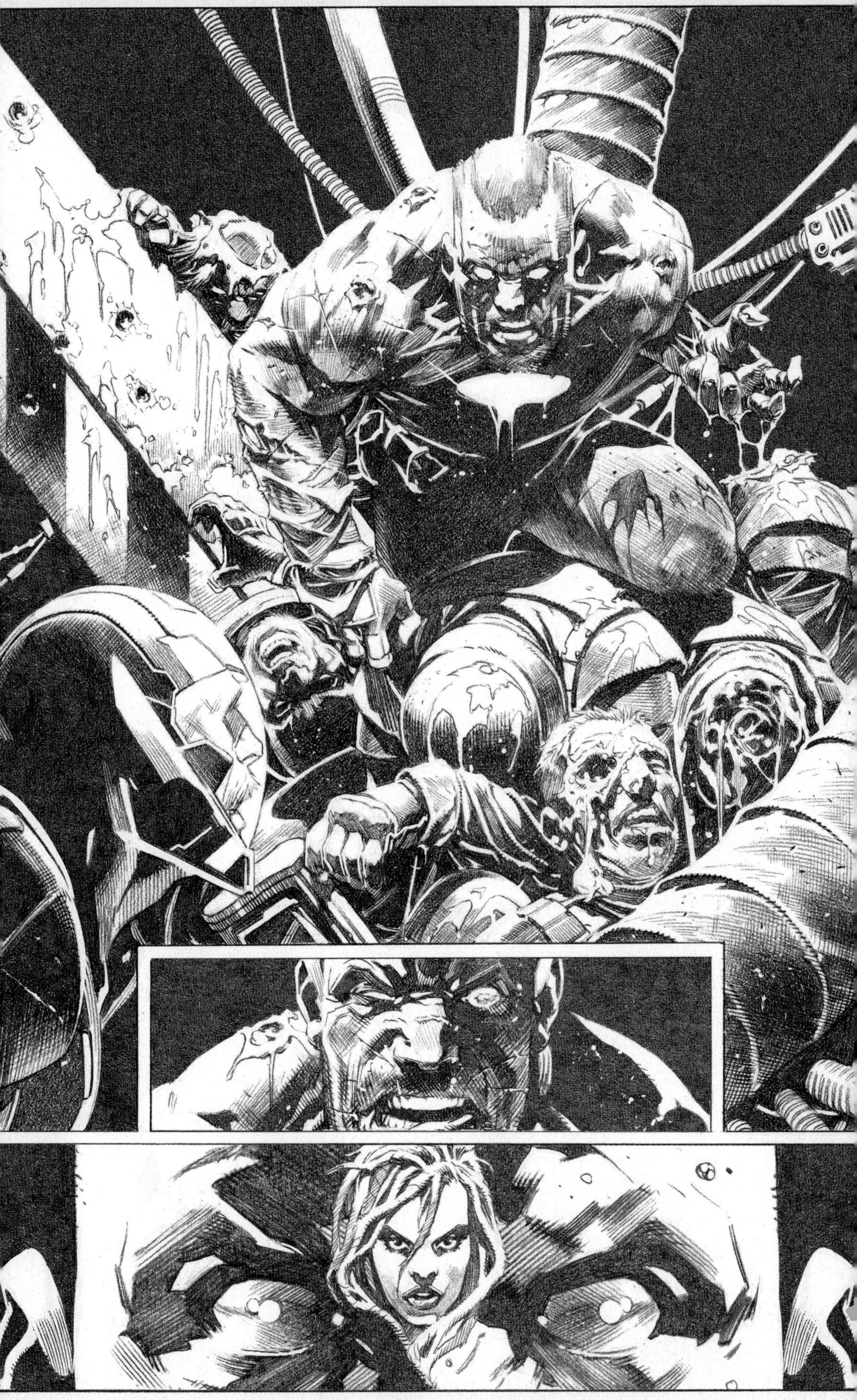

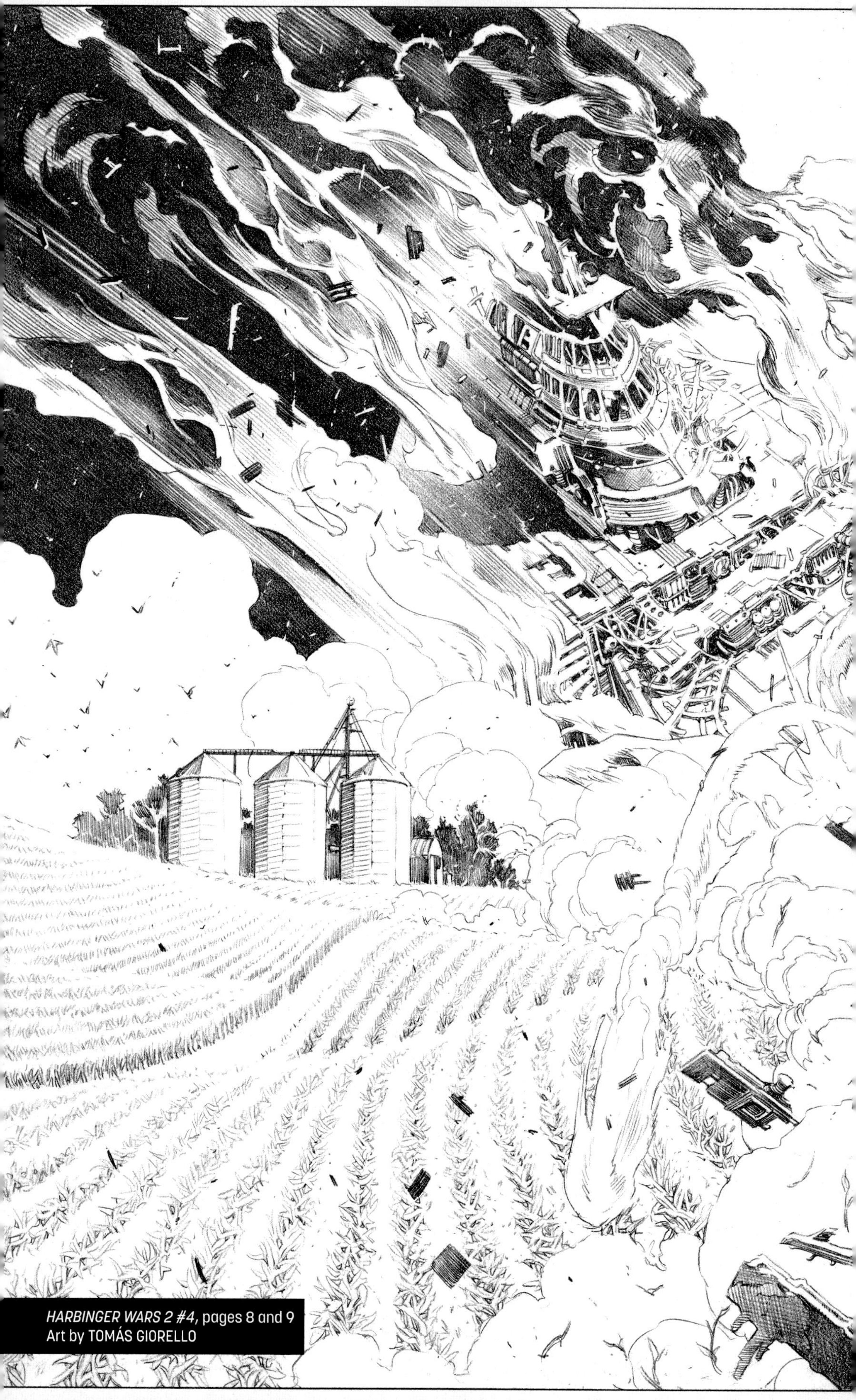

HARBINGER WARS 2 #4, pages 8 and 9
Art by TOMÁS GIORELLO

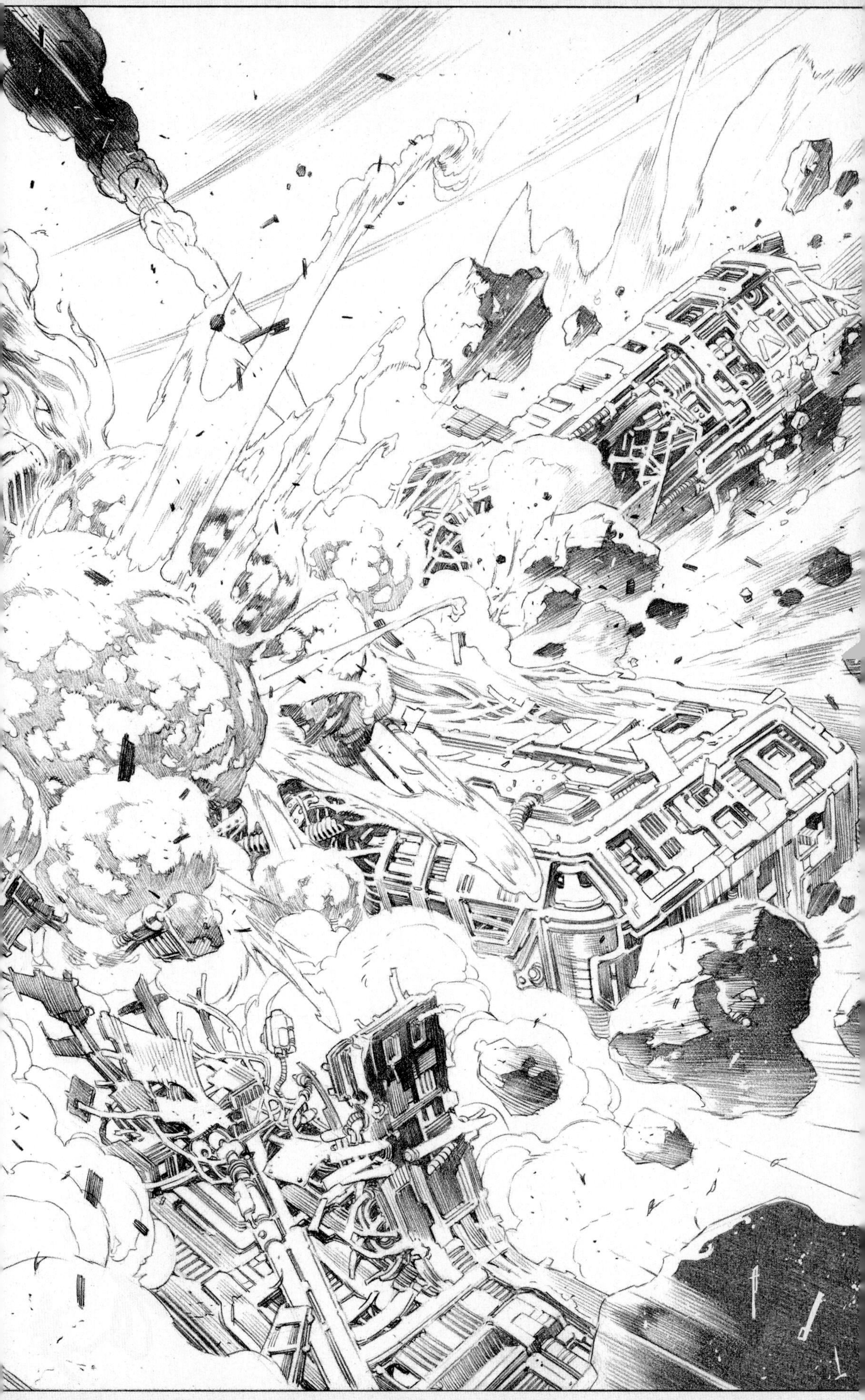

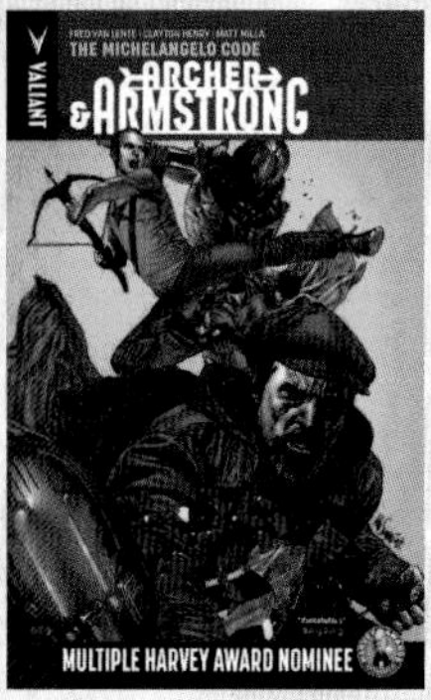
VALIANT
THE MICHELANGELO CODE
ARCHER & ARMSTRONG
MULTIPLE HARVEY AWARD NOMINEE
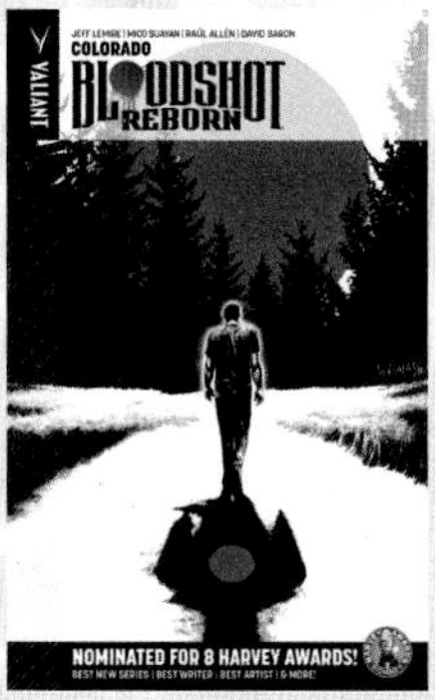
VALIANT
COLORADO
BLOODSHOT REBORN
NOMINATED FOR 8 HARVEY AWARDS!
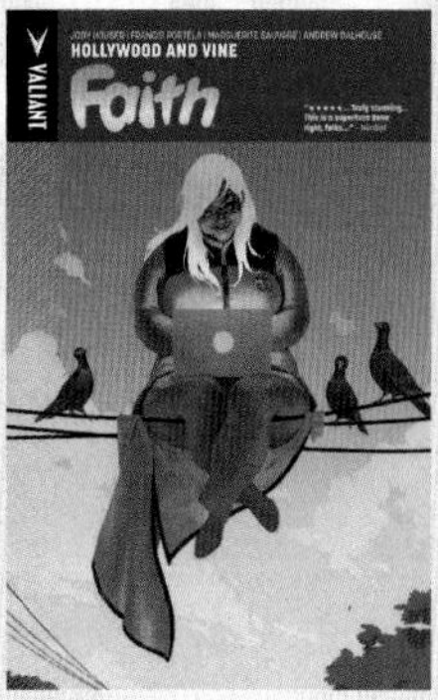
VALIANT
HOLLYWOOD AND VINE
Faith
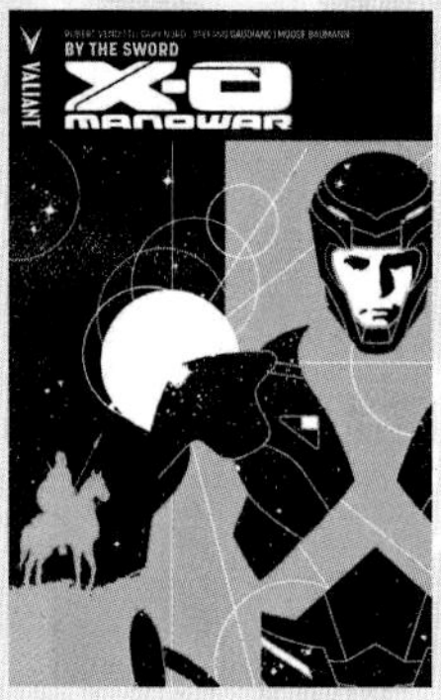
VALIANT
BY THE SWORD
X-O MANOWAR
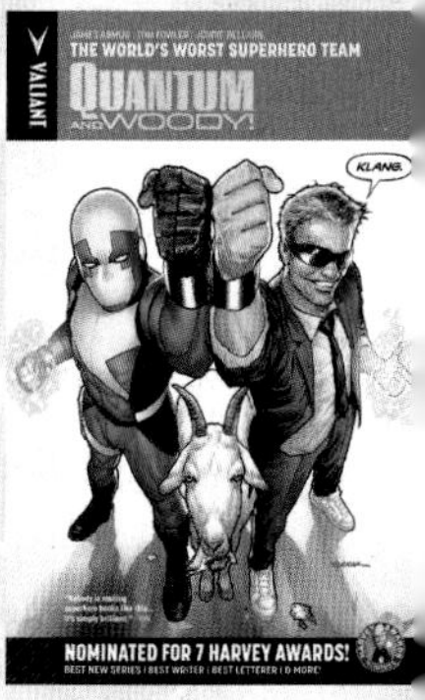
VALIANT
THE WORLD'S WORST SUPERHERO TEAM
QUANTUM AND WOODY!
KLANK
NOMINATED FOR 7 HARVEY AWARDS!

4001 A.D.
4001 A.D.
ISBN: 9781682151433
4001 A.D.: Beyond New Japan
ISBN: 9781682151464
Rai Vol 4: 4001 A.D.
ISBN: 9781682151471

A&A: THE ADVENTURES OF ARCHER AND ARMSTRONG
Volume 1: In the Bag
ISBN: 9781682151495
Volume 2: Romance and Road Trips
ISBN: 9781682151716
Volume 3: Andromeda Estranged
ISBN: 9781682152034

ARCHER & ARMSTRONG
Volume 1: The Michelangelo Code
ISBN: 9780979640988
Volume 2: Wrath of the Eternal Warrior
ISBN: 9781939346049
Volume 3: Far Faraway
ISBN: 9781939346148
Volume 4: Sect Civil War
ISBN: 9781939346254
Volume 5: Mission: Improbable
ISBN: 9781939346353
Volume 6: American Wasteland
ISBN: 9781939346421
Volume 7: The One Percent and Other Tales
ISBN: 9781939346537

ARMOR HUNTERS
Armor Hunters
ISBN: 9781939346452
Armor Hunters: Bloodshot
ISBN: 9781939346469
Armor Hunters: Harbinger
ISBN: 9781939346506
Unity Vol. 3: Armor Hunters
ISBN: 9781939346445
X-O Manowar Vol. 7: Armor Hunters
ISBN: 9781939346476

BLOODSHOT
Volume 1: Setting the World on Fire
ISBN: 9780979640964
Volume 2: The Rise and the Fall
ISBN: 9781939346032
Volume 3: Harbinger Wars
ISBN: 9781939346124
Volume 4: H.A.R.D. Corps
ISBN: 9781939346193
Volume 5: Get Some!
ISBN: 9781939346315
Volume 6: The Glitch and Other Tales
ISBN: 9781939346711

BLOODSHOT REBORN
Volume 1: Colorado
ISBN: 9781939346674
Volume 2: The Hunt
ISBN: 9781939346827
Volume 3: The Analog Man
ISBN: 9781682151334
Volume 4: Bloodshot Island
ISBN: 9781682151952

BLOODSHOT SALVATION
Volume 1: The Book of Revenge
ISBN: 9781682152553

BLOODSHOT U.S.A.
ISBN: 9781682151952

BOOK OF DEATH
Book of Death
ISBN: 9781939346971
Book of Death: The Fall of the Valiant Universe
ISBN: 9781939346988

BRITANNIA
Volume 1
ISBN: 9781682151853
Volume 2: We Who Are About to Die
ISBN: 9781682152133

DEAD DROP
ISBN: 9781939346858

THE DEATH-DEFYING DOCTOR MIRAGE
Volume 1
ISBN: 9781939346490
Volume 2: Second Lives
ISBN: 9781682151297

THE DELINQUENTS
ISBN: 9781939346513

DIVINITY
Divinity I
ISBN: 9781939346766
Divinity II
ISBN: 9781682151518
Divinity III
ISBN: 9781682151914
Divinity III: Glorious Heroes of the Stalinverse
ISBN: 9781682152072

ETERNAL WARRIOR
Volume 1: Sword of the Wild
ISBN: 9781939346209
Volume 2: Eternal Emperor
ISBN: 9781939346292
Volume 3: Days of Steel
ISBN: 9781939346742

WRATH OF THE ETERNAL WARRIOR
Volume 1: Risen
ISBN: 9781682151235
Volume 2: Labyrinth
ISBN: 9781682151594
Volume 3: Deal With a Devil
ISBN: 9781682151976

ETERNITY
ISBN: 9781682152652

FAITH
Volume 1: Hollywood and Vine
ISBN: 9781682151402
Volume 2: California Scheming
ISBN: 9781682151631
Volume 3: Superstar
ISBN: 9781682151990
Volume 4: The Faithless
ISBN: 9781682152195
Faith and the Future Force:
ISBN: 9781682152331

GENERATION ZERO
Volume 1: We Are the Future
ISBN: 9781682151754
Volume 2: Heroscape
ISBN: 9781682152096

HARBINGER
Volume 1: Omega Rising
ISBN: 9780979640957
Volume 2: Renegades
ISBN: 9781939346025
Volume 3: Harbinger Wars
ISBN: 9781939346117
Volume 4: Perfect Day
ISBN: 9781939346155
Volume 5: Death of a Renegade
ISBN: 9781939346339
Volume 6: Omegas
ISBN: 9781939346384

HARBINGER RENEGADE
Volume 1: The Judgment of Solomon
ISBN: 9781682151693
Volume 2: Massacre
ISBN: 9781682152232

EXPLORE THE VALIANT UNIVERSE

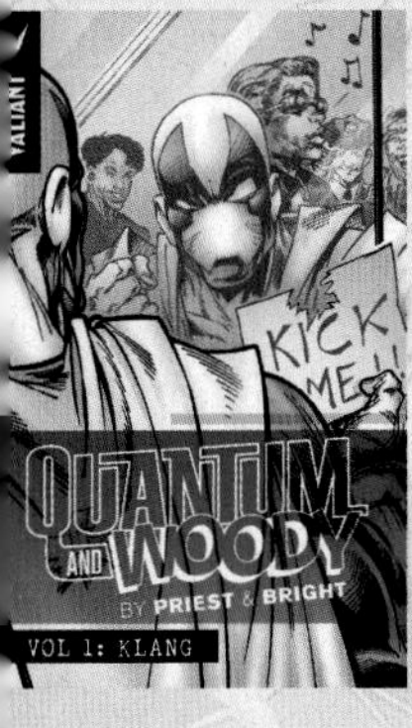
KICK ME
QUANTUM AND WOODY
BY PRIEST & BRIGHT
VOL 1: KLANG

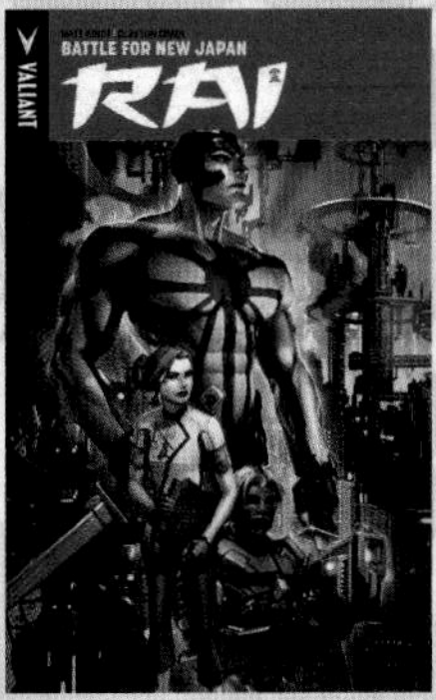
BATTLE FOR NEW JAPAN
RAI

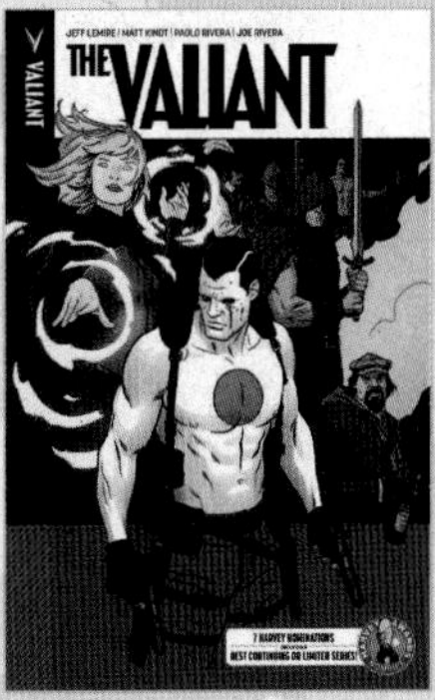
THE VALIANT

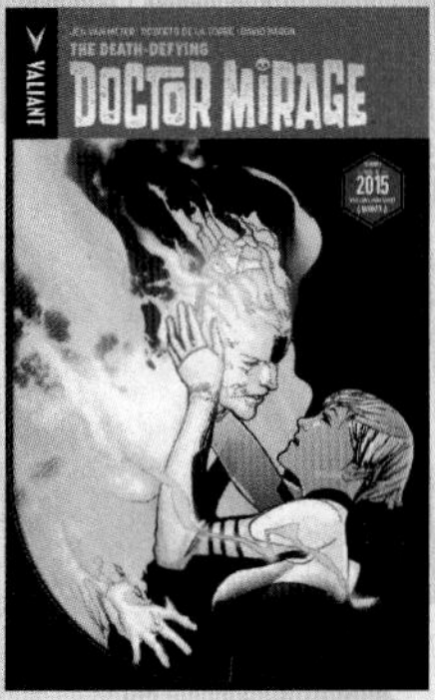
THE DEATH-DEFYING
DOCTOR MIRAGE

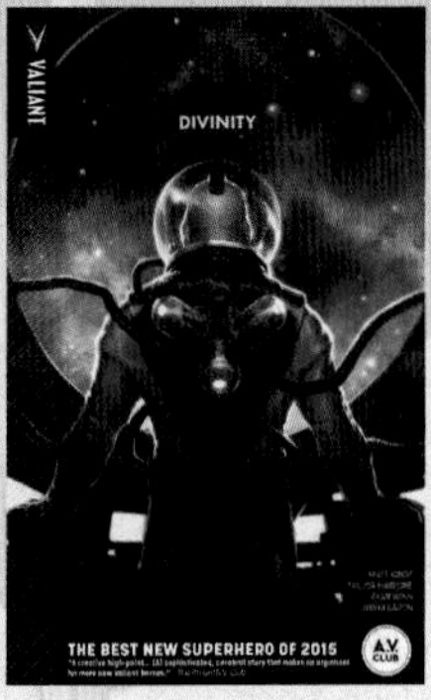
DIVINITY
THE BEST NEW SUPERHERO OF 2015

ARBINGER WARS
arbinger Wars
SBN: 9781939346094
loodshot Vol. 3: Harbinger Wars
SBN: 9781939346124
arbinger Vol. 3: Harbinger Wars
SBN: 9781939346117

MPERIUM
olume 1: Collecting Monsters
SBN: 9781939346759
olume 2: Broken Angels
SBN: 9781939346896
olume 3: The Vine Imperative
SBN: 9781682151112
olume 4: Stormbreak
SBN: 9781682151372

INJAK
olume 1: Weaponeer
SBN: 9781939346667
olume 2: The Shadow Wars
SBN: 9781939346940
olume 3: Operation: Deadside
SBN: 9781682151259
olume 4: The Siege of King's Castle
SBN: 9781682151617
olume 5: The Fist & The Steel
SBN: 9781682151792
olume 6: The Seven Blades of Master Darque
SBN: 9781682152119

INJA-K
olume 1: The Ninja Files
SBN: 9781682152591
olume 2: The Coalition
SBN: 9781682152812

UANTUM AND WOODY
olume 1: The World's Worst Superhero Team
SBN: 9781939346186
olume 2: In Security
SBN: 9781939346230
olume 3: Crooked Pasts, Present Tense
SBN: 9781939346391
olume 4: Quantum and Woody Must Die!
SBN: 9781939346629

UANTUM AND WOODY!
olume 1: Kiss Kiss, Klang, Klang
SBN: 9781682152690

UANTUM AND WOODY BY PRIEST & BRIGHT
olume 1: Klang
SBN: 9781939346780
Volume 2: Switch
ISBN: 9781939346803
Volume 3: And So...
ISBN: 9781939346865
Volume 4: Q2 - The Return
ISBN: 9781682151099

RAI
Volume 1: Welcome to New Japan
ISBN: 9781939346414
Volume 2: Battle for New Japan
ISBN: 9781939346612
Volume 3: The Orphan
ISBN: 9781939346841
Volume 4: 4001 A.D.
ISBN: 9781682151471

RAPTURE
ISBN: 9781682151891

SAVAGE
ISBN: 9781682152256

SECRET WEAPONS
ISBN: 9781682152294

SHADOWMAN
Volume 1: Birth Rites
ISBN: 9781939346001
Volume 2: Darque Reckoning
ISBN: 9781939346056
Volume 3: Deadside Blues
ISBN: 9781939346162
Volume 4: Fear, Blood, And Shadows
ISBN: 9781939346278
Volume 5: End Times
ISBN: 9781939346377

SHADOWMAN BY ENNIS & WOOD
ISBN: 9781682151358

IVAR, TIMEWALKER
Volume 1: Making History
ISBN: 9781939346636
Volume 2: Breaking History
ISBN: 9781939346834
Volume 3: Ending History
ISBN: 9781939346995

UNITY
Volume 1: To Kill a King
ISBN: 9781939346261
Volume 2: Trapped by Webnet
ISBN: 9781939346346
Volume 3: Armor Hunters
ISBN: 9781939346445
Volume 4: The United
ISBN: 9781939346544
Volume 5: Homefront
ISBN: 9781939346797
Volume 6: The War-Monger
ISBN: 9781939346902
Volume 7: Revenge of the Armor Hunters
ISBN: 9781682151136

THE VALIANT
ISBN: 9781939346605

VALIANT HIGH
ISBN: 9781682152799

VALIANT ZEROES AND ORIGINS
ISBN: 9781939346582

WAR MOTHER
ISBN: 9781682152379

X-O MANOWAR
Volume 1: By the Sword
ISBN: 9780979640940
Volume 2: Enter Ninjak
ISBN: 9780979640995
Volume 3: Planet Death
ISBN: 9781939346087
Volume 4: Homecoming
ISBN: 9781939346179
Volume 5: At War With Unity
ISBN: 9781939346247
Volume 6: Prelude to Armor Hunters
ISBN: 9781939346407
Volume 7: Armor Hunters
ISBN: 9781939346476
Volume 8: Enter: Armorines
ISBN: 9781939346551
Volume 9: Dead Hand
ISBN: 9781939346650
Volume 10: Exodus
ISBN: 9781939346933
Volume 11: The Kill List
ISBN: 9781682151273
Volume 12: Long Live the King
ISBN: 9781682151655
Volume 13: Succession and Other Tales
ISBN: 9781682151754

X-O MANOWAR (2017)
Volume 1: Soldier
ISBN: 9781682152058
Volume 2: General
ISBN: 9781682152171
Volume 3: Emperor
ISBN: 9781682152355
Volume 4: Visigoth
ISBN: 9781682152638
Volume 5: Barbarians
ISBN: 9781682152836

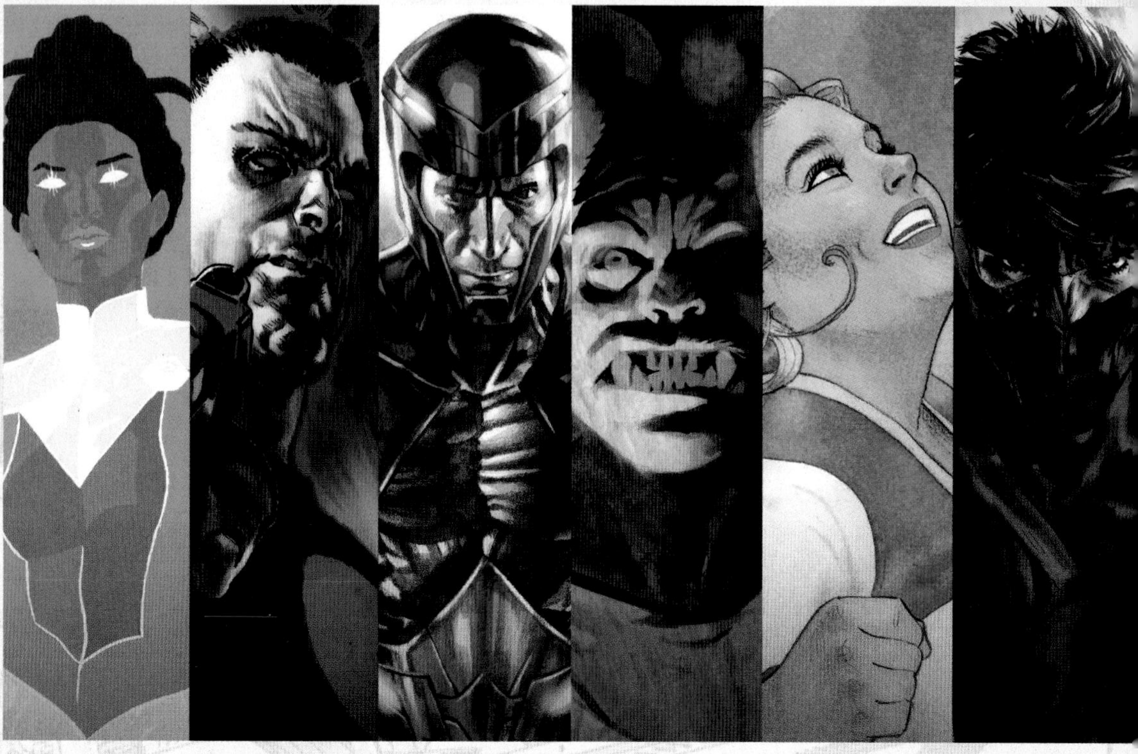

4001 A.D. DELUXE EDITION
ISBN: 978-1-68215-193-8

ARCHER & ARMSTRONG DELUXE EDITIONS
Book 1: ISBN: 978-1-939346-22-3
Book 2: ISBN: 978-1-939346-95-7

ARMOR HUNTERS DELUXE EDITION
ISBN: 978-1-939346-72-8

BLOODSHOT DELUXE EDITIONS
Book 1: ISBN: 978-1-939346-21-6
Book 2: ISBN: 978-1-939346-81-0

BLOODSHOT REBORN DELUXE EDITIONS
Book 1: ISBN: 978-1-68215-155-6
Book 2: ISBN: 978-1-68215-227-0

BOOK OF DEATH DELUXE EDITION
ISBN: 978-1-68215-115-0

THE DEATH-DEFYING DOCTOR MIRAGE DELUXE EDITION
ISBN: 978-1-68215-153-2

DIVINITY DELUXE EDITION
ISBN: 978-1-939346-92-6

FAITH: HOLLYWOOD & VINE DELUXE EDITION
ISBN: 978-1-68215-201-0

HARBINGER DELUXE EDITIONS
Book 1: ISBN: 978-1-939346-13-1
Book 2: ISBN: 978-1-939346-77-3

HARBINGER WARS DELUXE EDITION
ISBN: 978-1-939346-32-2

IVAR, TIMEWALKER DELUXE EDITION
Book 1: ISBN: 978-1-68215-119-8

NINJAK DELUXE EDITION
Book 1: ISBN: 978-1-68215-157-0
Book 2: ISBN: 978-1-68215-257-7

QUANTUM AND WOODY DELUXE EDITION
Book 1: ISBN: 978-1-939346-68-1

RAI DELUXE EDITION
Book 1: ISBN: 978-1-68215-117-4

SHADOWMAN DELUXE EDITION
Book 1: ISBN: 978-1-939346-43-8

UNITY DELUXE EDITION
Book 1: 978-1-939346-57-5

THE VALIANT DELUXE EDITION
ISBN: 978-1-939346-91-9

X-O MANOWAR DELUXE EDITIONS
Book 1: ISBN: 978-1-939346-10-0
Book 2: ISBN: 978-1-939346-52-0
Book 3 : ISBN: 978-1-68215-131-0
Book 4: ISBN: 978-1-68215-183-9
Book 5: ISBN: 978-1-68215-215-7

VALIANT CLASSIC

ARCHER & ARMSTRONG: THE COMPLETE CLASSIC OMNIBUS
ISBN: 978-1-939346-87-2

QUANTUM AND WOODY: THE COMPLETE CLASSIC OMNIBUS
ISBN: 978-1-939346-36-0

Q2: THE RETURN OF QUANTUM AND WOODY DELUXE EDITION
ISBN: 978-1-939346-56-8

VALIANT MASTERS: BLOODSHOT VOL. 1 - BLOOD OF THE MACHINE
ISBN: 978-0-9796409-3-3

VALIANT MASTERS: HARBINGER VOL. 1 - CHILDREN OF THE EIGHTH DAY
ISBN: 978-1-939346-48-3

VALIANT MASTERS: H.A.R.D. CORPS VOL. 1 - SEARCH AND DESTROY
ISBN: 978-1-939346-28-5

VALIANT MASTERS: NINJAK VOL. 1 - BLACK WATER
ISBN: 978-0-9796409-7-1

VALIANT MASTERS: RAI VOL. 1 - FROM HONOR TO STRENGTH
ISBN: 978-1-939346-07-0

VALIANT MASTERS: SHADOWMAN VOL. 1 - SPIRITS WITHIN
ISBN: 978-1-939346-01-8

X-O MANOWAR CLASSIC OMNIBUS
Vol. 1: ISBN: 978-1-939346-30-8

THE ROAD TO HWII AND BEYOND!

Read the full lead up and aftermath of Valiant's biggest, most ambitious and most impactful comic book event to date!

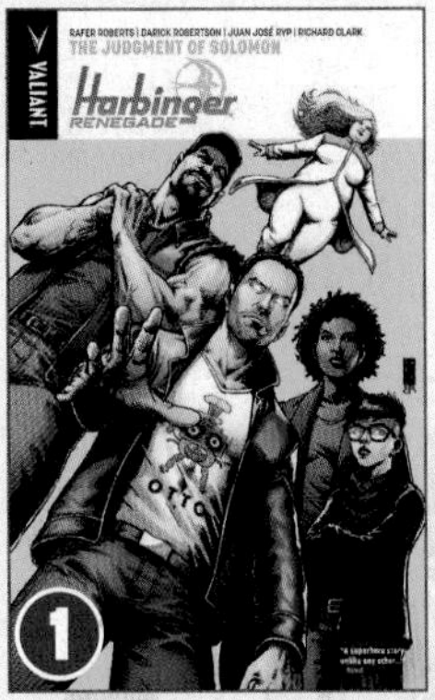
RAFER ROBERTS | DARICK ROBERTSON | JUAN JOSÉ RYP | RICHARD CLARK
THE JUDGMENT OF SOLOMON
VALIANT
Harbinger
RENEGADE
1

Harbinger Renegade Vol. 1: The Judgment of Solomon

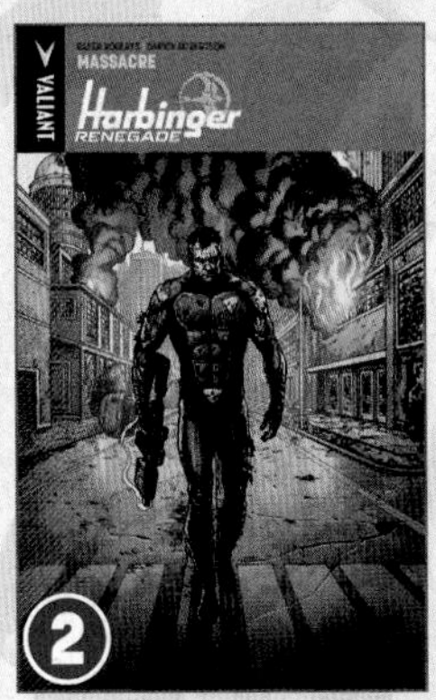
MASSACRE
VALIANT
Harbinger
RENEGADE
2

Harbinger Renegade Vol. 2: Massacre

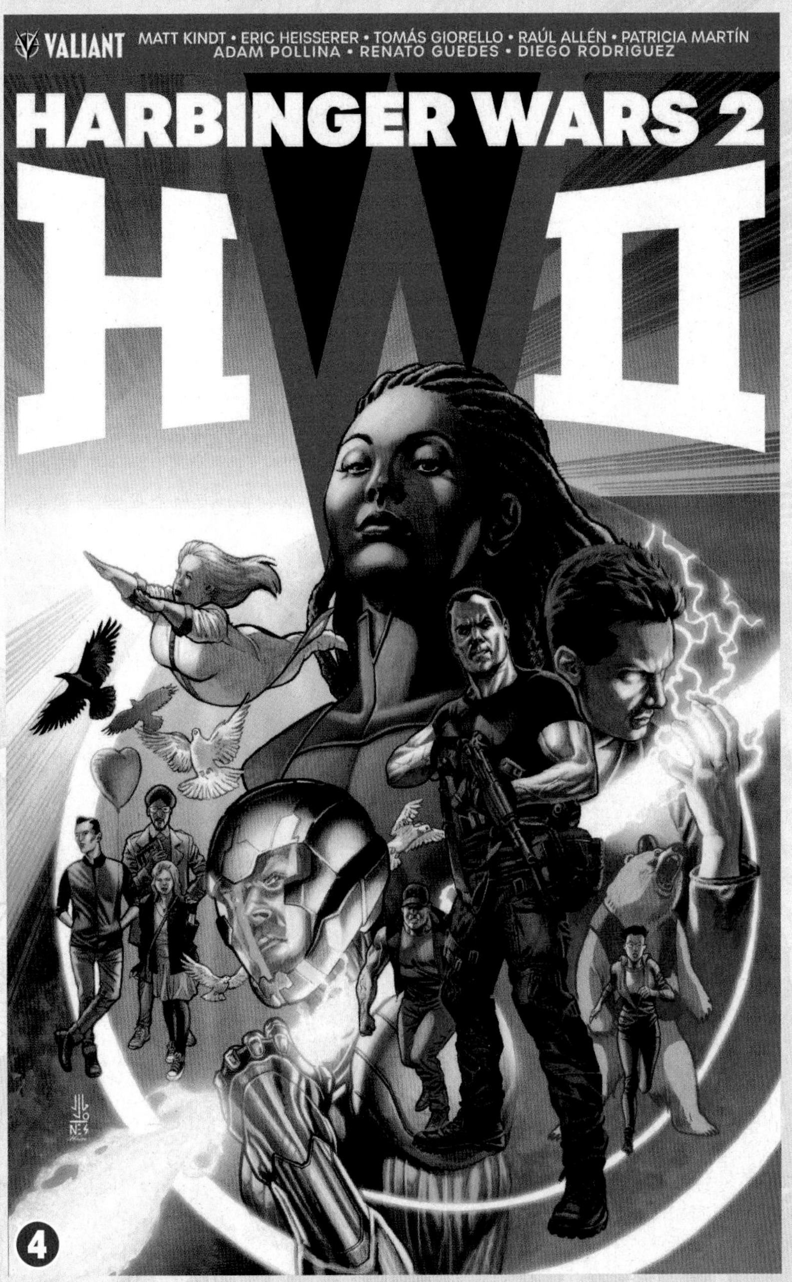
VALIANT
MATT KINDT • ERIC HEISSERER • TOMÁS GIORELLO • RAÚL ALLÉN • PATRICIA MARTÍN
ADAM POLLINA • RENATO GUEDES • DIEGO RODRIGUEZ
HARBINGER WARS 2
HWII
4

Harbinger Wars 2

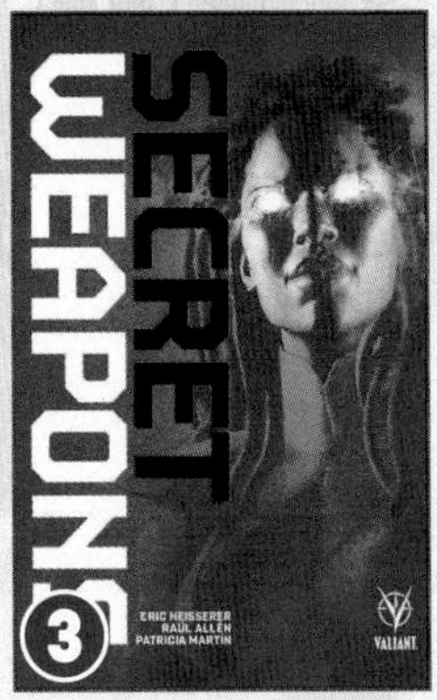
SECRET WEAPONS
ERIC HEISSERER
RAÚL ALLÉN
PATRICIA MARTÍN
VALIANT
3

Secret Weapons

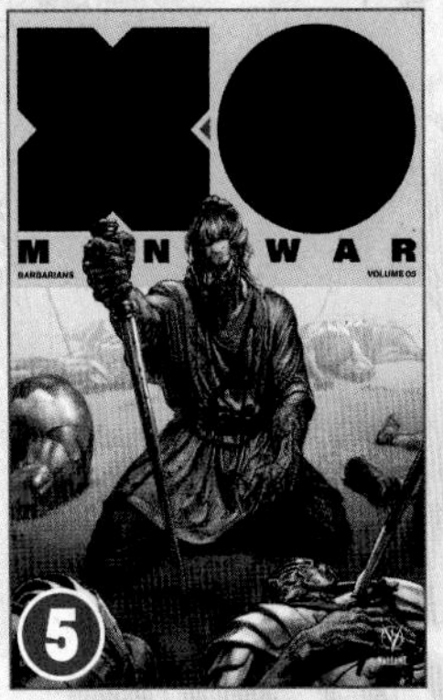
X-O
MANOWAR
BARBARIANS
VOLUME 05
5

X-O Manowar Vol. 5: Barbarian **(OPTIONAL)**

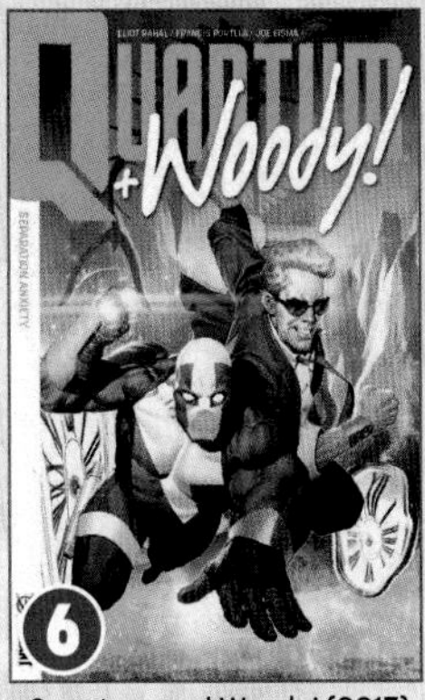
QUANTUM
+Woody!
SEPARATION ANXIETY
6

Quantum and Woody! (2017) Vol. 2: Separation Anxiety **(OPTIONAL)**

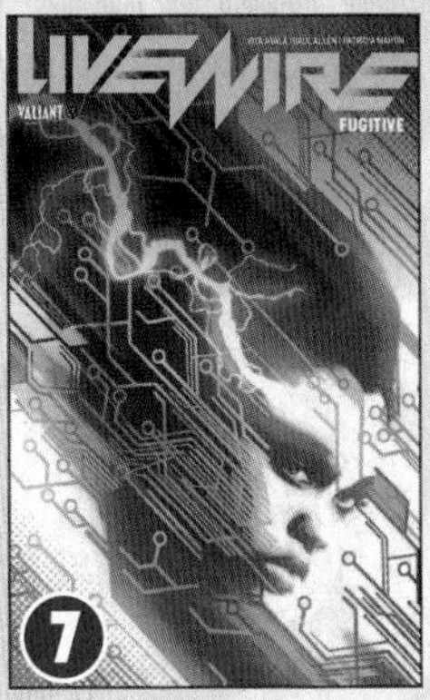
LIVEWIRE
VALIANT
FUGITIVE
7

Livewire Vol. 1: Fugitive

LIVEWIRE

VOLUME ONE: **FUGITIVE**

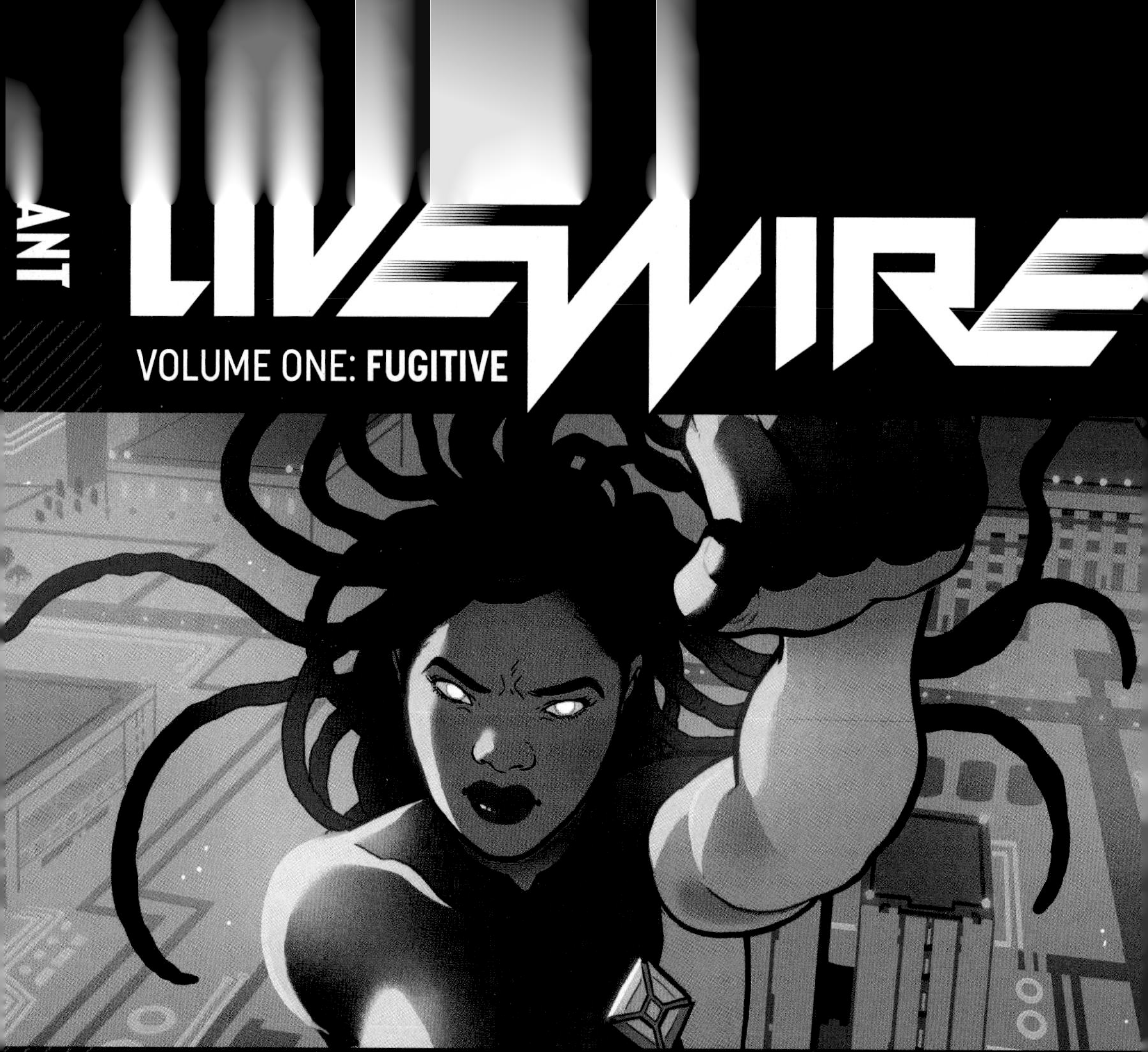

FOR THE FIRST TIME, LIVEWIRE TAKES CENTER STAGE!

Accomplice. Mentor. Savior. And now, Enemy of the State. Seeking to protect other vulnerable super-powered psiots like herself, Livewire plunged the United States into a nationwide blackout with her technopathic abilities, causing untold devastation. After choosing the few over the many, she must now outrun the government she served - and those she once called allies. With the whole world hunting her, what kind of hero will Livewire be...or will she be one at all?

Start reading here with the stunning new ongoing series from rising star Vita Ayala (*Supergirl*, *Submerged*) and fan-favorite artists Raúl Allén (WRATH OF THE ETERNAL WARRIOR) and Patricia Martín (SECRET WEAPONS) as they stand poised to launch the Valiant Universe into a new age of champions!

Collecting LIVEWIRE #1-4.

TRADE PAPERBACK
ISBN: 978-1-68215-301-7

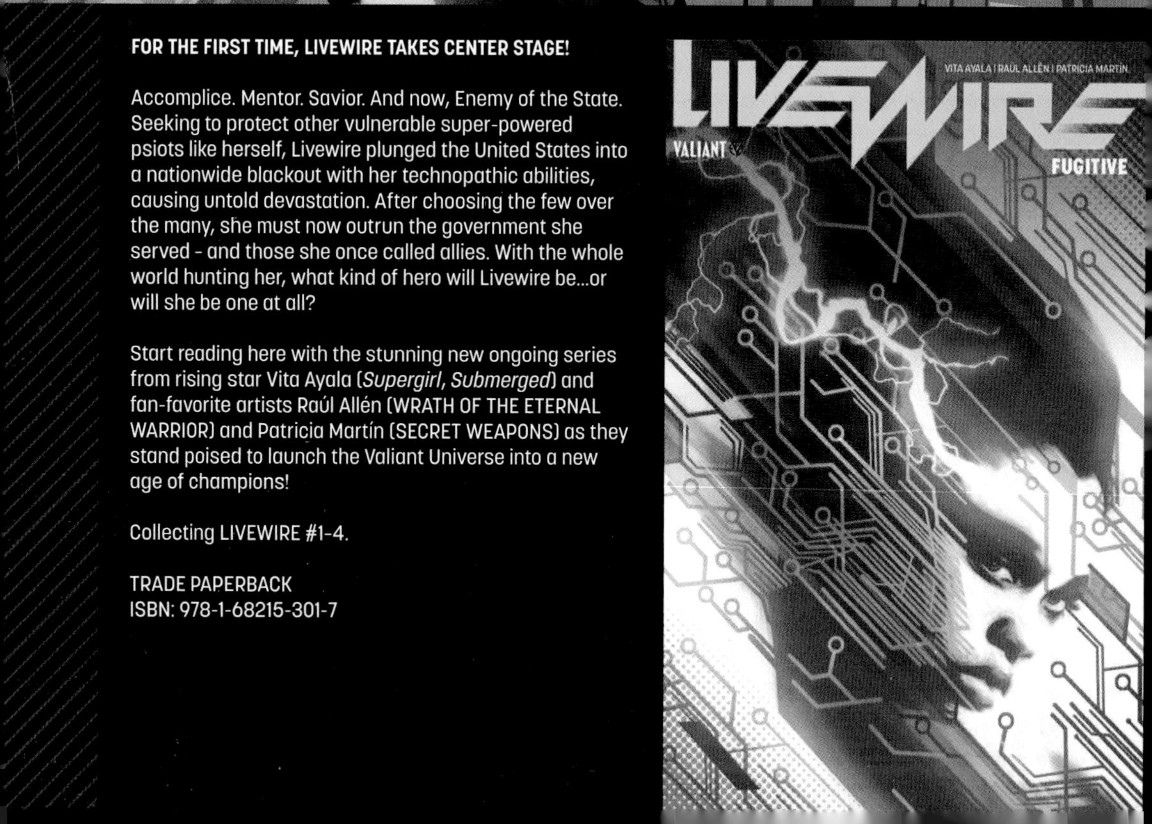
LIVEWIRE
VITA AYALA | RAÚL ALLÉN | PATRICIA MARTÍN
VALIANT
FUGITIVE